Rural Transport
and Planning

A bibliography with abstracts

David Banister

An Alexandrine Press book

MANSELL, London and New York

First published 1985 by Mansell Publishing Limited
(A subsidiary of The H. W. Wilson Company)
6 All Saints Street, London N1 9RL
950 University Avenue, Bronx, New York 10452

This book was commissioned, edited and designed by
Alexandrine Press, Oxford

British Library Cataloguing in Publication Data

Banister, David
   Rural transport and planning: a bibliography with abstracts.
   1. Transportation—Planning
   I. Title
   711'.7   HE151

   ISBN 0-7201-1692-9

Library of Congress Cataloging in Publication Data

Banister, David.
   Rural transport and planning.

   "An Alexandrine Press book."
   Includes indexes.
   1 Rural transit—Bibliography. 2. Transportation
and state—Bibliography. I. Title.
Z7164.T8B36   1985 [HE152.5]   016.3805'09173'4   84-21817
ISBN 0-7201-1692-9

Printed in Great Britain by
Butler & Tanner Ltd, Frome and London

Rural Transport and Planning
A bibliography with abstracts

Contents

Preface

Acknowledgements

Introduction   1

1. The context   5

1A   The rural context   10
1B   The transport context   28

2. Policy and planning in transport   33

2A   Great Britain   39
2B   The United States of America   61
2C   Europe   80

3. Accessibility and mobility   89

3A   Concepts and definitions   94
3B   Transport deprivation and needs   106
3C   Social groups   122
3D   Activities and telecommunications   137

4. Transport modes   151

4A   Conventional public transport—the bus   157
4B   Conventional public transport—the railway   186
4C   Unconventional public transport   197
4D   Private transport   239
4E   Waterways and freight   246

5. Methods and evaluation 251

5A Transport and regional development 257
5B Analysis methods 265
5C Investment appraisal and evaluation 285
5D Energy 313
5E Environment and safety 323
5F Engineering 329

6. Area-based studies 341

6A United Kingdom 345
6B Europe 364
6C USA, Canada, Australasia 372
6D Developing countries 387

7. Bibliographies 401

Other information sources 403
Selected periodicals 405

8. Additional entries 411

Subject index

Author index

Abbreviations

Acknowledgements

Many individuals have helped in locating the references and advising on those which should be included within this volume. I am grateful to them all—

Richard Balcombe, Mary Benwell, P Coquand, Mary Cawley, Enne de Boer, Dieneke Ferguson, Jackie Golob, Herr Heese, Wolfgang Heinze, Mayer Hillman, Keith Hoggart, Anne-Marie Hvaal, Rinus Jaarsma, NO Jørgensen, Britt Kihlman, Russ Kilvington, JA Kropman, Lewis Lesley, Carsten Løndal-Nielsen, Phil Lowe, Malcolm Moseley, H McGeehan, Laurie Pickup, Stephen Town, Stephen Woollett, Sue Wright

—particularly those from overseas who have helped with key references in their own countries. The monumental task of transforming references from over 1000 cards into typescript was undertaken by Christine Harris and Lizzie Bucknell helped with the editing and indexing.

David Banister

Introduction

'I keep six honest serving men,
They taught me all I know
Their names are why and when and where,
And what and how and who.'
Rudyard Kipling, 'Just So' Stories.

This annotated bibliography attempts to categorize the who, when, where and what of the Kipling passage quoted above. In addition the how and the why are alluded to in the sections at the beginning of each major section. Research on rural transport and planning has become an important issue in itself, and with the exponential increase in the number of publications available, a systematic review now seems appropriate. The focus is on the rural environment, but, because the distinction between rural and urban areas is difficult to make, some urban references have also been made. The size of the subject area has also made it possible to claim comprehensiveness in the coverage, and for every reference included in the bibliography one has been rejected. The purpose of this introduction is twofold. It will first outline the structure of the bibliography and secondly it will explain the referencing system that has been developed so that the reader can use the volume effectively.

There are six major sections, each of which is self-contained with some cross referencing between the sections. Each section has a short introduction that attempts to describe and highlight the main themes together with the principal publications. The abstracts are mainly descriptive, with comments and recommendations being restricted to the introductory text. The first section is the shortest, and outlines the rural context with some of the seminal texts that cover the main changes which have taken place in rural society as a whole over the last twenty years. This section is complemented by a similar description of the transport context in rural areas.

The second section covers the policy making and planning framework as it relates to rural transport in Great Britain, the United States of America and briefly Europe. The transport legislation is complex, but the main themes have been extracted with the rural elements tabulated. In the third section the focus is on access and mobility. Much research in the rural context has been initiated on the concepts of accessibility, mobility, deprivation, need and equity, and this work has been complemented by studies that have focused either on spatial inequalities or particular social groups or the decline of rural facilities. If research on transport in rural areas has a major contribution to make to other urban or social science research, it is in this area.

Many different means of transport have been used in rural locations and these are described in section four. The conventional bus and rail have been in common use for the last hundred years, but their futures may be limited.The private car has become almost synonymous with a rural life-style and this trend seems likely to continue. The numerous unconventional public transport alternatives may offer limited mobility to those without access to a car, and the rapidly growing literature on the subject is outlined in this section. Although analysis methods have not featured extensively in rural research, section five covers the applications of methods to rural transport problems both in a strictly analytical context and in investment appraisal and evaluation. This section on analysis also includes research on energy consumption in transport, environmental and safety issues as well as a short selection on engineering problems as they relate to rural areas.

The final section has grouped together those studies that have an area-based emphasis. Allocation has been difficult in some cases as particular publications could have been put into more than one section. The cross-referencing between sections has provided one means to get round this problem, but papers have only been allocated to this section if there is no other obvious location for them. Section seven covers bibliographies and selected information sources together with a short list of the principal periodicals.

The system of numbering is consecutive and continuous. Each major section has a number which is then followed by a letter to indicate the subsection. Similarly each reference in the bibliography is uniquely defined by two digits and the section and subsection identifier. Hence 3B always comes before 4B and 3C28 before 3C38. As a reference book this arrangement will help readers to find their way around the volume quickly and efficiently.

1   The context

1A   The rural context

Rural areas are in a continual state of change. The purpose of planning in this environment is to secure a stable and coherent pattern of land use in such a way as to produce the most life-enhancing pattern of activity for the community as a whole. Planning is the form of public intervention to secure this end (Robins [1A45]). Until recently most research and analysis had a distinct urban focus, but during the 1970s this situation was redressed (Cherry [1A11]). The two separate spatial strands have now come together as current research is questioning the premise that there is a distinct set of rural planning problems, particularly as the 'boundary' between rural and urban is becoming less apparent (Moseley [1A35]).

Many attempts have been made to come up with a definition of rural areas through statistical analysis of published data (e.g. Cloke [1A13] [1A14], Wytconsult [1A53]) or through the identification of key area characteristics (Blacksell and Gilg [1A5]). Blacksell and Gilg group rural areas into one of four broad categories, each of which has a distinctive set of planning problems. First there is the urban fringe that forms the buffer between truly urban and rural locations. Here the policy has been one of urban containment (Hall et al. [1A30]) even though pressures for incremental growth have been considerable, both for residential and industrial purposes.

The second area type is the agricultural lowlands. With the growth of incomes and car ownership levels, many former urban dwellers have moved into rural areas even though they continue to work in the neighbouring urban centres. Similarly some elderly people have sought retirement homes away from the city. The net result is that one has an unbalanced population profile as migration both in and out of rural areas is selective in social and demographic terms. There is the old-established resident who may be elderly or employed locally and who has had to accommodate to declining levels of service; on the other hand there is the recent migrant who may have urban-based life styles and only resides in the rural area playing no active part in the rural community. In effect one has communities within communities (Pahl [1A43]). Most recently however, it seems that many of the urban migrants are now becoming involved in local issues and are transforming and perhaps reviving rural community life (Bryant *et al.* [1A8]).

The two other area types cover the hill and remote uplands. Here there is a decline in the indigenous population with low employment opportunities and low income levels. However these areas do provide the major inland recreation resource as well as minerals and water supplies for the urban consumer. More recently, affluent urban dwellers have bought up and often renovated property for use as second homes or as retirement homes. Blacksell and Gilg [1A5] conclude that there are two planning approaches at work in rural areas. The statutory planning process operates in a rather negative way with its substantial powers of control over building, and it is accompanied by a diverse package of resource planning functions covering such interests as agriculture, forestry, recreation and tourism. These functions are not necessarily convergent.

In this short review of the rural context, certain themes will be selected to give an indication of the enormous range and diversity of research in rural areas. This introduction will form a focus for the transport contribution to the debate. In this respect, an outline will be given of the recent changes that have taken place in Britain and the demise of public transport in rural areas.

Settlement policy has features in many studies with arguments being stated for and against the key settlement. The economic case is based on the economies of scale that can be achieved in the provision of public services through concentration (Bunce [1A9], Cloke [1A15]). The most rigorous analysis of the policy has been carried out by Gilder [1A26], who concludes that the concept is only valid for certain services, not the whole range. Whatever economies of scale exist in theory may be completely out-weighed by the transition costs that would be incurred through writing off existing fixed capital. Others have argued that the policy has not been systematically thought out but that it was merely the means by which resources could be saved (Cloke *et al.* [1A19]). Nevertheless there does seem to have been a trend towards fewer, larger units, particularly with respect to the provision of services. For example, health care facilities have become characterized by group practices with large catchment areas and hospital facilities have become both more centralized and specialized (Rigby [3D29]). However the most recent evidence suggests that a reversal is now taking place with the growth of community initiatives (e.g. self-help bus schemes) and development control policies that favour village shops and post offices (Association of County Councils [1A1]. Rural Voice [1A46]).

The primary concern of rural planning has been with conservation and environmental issues rather than the means by which employment opportunities can be introduced (Gilg [1A28]). Employment in the primary sector, principally agriculture, has been declining at a rate of two to three per cent a year due to dramatic increases in efficiency. Drudy [1A24] has concluded that because there has been no alternative to agriculture, a vicious circle of decline has been initiated with the net result that emigration takes place and facilities decline. This employment-led cycle of decline is supported by evidence from elsewhere (e.g. Hodge and Whitby [1A32]) and some conclude (e.g. Beale [1A3]) that rural labour problems are the primary cause of rural depopulation in developed countries. Proposals to alleviate unemployment have mainly concentrated on the manufacturing sector with small industrial concerns making such products as furniture, scientific and electronic instruments and food processing. Some (e.g. Gilg [1A27]) argue that these industries are transitory and will go the same way as agriculture with the introduction of new technology. The service sector may offer opportunities or the rural resident may be resigned to a shorter working week, job sharing and more time to enjoy the countryside (Davidson and Wibberley [1A22]).

Housing is a third sector of much recent activity (Dunn *et al.* [1A25]). The availability of housing for local people has been affected by the demand for existing properties by urban migrants as retirement or second homes. Secondly, the already small stock of rural public housing is being considerably reduced through legislative changes that now allow council house dwellers to purchase their homes at advantageous prices. With the general increase in affluence and mobility, the rural housing stock no longer accommodates only the traditional rural worker. There are a wide range of other functions that it now serves and the pressures are likely to increase with the demographic changes that are taking place and the impact that micro-technology might have on the location decisions of both employers and residents (Bradshaw and Blakesley [1A7]).

Rural deprivation has emerged as a counter-part to urban deprivation (Walker [1A48]). It is difficult to identify the particular facets of rural poverty, but its characteristics are much wider than low income levels. Deprivation extends to the limited availability of employment and the absence of facilities and transport services, which lead to social isolation (Shaw [1A47]). Certain groups of rural residents have been identified as having particular problems, namely the elderly, the young, housewives and the disabled—perhaps amounting to nearly half the rural population (McLaughlin [1A37]). Some would argue that the rural resident benefits from a better environment and should be prepared to pay the price (Moseley [1A34]). These themes are taken up again in the transport context in Section 3 when the concepts of accessibility and mobility are discussed (Banister [1A2], Moseley [1A34]).

The study of the politics of planning in rural areas has perhaps offered some of the most original research. Sociologists have long been active in rural research (e.g. Bracey [1A6]), but recent work has opened new insights. Newby and his colleagues (Buttel and Newby [1A10], Newby [1A40], Newby et al. [1A41]) have focused on the mechanisms of rural decision-making and the primary role that certain groups such as landowners, farmers and the middle-class newcomers have on the outcomes of important decisions. It is argued that these groups, often in concert but sometimes in opposition, further their own interests at the expense of other local (but less cohesive and powerful) groups. The growth of the pressure group is one means by which community interests can be protected, but the same powerful alliances can still infiltrate these organizations (Lowe and Goyder [1A33]).

1B The transport context

Car ownership levels have continued to rise in rural areas despite increases in the prices of fuel and new vehicles. Trends are soon reestablished once the initial impact of price rises has been absorbed. In rural areas in Britain, about eighty per cent of households own at least one car, and the total level of vehicle ownership is much higher if bicycles and motorcycles are included: this compares with the national figure (1981) of sixty per cent of households with at least one car. Car ownership levels tend to be positively correlated with household income and negatively with population density (Rhys and Buxton [1B9]). Thus a household with a given income is more likely to own a car in a rural area than in an urban area.

Journey lengths in rural areas are on average about thirty per cent longer than those in all other areas. Shopping stands out as the trip purpose with the greatest difference, but in all cases rural people have to travel significantly further. Trip rates are however slightly lower, but the greater mean trip lengths give rural residents a total travel distance per week nearly twenty five per cent above the mean for all areas. The actual time taken to make a journey may not differ by so much as journey speeds are typically higher in rural areas (Banister [3A2]).

Public transport patronage has declined from peak levels in 1952 by about fifty per cent. At that time nearly forty per cent of all vehicular kilometres were by bus, but now the level is about eight per cent in rural areas. The two principal early reviews of the rural transport problem were made by Jacks (GB, Ministry of Transport [2A28]) and Thomas [1B10]. There were several reasons for this decline, the principal one being the increase in car ownership. Oldfield [1B6] has estimated that for every additional car, 300 bus trips were lost each year, and that the increase in car ownership accounted directly for about forty five per cent of the observed public transport patronage decline. The consequence of the decline in demand has been that bus operators have reduced the level of service provided, particularly frequency, and during the last four years alone fares have been raised by about thirty per cent in real terms. However, the fall in the annual vehicle kilometres has not been of a similar order (a nineteen per cent decline 1969–1980). Buses are now running emptier and so vehicle productivity has fallen despite increases in staff productivity (Rhys [1B8]). Overall, the number of passenger journeys on services run by the National Bus Company has declined by 38 per cent (1969–1980) (Bus and Coach Council [1B2]).

Railways in rural areas account for about 1100 M passenger kilometres a year with gross revenue amounting to £26M a year and direct expenses totalling £44M a year (Hodge [1B4]). The rural railway network was halved under the Beeching Plan (British Railways Board [1B1]) to about 5000 kilometres, and their present contribution to total rail travel is about four per cent. Most recently the

Serpell Committee (GB, Department of Transport [1B3]) has examined the railways' finances, and although certain savings can be made on current operations it seems that significant reductions in the size of the network will be required if the levels of financial support are to be lowered substantially. Inevitably this will mean the closure of rural railways. The most extreme option reduces the network from 17600 route kilometres to 2600 route kilometres (sixteen per cent) and the least extreme option reduces the network to 14600 route kilometres (eighty three per cent). In each case it is the rural routes that would be first to go as the average loadings per train are often less than thirty people and the service could be replaced by the bus. Bus operating costs can be as little as a quarter of rail operating costs.

A quiet revolution seems to have been taking place in the countryside and some of the principal issues have been highlighted, both in the broader rural context and as they relate to transport. Accessibility for those who have acquired or already own a car has been increased or maintained, but for those without access the situation is the reverse. Local facilities have closed and distances to be travelled have increased, but the vital transport links have also been curtailed. Thus, as in other sectors, there seems to have been a move from the public provision of transport (e.g. the bus) towards the private provision of transport (e.g. the car or the bicycle). These trends are apparent in both Great Britain and other developed countries (Organisation for Economic Cooperation and Development [1B7]).

1A Rural context

1A1 ASSOCIATION OF COUNTY COUNCILS (1979) *Rural Deprivation*. London: Eaton House, September.

This report contains the results and conclusions of the examination of rural deprivation carried out by the Association of County Councils. The terms of reference were to consider and report on: the nature and extent of rural deprivation in England and Wales; the difficulties and costs of providing rural services; the extent to which the allocation of resources reflects the scale of rural problems and the costs of overcoming them; the policies at present adopted by public authorities in rural areas; and ways in which public authorities could alleviate rural problems, especially if a fairer allocation of national resources were achieved. Part of the report examines the nature and extent of rural deprivation in England and Wales, the costs of provision, the allocation of resources and current policies. The present national allocation of resources is then discussed. Some ways by which public authorities could alleviate rural problems, given a more realistic allocation of resources, are also examined.

In the section on rural transport, essential needs are considered, which include good communications by rural industries. The scale, distribution and quality of transport opportunities in rural areas are discussed. Details are tabulated of the high road mileage in sparsely populated areas, and the decrease in passenger journeys made by public transport during 1965-75, with vehicle fleet remaining almost constant, is shown graphically. The relation between population decline and transport network is shown for Devon County, and the effects on a rural population of changes in motoring costs are discussed. Transport provision by local authority consists mainly of providing and adequately maintaining the highway network. This is reviewed in the light of increased vehicle loadings and financial resources available. Reference is made to the need for subsidizing uneconomic passenger services for various groups in rural communities. A description is given of unconventional passenger services and reference is made to the experience gained by TRRL RUTEX experiments. The need for extra financial resources is stated, and policies and actions which might be pursued are listed.

1A2 BANISTER, D.J. (1980) *Transport Mobility and Deprivation in Inter Urban Areas*, Farnborough: Gower.

This book reports on a major research project carried out in Oxfordshire on areas that are adjacent to the urban fringe. After an extensive review of concepts, definitions and previous research, the method and selection of parishes for household survey are outlined. Travel patterns and levels of access are described by location and the different social groups, and this is followed by a theoretical and empirical analysis of car availability and usage patterns together with an attitudinal survey of public transport. The attitudinal analysis also tests two new methodologies, one a gaming approach and the second conjoint measurement analysis, both developed specifically for the task. The concepts of latent demand, transport deprivation and accessibility are discussed both conceptually and in terms of measurement methods. The main empirical findings, plus

comments on methods and conceptual issues, are then placed within
a wider policy context so that recommendations for action can be
made. The policy issues covered are both national and local. Four
appendices cover further methodological points relevant to the main
text of the work and there is also an extensive bibliography.

1A3 BEALE, C.L. (1980) The changing nature of rural employment, in
Brown, D.L. and Wardell, J.M. (eds) *New Directions in Urban-Rural
Migration: the Population Turnaround in Rural America*, London: Aca-
demic Press.

1A4 BEST, R.H. (1981) *Land Use and Living Space*, London: Methuen.

Conventional wisdom suggests that good quality agricultural land is
being turned over to urban use at an increasing and alarming rate.
The evidence presented here suggests a contrary assessment, namely
that transfers of agricultural land to urban use have tended to decline; and that this has been particularly true since the mid 1970s.
A systematic study has been carried out on the amounts of land and
space that are available for various activities and whether changes
in the land-use structure are likely to have any effects on our land
resources and life-styles, particularly where food supplies are concerned.

1A5 BLACKSELL, M. and GILG, A.W. (1981) *The Countryside: Planning and
Change*, London: George Allen and Unwin.

This book investigates the underlying reasons for change in the rural
environment and the response of the government as reflected in the
powers assumed and rights granted to guide and direct rural development. The relationships between land use changes and public
policy are analysed with special reference to rural settlements.
Throughout the book there is recourse to case study material from
Devon to illustrate the main conclusions.

1A6 BRACEY, H.E. (1970) *People and the Countryside*, London: Routledge
and Kegan Paul.

This book is split into two main parts. The first provides the background information on population, migration, employment, mobility, government and planning, and the second part considers ways

in which the countryside should best be used in the 1970s, especially for leisure. The chapter on mobility describes the development of the roads and waterways up to the nineteenth century and then the more modern changes in the railway, bus and road system. Transport is seen as the key element in facilitating access to recreational opportunities.

1A7 BRADSHAW, K. and BLAKESLEY, E.J. (1979) *Rural Communities in Advanced Industrial Society*, New York: Praeger.

1A8 BRYANT, C.R., RUSSWURM, L.H. and McLELLAN, A.G. (1982) *The City's Countryside: Land and its Management in the Rural Urban Fringe*, London: Longman.

A wide range of regional contexts including the United States, Canada, France, the United Kingdom and Australia are used to illustrate the types of problems and the changing patterns of land use encountered in the rural-urban fringe. These area-based studies supplement separate chapters on residential development, agriculture, industry and commerce, recreational activities, infrastructure and institutions. As a fairly systematic approach is used, some of the conflicts between the different political groups and interest groups are not covered in depth, as similarities have been identified and not the differences in problems and approaches.

1A9 BUNCE, M. (1981) *Rural Settlement in an Urban World*, London: Croom Helm.

At a time when the resource shortages and operational difficulties of small settlements seem endemic, this book re-emphasises the continued significance of rural settlement forms. Over half the world's population still live in rural areas and the description covers the patterns of villages, their stagnation and decline, their changing functions and the future of the rural settlement.

1A10 BUTTEL, F.H. and NEWBY, H. (eds) (1980) *The Rural Sociology of the Advanced Societies*, London: Croom Helm.

Rural sociology is now in the midst of a number of important changes in theory, method and content; the contributors, from many Western nations, focus on all aspects of the subject, including the processes of cultural transformation, agriculture, labour, rural underdevelopment, rural poverty, land use planning and environmental problems, with particular emphasis on agricultural policy. The volume seeks to be comparative both in terms of the range of authors and the nature of the papers themselves. To that extent it breaks new ground as other studies have tended to be localized and parochial in nature.

1A11 CHERRY, G. (1976) (ed) *Rural Planning Problems*, London: Leonard Hill.

This book consists of a series of specially commissioned essays that were intended to redress the imbalance between urban and rural studies. Rural planning is not merely a question of protecting the countryside in visual and developmental terms or of providing facilities for outdoor recreation. It also embraces the question of recognizing and acting in areas of conflict in values and priority; whether these be employment, housing, population migration, village life, land use aspects or the provision of recreation and leisure facilities. Rather surprisingly transport does not feature prominently as it is only given five pages, even though it is recognized as a problem that has always existed in rural areas. The approach suggested is similar to that in other areas of community planning, namely that the State should shed some of its obligations to voluntary agencies. However what is evident is that transport solutions derived from a large scale urban society may not be applicable in small scale dispersed communities.

1A12 CHISHOLM, M. (1979) *Rural Settlement and Land Use. An Essay in Location*, London: Hutchinson.

This volume examines the relationships between agricultural settlements and factors such as distance, soil, slope and climate. The argument starts in the classical location theory of Van Thünen and covers the development of the village both in the developed and developing world.

1A13 CLOKE, P.J. (1977) An index of rurality for England and Wales. *Regional Studies*, **11** (1), pp. 31–46.

Rurality is defined in terms of selecting discriminating variables from which an index is formed using principal components analysis.

Distributions of four classifications of rurality are presented and both problematical rural areas and those suffering from extreme urban pressure are identified. Data generated are useful both for looking at possible solutions to problems in the different area types and as an aid to grouping areas with similar characteristics.

1A14 CLOKE, P.J. (1978) Changing patterns of urbanisation in rural areas of England and Wales, 1961–1971. *Regional Studies*, **12** (5), pp. 603–17.

Data generated by the construction of indices of rurality for 1961 and 1971 are used to describe the manifestations of rural change over this period. Particular emphasis is paid to processes of urbanization but 'ruralization' trends are also monitored. Analysis of inter-index change suggests some underlying uniformities in the processes of rurality dynamics over time. A cyclic or spiral model of rural change is proposed and both present and projected movements on the cycle are examined. Finally, practical applications of the cyclic model, both in terms of planning processes and in the understanding of rurality trends, are outlined.

1A15 CLOKE, P.J. (1979) *Key Settlements in Rural Areas*, London: Methuen.

Rural communities in Britain are in a crisis. The problems of providing essential services in a constrained economic climate and of conserving rural environments whilst protecting rural people, are of immediate importance in the countryside as a whole. Key settlement planning policies have long been regarded as a panacea for the ills existing in all types of rural area. Recently, however, many professionals have suggested that the key settlement approach has been short-sighted and that its continuation may well prejudice the long term health and stability of rural areas. The author examines in detail the history and theory behind key settlement policies and their practical application within the British rural planning system. The outcome of key settlement planning in two very different counties is measured and the specific conclusions from these case studies are fed into a discussion of the wider implications of the 'concentration-dispersal' debate. Finally the problems of rural policy evaluation and the future of key settlement policy are considered.

1A16 CLOKE, P.J. (1980) New emphases for applied rural geography. *Progress in Human Geography*, **4**, pp. 181–217.

1A17 CLOKE, P.J. (1983) *An Introduction to Rural Settlement Planning*, London: Methuen.

Following the initial post war emphasis on city rebuilding programmes in Britain, rural settlement planning has only slowly established itself as an equal in the partnership of town and country planning. The specific procedures of growth point nomination have evolved into a more flexible process that aims to cater for the needs of individual rural settlements. This book provides an introduction to the theory, practice and politics of rural settlement planning. It surveys the conceptual and ideological leanings of those who have developed, implemented and revised rural settlement practice, and gives details analysis of the literature of planning documentation so that an assessment of successful implementation can take place.

The focus of concern is over rural housing, employment, services and public transport, and how particular groups have been affected. Here the poor feature prominently. The shortfalls of rural planning and resource management are assessed, and some methods are presented through which rural communities can obtain a stable and equitable future.

1A18 CLOKE, P.J. and PARK, C. (1984) *Rural Resource Management*, London: Croom Helm.

The particular angle that this book takes on resource management is its synoptic view with a geographical treatment of physical, landscape and social resources, conflicts between them and approaches to integrated management. Drawing on British, European and North American material, the book has three main objectives: to offer an integrated review of the rural resources system; to isolate potential and actual conflicts between resources in the countryside and to analyse particular themes through a series of detailed case studies; and to explore various broad management techniques and their applicability to differing types of resource use and resource conflict.

1A19 CLOKE, P.J., AYTON, J.B. and GILDER, I. (1980) The key settlement approach. *The Planner*, **66** (4), pp. 98–9.

A series of three short responses on this issue. The conclusions reached suggest that a pragmatic or practical approach should be

adopted to key settlement policy and that through a robust framework of direct action some stability to the system can be introduced.
Consistency in approach, together with acceptance of the outcomes
should be the key points in application.

A20 CLOUT, H. (1977) Rural settlements. *Progress in Human Geography*, **1**
(3), pp. 475–80.

A21 COUNTRYSIDE REVIEW COMMITTEE (1977) Rural Communities—A
Discussion Paper, London: HMSO, Topic Paper No 1.

This discussion paper is the first report of the CRC that is intended
to stimulate public debate so that priorities for the rural areas can
be established. This one reviews the changing nature of rural communities and proposes various new initiatives that could be taken.

A22 DAVIDSON, J. and WIBBERLEY, G. (1977) *Planning and the Rural
Environment*, Oxford: Pergamon.

This book is about the changing fabric of the open countryside with
a central theme being the conflict of interests between some of the
major rural users and groups. The repercussions for the countryside
of changing activities and attitudes in five main areas of rural resource planning are examined: farming, forestry, leisure, the conservation of wild life and landscape. Their interactions are then
explored in the contrasting environments of the urban fringe and
the uplands. In the final section the development of rural planning
is discussed together with the major problems that have emerged.
The conclusion reached suggests that the rural environment is
changing at a rapid rate and that the characteristics of the present
countryside could rapidly disappear.

A23 DRUDY, P.J. (ed) (1976) *Regional and Rural Development: Essays in
Theory and Practice*, Chalfont St Giles: Alpha Academic.

Regional inequality is now widespread and its elimination has become an increasingly important part of government policy in many
countries. This inequality is particularly evident in depressed industrial and rural regions. This book brings together a series of perspectives and experiences from Britain and France so that the problems can be examined and the effects of policies analysed. Attention

is given to the growth point and industrial complex approaches to the development of lagging regions, and the role of various agencies responsible for regional and rural development is assessed.

1A24 DRUDY, P.J. (1978) Depopulation in a prosperous agricultural sub-region. *Regional Studies*, **12** (1), pp. 49-60.

It is little known that the phenomenon of depopulation is not confined to the marginal agricultural regions of Britain but is present in prosperous regions also. This paper examines the extent of depopulation in one such prosperous sub-region, North Norfolk in Eastern England. The process is shown to have accelerated during the most recent decade. Among the contributory factors are the agricultural adjustments which have caused a high rate of redundancy and the lack of employment alternatives to agriculture. It appears that the theory of 'cumulative causation' may have special relevance towards explaining the phenomenon.

1A25 DUNN, M., RAWSON, M. and ROGERS, A.W. (1981) *Rural Housing: Competition and Choice*, London: George Allen and Unwin.

This book explores the plight of the locally born or locally employed faced with spiralling house prices and strong and unequal competition from the richer commuter, the second home owner and the retirement migrant from the city. This study then examines the policy and planning issues through basic research and analysis.

1A26 GILDER, I.M. (1979) Rural planning policies: an economic appraisal. *Progress in Planning*, **11** (3), pp. 213-71.

One of the major principles upon which rural planning policies have been founded is that considerable savings in public service costs may be made if new development in rural areas is concentrated in a limited number of larger settlements rather than dispersed throughout the countryside. Whilst many doubts have been raised on this assertion and its validity, very little rigorous analysis has been undertaken. This study investigates the economics of rural service provision.

A27 GILG, A.W. (1978) *Countryside Planning, the First Three Decades 1945–76*, Newton Abbot: David and Charles.

The demands for the use of rural land have reached a degree of intensity where serious conflicts between the users of the countryside can best be resolved by a broadly-based approach to countryside planning. Focusing on the British experience in planning for agriculture, land use and settlement, forestry, water, recreation, conservation, building and landscape, the approaches adopted by different countryside planning agencies are examined within a common framework which compares and contrasts outcomes. The wider implications to be drawn from the first thirty years of countryside planning are highlighted at the end of each section and the book concludes with an assessment of the likely trends for the remainder of the century.

A28 GILG, A.W. (1983) Population and employment, in Pacione, M. (ed) *Progress in Rural Geography*, Beckenham: Croom Helm, pp. 74–105.

Because rural populations are so complex and dynamic, problems are posed in the collection of data and even a simple description of what is happening. This review paper begins by examining general descriptive studies at three spatial levels—the world, the country and local levels—before looking at some of the explanatory models that have been developed. Included here are density and population potential, rural migration studies and classificatory studies. In the second part, rural employment is outlined at the national and county level with a focus on the factual background and employment policies and proposals. Recent trends indicate that there may be a massive recolonization of the countryside during the rest of the century.

1A29 GREEN, R.J. (1971) *Country Planning: The Future of the Rural Regions*, Manchester: Manchester University Press.

1A30 HALL, P., DREWETT, R., GRACEY, H. and THOMAS, R. (1973) *The Containment of Urban England*, London: George Allen and Unwin.

Two volumes form the outcome of a five year study at Political and Economic Planning into the processes of urban growth in England after 1945, and the impact of the postwar British land use planning on those processes. The first volume has urban growth as its focus whilst the second concentrates on the planning system and its interaction with other actors in the development process.

1A31 HANRAHAN, P.J. and CLOKE, P.J. (1983) Towards a critical appraisal of rural settlement planning in England and Wales. *Sociologia Ruralis*, **23** (2), pp. 109–29.

The principal thrust of this paper is that in the light of continuing social deprivation in rural areas of England and Wales assessments of the statutory planning system have generally tended to understate the limitations inherent in the public policy process. The authors outline the narrow scope bestowed upon planners given their role as state officials, as functionaries of devolved government and as public servants charged inter alia with responsibilities for influencing the deployment of private resources. The conclusion is reached that future research should place greater emphasis upon the conflicts underlying policy decisions and their relationship to sustained inequity.

1A32 HODGE, I. and WHITBY, M. (1981) *Rural Employment*, London: Methuen.

The key to the depopulation of rural areas is seen as one of influence over the labour markets. Migration in search of work has been a major cause of rural decline, and its reversal to bring about economically viable communities must be related to the availability of employment in rural areas. Though recent demographic trends show signs of some recovery in rural areas, major problems remain. Rural economic policy's primary aim should be to establish socially viable communities.

1A33 LOWE, P.D. and GOYDER, J. (1983) *Environmental Groups in Politics*, London: George Allen and Unwin.

Since the 1960s environmental groups have emerged as a significant force in politics. Not only have they influenced legislation and official policy, but they have also aroused considerable sympathy among the public. In Britain, approximately one in ten of the adult population belongs to an environmental group. With an estimated

2.5 to 3 million supporters, the environmental movement is larger than any political party or trade union. It is thus a major social phenomenon as well as a political force.

The book is divided into three sections. The first section (four chapters) provides an overview of the size and diversity of the environmental lobby and its role in local and national politics. It also examines various ways of analysing and conceptualizing environmental groups. To understand the causes and consequences of organized environmental concern, the study is placed in a broad academic context, drawing insights from history, sociology and political science.

The second section comprises detailed case studies of five environmental groups—the Henley Society (a local amenity group), Friends of the Earth, the National Trust, the Royal Society for Nature Conservation and the European Environmental Bureau. These provide the reader with original material on a series of representative, local, national and international groups, as well as illustrating the application of the conceptual and analytical tools provided in the first section. For each group, its internal structure, resources and access to the political system are described as a basis for assessing its effectiveness.

Finally, the conclusions marshal the book's findings around three central themes: the reasons for the emergence of environmentalism as a political force; the relationship between the internal and external organizations of environmental groups; and the implications of their involvement in politics for other interests in society.

The book ends with speculation about the future. Despite the uncertainty with the current economic outlook, the environmental movement is a well-established feature of the political scene.

A34 MOSELEY, M.J. (1979) *Accessibility: The Rural Challenge*, London: Methuen.

The author sets out the problems, faced by planners, County Councils, education and health authorities, transport officials, and by those who live in rural Britain, of the inaccessibility of many areas of the country. For those two-car families who choose to live in the remoter villages, it matters little that the main town is only accessible by bus once a day. But for the poor, children, housewives, the elderly it can be a matter of some urgency when local shops, schools

and medical services are being whittled away in favour of larger
units in distant towns. This book, based on the author's report for
the Department of the Environment on rural transport and accessibility, reviews the process of decline which has led to this situation,
and considers the concept of accessibility and shows how it can be
developed into an analytical tool for measuring the success or failure
of alternative policies. The author details each policy option in turn:
the support of conventional bus or other transport services; the provision of mobile services; 'mini-outlet' policies; and the long-term
restructuring of the rural settlement pattern. He devotes a chapter
to the crucial fragmentation of decision-making bodies, which inhibits the necessary coordinated attack on the problem, and concludes with a chapter on 'the way ahead' which sets out his policy
for meeting the 'rural inaccessibility problem'.

1A35 MOSELEY, M.J. (1980) Is rural deprivation really rural? *The Planner*,
66 (4), p. 97.

This short paper argues that urban and rural deprivation are localized expressions of the same essentially aspatial problems. The focus
may be slightly different, but the problems are similar. To understand the causes of deprivation the scope should be set at the widest
possible level so that not just the deprived are investigated but
also the principal decision-makers, institutions and the providers of
finance.

1A36 McLAUGHLIN, B.P. (1976) The future of the village: a planner's
view. *Village*, 31, pp. 54–7.

A planner looks at planning attitudes to villages in the light of
county development plans and structure plans produced over the
last twenty-five years. The basic problems have been depopulation,
and the need to improve social amenities, educational and employment opportunities. Villages are classified into a four- or five-tier
system, ranging from a key village to small hamlets or 'outliers'.
Planners have over-concentrated on key villages and people have to
face the choice of moving to these or accept ever diminishing services. The author suggests an alternative policy, investing in groups
of villages on the principle of 'functional interdependence'. This will
require fresh thinking on rural employment and transport and a less
inflexible approach to both.

37 McLAUGHLIN, B.P. (1981) Rural deprivation. *Planner*, **67** (2), pp. 31-3.

The case for rural deprivation is argued on the grounds of a lengthy list of problems, notably: employment, service provision, accessibility, housing, and political ideology. The author argues whether the 'arithmetic of use' demonstrates the existence of rural deprivation or not, and concludes that more detailed research into the decision making patterns is required.

38 NATIONAL COUNCIL OF SOCIAL SERVICE (1979) Structure plans and rural communities, NCSS Report.

This desk study outlines the treatment of rural communities in a number of structure plans. It summarizes the main policies adopted in respect of nine key policy areas including transport. It then provides a systematic summary for each of the twenty-one structure plans reviewed with respect to the policy areas, and the final part of the report provides verbatim extracts to illustrate the main points.

39 NATIONAL EXECUTIVE COMMITTEE OF THE LABOUR PARTY (1979) Rural areas—an interim statement, March.

A review is presented of the problems of rural areas, in particular the inter-relationships between the different sectors and the importance of transport. Some tentative proposals are outlined—but these require both considerable financial commitment and political will.

40 NEWBY, H. (1979) *Green and Pleasant Land? Social Change in Rural England*, London: Pelican.

A generalized appraisal of the myth and reality of social change in rural England is presented. Although written from a sociological viewpoint Newby incorporates economic, historical and political viewpoints into the discussion. The first part is concerned with agricultural change, which it is argued is the root cause of rural social change. Considerable attention is given to changes in land tenure, the changing structure of the agricultural industry, and the continuing lowly position of the farm worker. The second part examines two recent national trends that have eroded the traditional agrarian society: changes in the social and occupational composition of villages, including the rural housing issue, and the conflict between economic rationality and environmentalism. The study concentrates on lowland, arable areas at the expense of the remoter uplands and the term 'rural' is interpreted as agricultural. Alternative applications are not examined, and this results in limited assessment of social groups other than the farming populations.

1A41 NEWBY, H., BELL, C., ROSE, D. and SAUNDERS, P. (1978) *Property, Paternalism and Power: Class and Control in Rural England*, London: Hutchinson.

The authors have explored the agricultural industry in Eastern England and investigated the attitudes and behaviour of business owners and entrepreneurs. Unlike most sociology, the focus is on the powerful rather than the powerless, the propertied rather than the propertyless and the wealthy owners of land rather than the landless rural poor. It penetrates the surface of English rural life and systematically investigates how farmers and landowners have retained control of the countryside in the face of recent social and economic change.

1A42 PACIONE, M. (ed) (1983) *Progress in Rural Geography*, Beckenham, Kent: Croom Helm.

Rural geography has a long tradition, but until recently it generally referred to studies concerned with agriculture or comprised historical analyses and descriptions of the settlement or land use patterns of the countryside. Although these areas of investigation retain their importance within the subject, rural geography has expanded over the last decade to encompass other lines of enquiry such as the systematic study of transport, employment, housing, assessments of development policies and attempts to develop theory and methodology in rural studies. This volume consists of a series of original essays on the full range of rural geography and planning issues so that the current state of the art can be reviewed. It includes a chapter on rural transport and accessibility (Banister [3A2]).

1A43 PAHL, R.E. (1964) Urbs in Rure: The metropolitan fringe in Hertfordshire, London School of Economics and Political Science, Geographical Papers No. 2.

This study covers the forces and patterns characteristic of the rural fringe of Greater London. This area, with 4.3 million people is considered a city in its own right, but only that part which lies in Hertfordshire (north of London) is described in detail. As well as the remnant of agricultural activity, there is a largely working class local commuting population interspersed with a predominantly middle class, car-owning group of commuters to London. These groups live in distinct areas and lead essentially separate existences and this is the principal conclusion from a social survey of three representative parishes. In the two parishes there is clear evidence of a real segregation by social class, occupation, commuting habits, education and pattern of social contacts. This sector of the countryside is therefore beginning to have essentially urban characteristics.

A44 RANDOLPH, W. and ROBERT, S. (1981) Population redistribution in Great Britain 1971–1981. *Town and Country Planning*, September, pp. 227–31.

This paper summarizes some of the main population changes in the last ten years. Total population increased by 0.4 per cent, but there has been a major shift away from the peripheral regions to the southern part of the country. To some extent this has been counterbalanced by loss in population from the conurbations. So the overall picture is one that suggests movement south, particularly to the new towns, and growth in urban fringe areas plus selective movement back to the more accessible rural areas (East Anglia, the South West and the East Midlands).

A45 ROBINS, D.L.J. (1983) Rural planning, in Pacione, M. (ed) *Progress in Rural Geography*, Beckenham, Kent: Croom Helm, pp. 226–49.

After outlining some current rural issues in Britain, the institutional framework for rural policy making is described with particular emphasis on recent developments such as structure plans and sponsored research projects. It seems that problems of rural planning do not align with the hierarchy of national parks, areas of outstanding natural beauty and the rest of rural Britain. Finally certain social problems are described before concluding on the scope for planning controls in agriculture which at present lies outside the statutory planning process.

A46 RURAL VOICE (1981) *A Rural Strategy*, London: National Council for Voluntary Organisations.

Outlines the purpose of Rural Voice. It is an alliance of eight national organizations representing rural communities. Between them they represent nearly 800,000 members, with branches in every village in the country and thus a wealth of experience of rural life. An eight point strategy is proposed with respect to energy and transport.

1A47 SHAW, J.M. (ed) (1979) *Rural Deprivation and Planning*, Geo Abstracts Ltd, University of East Anglia, Norwich.

This volume draws together the work of seventeen people who are centrally concerned with rural deprivation. There are eleven chapters which range from the political base of rural deprivation, through rural incomes, employment and services to innovations being introduced by some rural community councils.

1A48 WALKER, A. (1978) (ed) *Rural Poverty—Poverty, Deprivation and Planning in Rural Areas*, Child Poverty Action Group, Poverty Pamphlet 37, November.

The purpose of this collection of papers is twofold—first to redirect focus on the issues of poverty and deprivation from urban to rural environments so that policies can be developed that cover both types of location. Secondly it is to highlight the particular problems of the poor in rural areas where there is acute inequality in the distribution of facilities and access to them. There is a section on transport—see Coles [3B14].

1A49 WHITBY, M.C. and WILLIS, K.G. (1978) *Rural Resource Development. An Economic Approach*, London: Methuen.

The aim of this book is to suggest ways to improve decisions as to the allocation of public resources in rural areas. The decision making process is outlined in descriptive, predictive and evaluative contexts, and the conceptual basis of the local government planning system in Britain is summarized. These sections contribute to an understanding of the last two steps in the decision sequence, namely policy review and the process of choice. There are also chapters on land use, recreation and amenity, population, the labour market, settlement patterns, economic planning models, rural decisions and transport. The conclusion reached with respect to rural transport argues that the problem is part of the wider issues of economic policy and that it is intimately bound up with social objectives and planning policy. Transport needs to be evaluated, not in isolation, but as a component in the general rural economy.

50 WIBBERLEY, G.P. (1974) Development in the countryside. *Journal of Environmental Management*, **2** (3), pp. 199–204.

The discussion concentrates on two important elements of rural change, those taking place in the agricultural landscape and in the rural settlement structure. Agricultural changes have been beneficial in many ways—improved food output and efficiency, high farm income, output per man and per £100 capital, but these have been accompanied by a severe thinning out of the primary rural population, a scattering of service personnel, the rise of large owner-occupied farms and a reduction in the variety of natural fauna and flora. Old rural landscapes are being destroyed, farm buildings are becoming industrial in their structure and siting, and farm wastes and effluent are proving noxious. Changes in the rural settlement structure arise from the decline in the farming population, the increased mobility of the people and products of primary industry and the great increase in temporary and permanent residential use by middle class people. Villages have become places with rural facades rather than integral parts of the modern rural economy.

51 WIBBERLEY, G.P. (1976) Rural resource development in Britain and environmental concern. *Journal of Agricultural Economics*, **27** (1), pp. 1–16.

52 WOODRUFFE, R.J. (1976) *Rural Settlement Policies and Plans*, Oxford: OUP.

This concise book is a review of policies and plans prepared for rural settlements by county planning authorities in Britain since the 1947 Town and Country Planning Act. It concentrates on the spatial and geographical characteristics of policies and plans. The overall approach is historical, tracing the evolution of the concepts and methods used by planning authorities in devising policies and drawing up plans to solve problems such as providing rural areas with modern services and amenities or controlling residential development in villages. As a conclusion certain areas in which geographical research might be of value to rural settlement planning are suggested.

1A53 WYTCONSULT (1977) Rural typology study, Document 803, April.

The importance of distinguishing rural areas, one from another, in order to formulate rural transport policies was basic to the Rural Transport Study. Individual rural areas can be distinguished in many respects. The approach reported in this document describes a purely statistical technique for making such distinctions. (See Wytconsult [2A63]).

1B Transport context

1B1 BRITISH RAILWAYS BOARD (1963) *Reshaping of British Railways*, London: BRB.

The objectives of the famous Beeching Report were to determine the basic characteristics which distinguish the railway as a mode of transport, to determine the conditions that are favourable to the railways and to determine which part of the railways conform to these conditions and to shape the railways accordingly. A small part of the system accounts for most of the traffic and it was recommended that the network should be reduced by over 50 per cent (28000 route km to 13000 route km). Many rural services and other stopping services would be discontinued. The report concluded that if the whole plan (also included recommendations for freight and some improvements in efficiency) is implemented with vigour, much of British Railways' deficit will be eliminated by 1970.

1B2 BUS AND COACH COUNCIL (1982) The future of the Bus, A special report, November.

This report is designed to stimulate discussion on the role of the bus in society and how that role may be consolidated and developed. It is argued that the financial aspects are important but the overriding constraint is the absence of a coherent and consistent policy of long term investment and support. The report also covers other policy issues which require action if the bus industry is to operate efficiently, economically, and above all in the public interest. It is particularly important in the light of recent legislation that discussion should take place—the role of the bus in national transport policy has been taken for granted too long.

B3 GB DEPARTMENT OF TRANSPORT (1983) Railway Finances, Report of a Committee chaired by Sir David Serpell, London: HMSO.

This committee was appointed to examine the finances of the railway and associated operations, in the light of all relevant considerations, and to report on the options for alternative policies, and their related objectives, designed to secure improved financial results in an efficiently run railway in Great Britain over the next twenty years. In seven months of work the committee produced a financial analysis that may prove of crucial importance to the future of the railways. In the short term improvements in efficiency can take place through reductions in manpower, changes in management structures, and reductions in engineering costs, but in the longer term more significant decisions may have to be made. The levels of support will have to be increased unless the network is reduced in size, and to this end a range of alternative options is considered. The commercial railway would be only 2500 route kilometres in length whilst an option which maintained existing connections to the network of all communities above 25000 would leave a network of 13600 route kilometres. Even a high investment option would reduce route kilometres (from the present level of 17500 route kilometres) and would not show a satisfactory financial return.

B4 HODGE, P. (1979) Permanent way for rural trains. *Surveyor*, **154** (4548), pp. 12–14.

Rural deprivation studies have paid little attention to railways and they are seen by many as making no significant contribution to rural transport, lacking the flexibility and cheapness required for success. This paper argues that railways do have a positive role to play even though it may become an increasingly selective one specifically tailored to particular social needs.

B5 NASH, C.A. (1982) *The Economics of Public Transport*, London: Longmans.

The book indicates the manner in which economic analysis can be used as an aid in decision taking in long-range planning and also the daily management of public transport systems. Using detailed applications, the book demonstrates the usefulness of applying economic analyses to problems such as fare structures and level, service planning and investment decisions. Although the emphasis is on road and rail systems, which form the bulk of internal public transport systems, the methods employed can be applied to other transport modes. International comparisons are used to show the relationship between objectives, external circumstances, organizations and policy in the operation of public transport organizations.

1B6 OLDFIELD, R. (1979) Effect of car ownership on bus patronage. *Transport and Road Research Laboratory*, LR 872.

This report estimates to what extent the decline in national bus patronage over the past decade or so can be attributed to the effect of increasing car ownership. Data from the National Travel Surveys of 1964/5, 1972/3 and 1975/6 were examined to compare trip-making by bus in households owning no cars, one car, and two or more cars. From this it was estimated that in 1964, for every additional car, 380 bus trips were lost per year as the new car users travelled less frequently by bus, while by 1976 this loss had dropped to 300 bus trips. Over the period 1964-76, this direct effect of increasing car ownership accounted for just under 45 per cent of the observed decline in bus patronage. In addition to this, there is a 'second-round' loss of patronage as bus operators respond to the reduction in revenue by cutting services and increasing fares. If the services were required to break even, then this second-round loss would be almost as great as the patronage lost as a direct result of the newly acquired cars. However, in the period studied, bus services in the UK moved from break-even to an overall deficit approaching some 30 per cent of costs. Had break-even been maintained the decline in passenger trips would have been considerably larger than the observed drop, and it is estimated that the direct effects of increased car ownership would have accounted for 32 per cent of this larger loss. Second-round effects of car ownership would have accounted for a further 26 per cent, while the remaining 42 per cent would have been due to increased costs of operation and various background trends.

The national trend in bus patronage was analysed to estimate elasticities of demand with respect to fares, level of service and real income after the reduction in patronage due to increasing car ownership had been taken into account. A fares elasticity of -0.45 could be reliably established, but correlation between the trends in bus-kilometres run and real income prevented an unambigious determination of a service elasticity defined in terms of bus kilometres run.

B7 ORGANISATION FOR ECONOMIC COOPERATION AND DEVELOPMENT (1979) *Transport Services in Low Density Areas*, OECD, Paris, September.

An international road research group was set up by OECD to examine public transport systems, both conventional and innovative, implemented in low density areas as well as possible future improvements to these types of service. Due to the increasing number of dispersed and low density zones which have evolved within the last thirty years in OECD countries, the problem of public transport services in these areas is of increasing economic and social importance as the levels of urban accessibility provided depend to a large extent on whether or not the residents possess a private means of transport. Firstly, the report examines urban development patterns, activity distributions and trip patterns and highlights the share of trips made by public transport. It considers the set of transport problems related to these zones supported by a classification of different forms of transport services together with their characteristics, such as system availability and intrinsic accessibility, flexibility in time and space depending on the nature of the system, private or public. The report indicates the main factors to take into account in physical planning in order to promote improved operation of conventional or demand-responsive systems currently in use or under study. It deals in turn with the general conditions applying to public involvement in these areas, the social objectives assigned to public transport, the framework for adequate co-ordination and lastly, the overall problem of evaluating transport schemes for low-density areas. Finally, the report presents a number of conclusions and recommendations regarding methods for improving transport services in low density areas and priority research subjects in this field.

1B8 RHYS, D.G. (1972) Economic change in the rural passenger transport industry. *Journal of Transport Economics and Policy*, **6** (3), pp. 240–53.

The main result from recent structural changes in the bus operating and bus manufacturing industries has been the spread of one-man bus operation to urban and inter-urban services. One-man operation had long been a feature of rural bus services. Changes in the industries have resulted from official government involvement in the road passenger transport sector, and often reflect official policy in this field. The most significant developments in recent years have been capital grants paid to operators by the Ministry of Transport, the restructuring of the bus operating sector, and changes in vehicle design. It is intended to consider the interaction between these three developments and to examine the economic consequences.

1B9 RHYS, D.G. and BUXTON, M.J. (1974) Car ownership and rural transport problems. *Chartered Institute of Transport Journal*, **36** (5), pp. 109–12.

During the past few years the various threats to cut rural bus services have highlighted the problems of the provision of transport facilities in sparsely populated areas. This paper examines the determinants of the geographical incidence of car ownership, and attempts to use this analysis as a basis for policies to alleviate the 'rural transport problem'. In particular there is an investigation of whether a rural transport network based upon traditional public transport services is the best way of providing a passenger transport infrastructure, or whether a system based on the private motor vehicle could be superior.

1B10 THOMAS, D. St. J. (1963) *The Rural Transport Problem*, London: Routledge and Kegan Paul.

This was one of the first major studies on the problem of transport in rural areas. It has two chief aims: to demonstrate the importance, human and economic, of preserving some passenger public transport in country areas even at the cost of subsidy; and to discuss whether the resources available for train and bus services could not be used more effectively than at present. The book is in two parts. The first deals generally with the problem and possible solutions including the habits and needs of country people and of those who provide their transport. The second is devoted entirely to an outline of the original research made under the auspices of the Dartington Hall Trustees and of the Lake District Transport Enquiry.

2 Policy and planning in transport

2A Great Britain

About a quarter of the population of Great Britain live in rural communities and it has been recognized that they have particular problems of mobility (GB Department of the Environment [2A19]). Public transport patronage levels have declined from their peak over thirty years ago. The problem was first identified in the Jack Committee's Report (GB Ministry of Transport [2A28]) on rural transport services where it was concluded that 'the present and probable future levels of rural bus services are not adequate to avoid a degree of hardship and inconvenience sufficient to call for special steps'. The social function of transport was recognized and the suggestion was made for selective direct financial assistance.

The 1968 Transport Act, although concentrating mainly on urban transport issues, set up a system of direct grants for unremunerative services with central Government paying half provided that the service covered at least fifty per cent of its costs. Since then, the situation for the public transport operator has further deteriorated, despite many studies of the 'rural transport problem' initiated either by central government (GB Department of the Environment [2A16], [2A17], [2A18], or by other agencies (Hillman *et al.* [2A37], Rees and Wragg [2A53], Wytconsult [2A63]). The conclusions were all similar, namely that the demand for public transport services was so disparate and varied that it was difficult to match them together to form any sensible load.

Further measures were taken in the Local Government Act (1972) when the non-metropolitan county councils were directed to develop policies which will promote 'the provision of a coordinated and efficient system of public passenger transport to meet the country's needs'. Each county had to submit an annual Transport Policy and Programme (TPP) that made an estimate of transport expenditure for the following financial year, a statement of transport objectives, a strategy in outline for the next five years, a statement of short term investment proposals, and a summary of past expenditure. This document forms the basis for the allocation of the Transport Supplementary Grant (TSG), the principal means by which Central Government supports local transport expenditure (Chartered Institute of Public Finance and Accountancy [2A9], Gwilliam [2A30], Hounsome [2A40], Knight [2A46]).

The concern over rural transport issues was reinforced by the 1978 Transport Act as counties were now required to submit an annual County Public Passenger Transport Plan (PTP) which would provide a clear statement of objectives and policies for public transport together with the financial and resource commitments (Rigby [2A54]). Public transport in rural areas had taken on an explicit social function in that services should be provided to meet the 'needs' of the residents (Banister [3B6]).

During this period two other important initiatives were taking place. First the Government established sixteen rural transport experiments in Devon, North Yorkshire, South Ayrshire, and Dinefwr (in Dyfed). The areas selected were all 'deep' rural areas where conventional services were never likely to be viable and the purpose of the experiments was to test the impact of a relaxation of the licensing laws so that service innovation could take place (Balcombe [4C8], [4C10], Martin [4A48]). The second change was the Market Analysis Project, introduced by the National Bus Company as a selective service planning tool (Barrett and Buchanan [4A3], Cameron [6A8], and Jelley [4A39]). It arose from the necessity for rationalization and the avoidance of a piecemeal approach to service provision which was typical of many operations (GB Department of Transport [2A23], [2A26]).

Most recently the 1980 Transport Act has introduced radical changes in the provision of public transport services in rural areas with service deregulation (GB Department of Transport [2A27]). The debate has been vigorous at all levels (Banister [2A3], Dean [2A13], Hibbs [2A34], Winfield [2A62]) as the Act may end cross-subsidization of routes with rural transport moving back towards straight economic criteria for route assessment. Certain rural areas may have a very limited public transport service and the future of the conventional bus as a means of transport in these locations has been questioned. The most significant events in transport policy as it relates to rural areas have been summarized in table 2.1.

Table 2.1   Principal Transport Policy Changes and their Impact on Rural Areas—UK

	Date	Recommendations and actions
Jack Committee's Report on Rural Bus Services	1961	Selective direct financial assistance to unremunerative services. Fuel-tax rebate.
Beeching Report on the Reshaping of British Railways.	1963	Closure of 5000 km of rural railways.
Series of surveys in six areas	1963	To examine the problems of and the demand for rural transport services.
Transport Act	1968	System of direct grants with central government paying half where the services covered half its operating costs.
		Revenue grants to cover losses on unremunerative rail services.
		National Bus Company set up.
		School service contracts could now take fare-paying passengers if there is excess capacity.
		Fuel-tax rebates increased.
		New bus grants introduced.
		Concessionary fares.
Local Government Act	1972	Co-ordinating function for the county councils through the Transport Policies and Programmes.
		County councils to administer the distribution of the Transport Supplementary Grant.
Passenger Vehicle (Experimental Areas) Act	1977	Relaxation of the licensing laws in certain areas so that innovative services could be introduced.
	1977	Rural Transport Experiments set up in four 'deep' rural areas.
Transport Act	1978	County Public Transport Plans to co-ordinate passenger transport to meet the 'needs' of the public.
		Guidelines set for concessionary fares.
		Minibuses (8–16 seats) exempt from Public Service Vehicle Licences and Road

Table 2.1   Principal Transport Policy Changes and their Impact on Rural Areas—UK—cont.

	Date	*Recommendations and actions*
Transport Act	1978	Service Licences, provided that the drivers were from approved voluntary organizations.
		Traffic commissioners permitted to introduce short-term Road Service Licences.
		Car sharing allowed for payment.
Transport Act	1980	Major changes in bus licensing with deregulation.
		Small vehicles (fewer than 8 seats) no longer classified as Public Service Vehicles.
		Express services (minimum journey length over 30 miles) no longer required Road Service Licences.
		Road Service Licences 'create a presumption in favour of the applicant'.
		Trial Areas can be designated where there are no Road Service Licences.

Source: Banister [3A2]

2B United States of America

Nearly a third of the population of the USA live in rural or small urban communities away from the major conurbations. Although about 85 per cent of the households in these areas have at least one car, there are significant subgroups within the population that are disadvantaged. Over half of the rural poor do not have cars and nearly half the rural elderly are in a similar position. The net result is that these individuals are either dependent upon car drivers or public transport for their mobility. But less than one per cent of rural workers who work outside the home use or have access to public transport (Burkhardt [2B7]) and under one per cent of the nation's 20,000 towns that have populations less than 50,000 are served by fixed-route, regularly scheduled public transport services. Similarly many small towns (populations under 2500) have no taxi services.

   Federal response to these problems has been summarized in table 2.2. Here it can be seen that it was only in 1978 that significant resources have been allocated to rural public transport subsidies. Even then take-up of available appropriations was limited in the

first year, but this situation has been remedied in the
subsequent two years. By the end of 1980, over 500 projects for
capital and operating expenses had been approved. The federal
share of the costs for capital projects is 80 per cent, with the balance
being made up from state funds. The present administration
has stated that operating subsidies under Section 18 of the
Urban Mass Transportation Act should be reduced or even elimi-

*Table 2.2 Principal Transport Policy Changes and their Impact
on Rural Areas—USA.*

	Date	Recommendations and actions
Urban Mass Transportation Act	1964	Begins concern about transport provision for the disadvantaged, mainly the low income population.
Office of Economic Opportunity	1967	Authorized the use of funds to operate certain buses in a number of rural localities.
Bureau of Public Roads	1969	Study on the costs and benefits of rural transport.
Office of Economic Opportunity	1972	By this date over 50 local transport projects were being sponsored.
Federal Highway Act	1973	Section 147 set up the Rural Highway Public Transportation Demonstration Program. Grant aid for demand responsive transit and fixed route transit.
Federal-Aid Highway Amendments	1974	Amended as Section 103 with new regulations—by September 1975, the first 45 projects had been initiated with the first starting operation in March 1976. By 1979, 102 grants (132 projects) had been awarded at a cost of $25M.
National Mass Transportation Assistance Act	1974	Made available $500M for grants (1974-80) in non-urbanized areas, but eligibility was limited and rural services could not be subsidized (only $23M was actually allocated).
Surface Transportation Assistance Act	1978	Creation of the non-urbanized-area public transport programme.
Urban Mass Transportation Act	1978	Section 18 provides the first full-scale federal assistance programme for public transport in rural areas. Provided $75M (FY1979) in operating and capital assistance to public transport in non-urban areas, but only $8M taken up. The programme was authorized for a four-year period from 1979 to 1982.

Based on Burkhardt [2B7]

nated in the financial year 1983-4, and in rural areas the effects would be particularly severe (Wiese [2B49]). Capital support has already been reduced by $4B for the period 1982-5. Elimination of the Section 18 programme would leave many communities without any public transport and the problems of inaccessibility would be increased. The only short term alternative seems to be that the communities should themselves subsidize local services (Kaye [2B18]). The progress that has been made over the last eight years towards a more comprehensive planning approach that coordinated all rural transport services may be in danger of being wasted when these fundamental changes are implemented.

2C Europe

Under Article 3 of the Treaty of Rome (1957) the newly-formed EEC stated that 'the activities of the Community shall include ... the adoption of a common policy in the sphere of transport' (Lazarus [2C12]). However progress has been very slow with little agreement between the national and supranational dimensions in transport policy (Gwilliam [2C7]). The Commission's policy has incorporated three main elements: the elimination of discrimination, the integration of international transport, and the organization of the national transport market. As Whitelegg [2C17] has commented other important supranational issues such as transport and the quality of life, transport and energy, and transport and regional development have been ignored. Rural transport has been seen as a national issue and there are significant differences between European countries. For example, specific social concessionary fares are common in France, whilst general fare control for macro-economic reasons has been implemented in Italy and the Netherlands, as it was in Britain during the early 1970s.

A comprehensive review of national policies in transport as they relate to rural areas would be a difficult if not impossible task to achieve. Many issues raised in the contextual review (Section 1) of the nature of the rural problem as perceived by researchers in Britain can be transferred to other countries in Europe. Declining populations and unemployment, with selective migration back into rural areas, the contraction of rural services and facilities, and the demise of public transport are all familiar problems facing the planner. Recently, certain European countries have reviewed their transport policy in general and how it relates specifically to rural areas

—for example Ireland (McKinsey International [2C13], Coras Iompar Eireann [2C1]) and Sweden (Swedish Institute [2C15]). Other countries with different policies towards rural public transport have reassessed the benefits of providing high quality services to a limited number of travellers—for example the Netherlands (De Boer [2C2], De Kogel [2C4]) and Denmark (Kilvington [2C10]). In all countries, increasing concern over the future of public transport in rural areas is apparent and alternatives are being investigated—for example Germany (Heinze *et al.* [2C9]). The solutions are less apparent, and it seems that Britain may lead here, both in terms of the range of modes that have already been tested (Section 4) and in terms of the quality and quantity of research that has been carried out.

2A Great Britain

2A1 AWDAS, D. (1978) Rural transport coordination, in Cresswell, R. (ed) *Rural Transport and Country Planning*, London: Leonard Hill, pp. 119-38.

This is a review of some current transport and land use planning problems. The relationships and responsibilities of local authorities and operators are discussed with a more detailed analysis of travel concessions and school transport in the UK. Current practice in other European countries is included for comparative purposes.

2A2 BALL, R. R. (1976) The TPP: Assessing priorities. *Chartered Municipal Engineer*, **103** (12), pp. 226-32.

At a time of zero growth or even a decline in the financial resources available for transport it is more important to decide on priorities consistent with local authority policy. This paper suggests a way of carrying out such a procedure so that the objectives are explicit and the trade-off between the various elements is clear and unambiguous.

2A3 BANISTER, D.J. (1981) Self-help supersedes public transport. *Geographical Magazine*, **53** (11), pp. 725-8.

Public transport services now seem to be related to the price that passengers are prepared to pay and the social function of public transport has diminished. In this paper it is argued that personal mobility will increasingly depend on individual initiatives and private provision of services, rather than public provision.

2A4 BARROW, J. F. (1978) Public transport—a key issue in county plan making? in Cresswell, R. (ed) *Rural Transport and Country Planning*, London: Leonard Hill, pp. 8–16.

This paper outlines the statutory planning process and the ways in which transport is integrated. The Oxfordshire approach is itemized and the conclusions reached suggest that planners must find new solutions which are responsive to local initiatives and needs—convention and unconvention must be mixed.

2A5 BAYLISS, J. (1979) The public transport plan—the operator's viewpoint, Paper presented at the Conference on Public Transport Planning, Loughborough University of Technology, September.

An optimistic view of the PTP is presented as it seems to offer an opportunity to develop a strategy for local transport. However it does require responsibility and financial commitment from all the parties involved, so that some stability in the level of service can be provided.

2A6 BEESLEY, M.E. and GWILLIAM, K.M. (1977) Transport policy in the United Kingdom—A critique of the 1977 White Paper. *Journal of Transport Economics and Policy*, **11** (3), pp. 209-23.

The White Paper offers nothing theoretically or practically novel to resolve the perennial problem of securing allocational efficiencies in the transport sectors between road and rail modes. In that sense it must be viewed as a pretentious failure. Moreover, in the absence of such insights it shows all the earmarks of an uneasy compromise between the wish to promote efficiency via reliance on market forces and the perceived need to constrain expenditure and the difficulties of satisfying the pressures of the labour unions within the industry. At this more practical and opportunistic level its most significant advances appear to be in the recognition of the role of more 'unorthodox' transport modes in rural areas and of the need to provide a more rational and stable basis for subsidy management. But, at the end of the day, there is a feeling that the problems which gave rise to the White Paper—the financial problems of railways and of local public transport—remain fundamentally untouched by it. British Rail management must feel just as confused and insecure as ever about the absence of any clear framework in which to operate;

and those, in both urban and rural areas, who are most vulnerable
to the loss of public transport services must more than ever fear that
limited financial resources will be dissipated in an unhelpful across-
the-board subsidy of predominantly urban bus services.

2A7 BEETHAM, A. (1976) TPPs: Review and prospect from a public transport viewpoint. *Journal of the Chartered Institute of Transport*, **37** (7),
pp. 190–4.

This paper deals with shortcomings of TPPs in the non-metropolitan
counties from the viewpoint of the bus operator. Under the Local
Government Act 1972 these counties had the responsibility to plan
and make grants for co-ordinating passenger transport systems and
specific grants were replaced by a block grant, the Transport Supplementary Grant (TSG).

2A8 BLOWERS, A. (1978) Future rural transport and development policy,
in Cresswell R. (ed) *Rural Transport and Country Planning*, London:
Leonard Hill, pp. 45–60.

Many novel ideas are presented in this paper on the nature of the
rural transport problem and ways to tackle it. The goals of rural
policy are presented in terms of mobility, accessibility and societal
goals. The conclusions reached suggest a more positive role for the
planner where he should promote and anticipate change and not
merely react to it.

2A9 CHARTERED INSTITUTE OF PUBLIC FINANCE AND ACCOUNTANCY
(1976) Transport policies and programmes: The new planning
approach, Monograph, March.

The report was prepared by a working party set up to give guidance
on the new system of transport policies and programmes (TPP)
which the county councils are required to submit to central government. A survey of 1975/76 TPP submissions was made, and the
different weighting given to the main components by councils in
urban and in rural areas is illustrated. The effects of public policy
on individual transport requirements are described. Against a
historical background, the objectives of the new approach are outlined and advice on the preparation of TPP submissions is given. A
carefully arranged timetable, use of financial guidelines and moni-

toring of progress are recommended. The establishment of relationships between county councils and other bodies is discussed, and criticisms of the TPP concept and the transport supplementary grant (TSG) system are made. The opinion of the working party is that the TPP concept is sound and contributes usefully to forward financial and policy planning but no conclusion can be reached as to whether TSG is an effective grant.

2A10 COLLINS, B. (1980) Collaboration is better than conflict. *The Planner,* **66** (2), pp. 32-3.

The case of Nottinghamshire is discussed where there has been effective collaboration on transport between the County and District Councils. Transport consultative groups have been set up for each District and discussions have covered topics such as traffic management, public transport, highway proposals, transport aspects of major developments and local plans. A document has been produced on the layout of roads in residential areas by the joint collaborative groups.

2A11 COUNCIL FOR THE PROTECTION OF RURAL ENGLAND (1973) Transport coordination or chaos, CPRE Report.

This report was produced following a study of Britain's transport problems by a CPRE working party during 1973 and the findings were adopted as the Council's policy. The paper attempts to describe the CPRE's interpretation of an integrated transport system. It begins with a general discussion of the contemporary transport problem in this country and then, taking this as a background, examines different aspects of transport in turn and makes specific proposals. The problem of obtaining crude oil supplies was taken as the starting point for the survey.

The review calls for a common accounting system for roads, railways, waterways and air transport; a re-examination of the road programme in the light of possible oil shortages; and endeavours to calculate costs to the nation of acknowledged disamenities of roads and traffic.

2A12 CRESSWELL, R. (ed) (1978) *Rural Transport and Country Planning,* Conference Proceedings, London: Leonard Hill.

This volume contains a dozen conference papers which elaborate four themes: the link with wider issues in rural development, notably those relating to structure planning and to the alleviation of social deprivation; the financial context and more particularly the exigencies of the 'Transport Policy and Programme' (TPP) format of central-local government interaction; the actual operation of rural public transport and the difficulty of co-ordinating the various agencies involved; new rural initiatives, including reviews both of a variety of unconventional schemes up and down the country and the specific 'Rural Transport Experiments' (RUTEX) which operate within a new legal framework. In addition reviews of experience in the Netherlands (de Kogel [2C4]) and, briefly, in the rest of Western Europe (Awdas [2A1]), confirm the basic similarity of the situation across the Channel, with growing acceptance of the need for state intervention in rural transport in both a financial and a management sense.

A13 DEAN, N. (1980) The Transport Act 1980: Parish councils have an important role. *Local Council Review*, **31** (3), pp. 171-3.

Outlines the provisions of the Act relating to community-based transport initiatives and argues that they make it easier for parish councils to play an effective role in public transport provision. Recent initiatives in bus and other services are noted.

A14 ENGLAND, H. (1972) Rural transport: an opportunity not to be missed. *Commercial Motor*, 136, pp. 44-5.

The 1972 Local Government Act provides for the co-ordination of local authority transport requirements. Devon's county transport co-ordinating officer fears that too many councils will not only leave this too late but some may let slip even the existing arrangements. The result will be higher costs for local and county councils, and lost opportunities for rural public service vehicle operators.

A15 FAULKS, R. W. (1981) *Urban and Rural Transport*, Shepperton: Ian Allen.

A16 GB DEPARTMENT OF THE ENVIRONMENT (1971) Study of rural transport in West Suffolk, Report by the Steering Group.

2A17 GB DEPARTMENT OF THE ENVIRONMENT (1971) Study of rural transport in Devon, Report by the Steering Group.

These reports demonstrate the importance of public transport services in some form to particular groups of residents in rural areas.
A set of surveys was administered to determine the nature of the
problem and to examine ways to alleviate inaccessibility. Only 6 per
cent of the sample made regular use of public transport, mainly for
shopping trips, and 55 per cent made virtually no use at all. Furthermore, 36 per cent of the sample said that they were unable to make
trips that they want to make due to lack of public transport. This
was particularly true for leisure activities and for teenagers. The
conclusion from the West Suffolk report was that 'the real trouble
in rural areas seems to be that these 'residual' needs for transport
are so scattered and varied that it is difficult to envisage their being
matched together to form any sensible public transport load'.

2A18 GB DEPARTMENT OF THE ENVIRONMENT (1975) Review of Rural
Transport, PUPT1, London.

The review was primarily concerned with the problems of personal
mobility for those living in rural areas. But it was recognized that
there were also problems of accessibility from urban areas, in particular for leisure activities. In reviewing the situation, the report
pointed out that rural transport was not only, or even mainly a
matter of providing for journeys within rural areas, it was to do with
the links between rural and urban life and activities and it interacted
with wider networks of transport services.

The report reviewed rural population and the pattern of rural
life; the decline in public transport in rural areas; railways and
buses; alternative means of provision and an assessment was made
of need and minimum provision.

It was made clear that public transport in rural areas is, at
present, largely provided by bus but the limited extent and generally
low quality of bus services makes the use of these services crucially
dependent on private transport not being available. In recent years,
the rapid rise in car ownership has led to a structural decline in the
demand, while costs have been rising. The choice of the bus industry
has been whether to attempt to maintain service levels at costs which
will be reflected in escalating, often prohibitive, fares or to reduce

services in line with falling demand, which may imply an intolerable degree of isolation for certain sections of the community.

The differing operational items of service and the variety of the local pattern of demand point to the hopelessness of attempting any sort of panacea for rural transport. It is important that encouragement be given to the stimulation of local initiatives within a county's overall transport policy. It is recommended that Central Government should stimulate greater awareness among local authorities of what has been accomplished in some areas and require local authorities to have regard to the various ways in which better use of existing resources and better provision of services may be achieved in rural areas in their TPPs.

19 GB DEPARTMENT OF THE ENVIRONMENT (1976) Transport Policy: A Consultation Document, London: HMSO, 2 vols.

The basic principle of the document is that the country's transport system should become fully integrated, if it is to become economically viable. Rural transport is identified as a special case in that it is seen as a priority area for surviving transport subsidies. However, measures are suggested for enhancing cost-effectiveness. These include: the promotion of unconventional forms of passenger transport; some reorganization of the National Bus Company into more flexible and localised units; changes in the bus licensing system and the substitution of good bus services for heavily-subsidized rail services. The basic aim is to maintain minimum levels of service.

20 GB DEPARTMENT OF TRANSPORT (1977) Transport Policy, Cmnd 6836, London: HMSO

21 GB DEPARTMENT OF TRANSPORT (1977) Survey of concessionary bus fares for the elderly, blind and disabled in England and Wales— Local transport note 1/77, Department of Transport, August.

This report examines the coverage of schemes throughout the country, the variation in the generosity and type of scheme offered, eligibility conditions, factors affecting the take up of concessions and methods of calculating reimbursements.

22 GB DEPARTMENT OF TRANSPORT (1978) A guide to community transport, London: HMSO.

This has the clear aim of helping local people in rural areas to get together to organize and run their own volunteer transport services. Detailed legal, administrative and financial advice is given, particularly relating to community bus and social car schemes.

2A23 GB DEPARTMENT OF TRANSPORT (1978) Innovations in rural bus services, 8th Report from the Select Committee on Nationalisated Industries, Session 1977–78, HC 635, London: HMSO.

2A24 GB DEPARTMENT OF TRANSPORT (1979) Concessionary fares for elderly, blind and disabled people, Cmnd. 7475, London: HMSO.

2A25 GB DEPARTMENT OF TRANSPORT (1979) Transport policies and programme submissions for the 1980/81 TSG settlement, Circular 4/79, January.

This circular describes the arrangements for the Transport Supplementary Grant (TSG) with reference to the government policy for transport since the publication of the white paper (GB Department of Transport [2A20]). Counties, who were given general guidance, formed their own views on the appropriate level of expenditure. Advice is given on the bus and underground programmes, also local British Rail services. The use of market analysis to review fares and services is discussed and bus priorities and staggered working hours are considered. Proposals involving new rail investment require discussions with the railway board and regional offices. Environmental aspects of local roads and traffic management are discussed including better facilities for cyclists. Advice is given on policies affecting the operation of car parking facilities, freight transport is also mentioned, emphasizing the environmental advantages of rail carriage, and road safety is covered.

2A26 GB DEPARTMENT OF TRANSPORT (1979) Innovations in rural bus services: The Government's response, London: HMSO, Cmnd 7743.

Finance was considered to be the major problem. The government's intention of stabilizing public expenditure requires the maximum value for money. Higher productivity could be achieved by using the National Bus Company's (NBC) market analysis project (MAP). It was agreed that the present system of licensing can hinder the efficient development of new services and needs reform. New services, such as minibuses, shared cars and post buses, should be developed to supplement the existing network of conventional buses. Observations on specific recommendations include the need for regular discussions with the Association for County Councils on topics such as finance and the training of community bus drivers. The government would not agree to the recommendations that some of the NBC's debt should be written off, or to maintain the new bus grant at 50 per cent beyond 1981 (GB Department of Transport [2A23]).

A27 GB DEPARTMENT OF TRANSPORT (1980) *Transport Act 1980*, London: HMSO.

This Act has three main areas of significance for rural planning: the relaxation of controls over public transport, the use of school buses for fare paying passengers and the introduction of car sharing schemes. These are set out in the following sections:

Section 1 (Aims of the Act) 'The purposes for which this Part is enacted include

  (a) redefining and reclassifying public service vehicles;
  (b) abolishing road service licences for express carriages as redefined;
  (c) making it easier for applicants to obtain road service licences and restricting the power to attach thereto conditions as to fares;
  (d) providing for the designation of areas as trial areas in which road service licences are not required for stage carriage services; ...'

Section 2 (Conditions for private minibus/car schemes) '... a journey made shall not be treated as made in the course of a business of carrying passengers if

  (a) the fare or aggregate of the fares paid in respect of the journey does not exceed the amount of the running costs of the vehicle for the journey; and
  (b) the arrangements for the payment of fares by the passengers so carried were made before the journey began; ...'

Section 3 (Definitions of types of service) '...

  (a) a "stage carriage" is a public service vehicle being used in the operation of a local service;
  (b) an "express carriage" is a public service vehicle being used in the operation of an express service; and

(c) a "contract carriage" is a public service vehicle being used to carry passengers otherwise than at separate fares; . . . .'

Section 12 (Trial areas) '. . . a trial area is any area . . . in which road service licences are not required for stage carriage services.'

'The Minister may if he thinks fit make an order . . . so designating any area . . ., but shall not make such an order in respect of any area except on an application made to him by the local authority concerned.'

Section 32 (School buses) '. . . a local education authority may

(a) use a school bus, when it is being used to provide free school transport, to carry as fare-paying passengers persons other than those for whom the free school transport is provided; and

(b) use a school bus belonging to the authority, when it is not being used to provide free school transport, to provide a local bus service; . . . .'

Section 61 (The conditions for insurance cover to extend to car sharing) . . .' The conditions referred to are

(a) the vehicle is not adapted to carry more than eight passengers and is not a motor cycle;

(b) the fare or aggregate of the fares paid in respect of the journey does not exceed the amount of the running costs of the vehicle for the journey . . . to include an appropriate amount in respect of depreciation and general wear; and

(c) the arrangements for the payment of fares by the passengers or passengers carried at separate fares were made before the journey began.'

2A28 GB MINISTRY OF TRANSPORT (1961) *Rural Bus Services; report of the committee* (Jack Report), London: HMSO.

The report of a government committee enquiring into the decline of rural bus services since the war, and the associated problems for the bus operators and the community. Concluded that some form of financial assistance was essential to maintain many existing services and that this should be administered by the county councils. This study formed an important input to the relevant provisions of the 1968 Transport Act.

29 GUILD, A. (1981) No queue for trial area buses. *Surveyor*, **156** (4623),
pp. 12–13.

The Government's invitation to county councils to apply for trial
area status may prove to be more of a 'trial' than originally thought.
So far only a few councils have shown any interest and this paper
examines one such exception, namely Norfolk.

30 GWILLIAM, K. M. (1976) Appraising local transport policy: The new
regime. *Town Planning Review*, **47** (1), pp. 26–42.

The 'new regime' in local transport policy is by definition a set of
arrangements more in touch with local appreciation of actual transport problems. The roles of central government, local government,
the public, and transport operators have to be clearly defined; local
transport needs to be relocated into the responsibility of county
authorities with the integration of long term transport planning into
a structure plan open to public participation and inquiry; and short
term transport planning within the transport policies and programmes has to be consolidated with reformed local transport financing. In this paper, the author examines these aspects of local
transport policy and discusses the progress made in their implementation.

31 HAMILTON, T.D. and JOHNSON, W.B. (1979) Public transport plans
—3 Laying costs 'on the line'. *Surveyor*, **154** (4553), pp. 33–6.

This article considers the restraints under which local authorities
operate in the promotion of local rail passenger services, including
the overall control exerted by central government on local authority
expenditure. A summary is presented of the investment made by
Durham County Council in local rail and bus transport. Reference
is made to the difficulties of financing cross-boundary local rail services and the existence of similar inter-regional problems in France
is noted. Details are given of the improvements made to the Dar-
lington to Bishop Auckland branch line, particularly to the new
station at Newton Aycliffe New Town.

Feasibility studies are to be carried out for the restoration of
passenger services between Newcastle and Consett and for siting
stations along the route. The initial and running costs of such a
project are considered.

2A32 HAWKINS, M.R. (1978) The developing role of rural public transport. *Highway Engineer*, **25** (5), pp. 19–24.

Of the many inherited public transport problems currently facing county councils, one of the foremost concerns the future of public transport in rural areas. The paper outlines the background of the current problems of rural public transport which have been gradually eroded over a long period and the factors which led to this decline, together with the effects it is having on the rural counties and the policy of the county councils. Against this background, the paper describes the way in which the counties are setting about solving the problem of rural public transport by examining the policies adopted within the present legal and financial restraints and looks at possible solutions for the future, including the role of unconventional forms of transport and the need for modification in the legal framework.

2A33 HIBBS, J. (1972) Maintaining transport services in rural areas. *Journal of Transport Economics and Policy*, **6** (1), pp. 10–21.

To meet the changed pattern of demand for transport in rural areas, a case is proposed for the abolition of the road service licence and that small operations should take over with an increase in service flexibility. Car use and sharing should also be encouraged.

Car ownership is, and always has been, preferable to dependence on public transport. It has also increased in cost at a slower rate. The problem of transport in rural areas is one of transition—of providing for those without access to private transport, either because they are ineligible or unable to drive, or because the main breadwinner uses the only vehicle to get to work. The aim of policy for transport in the countryside is to achieve the provision of an adequate and viable service that forms an integral part of a self-regulating community. The author of this paper argues that much better use should be made of the private car for passenger transport, perhaps by means of fiscal incentives, and that the framework of public transport should be adjusted by abolishing the licensing system to allow bus operators to be more flexible.

2A34 HIBBS, J (1982) Transport without politics ... ? Institute of Economic Affairs, Hobart Paper 95.

In this paper the author questions the assumption that transport is special and cannot be left to the market as it requires close governmental control of its structure and management. A short section on rural transport argues that subsidy is not essential and that subsidy may only be necessary where hardship is evident. Smaller bus operating units are required plus marketing skills if deterioration is not going to continue.

A35 HILLMAN, M. (1975) Social goals for transport policy. Paper presented to the Conference on Transport for Society, Institution of Civil Engineers, November.

The paper suggests that social and ethical principles should be introduced more widely into the transport planning process and that it should become less mechanistic. It sets out goals based on these principles and draws on data from a variety of sources to question the suitability of current policies in the light of these goals. Alternative policies for the effective pursuit of the goals are set out, and some of the implications of adopting these are outlined.

A36 HILLMAN, M. (1982) An evaluation of transport policies in the 1970s. *Policy Studies*, **3** (2), pp 71–87.

The 1977 white paper on transport policy (GB Department of Transport [2A20]) recognized the need to improve the environment, conserve energy, minimize waste of expenditure, reduce accidents, and promote equity. This review of how Britain fared in relation to these objectives during the 1970s shows that little progress was made in the first half of the decade, and less in the second. It considers why things went wrong, and suggests that future transport policy should be based on planning to reduce the need for motorized travel.

A37 HILLMAN, M., HENDERSON, I. and WHALLEY, A. (1973) Personal Mobility and Transport Policy, PEP Broadsheet 542, London.

There are three important characteristics of personal mobility with which this broadsheet is concerned: its importance to the individual; the interactive effects of one form of travel on another; the importance of transport and land use in determining travel behaviour and the quality of people's lives. Thus the research investigates personal mobility from the points of view of the individual, the community, and policies affecting how people get about. The first chapters look at basic mobility needs and the different methods of travel, and report a survey carried out to determine the travel patterns of adults, teenagers, and primary school children; the later chapters are concerned with current policy. The conclusions present ideas for future policy and research emerging from the preceding chapters. One of the authors' survey areas is a rural parish in Oxfordshire.

2A38 HILLMAN, M., HENDERSON, I. and WHALLEY, A. (1976) Transport realities and planning policy, PEP Broadsheet 567, London.

The surveys which are analysed in this report were designed to explore alternative aspects of personal mobility and accessibility and to test the adequacy of some of the assumptions and techniques of current and past transport planning. It was pointed out that present transport planning is selective in not considering the travel patterns of all groups in the population, all the journeys they make, and all the methods of travel they use. The surveys therefore concentrated on these omissions: while hitherto car ownership has been treated at the household level, the surveys investigated the *personal* availability of cars; and whereas journeys have usually been aggregated to a total for the household, emphasis has been given here to *personal* travel (including that of children and teenagers). The research was thus concerned not with the movements of vehicles but with the movement of people and the way this reflects their personal mobility—their ability to get about on foot or cycle, the level of public transport service available to them and their option for travelling by car. The surveys also examined some of the effects of land use planning on travel patterns by focusing on the accessibility of facilities that are in daily use. The surveys were conducted in various parts of the Outer Metropolitan Area of South East England, some of which were clearly rural in nature.

2A39 HOLDER, A. (1979) Public transport plans—1 Fail 'needs' test. *Surveyor*, **154** (4551), pp. 7–9.

The Transport Act 1978 requires non-metropolitan county councils to produce public transport plans stating the needs for public transport in their areas. This article discusses the concept of transport 'needs' and the means by which they are determined. Distinctions are drawn between mobility and access, also between assessment of needs and the means for satisfying them. Basic needs, where the emphasis is on the characteristic of the individual, and general needs where the emphasis is on the characteristics of the transport and land use systems, are considered. The principal discussion is of the assessment of basic accessibility needs, and the author discusses the role of the individual, the elected member of local government and the professional officer who advises the council and implements its policies, in this assessment. The criteria upon which judgements are made, i.e. felt needs and normative needs, are considered.

A40 HOUNSOME, K.R. (1976) Local transport finance in England and Wales. *Local Finance*, **5** (5), pp. 23–6.

A broad picture is presented of the financial aspects of the transport scene in England and Wales. It sets out to indicate which parts of the nation's provision for transport are locally provided, where the responsibilities lie, how the provision of local transport is financed, and the framework of central government grant in aid of this expenditure.

A41 HOUNSOME, K.R. (1978) Transport in the county budget, in Cresswell, R. (ed) *Rural Transport and Country Planning*, London: Leonard Hill, pp. 74–92.

A comprehensive outline is given of the way in which the local authority budget is prepared and the submission of the TPP to the Department of Transport. It then goes on to discuss the allocation of the Transport Supplementary Grant and other county resources.

A42 INDEPENDENT COMMISSION ON TRANSPORT (1974) *Changing Directions: A Report from the Independent Commission on Transport*, London: Hodder.

This book presents a detailed discussion of all aspects of transport and concludes that significant changes in policy are required so that access to transport can be provided for all. Chapter nine covers rural transport and suggests certain policy initiatives that could be taken so that mobility deprivation can be reduced. Particular disadvantaged groups are identified, who together form a significant part of the total population, and their specific access problems are analysed.

2A43 JAMES, N. (1981) 1980 Transport Act: success or failure? *Buses*, **33** (318), pp. 400-3.

This review covers the effects of the Transport Act on road service licensing, developments in public transport trial areas (where no licensing is required) and in express and stage carriage services. It concludes that it is too early to form any real interpretations of the effectiveness of the Act in introducing competition into local bus services.

2A44 JONES, T.S.M. and WHITE, P.R. (1979) Public transport plans: A challenge. Proceedings of a Conference held at Oxford Polytechnic, May.

These proceedings summarize the current debate on transport policy and planning in rural areas. Included are papers on needs and their determination, approaches used by shire counties in the preparation of their public transport plans and a case study of one particular county's approach (Dyfed) to rural public transport.

2A45 KELLETT, J.T. (1971) Rural bus subsidies: A case history. *County Councils' Gazette*, 64, pp. 197-8.

This short paper summarizes the response of one county council (Cheshire) to the threat of bus service withdrawal. In some situations continued and increased subsidies should be paid prior to all other alternatives being investigated. Social and community need should be considered as well as the economic viability of a particular service.

2A46 KNIGHT, V.A. (1978) Priorities in Transport Policies and Programmes (TPPs), in Cresswell, R. (ed) *Rural Transport and Country Planning*, London: Leonard Hill, pp. 107-18.

The present system of financing local transport is outlined both in principle and in practice with examples taken from Cheshire.

2A47 LEACH, S. and MOORE, N. (1979) County/District relations in Shire and Metropolitan counties in the field of town and country planning: a comparison. *Policy and Politics*, **7** (2), pp. 165-79.

A review is presented of the current meagre literature on inter-organizational relationships that emphasizes the limits of certain approaches (in particular Evans' model). An alternative framework is proposed that brings together a series of concepts from the literature on inter-organizational coordination, the relationship of an organisation to its environment, and the role of choice and individual action in understanding how organizations work. There are a series of examples taken from both shire and metropolitan county/district situations. The framework is finally used as a basis for the discussion of the likely impacts of the Government's proposals for organic change in local government.

148 MACKIE, P.J. (1980) The new grant system for local transport—the first five years. *Public Administration,* **59** (2), pp. 187–206.

When local government was reorganized in 1974, and responsibility for local transport passed to the new metropolitan and shire county councils, the Government took the opportunity of revising the basis on which local transport expenditure is supported by Exchequer grants and loans. Prior to 1974, expenditure on local transport was aided in a general way by the Rate Support Grant (RSG), and specifically by a series of grants on various types of expenditure. Since then, the specific grants have been replaced by a block grant, the Transport Supplementary Grant (TSG). The aim of this paper is to review the way in which the new system has worked, against the objective which it was originally designed to meet.

149 MACKIE, P.J. and GARTON, P.M. (1979) The financing of local transport, University of Leeds, Institute for Transport Studies, Working Paper 117, August.

This background paper provides a description of the administrative and financial relationships between central and local government. It outlines the current situation and the changes that have taken place since local government reorganization in the sources of income and the patterns of expenditure.

150 METCALF, A. (1972) Managing rural bus services, in Local Government Operational Research Unit and Royal Institute of Public Administration Seminar on Planning Rural Transport, August, pp. 21–4.

As the rural transport problem continues to grow, it will become increasingly important to be able to assess, much more accurately than can be done at present, the likely effects any change in existing routes will have on the people most concerned. On the basis of its experience in urban bus transport—and taking into account the important differences between town and country—the Unit believes that a method could be developed of providing authorities with just this type of information. To this end a 2-stage study has been proposed to develop and apply the method. The aim of the first stage would be to develop a generalized rural transport model. This could then be adapted for use in any part of the country. The second stage would be to 'plug in' this model to the particular requirements of any individual authority that wanted to use it.

2A51 MILLS, D. (1975) Goals and objectives of rural transport planning, in Wilmers, P.H.M. and Moseley, M.J. (eds) Rural Public Transport and Planning, Regional Studies Association, Discussion Paper 4.

In considering a rural public transport strategy it is important to distinguish between the role of such transport as an agent of change in the distribution and composition of rural populations, and as a means of ensuring equity and adequacy for present-day rural residents. The case for emphasizing transport in the latter context is strengthened by the lack of success of rural settlement strategies, since the War, which has in turn adversely affected both the accessibility and the utilization of service outlets.

2A52 McMILLAN, A.W. (1978) The role of structure plans and local plans in transport planning. *Traffic Engineering and Control*, **19** (6), pp. 294–5.

This paper suggests how the comprehensive planning of land use and transport may be achieved within two-tier local government.

2A53 REES, G.L. and WRAGG, R.F.W. (1976) The problems of rural transport. *Highway Engineer*, **23** (6), pp. 14–19.

A survey of 1200 households in Merioneth undertaken to identify the demand for transport showed that over 64 per cent of households had the use of a car. Data on trip behaviour showed that fewer than 10 per cent of all trips were made by public transport, while over 65 per cent were made by car. Forecasts of future usage predicted a further decline in public transport trips. However, although few people used public transport, the study showed that there was still a social need to maintain the service if hardship was to be avoided. An appraisal of public transport operations showed that for small passenger flows the railways of rural Wales were inefficient and not the least cost solution. For the bus industry large variations in costs and efficiency were found between the National Bus Company and independent operators. A number of policy options to improve the efficiency of public transport were examined. These indicated that for external trips a specially designed bus service was preferable to the present rail system. For internal trips improvements to the bus service might be made at little social cost, but large savings in resource costs.

54 RIGBY, J.P. (1980) Public transport planning in the Shire Counties: An evaluation of the public transport plan as an aid to transport policy making. Oxford Polytechnic, School of Town Planning, Working Paper No. 46, June.

This research document enumerates a series of attempts over the last decade to improve the planning and provision of public transport. Particular emphasis is placed on the PTPs and the requirement in the Shire Counties to produce these annual reports.

55 SCOTTISH DEVELOPMENT DEPARTMENT (1975) Transport policies and programmes: guidance on rural passenger transport, SDD, Edinburgh.

A guidance note has been produced for Scottish regional and island councils, and it deals with rural passenger transport. The guidance takes particular account of the fact that while on the one hand the problems in rural transport facing authorities are increasing, inevitably, in the present situation of public expenditure restraints, the resources available to deal with these must be limited. The note considers provision of transport services, British Rail, Scottish Bus Group, Post Office, rural social transport, Traffic Commissioners, Highlands & Islands Development Board, school buses, vehicles of local authorities and other bodies, and demand estimation.

56 SEARLE, G. (1982) Co-ordinating public transport in rural counties: summary of the Lewes study approach. Department of Transport, Economics Local and Roads Transport Division, Paper 26.

Transport is essentially an intermediate good. People travel with some other activity as their objective. This paper addresses the basic question about how a rural county council can determine what public transport, in the broadest sense, it will provide or support, bearing in mind limited resource availability. A flexible method is developed to examine bus services, train services, 'needs', spatial requirements and accessibility. The scale of the problem is indicated on maps and then a comprehensive view is taken of how these needs can be met—once these have been matched up, then scarce resources can be allocated to meet 'needs'.

2A57 SMITH, D.R. (1975) The role of the Traffic Commissioners. *District Council Review*, February, pp. 38-9.

One of the principal aims of the 1930 Road Traffic Act which established the Traffic Commissioners was to rationalize an industry in which proliferation of services, duplication and waste was rife at the time. For more than 30 years this aim was admirably achieved. Like the industry itself, the role of the Traffic Commissioners is now being overtaken by events. In the totally different context in which public transport operates today, due to the proliferation of the private car, the process of rationalizing and simplifying the process of public participation and consumer control should come soon.

2A58 WARBURTON, S. and TROWER-FOYAN, M. (1980) Public transport in rural areas: The increasing role of central and local government. Transport Operations Research Group, University of Newcastle upon Tyne, Research Report.

2A59 WELLS, G. (1979) Highway and transportation planning in England. *Transportation*, **8** (2), pp. 125-40.

This article presents an overview of highway and transportation planning in England. It covers the division of responsibilities between central and local government; the organization of the department of transport; the planning, financing and implementation of road schemes, both local and national. A very brief review of transport legislation is included. This paper was printed before the UK general election of May 1979. The Department of Transport is now responsible to the Minister of Transport. The minister has similar responsibilities to those previously exercised by the Secretary of State for Transport as referred to in this paper.

60 WILMERS, P.H.M. and MOSELEY, M.J. (eds) (1975) *Rural Public Transport and Planning*, Regional Studies Association, Discussion Paper 4.

The conference stemmed from the feeling that rural public transport had been ignored for too long by those involved in the field of rural planning. Secondly, interest in rural public transport was growing as an awareness of the size of the problem increased. In his introduction Wilmers suggested that two fundamental factors had emerged:

i the 'resource factor': public transport, particularly in rural areas, was not receiving a fair share of the national transport budget. If adequate mobility was to be provided, more resources would be required.

ii 'the attitudes factor': this to some extent explained why rural transport was starved of resources. The attitude in question was that transport meant roads, railways were a historic accident and buses were for a tiny, and relatively unimportant, residual minority.

The attitude required was that of a corporate planner to produce an overall package of policies designed to answer present and future needs. Local authorities and Central Government should think positively about rural public transport expenditure as a means of buying welfare for the community. The papers developed some positive approaches and the final discussion was also reported.

61 WINFIELD, R. (1979) Public transport plans—2 An effective planning discipline. *Surveyor*, **154** (4552), pp. 26-8.

Progress made by local authorities in policy development for the provision of co-ordinated and efficient public transport is considered. Reference is made to the value and purpose of annual Public Transport Plans (PTPs) considering the work and cost involved, the planning previously undertaken by local authorities, and their assessment of transport needs and how they may be met. The results of a survey into the effectiveness of PTPs in their first year are presented and analysed. It appears that policies have been affected little, although more comprehensive assessment of transport needs has been made. Instead of an annual plan, a three or five yearly review of public transport is suggested with discussions of the document in the intervening years. The establishment of local authority transport units responsible for meeting the various public transport needs is recommended.

2A62 WINFIELD, R. (1982) Public transport planning: the end of an era? Welsh Consumer Council, Cardiff, December.

Bus operation in Great Britain underwent considerable change during the 1970s. This report proposes that further changes are necessary; first an emphasis on accessibility rather than on provision of transport and second, that the provision of transport should be considered on an hierarchical basis. It is proposed that accessibility should be planned by district councils and that responsibility for local rail services and regional road passenger transport should be transferred to newly created regional passenger transport authorities. Although reorganization onto an hierarchical basis could be said to undermine the traditional concept of an integrated system, it is considered that this approach would be more responsive to the changing needs of the consumer and would provide better public accountability.

2A63 WYTCONSULT (1977) Rural transport policies, Interim Report 4, May.

This report summarizes the main findings of the transport study with respect to rural areas under the eight stated objectives.
  - an understanding of the interdependence of the communities and their present travel characteristics.
  - a detailed examination of present transport services.
  - the compilation of a data base.
  - the mismatch between the demand for and supply of transport services.
  - the implications of present transport provision on the social, economic and other planning issues.
  - the development of policies to alleviate the problems identified.
  - an evaluation of the series of policies.
  - the design of monitoring procedures to enable the studies to continue over time, particularly whilst policies are being implemented.
In effect the classic conventional transport planning process of survey, analysis, and plan is being applied to the rural communities in West Yorkshire.

2B United States of America

31 BENACQUISTA, R.J. (1978) Procedures and experiences in the evaluation of rural highway public transportation demonstration program. *Transportation Research Record*, 696, pp. 69–71.

The Rural Highway Public Transportation Demonstration Program projects funded under section 147 of the Federal-Aid Highway Act of 1973 are being evaluated on the basis of an extensive reporting procedure. Three categories of information—statistical, narrative and detailed passenger survey data—are being collected. Statistical data on project operating characteristics are collected monthly, and narrative reports are submitted each quarter, at the end of the first year, and as a final report. After Federal Highway Administration analysis, the monthly statistical data are summarized quarterly in computer-tabulation form and distributed back through the field offices and the states to the project personnel. One year (January–December 1977) of statistical data have been reported back to the projects by this mechanism. Peer groups have been established that contain projects that, based on population density and size of vehicle fleets, are similar. Although all projects are required to be able to meet the service needs of elderly and handicapped riders, some projects have been more successful than others. The predominant one-way trip purposes were work, shopping, and school and education. Data for the fourth quarter of 1977 showed that drivers' wages account for more than half of the operating costs. Eighty per cent of the funding comes from federal sources, the states contribute thirteen per cent, and local and private agencies contribute seven per cent. The statistical-evaluation results were remarkably steady throughout 1977; no significant fluctuations were identified.

32 BERG, W.D. (1974) More efficient local rural road administration. *American Society of Civil Engineers Transport Engineering Journal*, **100** (11), pp. 975–83.

There is currently debate in the USA over whether responsibility for rural roads should be left with the small local government units or whether the function should be given to larger and more economically efficient units. This article presents a case study analysis of the Illinois Township Road System undertaken in order to identify the relative efficiency of local rural road administrative units.

2B3 BREEN, D.A. and ALLEN, B.J. (1979) Common carrier obligation and the provision of motor carrier service to small rural communities. Washington State University, Department of Economics, Pullman, Washington D.C.

2B4 BUNKER, A.R. and HUTCHINSON, T.Q. (1979) Roads of Rural America, Economics, Statistics and Cooperative Service, ESCS-74, December.

The six articles cover public policy issues, identify research needs in rural road transport, suggest methodologies and report results of completed studies in rural road utilization. Jerry E. Fruin cites reductions in the real value of revenues for rural roads and highways and suggests three solutions: road abandonment, ad valorem fuel tax, and improved management. William Easter and Harold Jensen review the demand and cost estimation of transport, especially as applied to older rural Americans. Malcolm Kirby, Peter Wong, and Wallace Cox describe and apply an optimizing network model for planning and analysing transport investments and, in an appplication to a timberwood product problem, showed a large efficiency gain over manual computations. Marc Johnson develops a surprisingly simple technique of benefit measurement for five types of incremental rural road improvement projects. From a court centralization experience in Michigan, Joseph Broder shows that centralization of services (bringing people to services) resulted in increased costs or reduced services to rural residents as compared to the services being distributed in local communities. Norman Walzer and Ralph Stablein review the condition of locally maintained roads and bridges in a region in Illinois, estimate costs to bring them up to standards acceptable to local officials, and discuss financial problems that may be encountered.

2B5 BURKHARDT, J.E. (1978) Costs of rural public transportation services. *Transportation Research Record*, 696, pp. 27-31.

Typical costs for rural transport operations and the factors that influence such costs are examined. Until now, few hard data have been available for the purpose of describing rural transport costs. The data used in this research are taken from applications for funding and actual operations performed under Section 147 of the Federal-Aid Highway Act of 1973, the Rural Highway Public Transportation Demonstration Program. The following aspects of rural transport costs are investigated: general cost ranges and what constitutes average and 'good' costs, factors that affect the cost of operations, and the characteristics of the most economical and most expensive hypothetical system designs.

B6 BURKHARDT, J.E. (1979) A section 147 rural public transportation demonstration manual, Number 2, Planning rural transportation systems. Econometrics Incorporated, Bethesda, Maryland.

B7 BURKHARDT, J.E. (1981) Rise and fall of rural public transportation. *Transportation Research Record*, 831, pp. 2–5.

The long process of developing a viable programme of federal aid to help overcome rural transport problems is reviewed. Despite its successes, the Section 18 programme (the Urban Mass Transportation Act of 1964) is now under attack. A series of proposals have been advanced that would effectively destroy the programme's usefulness and, ultimately, the programme itself. Unless the important decision makers can be made aware of crucial rural transport interests, the Section 18 programme may be emasculated by the budget cutters.

B8 BURKHARDT, J.E., LAGO, A.M., CEGLOWSKI, K.P. and MONTOULIEU, C.F. (1978) Impacts of rural transit funding options. *Transportation Research Record*, 661, pp. 7–14.

This paper summarizes a study undertaken to assist the Urban Mass Transportation Administration (UMTA) in programming non-urban transit funds available through the National Mass Transportation Act of 1974. The study produced estimates of the amount of transport provided and probable assistance levels under a variety of possible funding options. It was found that the supply of rural transport services available in the next few years will vary significantly according to the type and amount of financial assistance available from UMTA, that assumptions about the useful life-span of vehicles significantly affect overall costs and administrative burdens, and that the transit assistance programme with the most benefit to rural areas would be flexible depending on local conditions and would include some assistance for operating costs.

B9 CEGLOWSKI, K.P., LAGO, A.M. and BURKHARDT, J.E. (1978) Rural transportation costs. *Transportation Research Record*, 661, pp. 15–20.

This paper presents a rural transport cost model which was developed while determining potential future demand for UMTA capital and operating assistance in rural areas. The model is designed to account for all costs incurred in the operation of a rural transit system, with considerations given to regional location, firm size and public/private ownership characteristics. The bulk of the data used to develop this model came from the Section 147 Demonstration funded by FHWA and UMTA. By combining the cost information and the information available on operating characteristics, a standardized cost per vehicle mile can be calculated for a given vehicle type. Several conclusions regarding costs are noteworthy: total operating costs per vehicle mile are highest in the Northeast and Pacific coast states; in rural transit operations, the bulk of the total system costs are directly attributable to drivers' wages, overhead costs, and vehicle capital costs; economies of scale are not obvious in rural transport operations.

2B10 COLLINS, J. (1982) Transit ownership/operation options for small urban and rural areas, National Cooperative Highway Research Programme, Synthesis of Highway Practice 97, Transportation Research Board, Washington DC.

Public transport services in rural and small urban areas have several common characteristics. These services are important to a broad spectrum of public agencies, are usually multi-jurisdictional, are established to meet a variety of special transport needs, and are extremely dependent on financial support from sources other than fares.

Ownership means holding titles to vehicles and related equipment and facilities. Operations are the day-to-day activities such as scheduling drivers, dispatching services, and maintaining vehicles. The most common ownership and operations options are publicly owned and operated, publicly owned and privately operated, and privately owned and operated. In some cases a publicly owned and operated system may also use a private company to manage day-to-day operations. Also, many privately owned and operated systems are publicly subsidized.

Public ownership options allow greater orientation toward service to the entire public and offer a better position for short- and long-term planning, which may lead to greater coordination and consolidation of transport services. Public ownership can take advantage of tax exemptions and may eliminate state public utility commission involvement in setting routes and fares. On the other hand, public ownership may entail political interference that affects management and operations, especially where the service is publicly operated, and financing may be difficult during times of fiscal austerity. Public ownership may not be suitable in some areas because it requires a public entity to be involved in a function with which it has little experience. The degree to which the various advantages and disadvantages of public ownership occur is affected by the type of public ownership (city, county, or authority).

Private ownership permits easier implementation of new services. Because public employees are not involved, there is less potential for political interference. Where service is publicly subsidized, a public official is needed to administer the contract and monitor the service. However, private ownership may not be able to take full advantage of local, state, and federal tax exemptions.

Before evaluating the various ownership and operation options, three questions should be answered: what are the public transport needs? Should public funds be used to meet those needs and if so, what funds are available? Do current laws permit creation of special organizations, such as authorities?

The evaluation of options should include a detailed study of costs, especially those related to personnel, and the noncost factors, such as coordination of services, potential for political interference, time to implement the option, and problems of adding employees to a public payroll. A framework, which includes a flow chart and two matrices, is suggested for formulating and evaluating the options. The flow chart is a logical, systematic method of answering questions regarding needs and availability of funds, owners and operators. Use of the flow chart should result in identification of several potential ownership/operation options. The matrices are then useful in evaluating the cost and noncost factors for each option. A recommendation of this synthesis is that a systematic study be conducted to examine the relationship of the ownership/operation option to overall system efficiency and effectiveness in small urban and rural areas.

11 CUTLER, D. A. (1978) Statutory barriers to coordination. *Transportation Research Record*, 696, pp. 20-3.

This paper reports on an initial investigation of statutory barriers to coordination, especially concerning transport, evident in seven pieces of federal legislation. Using data collected from three American cities, the study found that most of these statutes encouraged or mandated various forms of coordination. All included provisions that could prove to be barriers to coordination, such as inconsistent federal-local matching ratios, differing definitions of a handicapped individual, differing planning cycles among the programmes included in this study, and state and local interpretations of federal audit provisions.

2B12 FORKENBROCK, D.J. (1981) Planning for transit development in an era of fiscal scarcity. *Transportation Research Record*, 831, pp. 33-7.

An approach to transit development planning is presented that grew out of a research effort to formulate planning guidelines for the Iowa Department of Transportation for application to small urban and rural areas. A critique of the transit planning process is presented. It is concluded that planners must act not only as technical experts but also as facilitators who strive to ensure that local preferences and needs are reflected in the service ultimately provided. A 'budget-constraint' approach to transit development planning is then laid out. Through surveys of transit users, the general public, business leaders, and political officials, views regarding goals and objectives are obtained. The results of the survey are discussed in a public meeting, where those in attendance may express their views. Out of these contacts with the public, the planner formulates and ranks a series of social objectives for transit in the area. The objectives constitute a basis for generating developmental alternatives. Each of the several alternatives is aimed at attaining the same objectives, but they vary in scale and, hence, in cost. Decision makers are thus able to perceive the incremental benefits and costs of moving from the smallest to larger alternatives. The approach allows citizen views to become the basis for the transit plan, and decision makers are enabled to make informed choices rather than merely respond to a finalized plan.

2B13 FORKENBROCK, D.J. (1981) Transit assistance allocation: further research findings. *Transportation Research*, **15A** (5), pp. 363-65.

Earlier work on the allocation of transit operating assistance at the state level in the U.S. is extended. As before, available resources are first distributed to three categories of transit systems: large urban, small urban and rural. The intra-category allocation now considers ridership and revenue miles using a multiplicative (Cobb-Douglas) function, rather than an additive relationship. The result is that systems which score high on one measure but low on the other receive less funds than systems with output more in line with specified weights for the measures. A comparative application of the two versions to data on small urban systems within the State of Iowa illustrates the advantage of the multiplicative model.

14 GARLAND, A. D. and GARRITY, R. (1978) State role in rural public transportation. *Transportation Research Record*, 696, pp. 6–10.

This paper reports on the efforts of various states to be more deeply involved in providing transit services in rural and small-town areas. Current state involvement, innovative programmes initiated in a few states, existing problems, and future programmes are discussed. Most of the information presented in this paper was obtained from a survey of all states by the North Carolina Department of Transportation. The survey results suggest that one of the most significant problems to be solved is the fragmentation of services due to the multiplicity of federal programmes funding rural transport—until now an issue dealt with at the local level.

15 HAYES, J. (1979) A section 147 rural public transportation demonstration manual, Number 4, Rural public transportation vehicles, Michigan Department of Transportation, Lansing, Michigan.

16 HUDDLESTON, J. and WALTON, C. M. (1976) Interurban transportation policy and the rural community. *Transportation Research Record*, 617, pp. 7–12.

Interurban transport systems are designed primarily for the purpose of moving people and goods between metropolitan centres. However, the effect of these systems on the nonmetropolitan areas, which they also serve, raises the expectations and sometimes frustrates the hopes of the residents in small urban places. Since current policy trends have placed the transport planner in the role of serving general social goals, this paper examines some of the resentments of small town residents that have resulted from their previous experiences with the development of the Interstate Highway Programme. So that interurban transport systems in the future may better serve the areas they affect, three policy proposals are offered to enhance the relation between transport agencies and small communities: an expanded notion of direct responsibility for the impacts of new facilities; an extension of technical assistance to small communities; and an expanded advisory role that involves greater cooperation among small communities, transport agencies, and other planning and advisory agencies.

2B17 HYNES, C. (1976) Small business and deregulation of the motor common carriers. *Transportation Journal*, **15** (1), pp. 74–86.

The author fears that if US federal regulation of the road haulage market were to be stopped and carriers were allowed pricing freedom they would concentrate on the profitable traffic between metropolitan areas, reduce the service to rural areas and set their rates too high for small businesses. Ninety-seven per cent of businesses in the USA are small and 33 per cent of these are in small urban or rural areas. The 1970 Urban Growth and New Community Act was designed to divert development from the metropolitan areas and encourage the economic stability of rural areas. Relieving carriers of their legal duty of supplying these areas with adequate transport would lead to the collapse of many small rural businesses with harmful effects on the local economy.

2B18 KAYE, I. (1978) Rural development policy and rural public transportation. *Transportation Research Record*, 696, pp. 10–14.

The transport systems that serve rural people and their communities continue to dwindle. Local communities affected by the diminution of these transport resources are under pressure to raise local money to subsidize the air service, the rail service, and intercity bus lines, to maintain their off-system roads and bridges in usable condition, and to provide whatever forms of public transit may be achievable. The competition for local funds is one of the problems to be faced if a small-town and rural-area public transit programme is, as seems likely, at last obtained from Congress. Because the lack of accessibility to jobs, training, and other essential services will continue to be be a major obstacle to a rational rural development policy, comprehensive planning and the maximum feasible coordination of transport resources must be given high priority.

B19   KEMP, J.B. (1978) Federal regional councils and the uniform cost-accounting project. *Transportation Research Record*, 696, pp. 57–8.

The General Accounting Office (GAO) has identified 114 federal programmes that provide federal assistance for passenger transport and has concluded that there are no statutory or regulatory instructions that specifically prohibit the coordination of transport resources. It has, however, identified a number of hindrances to coordination. This paper focuses on the development of a common cost system that should increase coordination between agencies and providers of transport.

B20   KETOLA, H.N. (1979) A section 147 rural public transportation demonstration manual, Number 3, Rural public transportation coordination efforts, Applied Resource Integration Limited, Boston, Massachusetts.

B21   KIDDER, A.E. (1978) Sources of non-federal support for public transportation programs in non-urbanized areas, North Carolina Agricultural and Technical State University report for the Urban Mass Transportation Administration, UMTA–MC–11–0004–782, June.

The purpose of this study was to find out the extent to which states and localities are spending nonfederal funds in support of public transport in non-urbanized areas. A survey was administered to state officials in transport or highways departments, to social service agencies of the state whose budgets include significant funding for client transport, to ascertain current and projected expenditures. This report presents the results of a survey of twenty-five states, estimating the extent of nonfederal support for public transport programmes in rural areas. The survey found $36 million of state funds, and three million dollars of substate funds supporting public transport in these areas. Based upon these figures, it is estimated that at least $78 million are spent annually from nonfederal sources, and that the trend in such funding is upward. Passage by Congress of operating assistance programmes for rural areas would enlarge the figure. The principal focus of nonfederal funding is to match social service based budgets used to enhance mobility of the transport dependent in

non-urbanized areas. Two dollars of 'special service' transport
money is spent at the state level for every one dollar of 'general
service' public transport in non-urbanized areas.

2B22 KIDDER, A.E. (1978) Nonfederal funds for public transportation:
special reference to non urban areas. *Transportation Research Record*,
696, pp. 31–4.

From a sample of 25 states, it was observed that only 3 per cent of
the non-federal funds for public transport that serve the general
public are expended in non-urban areas. Furthermore, the extent of
support for public transport in rural areas varies widely; the more
affluent states are more likely to support programmes for the non-
urban sectors. Thus, the more wealthy sections are likely to benefit
from a federal support programme that requires substantial local
contributions. Far more important from a dollar standpoint is the
social service agency non-federal support, which in many rural areas
is the only source of funds for transport, albeit client-oriented mobility. Evidently the need for mobility support for disadvantaged
groups is recognized by state and local groups. However, there has
been little coordination among social service funds for public transport by state governments; congressional action to provide stronger
incentives for such coordination would be advantageous.

2B23 KIDDER, A.E. (1979) Usage of revenue sharing for public transportation in rural areas, North Carolina Agricultural and Technical
State University, Transportation Institute, Greensboro, North Carolina, Final Report DOT-I-79-3, July.

The purpose of this study is to explore whether rural towns and
counties use portions of their revenue sharing monies in support of
public transit operations, or other forms of public transport such as
road construction and maintenance in contrast to public transit.
This topic is of interest because the current demonstrations of public
transport programmes in rural areas are supported principally out of
federal demonstration funds of the US Department of Transportation, Federal Highway Administration, and face the possibility of
funding termination unless sufficient local financial support is
forthcoming. The topic is additionally relevant to discussions of the
impact of new legislation making broader federal assistance available
to public transport in non-urbanized areas. The latter funds are

dependent upon the availability of local matching funds to under-gird federally supported programmes. Also published in 1981 as *Transportation Research Record*, 813, pp. 6–10.

B24 LARSON, R.A. (1979) Impact of Federal Highway Policy on County Road Programs. *Transportation Engineering Journal*, ASCE, **105** (TE1), pp. 23–30.

County road agencies have become dependent on federal aid to construct and maintain a minimum network of usable roads. County roads programmes will be critically impacted by future federal transport decisions regarding post-Interstate System funding levels, Federal aid programme structure, the Federal Highway Trust Fund, Transportation System Management and energy conservation. This dependency is highlighted in a case study of the Wayne County Road Commission.

B25 MAGGIED, H.S. (1978) Georgia's critical rural public transportation needs. *Transportation Research Record*, 661, pp. 40–2.

This analysis is designed to identify public transport needs of Georgia's rural transport disadvantaged including elderly Georgians 60 years of age and older, and the handicapped under Section 16(b)(2) and Section 147. Approximately 12 per cent or a half million of Georgia's population are over 60 years of age. One quarter of this group is handicapped numbering around 130,000. It is estimated that 1.5 per cent of Georgia's under 60 population, or 60,000, are handicapped. Georgia's rural population approximates two million people. The rural target population, this study's focus, slightly exceeds 400,000 of which 34 per cent are transport deficient. Subsequently, rural Georgians require 611,300 trips to satisfy 135,400 rural transport deficient citizens. This analysis provides a cursory view by use of a broad-brush sketch plan as many data gaps exist and the estimates are crude. Therefore, reliance on a professional 'best-judgment' to identify Georgia's transport needy predominates.

B26 MARKVE, K. (1979) Transportation planning for rural America. Upper Great Plains Transportation Institute, North Dakota State University, North Dakota, Report TES 5, December.

Transport planning for rural areas is important in view of the fossil fuel shortage and its impact on the transport of goods and services in low density areas. A systematic planning process must first determine the limits of the problem area, as well as the objectives of the people in the designated system. Physical constraints (river, rail crossings, etc.) and legal requirements must also be defined. Possible economic and political resources to support alternative solutions should be investigated, and the decision maker and the decisions to be made should be identified. Aspects of planning which are stressed are continuity, flexibility, simplicity and the reduction of intermodal conflict points. A primary purpose of planning is to relate service to maximum demand, which involves plotting maximum demand and the minimum resistance to it. This report discusses the wise use of land, planning for pedestrians, bicycles, pedal cars and mopeds, and planning for transit (routing, marketing and management). Problems related to the highway and parking in small urban areas are also discussed. The three phases of plan implementation, citizen participation/public relations, developing a continuing planning programme, and evaluation alternatives are also covered.

2B27 MOORE, D.H. (1978) Funding, insurance and regulation developments in Oregon. *Transportation Research Record*, 696, pp. 41-3.

This paper identifies funding, insurance, and regulation as the three major problems confronting rural public transport in Oregon. Solutions to these problems on the state, federal, and local levels are suggested, along with future national possibilities for reducing insurance difficulties.

2B28 MORGAN, R.D. (1978) Rural highway public transportation demonstration program: intergovernmental relations. *Transportation Research Record*, 696, pp. 72-3.

The changes in the traditional role of the Federal Highway Administration (FHWA) are described particularly as it affects rural communities. The initiatives taken include the Rural Highway Public Transportation Demonstration Program which involved $25 million over two years. Certain examples are outlined and the conclusions reached suggest that some of the initiatives can be viable as well as providing a social transport service to those without access to a car. Many of the demonstration projects seem likely to continue with or without selective assistance.

B29 McGILLIVRAY, R.G., ERNST, U., OLSSON, M.L. and TOLSON, F. (1979) A section 147 rural transportation demonstration manual, Number 1, Rural public transportation services and performance, Urban Institute, Washington DC.

B30 PANEBIANCO, T.S. (1979) A section 147 rural public transportation demonstration manual, Number 5, Marketing rural public transportation, Florida Department of Transportation, Tallahassee, Florida.

B31 POKA, E., MARING, G., DAVISON, P. and BENACQUISTA, R. (1978) Rural highway public transportation demonstration program evaluation—progress report. *Transportation Research Record*, 661, pp. 28-31.

Section 147 of the 1973 Federal-Aid Highway Act established the Rural Highway Public Transportation Demonstration Program which authorized funds to encourage the development, improvement, and use of public transport for residents of non-urban areas, so as to improve access to employment, health care, retail centres, education, and public services. Total funding of $24.65 million for FY 1975 and 1976 permitted the selection of 102 projects from more than 500 applications. Ninety-eight of the projects have been authorized to proceed with about three-quarters in actual operation. A variety of organizational arrangements, service types and sizes are being demonstrated. There is a significant evaluation component to the programme which will provide needed information for future decisions regarding possible national programmes for rural transport. The results of the first two quarters' evaluation, although preliminary, show performance measures comparable to or better than previous rural public transport projects. It is significant to note that over half of the initial projects studied were performing according to pre-project estimates of ridership and service.

B32 RAO, K. and LARSON, T.D. (1982) Highway fiscal and program management for the 1980s. *Transportation Engineering Journal*, ASCE, **108** (TE2), pp. 183-95.

The 1980s are a time of rapid change to most transport agencies in the USA—change in a funding base, which has remained essentially stable for the last 60 years, and change in programmes at both state and federal levels as efforts are made to recapitalize our vast highway network. Fiscal and programme management strategies are described for responding to this change, and various efficiency improvements and management methods for both intra- and inter-agency communication are described.

2B33 REICHART, B.K. (1976) Non-urbanized public transportation: a federal perpective. *Transportation Research Board*, SR 164, pp. 157–62.

A selected number of demonstration projects are described which were identified for funding by the Federal Highway Administration and the Urban Mass Transportation Administration. This study of 45 projects which were designed to demonstrate how the mobility of non-urbanized residents may be improved, provides information that will be useful to both federal and state governments in framing future policies and programmes to meet the public transport needs of rural areas. The projects represent a wide variety of schemes ranging from fixed-route, scheduled general services to an assortment of demand-responsive van operations and an institutionalized volunteer transport concept. The New York, Pennsylvania, Tennessee, Oklahoma, North Dakota, California, and Oregon projects reviewed here, indicate that the question of the provider of the service depends on many local conditions and experiences. The importance of the state's role as co-ordinator is emphasized. Localities must explore all existing transport resources particularly because federal assistance programmes will be service-oriented and will emphasize improvement of services to meet the needs. Comments are made related to the planning required to develop service-oriented approaches. Comments are also made on the nature of the financing. The studies show that paratransit, because of its ability to adapt to various needs, will contribute significantly to the effort to provide public transport in rural and non-urbanized areas.

2B34 REVIS, J.S. (1978) Transportation problems of the elderly and handicapped: An overview of American experience. Paper presented at the International Conference on Transport for the Elderly and Handicapped, Loughborough University of Technology, pp. 10–19.

This paper reviews the experience in the United States since 1970 as regards the transport problems of older and handicapped Americans. The paper identifies the basic nature of the problem in terms of low income, low levels of car ownership, poor transit availability, and system design problems. The paper then reviews the scope of the problem in terms of the number of elderly and handicapped, their location geographically and in terms of urban and rural places, and explores some of the implications. A review is undertaken of the transport systems presently serving the elderly and handicapped including public transit, taxis, school buses, personal transport via the automobile, special and private systems. The basic characteristics of each of these systems is described covering service, operating levels and costs. Finally, the paper presents an evaluation of present U.S. systems discussing three levels of system activities: funding, institutional, and planning and operational problems. The paper draws some basic conclusions of relevance for other countries.

335 REVIS, J.S. (1978) Coordination, costs, and contracting for transportation services. *Transportation Research Record*, 696, pp. 46–54.

Studies of contractual and cooperative agreements among US social service agencies that provide transport services have shown that one of the most serious barriers to coordination among agencies is lack of knowledge about transport costs. In this paper, categories of transport costs and services developed by the Institute of Public Administration as cost-accounting guidelines for transport projects are identified and defined. The issue of allocation of data collection responsibilities among the personnel of transport projects is discussed. Cost accounting and reporting systems developed under Section 15 of the Urban Mass Transportation Act of 1964 (as amended) are related to the Institute of Public Administration guidelines to provide a basis for cost-sharing agreements among transport agencies.

336 ROBINSON, L. (1981) Rural public transportation: an Alaskan perpective. *Transportation Research Record*, 831, pp. 6–11.

The development and current role of public transport in the state of Alaska are discussed. The state role in public transit began in 1975, with the hiring of a planner to manage federal transit assistance programmes in the state. Statewide annual ridership in 1975 was 500,000 trips, and annual system capital and operating expenses were $750,000. In 1980, annual ridership had risen to 6 million trips and system fiscal requirements amounted to $20 million. Data indicate that there is significant potential for growth of the statewide public transport system, largely because of the high density of population in most Alaskan communities. Steps being taken to ensure the future credibility of Alaska's public transport programme in the areas of planning and policy-making are outlined. Finally, the Alaska experience is related to national issues, including the need for a uniform and effective method of apportioning federal transit funds.

2B37 ROBLIN, R.A. (1981) Organisational planning for contracted rural public transit services. *Transportation Research Record*, 831, pp. 28–33.

A framework for organizing a transit authority to contract with the private sector for service delivery is presented. It is based on a case study of the Franklin County, Massachusetts, Regional Transit Authority. Public pressure is mounting for a reduction in the size of government and the return of many functions to the private sector. Transit authorities in rural and small urban communities can meet this challenge by contracting with private-sector organizations for the delivery of transit services. Use of contracted services will change the focus of the authority's management. Based on a clear division of functional responsibilities between the authority and the contractor, planners must construct an organizational framework to reflect the authority's functions and to provide the managerial skills required to direct the contractor and evaluate performance. Overemphasizing any single area of skill will diminish the effectiveness of the authority in meeting local transport needs.

2B38 SALTZMAN, A. (1978) Overview of rural transit planning and implementation. *Transportation Research Record*, 696, pp. 14–16.

A typical planning and implementation process for rural transit systems is summarized. Specialized rural transit systems usually are initiated when local authorities perceive and define a transport problem. The next step in the process is a needs and feasibility study in which efforts are made to determine whether or not a system should be started. After financial and political support are obtained, the system must then be designed and implemented. Finally, a continuous evaluation of whether the system is solving the perceived local transport problems is necessary. The synthesis of the planning and implementation process that is described in this paper was developed from extensive information on special rural transit systems that was gathered by field visits to 12 systems and from data on other operations.

B39 SMERK, G.M. (1980) Transportation and transit planning for small and medium-sized urban communities. *Transportation Research Board*, SR 187, pp. 18-21.

B40 SMERK, G.M. (1981) A profile of transportation in the United States. *Transport Reviews*, **1** (2), pp. 101-26 and **1** (3), pp. 209-24.

This extensive review of transport in the United States starts with the geographical background and a discussion of some of the population and economic trends together with their possible impact on transport. Each of the major modes of transport—railways, waterways, roads and airlines—is covered briefly in a discussion of current problems and trends. A special section covers public transport. The regulation of transport by independent commissions is discussed and recent trends towards deregulation are covered. The difficulty of formulating a national policy in a nation where private ownership is the rule provides an introduction to issues associated with the high cost and potential shortage of petroleum-based sources of energy.

B41 STONE, J.E. and HOEL, L.A. (1980) Implementation planning of integrated transit services for small urban and rural areas. Volume II: Community review and evaluation. Virginia University, Urban Mass Transportation Administration, Final Report UMTA-VA-009-81-3, September.

This research focuses on tasks for taking technically feasible preliminary transit options to a local community and translating these plans into an implementable programme. This planning phase, referred to as implementation planning, addresses the following planning considerations: Financial Planning; Management and Organization; Institutional Roles; Regulatory Reforms; and Citizen Participation. The specific problem addressed concerns an evaluation of the requirement for implementing transit alternatives in a low density area and securing a community consensus. In this report, a model is developed to facilitate public participation in the evaluation of public transport system alternatives. The model addresses the related problems of community participation in: selecting the most preferred combination of service alternatives with respect to the technical, financial, institutional, and other constraints; establishing transport service priorities with respect to future scenarios; and developing a timetable for their implementation. The combination of these three related problems allows their interactions to be studied and tradeoffs to be specified.

2B42 SULLIVAN, B.E. (1974) An analysis of the demand for the supply of rural public transportation: The case of Alberta. Unpublished PhD Thesis, Stanford University, Stanford, California.

2B43 TENDLER, J. (1979) New directions in rural roads. Agency for International Development, Report No. 2 AID-PN-AAG-670, March.

The paper examines rural road projects in the light of the Agency's 'New Directions' mandate to improve the position of the rural poor. Attention is focused in particular on the relative merits of labour-based vs. equipment-based construction techniques. Although equipment-based techniques are traditional in donor-recipient projects and often prove administratively or financially more attractive to both, labour-based techniques more greatly benefit the poor by generating employment and by reducing costs.

2B44 TUDOR, D.N. (1981) Use of unrestricted federal funds of the Section 18 Program. *Transportation Research Record*, 831, pp. 18–23.

South Carolina's use of the Federal Highway Administration Section 18 programme provision that allows the use of unrestricted federal funds as local match is analysed. Answers are provided to the following three questions: can a definition of unrestricted federal funds or a list of preapproved federal funding sources be provided? What are the mechanics of using the unrestricted federal funds for matching purposes? How can the match maximums be calculated? Two case studies that include a complete range of use of unrestricted federal funds are discussed.

2B45 UNDERWOOD, W.C. and McKELVEY, D. (1979) State of the art in rural public transportation, Urban Mass Transportation Administration, DOT-I-79-19, September, pp. 3–5.

It is noted that rural persons, especially the elderly and the poor, are without a car, that the taxi and intercity bus systems in rural areas are inadequate, and that rural economic development and rural-to-urban commuters are increasingly dependent on public transport. Local officials are giving attention to rural transport issues and taking advantage of emerging technical and funding opportunities. However, technical and fundings aid is limited so that the identification of priorities and choosing the best transport mix are critical. Local decision-makers are learning that they should not consider Section 18 or publicly owned transport as a panacea for rural mobility. Specific Section 18 issues that state governments are facing are listed. The US Department of Transportation is finalizing regulations for the Surface Transportation Assistance Act Section 18 programme and developing technical materials and workshops for states and systems. Despite everything, progress in rural mobility has been limited by inadequate communication both among and between the levels of decision-making. The need for comprehensive information exchange is also emphasized.

346 US DEPARTMENT OF TRANSPORTATION (1976) *Rural Passenger Transportation*, Washington D.C.

347 US DEPARTMENT OF TRANSPORTATION (1979) Proceedings of the Fourth National Conference on Rural Public Transportation. Transportation Research Board, DOT-I-79-19, September.

At present there is a fairly substantial period of transition for rural transit services. The Section 147 Demonstrations were in many cases winding to a close, and a landmark series of reports on their results was under preparation. The Congress had passed the new Section 18 programme, which for the first time provided both capital and operating support for rural public transportation services. Although only $75 million in FY-1979, the Section 18 money represented a 'coming of age' for rural transit. To top things off, the White House was putting the finishing touches on a Rural Transportation initiative, which was formally announced shortly after the conference. The papers presented at the conference reflect the transition taking place. Many attempted to assess the results of the Section 147 demonstrations, and speculated about their long-term implications. A major theme of the conference was coordination, and how it could be accomplished. This reflects the limited amount of Section 18 funds and provided an option for stretching available resources. A number of papers also dealt with the role of the states in managing rural transport programmes reflecting the emphasis which Section 18 places on this function. This volume contains most of the papers presented at the Fourth National Conference. (e.g. Underwood and McKelvey [2B45])

2B48 US DEPARTMENT OF TRANSPORTATION (1981) Transportation research and technical assistance for rural and small urban transportation systems, Washington DC, 81 pp.

2B49 WIESE, A.E. (1981) Reaganomics spelling trouble for transit. *Mass Transit*, **8** (10), pp. 6–10, 32.

2C Europe

2C1 CORAS IOMPAR EIREANN (1981) *Review of the McKinsey Study*, CIE, Dublin.

This report forms the response of CIE to the McKinsey Study [2C13]. In particular, issue is taken on the recommendations that the CIE should be replaced by three new companies to run the major businesses (Railways, Provincial Bus Services, Dublin City Bus Services), and with respect to rural services where 217 of the present 284 provincial bus routes should be replaced by private operators with mini-buses. The CIE analysis suggests that each of these conclusions are invalid and that the existing arrangements should continue with even stronger links between the principal transport undertakings.

2C2 DE BOER, E. (1981) Social public transport in rural areas? Some results of research into the impact of reduced services on users of rural transport. Paper presented at a Conference on New Directions in Transport Planning Research, The Hague, November, (in Dutch).

The Netherlands has an elaborate system of rural public transport. The level of service of each line is regularly adapted to rising or falling passenger numbers according to national standards, the so-called NVS criteria. The application of these standards enhances a steady growth of strong (frequent) connections and a steady decline of weaker ones. In 1981 the NVS was applied somewhat more strictly than usual for reasons of economy. Particularly in the province of Friesland this caused serious decline on weaker lines. The impact on (former) passengers is investigated in a before and after study performed in the concessions of two bus companies (FRAM and GADO). A number of outcomes of this research are presented and the results are rather alarming as the average passenger has difficulty in adapting to the new situation since he can hardly ever change to other means of motorized transport. Policymakers should be aware of this, and some provincial influence on the level of service seems to be advisable.

C3 DE BOER, E. and KLINKENBERG, J. (1983) Developing an integrated network of conventional public transport, specialist and community transport, Paper presented at the PTRC Annual Conference, Sussex.

Rural public transport is declining gradually in sparsely populated parts of the Netherlands. This is due in part to a steady depopulation of small villages but decline is selfsustaining and confirmed by the national standards for level of service (NVS) based on mean ridership levels. In 1981 an application of somewhat stricter standards (for reasons of economy) caused considerable decreases of the level of service in some areas. A before and after study was undertaken by the first author on about 40 buslines. It was subsidized by two provinces—worried about liveability of the countryside—and carried out in cooperation with the regional bus operators—worried about their prospects. Two-thirds of the passengers experienced problems, and those on weak lines with a sharply decreased level of service were severely affected. Regarding the apparent value of rural transport for its users we set out to develop a transport system integrating conventional public transport with specialist and community transport. Its purpose was threefold: to increase the general level of service without increasing deficits, to serve the needs of different user-categories as indicated by the study mentioned, and to protect conventional public transport. This might be attained by dropping traditional geographic (and legal) boundaries between different systems and by utilizing different components dependent on changes in volume and character of demand during the day and the week. The second author surveyed transport provisions in an area of approximately 160 km² and designed a new network.

2C4 DE KOGEL, C. G. (1978) Rural transport policy in the Netherlands, in Cresswell R. (ed) *Rural Transport and Country Planning*, London: Leonard Hill, pp. 17–30.

The paper describes public passenger transport in the Netherlands with a particular emphasis on bus operations in rural areas and the associated development policies. The organizational structure is presented with particular case studies to highlight the differences between the three tiers of government.

2C5 ECKMANN, A. (1981) Rural passenger transportation in the Netherlands. *Transportation Research Record*, 831, pp. 69–75.

The close relation in the Netherlands between rural passenger transport, national transport policy, and rural development objectives is described. Although Dutch cities are geographically close to one another, they remain physically separated by rural countryside as a result of strict land use control. More than one-third of the total population lives in rural areas or small towns. A high level of demand for intercity trips gives rise to high frequency and capacity of service for rural passenger travel, by both train and bus. The nationwide regional bus network is more extensive than the rail system and trip lengths are shorter. Official Dutch transport policy seeks to maintain the distinction between intercity rail service for lengthy trips and regional bus service for rural trips and for travel on small urban transit systems. In developing new transportation facilities, including highway construction, the national plan for transport seeks to restrain further migration of city dwellers to rural communities. For the convenience of existing rural transit travellers, central government policy is designed to relate frequency of bus service to observed levels of passenger demand. Alongside the Dutch policy of extensive national transport service has been a recognition that traffic and transport are essential elements in regional development planning. Improved passenger transport in rural areas has helped to preserve the rural way of life by affording access to important urban jobs and services. The lesson of the Dutch experience is that rural transport is most effective when integrated with national transport policy and linked to clear objectives for rural area development.

2C6 EUROPEAN CONFERENCE OF MINISTERS OF TRANSPORT (1977) Organisation of regional passenger transport, ECMT, Paris.

This review examines regional transport needs, the organization of undertakings, the role of the authorities, regular special-purpose vehicles and services, the function of national railways, intermediate forms of transport and fares.

C7 GWILLIAM, K.M. (1980) Realism and the Common Transport Policy of the EEC, in Polak, J.B. and Van der Kamp, J.B. (eds) *Changes in the Field of Transport Studies*, The Hague: Martinus Nijhoff, pp. 38–59.

It seems that there is deadlock between the incompatibilities of existing national transport policies and those which the EEC Commission has been attempting to develop. This paper attempts to resolve some of these dilemmas. The nature and scope of transport policy is outlined prior to a resumé of UK transport policy and the essential elements of EEC transport policy. The inconsistencies in stance and content between the national and EEC policy levels are identified as the basis for the recommendations made for the reconciliation between the two policy levels.

C8 HEINZE, G.W. (1982) Travel behaviour in rural areas: A German case study. *International Journal of Transport Economics* 9 (2), pp. 193–203.

The discussion of necessary and possible improvements in the provision of transport in sparsely populated rural areas continues to be characterized mainly by hypotheses which display a broad spectrum of varied ideas. This has severe repercussions on forecasts made and instruments used as well as on their feedback into the process of developing objectives. This problem made itself felt particularly in the preparation of a major study project on the possibilities and limits of improvements in the transport services in sparsely populated rural areas. The authors tried to obtain concrete information on the actual transport services provided by means of primary surveys carried out in selected, representative partial areas in Lower Saxony. More attention should be paid to constitutional and social aspects of supplying marginal groups with public transport.

C9 HEINZE, G.W., HERBST, D. and SCHÜHLE, U. (1982) *Verkehr im ländlichen Raum*, Hannover: Curt T. Vincentz Verlag, p. 560 (in German). (Transport in Rural Areas.)

This book forms a major contribution to the literature on transport in rural areas and represents a thorough review of the German experience. Having outlined the definitions and nature of rural areas, their particular transport problems are identified, principally one of accessibility for those with and without the private car. Different approaches to the analysis of both local and regional accessibility are presented with the conclusion that real journey times are low. On the supply side of the question it seems that public transport has improved rather than deteriorated over time in the particular areas that have been selected for case study investigation. Policy issues are raised under the three headings of infrastructure, transport capacity, and subsidization. Various initiatives have been taken which include tax reductions for public transport operators, cooperative ventures, and schools transport services being made available to all users. Public transport services are provided by many agencies and this presents a highly heterogeneous picture. Some of the legislation is summarized as it relates to rural areas, particularly the integration of public transport provision and the organizational and regulatory conditions. The final section of the volume examines opportunities for the future. Paratransit modes are covered together with the increased use of taxis or hire cars as alternatives to conventional public transport. Car sharing and car pooling schemes also seem to have some potential in this context. A model concept for integrating public transport and car pools is developed which is designed for the specific conditions of rural areas and which goes beyond existing types of organization. It is extremely difficult to establish any findings on the development of public transport in rural areas and the possibilities for action are limited given the cyclical nature of economic problems and their structural nature. The mobility situation in rural areas involved a varied and largely unresearched spectrum of substitution and complementarity in processes that constitute a complex phenomenon. Transport is only one of the measures that can be used to influence the mobility problems of rural residents.

2C10 KILVINGTON, R.P. (1981) The organization and operation of public transport in Denmark and the Netherlands: an international comparison with the United Kingdom. Paper presented at the PTRC Annual Conference, Warwick.

This paper examines the organization and operation of public transport in two of the EEC countries and seeks to draw comparisons with the United Kingdom. The organization of transport, fares and subsidy policies and patronage trends are outlined for the two European countries and comparisons are drawn in terms of the relative success of the different approaches to public transport provision in each individual location.

211 LAUDENBACH, A. (1980) Transport policies and new regional planning requirements. Council of Europe, European Regional Planning Study Series No. 34, Strasbourg.

Changing transport needs and recent developments in the transport sector are discussed in the light of two emerging constraints—energy saving and the protection of the environment. The consequences of the latter are examined for regional planning and transport authorities, but the conclusion reached is that new considerations should encourage a reformulation of objectives in a context of moderate economic growth.

212 LAZARUS, P.E. (1978) The implications of EEC transport policy for the UK. *Highway Engineer*, **25** (4), pp. 2–7.

Although the Treaty of Rome identifies transport as one of only three areas in which the Community should develop a common policy, progress has been extremely slow because of the different philosophies of individual member states. The result is a lack of any broad agreement on overall objectives and a concentration on detailed, and often unrelated, issues with the intention of developing these, eventually, into a coherent policy. The paper reviews progress so far and covers some of the current developments on a number of these detailed proposals.

213 McKINSEY INTERNATIONAL (1980) *The Transport Challenge—The Opportunities in the 1980s.* A report for the Minister for Transport, December, Dublin: Stationery Office.

This report forms a major review of transport in Ireland. The first part summarizes a series of detailed studies that have been made on current policy issues, particularly on the question of evaluation of public transport alternatives, and on the legislative and institutional

framework for transport. The conclusions reached suggest that there
are fundamental problems in a structure that has developed over
many years and that reform must take place. Individual transport
problems—grouped into separate national, urban, and rural categories—can only be successfully tackled after such a reform has been
achieved. Among the institutional changes suggested are the dis-
establishment of CIE as an entity, the combination of national roads
and rail infrastructure and service functions in the Department of
Transport, and the restructuring of relationships between the operators and the Department of Transport with a continuous review in
all areas. Recommendations for public transport operations are
listed under three headings—the railways, urban buses, and rural
buses. In the last heading, two main suggestions are made. Service
levels and costs should be adapted more closely to demand levels
through the use of small vehicles and unconventional modes. The
management approach should be altered by the creation of a rural
transport unit in the Department of Transport to administer the
changes suggested in point one and the levels of subsidy, and to
introduce some elements of competition in service provision.

2C14 ORGANISATION FOR ECONOMIC COOPERATION AND DEVELOPMENT
(1977) *The Future of European Passenger Transport*, 3 vols, OECD,
Paris.

This forms the final report of the OECD study on European intercity passenger transport requirements. It describes the study, including the approach and the assumptions adopted, and presents the
results, and the two volumes of appendices contain explanatory matter and maps.

2C15 SWEDISH INSTITUTE (1980) Transport policy and traffic trends in
Sweden. Fact sheets on Sweden.

A new joint body, representing the county council and all local
councils in the county, has now taken responsibility for local and
regional public bus transport. At the same time a new system of
state subsidies has been introduced that pays the cash straight to the
regional transport authority.

2C16 VERHOEFF, J.M. (1980) Governmental financial support for regional
public transport, *Economisch Statistische Berichten*, **65** (3249), pp. 404–
10 (in Dutch).

Financial support for regional public transport is theoretically based on four concepts: temporary financial aid to enable undertakings to regain a profitable market-share; financial aid to compensate for a decline in transport demand; financial aid to assure the continuation of public transport services; and temporary financial aid to be able to nationalize public transport undertakings. The second concept refers to the additional costs of public transport as a result of improvement measures taken by the government. In this case government support is needed. The amount of additional costs is determined by using the average utilization factor in public transport as a criterion. Groups of public transport undertakings are discerned which suffer differently from government improvement measures. The advantages and disadvantages of the principles applied are discussed. The third concept refers to government standards concerning production costs and quality of service. In order to stimulate efficiency of public transport its production costs must be covered by an appropriate tariff structure. Additional costs might occur if the quality of service is to be maintained. The first and fourth concepts are said not to be of any relevance as long as the two other concepts can be used. The article concludes with a description of the choice between relevant concepts and a description of the present application of the concepts in the Netherlands.

217 WHITELEGG, J. (1979) The Common Transport Policy: A case of lost direction? *Transportation Science*, **13** (4), pp. 343–57.

While the Common Transport Policy has made significant progress in the 'regulation', 'harmonization', 'charging for infrastructure', and related areas, it has failed to recognize the wider environment of transport and in particular the ways in which transport policies are inextricably linked with other policies of the EEC. Successive policy statements are examined to illustrate how the EEC's view of transport can be seen as increasingly narrow and unrelated to the central issues of community development in the period immediately preceding economic and monetary union. While very critical of EEC policy the underlying assumption is that transport is a core policy through and with which one can advance the central issues, as long as the links between policies are understood and the administrative machinery reflects this.

3 Accessibility and mobility

3A Concepts and definitions

The conventional land-use transport planning process, as used and developed for studies in major urban areas, is not suitable for application in rural areas. The main reason for this is that conventional approaches rely on actual demand levels as the basic input to predictions of future demand. In the rural context, it is unrealistic to assume that the total number of trips made by a household is independent of the quality of transport provision available to that household (Moseley [3A21]). The basic problem in rural areas is that many strongly felt desires for movement are frustrated because of the imperfections of the market (Banister [3A1]).

Consequently most of the research on transport in rural areas revolves around the twin concepts of mobility and accessibility. Mobility can simply be defined as the ability of an individual to move about. This ability can operationally be examined in two parts, the first of which relates to the amount of travel which is actually made in terms of the numbers of trips by all modes (including the walk mode) for all purposes (including multipurpose trips). The second part covers the ease of movement which is much harder to quantify. It would include personal characteristics (age, sex, socio-economic variables, physical disability), whether the car is available or not (either as a driver or a passenger), the ability to drive a car and the availability of public transport services and other modes (motor cycle and pedal cycle).

So personal mobility has been defined as a function of two variables. The first is the tangible realization of travel demand in terms of actual movement, whilst the second is a personal categorization which acts as a constraint upon the first, and can be interpreted as the potential for movement. With this definition, it is recognized that not everybody wants or requires the same level of mobility. (Koushki and Berg [3A14], Moseley [3A20], Skelton [3A29]).

Increasingly, however, the focus of attention has switched from a concern with mobility to one over accessibility. Transport is now seen as the means to an end and not an end in itself. People travel because they derive benefits at their destination which exceed the costs of travel; thus if transport is treated as a derived demand, consideration must be given to the distribution of facilities as well as the transport links and the spatial and social characteristics of the population. Transport accessibility can be defined as the ability of people to get to or be reached by the opportunities which are perceived to be relevant to them (Jones [3A13]).

Conventionally, accessibility can be considered in two ways. Locational accessibility is either a comparative measure which weighs units of separation against the number of destinations, or as a composite measure which combines the two factors into a single index. Comparative measures of accessibility are numerous and indicate the increasing number of opportunities which become accessible with distance (Mitchell and Town [3A18], Moseley et al. [3A23]). Composite accessibility is usually based on the gravity model where accessibility is a function of the attractiveness of the destination and the distance to be travelled (Baxter and Lenzi [3A3], Hansen [3A8]). The applications are common in the transport planning situation where the variations on the basic theme are numerous (Daly [3A6], Johnson [3A10], Morris et al. [3A19], Pirie [3A27]).

Secondly, there is personal accessibility where the unit of study is the individual rather than the location. Here the individual is limited by the available modes of travel and communication, and these are modified by the person's perception and determined by the individual's activity demand pattern. Perhaps the best example is the time-space school of geography at Lund in Sweden; most of this research has concentrated on the urban situation, but there are some examples of rural applications (Lenntorp [3A15], Martensson [3A16]). Each individual has his own 'action space' which limits the activities he can take part in, and the objective of the approach is firstly to determine the dimensions of the 'action space', and secondly to expand it or to place more opportunities within it.

Accessibility is very unequally distributed in rural areas, both between different locations and within individual locations. Research has almost exclusively concentrated on the demand and 'need' elements of particular consumers. The producers or suppliers of services have not yet come under the researcher's microscope (Moseley [3A22]).

3B Transport deprivation and needs

Much research effort has been directed towards the questions of deprivation and needs to ensure that available resources are properly allocated. The arguments have revolved around the actual nature of needs and whether they can be measured (e.g. Koutsopoulos [3B17], Rawson [3B31]). One line of enquiry (Banister [3B5]) suggests that needs are essentially conceptual in nature and that any attempt to analyse the problems of rural transport in terms of a needs based approach should place the transport element within the wider context of rural problems. Transport need in the broadest sense is one manifestation of the 'rural problem'.

Other research has ignored the fundamental concepts of need and has attempted to find an operational tool. Minimum levels of service have been the most commonly devised method where every rural community should be entitled to a given level of public transport provision if it comes up to certain population thresholds (Beetham and Robertson [3B8], Peat, Marwick and Mitchell [3B28], [3B29], Rühl et al. [3B33], Winfield et al. [3B39]). Other studies have examined particular communities (Coates and Weiss [3B13]), or particular 'client' populations (Bailey [3B3]). Some of the problems with the measurement of needs have been well illustrated by Bird [3B10]. In a comparative analysis of six index methods used to identify transport need she concluded that 'even when the type of information included and the method of construction used are similar, the results are often quite different'. The suggestion is made that the output is not consistent when applied to different sets of data. Deprivation is somewhat easier to measure; perceived or relative deprivation occurs when a person compares his position with another person's and he perceives that a good or service is being received and he wants it and regards it as feasible that he should have it (Banister [1A2], Coles, [3B14]). Deprivation can also be examined from the decision makers' perspective when indices of multiple deprivation are constructed either in the transport context or a wider social context (Connor [3B15]). The indicators of both 'needs' and deprivation used by the county councils in their submission for transport related grants (Sections 2A and 6A) are mainly aspatial and based on minimum levels of service. Further research may be required to determine a social group based measure, perhaps within a particular spatial context with the local community having an active role to play.

3C Social groups

It is clear that rising prosperity and substantial increases in car ownership in rural areas have not solved mobility and accessibility problems for all rural residents; indeed it could be argued that it has increased the difficulties for certain sectors of the community. Studies have concentrated on all the carless population (Briggs and McKelvey [3C5]) or on certain groups within the population and the difficulties they have in gaining access to facilities.

The concern of public policy is to provide some public transport service for those without access to a car. As Hillman *et al.* [2A37] have suggested, there will always be a substantial part of the population without access to their own car and will be dependent upon others for their mobility. Studies have tended to concentrate on three main groups of rural residents; the elderly are perceived as having particular problems with studies being carried out by the national organizations (Age Concern [3C1]) and universities (Notess *et al.* [3C24] and Wachs and Blanchard [3C36]). The problem is not just one of the supply of a service, but whether the elderly can afford to use it and whether it satisfies their particular requirements. Much has been achieved through sensitive planning and concessionary fares (GB Department of Transport [3C14]) but many elderly people still suffer from isolation.

The second group are young people in rural areas, and in particular their travel to school. Increasing concern over the cost and safety of school journeys has led to a series of studies (Rigby [3C31]) that review the most recent trends. Other studies focus on the methods that can be used in planning and design of school transport routes (Demetsky *et al.* [3C11]). With the concentration of facilities and the demise of the rural primary schools, both the costs and distances to be travelled to school are likely to increase.

The final group are the rural poor and those with some handicap. Ambulance and social services transport play a limited role in alleviating some of these problems and the voluntary sector has become more important (Bailey [3C3]). However a broader based approach is really required through the use of special vehicles (Dallmeyer and Surti [3C10]), the private car and taking services to the people rather than people to services (e.g. Moseley and Packman [3D22]). Other disadvantaged groups in the rural context are housewives and non car owning households, but less work has been carried out here. Through the identification of specific subgroups within the population, analysis can take place and recommendations made so that particular social policy initiatives can be taken.

3D Activities and telecommunications

Throughout this part of the review it has been emphasized that travel in rural areas should be seen as a means to participate in a particular activity. Demand is often not realized because suitable opportunities, both transport and non-transport, do not exist. In this section research on access to specific activities is presented together with some of the recent work on the impact of telecommunications.

One persistent feature with respect to the provision of facilities has been the trend towards concentration into fewer, larger units. These units, particularly shops, are sometimes located in the urban centres and not locally with the result that distances to be travelled have increased (Moseley and Spencer [3D23]). One alternative has been to take the services to the customer (Moseley and Packman [3D22]). Another initiative has been taken to encourage local residents to retain existing services or to set up community based schemes (National Council for Voluntary Organisations [3D24] and Woollett [3D42]). Health care facilities have become characterized by group practices with large catchment areas and hospital facilities have become both more centralized and specialized (Rigby [3D29], Welsh Council [3D39]). However there is evidence to suggest that a reversal is now taking place with the growth of community hospital facilities (Hayes and Bentham [3D16]). Concentration has also resulted in the closure of local facilities including schools, post offices, and petrol stations (Taylor and Emerson [3D34]). All these changes have resulted in a decline in the levels of local accessibility with an increase in the requirements for transport.

Traditionally, rural accessibility has been defined in terms of physical access to employment, services and facilities, and attention was concentrated on the movement of people and goods through the transport system. The advent of telecommunications could fundamentally change the demand for travel as many more exchanges in rural areas could take place by non-physical means (Clark and Unwin [3D6] [3D9]). In the short term it seems likely that established services will spread (such as the telephone), suggesting that some travel substitution may take place (Kraemer [3D19]). However a more likely scenario will be that travel patterns may change with a growth in overall levels of demand (Miller [3D20]) as people expand their range of contacts.

Social aspects of telecommunications use have only recently emerged as an important research area (Clark [3D5]). A more immediate impact is the opportunities that telecommunications afford to access and provide services, particularly information services, remotely (Edwards [3D12], Short [3D32]). Dispersal may take place in the location of certain types of business activity as residents in rural areas could work from local neighbourhood centres rather than travel to a central office (Christie and Elton [3D3]). Similarly, education and health care diagnosis could be carried out at home through home-based terminals that could operate in both an active or passive capacity (Dhillon et al. [3D11], GB Departments of Environment and Transport [3D15]). The consequent increase in leisure time from the reduction in travel to work may then be taken up with new activities that could either be home-based or require travel. The technology is available, but little is known about the actual effects on rural areas and lifestyles. Perhaps telecommunications should be given as much attention as the car and other forms of transport as a means by which rural inaccessibility can be reduced.

Many other studies which include aspects of mobility and accessibility, but involve particular modes of transport, both private and public, are covered in Section 4. Area based studies that do not develop methodologies but are concerned with applications have been grouped in Section 6.

3A Concepts and definitions

3A1 BANISTER, D.J. (1980) Transport Mobility and Deprivation in Inter Urban Areas: Research Findings and Policy Perspectives. University of Reading, Department of Geography, Geographical Paper 71.

This paper summarizes a two year research project which was designed to investigate the patterns of mobility in areas which are separate from, but within the influence of, an urban area (defined as inter-urban). A large proportion of non-urban Great Britain comes within this definition. Having determined the present mobility patterns, particular issues such as attitudes towards public transport, car availability, car usage, car sharing, and levels of access are all investigated. This analysis involves a detailed household survey of six parishes which had been selected by cluster analysis to give representation to the different 'types' found in the study area of South Oxfordshire.

In addition to the empirical analysis, two new techniques were used to test policy questions as perceived by the respondents in the survey parishes. The first concerned trade-off analysis of policy alternatives and the second covered consumer preferences for characteristics of alternative modes. The findings from these methods are included in the sections on latent demand and deprivation and evaluation. The whole research is placed within both the national and local policy context, highlighting the transport policy adopted in Oxfordshire.

A2 BANISTER, D.J. (1983) Transport and accessibility, in Pacione, M. (ed) *Progress in Rural Geography*, Beckenham, Kent: Croom Helm, pp. 130-48.

This extensive review paper defines transport mobility and accessibility within the context of rural areas and recent changes in transport policy. The situation is one of continual change and this has been reflected in certain policy initiatives that have been taken over the last five years. The alternatives available to planners and operators are stated and the conclusions that are drawn seem to indicate that the role for conventional public transport in rural areas may be limited. Policy should explicitly consider alternatives including the better use of the private car and non transport options. The paper concludes with a set of proposals for transport and accessibility in rural areas.

A3 BAXTER, R.S. and LENZI, G. (1975) The measurement of relative accessibility. *Regional Studies*, **9** (1), pp. 15-26.

This paper presents a method of arriving at an accurate distance matrix at the urban scale using abstract network patterns incorporating the geographical constraints. This obviates the need for expensive digitization and analysis of the road network as a pre-requisite in the compilation of the distance matrix.

3A4 BENWELL, M. (1977) Accessibility in the design of local transport policies, in Williams, A.F. (ed) *Transport and Public Policy*, Transport Study Group, Institute of British Geographers, Vol. 2, pp. 114–27.

While there is considerable agreement about the nature of the changes which have recently taken place in transport planning, there is, as yet, no set of widely acceptable new techniques for making transport decisions. This paper outlines the potential applicability of an accessibility framework for the development of techniques appropriate to normative transport planning.

3A5 COLES, O.B. (1976) Improving rural accessibility: a pragmatic approach. Proceedings of the PTRC Annual Summer Meeting, Warwick, July.

This paper outlines certain policy avenues which might fruitfully be explored by those concerned with improving rural accessibility. In particular, attention is devoted to policies which avoid, on the one hand, the commitment of substantial additional resources to conventional public transport, and, on the other, reliance upon unconstrained market forces as a means of resource allocation. This is considered to be advantageous, because, it is argued, both the latter policies may be associated with resource misallocation. The paper is organized in four sections. First, rural policies bearing upon transport and accessibility are reviewed. This is clearly essential since no policy discussion can take place 'in vacuo'. Second, the shortcomings of a total reliance upon conventional forms of public transport or on market forces are enumerated. Third, some possible means of escaping from such reliance are outlined. Finally, some general lessons about rural accessibility policy are suggested.

3A6 DALY, A.J. (1975) Measuring accessibility in the rural context. Proceedings of a Seminar on rural Public Transport, Polytechnic of Central London.

Suggests that an objective measure of accessibility can give useful insight for the rural planning process. The author then presents the measure Local Government Operational Research Unit developed in the study carried out in West Yorkshire and goes on to discuss the properties and use of the measure. The measure has the properties that the introduction of any new alternative—destination or mode—will increase the accessibility, as will any improvement in any existing alternative. The extent to which the accessibility is improved, however, depends on the importance of the alternative that is improved. That is, an improvement that still leaves an alternative little used will have little impact on the accessibility. This desirable feature follows from the compatibility of the accessibility measure with standard transportation planning models.

47 GARDEN, J.M. (1978) The mobility of the elderly and disabled in Great Britain: An overview. Paper presented at the International Conference on Transport for the Elderly and the Handicapped, Loughborough University of Technology, pp. 27-32.

This paper summarizes some of the developments of the past ten years which have brought benefits to elderly and disabled people with mobility problems. In the case of the elderly it identifies concessionary fares schemes as having been of considerable importance despite the unfairness of their distribution and value. It is argued that the elderly could be further helped in the future, if the results of recent research on vehicle design, lead to new generations of public transport vehicles which are accessible and comfortable for the widest possible span of passenger capabilities. Those disabled people who are unable to use public transport are now being helped by a new form of benefit called the 'Mobility allowance' which is described. However, despite much goodwill the needs of the elderly disabled are inadequately met and this is identified as an important problem to which solutions have yet to be found.

48 HANSEN, W.G. (1959) How accessibility shapes land use. *Journal of the American Institute of Planners*, **25** (2), pp. 73-6.

An empirical examination of the residential development patterns illustrates that accessibility and the availability of vacant developable land can be used as the basis of a residential land use model. In this seminal paper, the author presents an operational definition and suggests a method for determining accessibility patterns within metropolitan areas. This is a process of distributing forecasted metropolitan population to small areas within the metropolitan region. Although the model presented is not yet sufficiently well refined for estimating purposes, the concept and the approach may be potentially useful tools for metropolitan planning purposes.

3A9 HUDSON, W.R. and WALTON, C.M. (1974) Transportation to fulfil human needs in the rural/urban environment. Society of Automotive Engineers, Pennsylvania, SAE Paper 740026.

This paper presents background and initial findings on a multi-disciplinary programme sponsored by the US Department of Transportation, University Research Program which considers transport problems involving urban and rural travellers and relates to all modes of travel. Work reported in this paper includes: evaluation of transport problems related to providing essential services to rural and urban dwellers; study of the effect of inter-urban transport systems on the rural environment and the development or demise of the small rural communities; study of the movement of goods and freight in the south west including the impact of the new Dallas–Fort Worth regional airport; development of methodologies for considering human response to the quality of ride and service in developing criteria for the various transport modes in both urban and rural areas and study of human response in developing methods of evaluating possible modal choice decisions in both urban and rural areas. While these are broad programme areas, preliminary results are reported herein which indicate the potential of multidisciplinary university research.

3A10 JOHNSON, R.J. (1966) An index of accessibility and its use in the study of bus services and settlement patterns. *Tijdschrift Voor Economische en Sociale Geografie*, **57** (1), pp. 33–8.

In NW Yorkshire, bus services are taken as an accurate measure of short-distance movement and an index constructed based on the extent to which the services meet the needs of work, shopping, and entertainment; shopping being the chief item. A definition of urban hinterlands, based on the frequency of buses reveals great variations in urban dominance. While town distance and size are the principal factors influencing bus services, general correlation exists between rural population, settlement pattern, and the amount of bus traffic. The paper presents two new methods of measuring accessibility by bus and suggests that the results obtained could be of use to rural development planners.

1 JONES, A.D. (1977) Rural accessibility: its measurement and improvement. Unpublished MSc Thesis, Department of Town Planning, UWIST, Cardiff.

2 JONES, P.M. (1975) Accessibility, mobility and travel need. Some problems of definition and measurement. Research Note 4 and Paper presented to the Institute of British Geographers, Transport Geography Study Group, Birmingham.

3 JONES, S.R. (1981) Accessibility measures: a literature review. *Transport and Road Research Laboratory*, LR 967.

Accessibility is a term often used in transport and land-use studies and the main aim of this report is to survey the range of measures of accessibility that have been proposed. Accessibility is seen as being concerned with the opportunity available to an individual or type of person at a given location to take part in a particular activity or set of activities. However various other interpretations of the term accessibility have been made and in order to survey the range of indices to which the term accessibility measure has been applied it is necessary to consider also the range of definitions that have been given to the term accessibility. The advantages and disadvantages of the various measures are discussed. No single 'best' measure is identified; rather the choice depends on the type of problem being studied and the resources available. Some consideration is given also to the areas of study in which accessibility may be a useful concept.

14 KOUSHKI, P.A. and BERG, W.D. (1982) Improving rural mobility— a practical approach. *Transportation Quarterly*, **36** (4), pp. 631–42.

The need for public transport services to supplement the private car in small towns and rural communities is readily apparent, particularly for certain groups within the community. The provision of paratransit services to isolated areas to give a link to a neighbourhood town is seen as one way to improve rural mobility. To provide a successful case of implementation these new services have to be coordinated within existing paratransit services without additional cost and one such scheme is evaluated in this paper.

3A15 Lenntorp, B. (1981) A time-geographic approach to transport and public policy planning, in Banister, D.J. and Hall, P.G. (eds) *Transport and Public Policy Planning*, London: Mansell, pp. 387-96.

First a general background to the time-geographic approach developed at Lund is outlined in a theoretical manner. This is followed by two case studies, one in an urban context and the other that describes the daily production in the dairy farming industry over a period of time.

3A16 Martensson, S. (1974) Quality of life—possibilities for individuals and households to carry out daily programs in different types of regions. Department of Geography, University of Lund, Sweden.

This is a summary in English of a Swedish study which employs the concepts and techniques of 'time-space geography'. Three rural areas are studied in depth, with a view to establishing what activities are possible for people in different circumstances and different locations, given alternative locations of activities and assumptions about transport availability.

3A17 Mitchell, C.G.B. (1979) Concepts and definitions of accessibility, in *Mobility in Rural Areas*, Proceedings of a Conference held at the Centre for Transport Studies, Cranfield, pp. 49-58.

The concepts and definitions of mobility and accessibility are presented together with a review of measurement techniques. These methods can be equally well applied in nonrural areas and it is concluded that the evidence is not yet clear as to which measure correlates best with perceptions of the ability of people to reach activities.

3A18 Mitchell, C.G.B. and Town, S.W. (1977) Accessibility of various groups to different activities. *Transport and Road Research Laboratory*, SR 258.

The population has moved out to the edge of towns in the suburbanization process while services have increased in size and reduced in number by grouping in centres for economic reasons. New employment has moved to the edge of towns. Generally the main trips have increased in length over the years along with the increase in car ownership. The importance of motorized travel compared with walking varies with the distance travelled which depends upon the activity and the personal characteristics of the traveller. Education and shopping trips are shorter than work and social trips and they are usually on foot and are likely to be made by women and children. Distance tends to increase with motorization. Car ownership tends to vary directly with socio-economic grouping with more professional and managerial workers having cars and fewer semiskilled and unskilled workers having them. Of those old enough to hold a driving licence there are approximately 64 per cent of males and 21 per cent of females who do. There are three groups who generally do not have access to car driving—they are the young, the old, and housewives.

19 MORRIS, J.M., DUMBLE, P.L. and WIGAN, M.R. (1979) Accessibility indicators for transport planning. *Transporation Research*, **13A** (2), pp. 91–109.

Both perceptual and measurable specifications of accessibility are reviewed and their relevance to transport planning established. The wide variety of analytical forms which can be used to quantify different aspects of accessibility are categorized and grouped by conceptual basis. The different forms of accessibility index are then related to underlying theories which link consumer demand, evaluation and accessibility.

20 MOSELEY, M.J. (1979) Rural accessibility: the role of the motor car. *Highway Engineer*, **26** (6), pp. 18–19, 25.

Rising car ownership in rural Britain has greatly improved the accessibility enjoyed by some residents, while worsening that of others by undermining public transport and village services such as shops and pubs. Disadvantaged groups within the community are identified: they include many women, the elderly, and the young. Still higher levels of car ownership are to be expected and this resource can, to some extent, be harnessed as a community resource. But devoting the bulk of available resources to road building and maintenance implies social inequalities and a rigorous evaluation procedure embracing the full range of policy options is urgently needed.

3A21 MOSELEY, M.J. (1979) Rural mobility and accessibility, in Shaw, J.M. (ed) *Rural Deprivation and Planning*, Norwich: Geo Books, pp. 137-45.

This paper looks at the causes, consequences, and policy implications of the deterioration in rural accessibility which forces attention as much upon rural services as upon modes of travel. Some myths about rural mobility which underlie the widespread reluctance to improve accessibility and the organizational fragmentation which inhibit any attempts to do so are examined. A range of policy options is considered and it is argued that for every local situation the widest range of alternatives should be assessed.

3A22 MOSELEY, M.J. (1981) The supply of rural (in) accessibility, in Banister, D.J. and Hall, P.G. (eds) *Transport and Public Policy Planning*, London: Mansell, pp. 183-8.

The paper argues that a new thrust in rural research is required if significant further understanding is to be achieved. The focus has been on the individual and the demand side, not on the producers of inaccessibility. Research should now switch to an analysis of policy formulation and implementation, on the political context of decision making and studies of the decision makers themselves at all levels. A shift from behaviouralism to managerialism must be followed by a wider analysis of the whole political and economic context.

3A23 MOSELEY, M.J., HARMAN, R.G., COLES, O.B. and SPENCER, M.B. (1976) Rural Transport and Accessibility. Final Report to the Department of the Environment.

The final report of an intensive research project carried out in Norfolk in 1975 and 1976 for the Department of the Environment. The study aimed to take both a long view (looking back to the 1950s, and forward to the 1980s) and a broad view (including non-transport issues) of the rural accessibility problem. The context of change in the rural areas of Great Britain is examined in detail and informed speculation about the future discussed. Response to change and ability to adapt to new circumstances are considered before the nature of the rural accessibility problem (essentially the inability or difficulty of carless rural residents to gain access to the services or facilities that are relevant to them) is analysed in greater depth. The problem has to be defined in terms of disadvantaged groups within the rural population and the constraints which impede their mobility and access to facilities. The concept of accessibility is developed and then used to assess alternative strategies for meeting the needs of rural populations. The organizational and financial fragmentation which inhibits the implementation of a comprehensive approach is described. Finally policy recommendations are made, with the conclusion that there can be no single solution universally applicable in every situation. Volume 2 contains ten appendices and a very extensive annotated bibliography (Section 7).

24 NUTLEY, S.D. (1981) The evaluation of accessibility levels in rural areas: an example from rural Wales. Welsh Office, January.

After a brief review of previous analytical techniques used to evaluate accessibility, details are given of the method used in this report. It is based on a comparison between the location of population and the location of facilities/activities to which people seek access. The input variables are population disaggregated into social groups, car availability, functions (activities/facilities/services), times at which functions are available, time budgets of social groups, acceptable time at destination, frequency, and maximum walking distance. This framework has five dimensions, between which the data can be manipulated: sample settlements, social groups, functions, car-owning and non-car owning groups, time (either a simple comparison of two time periods or before and after a specific policy implementation). The analysis is conducted on the basis of individual settlements, normally rural villages. The first objective is to assess the ability of each of the social groups to avail itself of the functions it needs in accordance with the time and transport standards set. Thus each social group/function combination is classified as accessible or not accessible. The manner in which decisions are taken as to whether one activity is accessible to one social group is plotted in flow charts incorporating the time and transport standards. This procedure is significantly different for 'car users' and 'non-car users'.

25 NUTLEY, S.D. (1985) Planning options for the improvement of rural accessibility—the use of the time space approach, *Regional Studies*, **19** (1).

Using a time-space approach, it is explained how the evaluation of current accessibility problems in rural areas can be carried forward into planning 'solutions'. Forty planning options are presented for improving access standards in a small case study area in rural Wales. These include conventional bus services, various 'unconventional modes', and several 'non-transport solutions', plus combinations of these. Social benefits of each plan are expressed by the additional accessibility provided, and hence costs and benefits can be presented in a comparable manner, and the most appropriate options recommended.

3A26 OXLEY, P.R. and SEATON, R.A.F. (1979) Conference report—Mobility in rural areas. *Traffic Engineering and Control*, **20** (7), pp. 364-5.

3A27 PIRIE, G.H. (1979) Measuring accessibility: A review and proposal. *Environment and Planning A*, **11** (3), pp. 299-312.

An attempt is made to clarify some of the confusion about the notion of accessibility by examining its limitations, strengths and conceptual bases of distance, topological, gravity, and cumulative opportunity measures of accessibility. In their aggregate and disaggregate states the measures are practical, enabling measurement into the future and measurement with a minimum of data, but the assumption that all nodes are potential destinations and all origins are known severely restricts the meaning and uses of the measures. Time space measures of accessibility do not make these assumptions but they are data hungry. It is proposed that accessibility be thought of as a vacancy in an activity routine and that it be measured in terms of the disruption involved in creating it.

3A28 PIRIE, G.H. (1981) The possibility and potential of public policy on accessibility. *Transportation Research*, **15A** (5), pp. 377-81.

The development of measures of accessibility has proceeded largely independently of concern for the ways in which public policy makers respond to analytic research. Academic interest in accessibility is not necessarily paralleled by a public interest and the former cannot be expected to have a ready-made market or to promote public policy of its own accord. Public policy on accessibility will only be forthcoming if accessibility is a well politicized issue. If improved accessibility can be achieved as part of other programmes, then there is little likelihood of public policy being addressed to accessibility exclusively. If conditions are such that public policy on accessibility is a possibility, sound policy-relevant research is still not a guarantee of programme success. Successful implementation of public policy relies in part on identifying those who have actual and not merely nominal control over outcomes. Political viability is also vital to the working of accessibility policy. Public policy imposed from above is unlikely to succeed in the context of a pluralist society honeycombed with special interest groups committed to participatory problem solving. Reflecting on the possibility of formulating and implementing an effective policy on accessibility suggests the importance of giving as much attention to the development of a conceptually robust and incisive notion of accessibility as to the improvement of accessibility measures.

129 SKELTON, N.G. (1979) The investigation of travel. *Transportation Planning and Technology*, **5** (2), pp. 115-22.

This paper discusses a number of theoretical points related to the investigation of travel characteristics, with particular reference to the elderly. It starts by discussing a number of basic terms, pointing out their relationships and discussing their implications for research and policy. It is argued that, in the context of social policy on transport, travel should be investigated in the light of the activities to which it gives access, rather than as a phenomenon in its own right. Another important aspect of travel is the way in which it is constrained, through the limitations of the person or of the transport system. The difficulties of isolating the effects of travel constraints are pointed out. The paper concludes with a discussion of some ways in which 'need' may be defined and assessed.

130 VICKERMAN, R.W. (1974) Accessibility attraction and potential—a review of some concepts and their use in determining mobility. *Environment and Planning A*, **6** (6), pp. 675-91.

Various concepts of attraction, accessibility, and potential are examined with the object of reaching a definition of each. Multivariate analysis suggests that the influences of conventional accessibility indices are concealed by collinear socioeconomic variations. When these are separated there is a more pronounced relationship.

3A31 WIBBERLEY, G.P. (1978) Mobility and the countryside, in Cresswell, R. (ed) *Rural Transport and Country Planning*, London: Leonard Hill, pp. 3-7.

This introduction begins on an optimistic note that stresses the tremendous technical developments which have greatly increased the mobility of most people in the last 100 years. Rural areas have been characterized by a greater differentiation between the privileged and the disadvantaged and several groups now constitute the rural transport poor—pensioners, others on low incomes, children and housewives. Poverty and policy options are considered briefly.

3A32 WYTCONSULT (1977) Social research in rural areas, Document 804, April

The methodology used in the research programme Wytconsult [1A53], [2A63] is discussed in detail in this document. Much of the data was gained from loosely structured in-depth interviews which were carried out according to a brief, but which were free ranging in the sense that relevant issues emerging could be probed in depth. Over 350 interviews were conducted covering a wide cross section of the population. The physical size of the Rural Study Area precluded complete coverage of the County. An attempt was made to include any 'complicated' areas and representative locations.

The remainder of the document discusses the results and conclusions of this fieldwork and is divided into two parts. The first section covers general themes and is concerned mainly with the changes occurring in rural West Yorkshire associated with urban expansion and the cultural trend towards living away from the urban area of employment. The report discusses these changes, and the lifestyles of the different types of villages with reference to particular areas.

The final section of the report looks in detail at the transport themes which affect life in rural areas. Topics discussed include public transport fares, the expectations of the public with regard to adequate services, and the image of public transport.

3B Transport deprivation and needs

3B1 ANON (1978) Methods for measuring rural transportation needs and demand. *Transportation Engineering*, **48**, May, pp. 39-46.

The objective of the Committee on Rural Transportation Needs is to survey the state-of-the-art literature on rural public transport needs and demand, and to synthesize currently available methods for needs estimation and demand forecasting. The scope of the study is focused on pre-implementation planning rather than post-implementation evaluation of a demonstration project. Distinction is made between the need versus potential demand for rural public transit services.

3B2 ASSOCIATION OF TRANSPORT CO-ORDINATING OFFICERS (1976) Findings of the standards of service working party, (Chairman N. Archibald) Association of Transport Co-ordinating Officers.

The terms of reference of the Working Party were 'To consider and recommend criteria for enabling bus service network comparisons to be made and standards by which quality of service can be judged, as a basis for comparing standards of service with levels of need with specific reference to measures of network, quality and usage'. The report concentrates on rural areas, and after a study of provision in a number of rural counties, the authors come out strongly against any attempt to impose nationally any minimum levels of service provision.

3B3 BAILEY, J.M. (1979) Public transport plans—4 Social transport based on 'need'. *Surveyor*, **154** (4554), pp. 14-16.

Four main groups of transport services are discussed, and the three links between them (client, supply, and legal) are considered collectively. A description is given of the ambulance service, vehicles operated, and statistics of emergency and non-emergency services. The organization and financing of the hospital car service is mentioned together with those of voluntary transport organizations. The social service transport provided by local authorities is discussed with brief reference being made to education transport and voluntary transport services concerned with socio/recreational activities. The scope of 'needs' assessment is defined and methods for its measurement are considered. The transport functions of the main operators, including passengers and goods, are tabulated, and the possibility of greater co-ordination of the services is discussed. Examples are given where this has successfully taken place.

3B4 BANISTER, D.J. (1980) Transport mobility in inter-urban areas: a case study approach in South Oxfordshire. *Regional Studies*, **14** (4), pp. 285–96.

Transport mobility is examined within the context of one particular interurban area which itself is typical of many 'rural' areas in England and Wales. Part of the analysis is concerned with an estimation of consumer preferences for mode and policy alternatives and the methodologies used are outlined. This type of case study approach is then linked to the demands of policy makers and a total-welfare approach is suggested for the provision of 'rural' services, including transport. Finally, certain priorities for further research are noted and conclusions are drawn about the usefulness of the case study approach.

3B5 BANISTER, D.J. (1982) The response of the Shire Counties to the question of transport needs. *Traffic Engineering and Control*, **23** (10), pp. 488–91.

This paper attempts to review the responses from the non-metropolitan counties to the changes in policy and the requirements to make an explicit statement on transport needs. The conclusion reached suggests that none of the three different groups of methods is adequate—minimum levels of service, demand measures, or local based measures—and that an operational tool for transport planning is still sought.

3B6 BANISTER, D.J. (1983) Transport needs in rural areas—A review and proposal. *Transport Reviews*, **3** (1), pp. 35–49.

Decision makers have been concerned with the decline of public transport in rural areas and ensuring that the needs of those without access to a car are met. This paper is divided into three main parts. The first reviews the responses from the 39 non-metropolitan counties in England to the statutory requirements of a statement on need and the extent to which they could be satisfied within the current transport planning framework. The second part examines the conceptual problems raised in the definitions and measurement of need, both from the responses of the counties and from an investigation of different theoretical perspectives on need. The final section argues that the concentration on the measurement of need may be misplaced, and that needs should only be considered at the conceptual level with the purpose of providing a perspective within which policy makers can consider the outcomes of particular decisions.

B7 BEBBINGTON, A.C. and DAVIES, B.P. (1980) Territorial needs indicators: a new approach. *Journal of Social Policy*, **9** (2), pp. 145–68 and **9** (4), pp. 433–62.

B8 BEETHAM, A. and ROBERTSON, D.M. (1978) Criteria for minimum levels of service for rural public transport. Paper presented at the PTRC Annual Summer Conference, Warwick, July.

This paper summarizes the main findings of the Peat, Marwick and Mitchell (1977) report on minimum levels of service [3B28].

B9 BENWELL, M. and WHITE, I. (1979) Car availability and transport need: an approach to the development of an appropriate indicator for transport planning. *Traffic Engineering and Control*, **20** (8/9), pp. 410–18.

This paper reports a preliminary piece of research on a method for measuring the extent of car availability and its relationship to travel behaviour in a rural area of Northamptonshire. The research developed a detailed personal descriptor of car availability. This was defined in terms of an individual's access to a car by time of day and number of days a week. These periods were, in turn, described in terms of whether access to particular activities was possible at that time. A check on the use of this set of indices, by relating them to behaviour, yielded results which appear intuitively reasonable. Further refinement of the method, and testing of its generalizability, may offer one way into the difficult problem of developing theoretically sound transport indicators from existing secondary data.

B10 BIRD, C.M. (1981) Analysis of six techniques to identify need for public transport. *Transport and Road Research Laboratory*, LR 1027.

This report describes the analysis of six index methods which have been developed to highlight areas of need for public transport services. The six methods were applied to three data sets, collected in Strathclyde, Gwent, and Hampshire and consisting of population information from communities, enumeration districts, and parishes respectively. The communities in each data set were then ranked by their scores from each method and the rankings analysed. These rankings of communities by different index methods were compared in a graphical way and also by calculating rank correlations. A sample of communities from the Strathclyde data set were also studied individually to see how they had been ranked by each index.

Analysis of results did not reveal consistent trends in most cases for all three data sets. It was also difficult to predict likely results from the information used and the forms of the techniques. The more complex the index, and the more apparently relevant the information included, the harder such predictions became. Many arbitrary effects were found arising from both the form of the various index methods and from population characteristics within the data sets themselves.

3B11 BUCHANAN, M. and LEWIS, K. (1980) Do we need 'needs'? *Surveyor*, 155 (4614), pp. 8–10.

Studies to determine transport 'needs' in forms of public transport could be largely irrelevant and an alternative approach to public transport is required. A new approach must be based on the provision of good accessibility to a wide range of activities, promote a more equitable distribution of incomes, minimize the contribution from public funds, improve incomes and working conditions of transport employees, promote road safety, improve the environment, conserve oil, and promote land use objectives. These broad aims have been incorporated into an appraisal method known as busmodel, designed to run on a low-cost microcomputer. Standard bus company management information and market analysis type origin/destination data are utilized in the model. 'Need' does not have to be defined because the policy maker decides what social cost/benefit ratio is required from a given public expenditure. Weights are given to the benefits to be given to different passenger groups such as the aged and schoolchildren. Busmodel is then used to derive the optimum combination of services, service levels, fares and subsidies for a given set of criteria.

3B12 CHAVIS, L.K. (1974) Needs and potentials for transit in rural areas. Virginia Inter-University Transportation Study Group, Washington.

Many rural areas, even those fairly close to large cities, suffer from lack of employment centres, health facilities, and the like. This dearth of local opportunities can be made up, in part, through better public transport services. The study summarizes the 'needs' and potentials for transit in several rural counties in the Richmond (Va.) region. The 'needs' are specified in terms of lack of employment centres, banks, hospitals, health services (including doctors and hospitals), libraries, recreation programmes, and, of course, existing transit services. Car ownership is also considered. It is concluded that several counties have a high potential for transit based on the above factors.

B13 COATES, V. and WEISS, E. (1975) Revitalization of small communities: transportation options. George Washington University, Final Report DOT-TST-76-80, December.

This is a final report of a two-year policy-oriented, interdisciplinary study of the long-range trends affecting small towns in non-metropolitan areas, the effects of transport availability and systems on their viability and vitality, and their needs and problems related to transport. The study concludes that the role and functions of rural small communities are changing as America becomes a 'post-industrial' society. The majority of small towns were found to be viable as a human habitat offering a quality of life desirable to many Americans, but vulnerable over the long term to structural changes in society and the economy which may result from rising energy costs or energy shortages. Lack of mobility (local transport alternatives) for those who lack access to an automobile was identified as the most severe transport problem for small towns at present. The study also concluded that rural areas need special consideration in formulating national energy policy, transport policy, and welfare policy.

B14 COLES, O. (1978) Transport and rural deprivation, in Walker, D. (ed) Rural Poverty—Poverty, Deprivation and Planning in Rural Areas. Child Poverty Action Group, Poverty Pamphlet 37, November, pp. 78–91.

Concentrates on three issues: the relationship between rural transport and rural deprivation; the conceptual framework used to model travel behaviour; the trends relevant to transport associated rural deprivation. Problems of accessibility for the rural poor reflect both the deterioration in public transport and the increasing concentration of other services and amenities. It is suggested that a more comprehensive approach to transport planning is essential.

3B15 CONNOR, J. (1980) Rural deprivation. *County Councils Gazette*, **73** (3), pp. 88–92.

Lincolnshire County Council is looking for ways of tackling the difficulties that are being created by change in the countryside. Four villages have been selected for the first application of the rural change project. Intensive local discussions were followed by the formation of local committees so that problems can be identified and responded to at an early stage. Public transport was one of the first to be tackled.

3B16 KILVINGTON, R.P. (1980) Meeting the transport needs of persons in rural areas: The British experience. Proceedings of the World Conference on Transport Research, London, April.

Although public transport planning in rural areas has become an important area of transport planning over the last decade, no acceptable resolution of the concept of social need has been derived. Political and financial stringency has played a major part, but the researcher has not produced the answers. The author argues that it is still worthwhile pursuing the target as 30 per cent of households will still be without any access to a private car. With the centralization of facilities and the demise of conventional public transport, the maintenance of an appropriate socially oriented network remains crucial.

3B17 KOUTSOPOULOS, K.C. (1980) Determining transportation needs. *Traffic Quarterly*, **34** (3), pp. 397–412.

The examination of the distribution according to need concepts is the subject of research reported here. Specifically, this article has three objectives: to examine the use of this concept in transport and to determine its shortcomings; to develop a framework that can be used in identifying transport needs; and to operationalize this concept by developing indices for determining the transport needs of various groups and in evaluating the transport services offered to them. Overall, this framework constitutes: a contribution to the relatively new behavioural school of transport research; a reaffirmation of the notion that travel patterns, contrary to traditional research in transport planning, are not independent of the activities that travel serves; a departure from existing ways of determining transport needs in that these needs are considered as traveller specific, resulting from the individual's inability to adjust their aspects of travel; an understanding that 'transport needs' is actually a set or groups of needs differentiated in terms of the various members of an individual's travel space and activity space; and a realization that this framework can be made into an invaluable transport planning tool.

18 KOUTSOPOULOS, K.C. (1980) Concept of transportation need revisited. *Transportation Research Record*, 761, pp. 66-9.

A new approach in considering the concept of transport need is suggested based on the notion that need can be determined by considering the inverse of one's ability to adjust, for a given trip purpose, to aspects of this trip in response to mobility constraints. By using this criterion, two indices of need (effectiveness and efficiency) can be constructed. The application of this approach to data on the handicapped in four areas (two urban and two rural) in Iowa indicates that the needs of the handicapped are equally met in all four areas; however, the rural systems are less efficient than the urban ones in meeting that challenge. These results are in contrast to the results of the traditional approach (existing demand met), which show great spatial discrepancies between urban and rural areas.

19 LAGO, A.M. and BURKHARDT, J.E. (1978) Rural transportation needs and demands: definition and measurement in the case of the rural elderly, in Ashford, N. and Bell, W. (eds) *Mobility for the Elderly and Handicapped*, Proceedings of the International Conference on Transport for the Elderly and Handicapped at Cambridge, April, pp. 269-79.

20 LEE, J., TAMAKLOE, E.K.A. and MULINAZZI, T. (1981) A public transportation needs study for the low density areas in a five-state region in the Midwest (Iowa, Kansas, Missouri, Nebraska and Oklahoma), Executive Summary. Kansas University, Urban Mass Transportation Administration, UMTA-KA-11-0001-81-1, April.

This report is concerned with the Public Transportation Planning Process for low density areas. The study area is the five-state Midwestern region of Iowa, Kansas, Missouri, Nebraska, and Oklahoma, referred to in the report as the target region or the Midwest. The main research objectives of the study are: to study the performance characteristics of transit systems in the target areas and compare these with the characteristics of corresponding systems in other regions of the United States; to develop a planning methodology for estimating the amount of travel for public transport and evaluating alternative transit systems for low density areas in general and for the target region in particular; and to utilize the views and input from local officials and transport agency personnel in deriving such a methodology for their use. This report outlines a systematic approach by which travel demand for rural public transport as well as the selection of appropriate public transport systems to meet rural travel patterns can best be determined. The major conclusions of this study are that there are two mutually exclusive groups of transit clientele; a group who 'needs' the service and another group who 'demands' the service. Therefore, the method of estimating actual travel by these groups should be considered separately, although they jointly constitute the overall estimated ridership and that a methodology which can incorporate the estimation of all the components of travel requirements for rural public transport within the framework of incremental analysis would be useful.

3B21 MADDOCKS, T. (1975) Mobility and accessibility problems in a small rural village. *Reading Geographer*, **4,** pp. 70-5.

This paper describes a survey of residents of a small village in Devon. Its aim was to examine residents' needs for access to particular services and their ability to reach them. The national context of declining bus services and increasing car ownership is outlined along with the scope of the survey, which collected data on car ownership, individuals' access to cars, and the availability of bus services. The problems of travel and limited choice of opportunities for non-car-owners are described in respect of each major trip purpose—work, shopping, social, recreational, and welfare. The author concludes that the level of access to welfare services is exceptionally poor for the area's residents. Survey results also indicated that bus users were willing to pay more for the service and that all residents were willing to provide higher subsidies for public transport. It is suggested that there will be a continuing need to provide for those with limited car access.

22 MILLIKIN, N.H. (1971) Assessing transit needs in small communities. *Transportation Research Record*, 638, pp. 47–8.

Mobility in rural and small urban areas is generally limited to one mode, the private car. Most government efforts to improve the mobility of rural area residents have resulted in upgrading the roadways, causing greater dependence on the car mode. But this type of assistance does very little for the poor, young, elderly, and handicapped. They cannot usually avail themselves of private transport. Many cannot afford to buy a car without depriving themselves and their families of more critical goods and services. Many others are stranded at home because someone else in the family is using the only automobile, usually to go to work.

The first objective was to develop a methodology that would be useful in determining the location and magnitude of public transport needs in rural and small urban areas. The methodology would be applied to:

1. Suggesting a uniform approach for determining transit needs, and
2. Recommending public transport legislation and implementation programmes to effectively use existing and future resources.

The second objective was to provide training opportunities for department employees to gain experience in public transport planning activities.

23 MILLIKIN, N.H. (1978) Public transportation needs of rural and small urban areas. California Department of Transportation, Division of Mass Transportation, Sacramento, California, Final Report UMTA-CA-09-8001-79-3, October.

The study describes the development of a model to predict potential patronage for transit in rural and small urban areas of less than 50,000. Patronage was developed through a home interview survey in which respondents were asked to rank relative satisfaction with their trip making ability. This information was then related to their socioeconomic characteristics and desire to make trips. This was done for ten representative sites in California. A procedure was then developed to match the representative sites to similar areas, which is known as a site pairing technique. One study objective was to develop a methodology useful for determining the location and magnitude of public transport needs in rural and small urban areas. The methodology could have application to suggesting a uniform approach to determining transit needs and to recommending public transport legislation and implementation programmes to effectively utilize existing and future resources. Another study objective was to provide training opportunities for the California Department of Transportation's (CALTRANS) employees to gain experience in public transport planning activities.

The study points out that in interpreting the results of the survey, one has to use caution, because the model estimates potential patronage, and not demand. Thus, the figures obtained are, at first glance, quite high. The study concludes that the site-pairing technique has potential to save considerable amount of effect when analysing many locations.

3B24 MIX, C.V.S. and DICKEY, J.W. (1974) Analysis of the need for a rural transportation system. Interim report, Virginia Inter-University Transportation Study Group, Washington.

The study defines and develops tools for analysing the 'need' for rural public transport. Using Madison County, Virginia, as an example case, the study first defines travel demand, latent demand, travel 'wants', and diverted travel. Five techniques are analysed for making demand and need forecasts (accessibility, gap analysis, attitude surveying, committee estimates, demonstration projects). It is concluded that full-scale O-D surveys and analyses are too expensive, and that a combination of committee estimates and demonstration projects may be the best forecasting method.

3B25 NUTLEY, S.D. (1978) Transport and accessibility in the North West Highlands and Islands—with an evaluation of methodology. Unpublished Ph.D. Thesis, Department of Geography, University of Aberdeen.

3B26 NUTLEY, S.D. (1980) The concept of 'isolation'—A method of evaluation and a West Highland example. *Regional Studies*, **14** (2), pp. 111–24.

The term 'isolation' is widely used in everyday speech, and has considerable spatial implications, but has undergone very little conceptual discussion. Relevant 'isolating' factors are considered in general terms and in the specific context of the West Highlands. A methodology is borrowed from landscape evaluation and suitably adapted. The major problem is finding a realistic surrogate for 'isolation' to act as dependent variable. The analysis is repeated using 'objective' and 'subjective' dependent variables, the latter producing the more consistent results.

27 OCHOJNA, A.D. and BROWNLEE, A.T. (1977) Simple indices for diagnosing rural public transport problems. *Traffic Engineering and Control*, **18** (10), pp. 482–6.

The wide range of settlement types in the rural areas of the Strathclyde region has resulted in a variegated public transport network serviced by numerous modes—bus, train, ferry, postbus, and aeroplane—run by many undertakings and offering different levels of accessibility. Three simple indices were developed to assess public transport provision in rural areas and this paper compares the construction of the indices with their performance in practice. The first estimates the demand, the second the supply, and the third is the ratio of one over the other.

28 PEAT, MARWICK AND MITCHELL (1977) An initial report on minimum levels of service for rural public transport, prepared for the National Bus Company, April.

This report summarized responses from 38 counties to a questionnaire on rural public transport. The difficulty of measuring minimum levels of service is extensively discussed with the main conclusion being that greater discipline is required for the allocation of limited resources. The responses were varied but throughout the report it is emphasized that transport does not itself produce any material benefits to the users or the community. It only serves to facilitate access to other activities and facilities, and the assessment of need for transport must in turn relate to a statement of the objectives of the community to be fulfilled in part through public transport policy.

3B29 PEAT, MARWICK, MITCHELL AND COMPANY (1980) The assessment of needs for rural public transport. Blackfriars, London.

The report discusses the findings of a study, commissioned by Dyfed County Council, into the need for rural public transport. Much of the work of county councils on rural transport has been directed towards short-term gains to be made by bus network rationalization to avoid major reductions in level of service. A review of rural transport needs was made necessary by the intention of central government to support rural bus services by subsidies but only where social needs have been demonstrated. The first phase of the study was concerned with a series of discussions held with groups of residents, including elderly persons and those without daily access to private transport. The second phase was concerned with confirming these transport needs by consultation with local community representatives. Conclusions provide a detailed definition of public transport needs of rural areas according to population groups. It is suggested that county councils should deploy available resources to meet as many as possible of the defined primary and secondary transport needs as a matter of policy.

3B30 PRITCHARD, B. (1974) A study of travel patterns and needs in a village which has no public transport or shops. Unpublished MSc Thesis, Centre for Transport Studies, Cranfield.

This thesis studies the problems of rural transport in the village of Newton Blossomville, Buckinghamshire. The first chapter introduces the problems of rural transport, reviews previous work, and locates a new area of study. This is the study of a village which has no shopping facilities and is not served by public transport. There follows a description of the village of Newton Blossomville, why it was chosen, where it is, and what are its present services and the survey which was undertaken in the village. It gives a demographic description of the village and its inhabitants and describes the current travel patterns of the villagers from information received in the survey. Next the concept of need is introduced in order to measure trips which are unmade by villagers at present. It discusses a number of possible methods for the measurement of need, selects one and applies it in Newton Blossomville to establish a pattern of latent demand for public transport. The powers and duties of county and district councils are outlined and how Buckingham County Council uses and fulfils them. It then reviews some of the possible transport and non-transport solutions to the problems of rural transport and finally the application of these solutions to Newtown Blossomville is assessed.

31 RAWSON, J. (1981) Needs—a notion much misused. *Surveyor*, **156** (4652), pp. 8–10.

The author suggests that social research techniques provide the only method of finding out how the present public transport system is used and how it is viewed. The investigation and monitoring of needs should be explained in any government guideline on methodology. Several aspects of need and the provision of public transport are discussed. It is suggested that the meaning and interpretation of need often results in unsatisfactory definitions. Need-based methodology is founded on three considerations: the public service tradition in British transport; the ample evidence of current need for public transport services; and these needs will increase if future public policies fail to respond to them. Since needs are relative they should be defined with reference to standards or thresholds as to what is an acceptable level of service. Who are in need, and what standards or thresholds of acceptability should be adopted, must be assessed from studies of the viewpoints of local residents, especially the elderly and disabled, public transport operators, teenagers, housewives, and working adults. It is hoped that the government will take a long-term view of needs, rather than an expedient one based only on financial restraint.

32 ROBERTSON, D.M. and WINFIELD, R. (1980) Just what are the needs of rural areas? *Surveyor*, **155** (4593), pp. 23–4.

This paper describes the approach to the measurement of needs in Dyfed (Wales). Three types of evidence were used—from the views of local residents, from existing travel patterns of rural residents, and from the priorities of local representatives. The assessment is limited both by data and by interpretation of the concepts of needs, but primary and secondary needs are described.

33 RÜHL, A., BAANDERS, A. and GARDEN, J.M. (1982) Assessment of society's transport needs mobility of persons. A report to the 9th Symposium on Theory and Practice in Transport Economics, Madrid.

This paper presents some first impressions on the methods that could
be used to establish transport needs of society, building up from the
individual level. Discussion also revolves around the ways in which
these needs can be met, given that they can be identified in the first
place. Inequalities exist in society from unequal satisfaction of transport needs and means are required for their assessment. It seems
likely that those without access to cars will be unable to obtain a
reasonable degree of satisfaction of their transport needs. Methods
for analysis are not available at present and this paper tries to accept
the importance of the needs issues and suggest priorities for future
research.

3B34 STANLEY, P.A. and FARRINGTON, J.H. (1981) The need for rural
public transport: a constraints-based case study. *Tijdschrift voor Economische en Sociale Geografie,* **72** (2), pp. 62–80.

The legislative rationale for subsidy payment to rural bus services
and the actual allocation are examined. An alternative approach is
developed based on the analysis of three sets of constraints affecting
accessibility, namely the socio-economic characteristics of the population, the location and type of facilities, and the public transport
system. Application is tested in Skye and Lochalsh District in Scotland.

3B35 STAPLETON, B. and RICHARDS, P.J. (1982) Transportation, mobility
and satisfaction of basic needs, in Richards, P.J. and Leonor, M.D.
(eds) *Target Setting for Basic Needs.* Geneva: International Labour
Organisation, pp. 105–30.

This paper focuses on the problem of establishing degrees of need
for transport and mobility among the poor in rural areas. The main
points covered are the definition and quantification of the need for
access to service points and of basic rural transport, the effects of the
road programmes on the local economy, and the problems of planning, site selection, and upgrading. Case material from Bangladesh
is used.

3B36 STONE, K.H. (1972) The concept of isolation. *Geoforum,* 11, pp.
74–7.

Though isolation is a commonly used term, does it have a universal
meaning so it is understood easily? There are many different kinds

of isolation, each with important characteristics. Each type varies from place to place, person to person, and from time to time. Do we not need to recognize these differences and speak in terms of kinds and degrees of isolation rather than simple remoteness or non-remoteness? This paper discusses all these issues in a conceptual review.

7 WARBURTON, S. and TROWER-FOYAN, M. (1981) Rural public transport need, demand and provision: an overview. Transport Operations Research Group, University of Newcastle upon Tyne, Research Report 43.

The development of rural public transport in Britain is described and the elements which make up the rural transport 'problem' are discussed. The legislative background to local authorities' involvement with the definition of transport 'needs' is reviewed and an appendix briefly summarizes the approach adopted by each English and Welsh Shire County.

The relevance and definition of needs are considered, and some of the main studies of the subject are described. It is concluded that a needs-based approach to the provision of public transport and the allocation of transport subsidies in rural areas is not inconsistent with an economic evaluation framework. Such an approach offers advantages over an approach based on analysis of current demand.

38 WICKSTROM, G.C. (1971) Defining balanced transportation—a question of opportunity. *Traffic Quarterly*, **25** (3), pp. 337-49.

It is argued that the failure to improve public transport services has arisen from the lack of objectives and goals. Standards are required for new systems and integration of existing travel modes must be considered in the planning process.

39 WINFIELD, R.C., DODD, A. and ROBERTSON, D.M. (1980) Dyfed establishes its transport needs. *Transport*, **1** (5), pp. 17-19.

The article describes a study carried out by Dyfed CC to establish the transport needs of rural areas. The need for public transport can be evaluated in terms of what is required to avoid hardship to individuals and to maintain the well-being of a rural population. The definition of transport needs developed by Peat, Marwick,

Mitchell & Co. is based on population groups needing access to facilities or centres of activity. Transport needs can be judged by evidence of travel patterns and transport problems. Three main types of evidence were used to define public transport needs of rural areas: evidence of local residents; travel patterns of a rural population; and evidence on views and priorities of local council representatives. It was concluded that transport needs should be defined as primary and secondary classes of need which are detailed. The approach to the definition of rural transport needs is capable of wider application and adaptation to similar areas.

3C Social groups

3C1 AGE CONCERN (1973) Age Concern on Transport. National Old People's Welfare Council, London.

This reports the findings of a survey of a large number of local authorities. The survey was designed to find out how old people are restricted by inadequate travel facilities. There is a marked difference between urban and rural problems; the former involve fares, limitations on the use of concessions, vehicle design, service reliability, and driving standards. Problems in rural areas concern the level of service, the lack of concessionary fare arrangements, fare levels, and limitations on the ability to shop and attend health centres or doctors as a result of poor services. Discussions were held with interested parties in order to formulate policy. Various extensions of the concession are suggested including financing the scheme from central government. Improvements on step heights are imminent and suggestions for special seating at the front of buses have been made. General difficulties of entering and leaving the bus are discussed along with the lack of conductor assistance implicit in one-man operation. The principal improvement in rural areas involves coordination of all types of local services.

3C2 ALLARD, M.A. (1979) Rural transportation for human services: a guide for local agencies. Human Services Research Institute, National Institute of Mental Health, June.

The development of rural transport programmes to facilitate access to needed human services is frequently mentioned in the literature but there is no one document that specifically addresses the transport needs of mental health agencies and/or other persons and entities concerned with the delivery of rural mental health services. This monograph attempts to synthesize some of the current literature on rural transport and human services with a focus on the way in which such information can be of use to mental health systems in rural areas. Included are: an overview of the characteristics of rural populations; a summary of certain key Federal programmes; a discussion of several approaches to delivering rural transport services; a presentation of some of the resource and planning issues; and additional resource material.

3 BAILEY, J.M. (1979) Voluntary and social services transport in Birmingham, Redditch and Bromsgrove. *Transport and Road Research Laboratory*, SR 467.

This report is concerned with the use of small vehicles for providing communal transport as a form of welfare. A postal survey, supplemented by personal interviews, was carried out in Birmingham to identify the pattern of transport provided by voluntary organizations. Data were collected on vehicle-type, cost and finance, drivers, users, trip purposes, and the development of the service. It appeared that most services were associated with some social or recreational service provided for particular clients, although the characteristics of clients varied considerably between different voluntary organizations. Journeys to suit personal requirements were less common, and there was little diversion from public transport. Levels of vehicle utilization varied considerably, and the potential for improving the provision of such transport by better co-ordination between organizations is discussed. The operation of Social Services Department transport in two areas was also studied. This is a sector of transport provision which has grown in a relatively unplanned way in recent years, as a function ancillary to domiciliary and day-care provision. A number of problems for both types of transport supplier are identified in the context of fleet management, organization, and finance.

4 BAILEY, J.M. (1979) Social transport based on need. *Surveyor* **154** (4553), pp. 33-6.

Declining patronage and increasing costs have made conventional public transport services non-viable in many areas. Four groups of service are discussed—local authority social services transport; education transport; the ambulance service and voluntary transport services. Each type of service is related to the context of the client group often disadvantaged in some way, the supply link as to who organizes and pays for the service and any legal constraints which are in operation.

3C5 BRIGGS, R. and McKELVEY, D. (1975) Rural public transportation and the disadvantaged. *Antipode*, **7** (3), pp. 31–6.

Various planning responses to the transport problems of the disadvantaged (the poor, the young, the elderly and the disabled) are criticized for being too few, too small in conception and application, badly coordinated and for being urban biased. More appropriate solutions, it is argued, though linked primarily to the traditional concept of transporting people rather than goods and services, should incorporate more direct subsidizing of people rather than the transport system, and place emphasis on flexible, energy-efficient automobile transport supported by appropriate public transit systems.

3C6 BRIGGS, R. and VENHUIZEN, D. (1976) Characteristics and costs of pupil transportation. *Traffic Quarterly*, **30,** pp. 303–23.

This article presents a study of school bus systems in Texas. The data are used to develop a model for predicting actual pupil transport costs by school district. The model is compared with other models for predicting the costs of urban transit. Data on the costs of rural and urban pupil transport are used to give some indication of how costs of urban and rural public transport might compare; because of the scarcity of public transport in rural areas of the USA little is known about their operating costs.

3C7 BURKHARDT, J.E. (1972) A study of the transportation problems of the rural poor. Bethesda, Maryland, Resource Management Corporation Report, UR-171, 2 vols.

3C8 CRAIN, J.L. (1976) Role of paratransit in serving the needs of special groups. *Transport Research Board*, SR 164, pp. 183–92.

This paper discusses each of the four transit-dependent groups identified as in need of particular service provision—the elderly, the handicapped, the young, and the poor. The focus is on the contri-

bution that a wide range of unconventional modes of transport can
have on their low mobility levels.

CROSS, K.W. and TURNER, R.D. (1974) Factors affecting the visiting
pattern of geriatric patients in a rural area. *British Journal of Preventive Social Medicine*, **28,** pp. 133-9.

For a period of one week, all visitors to Shropshire patients in geriatric units were interviewed about the method, duration, and starting point of their journey to hospital. These data, together with
those of the patients, were used to examine the extent to which the
duration of hospital stay, and the 'crow-fly' distances of patients'
and visitors' homes from the hospitals, affected visiting rates. The
pronounced effect of the first factor underlines the need to consider
separately those patients requiring assessment and rehabilitation
from those requiring mainly custodial care when the siting of hospitals for geriatric patients is being planned. The visiting pattern for
the former type of patient was not materially affected by the distance
of the patient's home from hospital (within a range of 0-32 kilometres), whereas visiting rates for long-stay patients decreased rapidly as distance increased beyond 16 kilometres.

DALLMEYER, K.E. and SURTI, V.H. (1976) Transportation mobility
analysis of the handicapped. *Transportation Research Record*, 578, pp.
40-5.

Handicapped people are one of the neglected minorities of transport
planning. For decades, their needs in transport have been neglected
in favour of the needs of the overwhelming majority. This has meant
that, in a society in which mobility is a prerequisite of living, the
handicapped are forced to travel very little and either depend on
their friends and family for transport or pay the high cost of special
transport. Handicapped people make up about 11 per cent of the
population. They are, though, divided by numerous disabilities each
of which has its own special limitations. This paper studies the mobility of the handicapped in terms of broad functional classification.
In terms of individual personal mobility, a 6-step classification from
needing a person's help in moving to no limitations is analysed. The
analysis also includes means of travel, number of trips made, cost of
travel, opinions on the adequacy of current conditions, and possible
improvements. Handicapped people, especially those with severe

handicaps, made fewer trips, depended more on family and friends to drive them, used more expensive travel modes, and were willing to pay more for any new transport than the average citizen. Furthermore, it was found that improvement in transport will have to be of at least three types: improvements for the ambulatory, improvements for those in wheelchairs who can travel two or more blocks (negotiate curbs), and improvement for those in wheelchairs who cannot travel two or more blocks. Improvements would range from relatively minor bus modifications, such as lower stairs, to new, special door-to-door services.

3C11 DEMETSKY, M.J., HARGROVES, B.T. and SZE MING CHAN, M. (1981) Evaluation of pupil transportation routing procedure. *Transportation Research Record*, 797, pp. 73-6.

The process of choosing a method for reviewing and designing the route structure of pupil transport systems for rural and suburban areas was investigated. The available techniques for school bus routing were reviewed and divided into three general categories: manual procedures, computer-assisted manual design methods, and computerized design programs. An evaluation framework is presented for application by school districts in selecting the most appropriate school bus routing procedure to use in their areas. The application of the evaluation model in a selected school district is described, and the study results indicate that the computer-assisted methods are best suited for the majority of school districts, except for only the very large and very small areas. Future work should be directed to improving on these interactive computer-assisted methods.

3C12 ECKMANN, A. (1978) Identifying and serving the elderly and handicapped in rural areas. *Transportation Research Record*, 696, pp. 87-8.

Transport of the elderly and handicapped is supplementary to the main objectives of urban transit but fundamental to rural public transit. Conventional mass transit for journey-to-work travel is not feasible in rural areas because places of employment are widely dispersed and residences of workers are even more widely scattered. Experience shows that the rural transport-disadvantaged commonly use carpools and other shared-ride concepts for journey-to-work between several residences and individual places of employment. Job-centred van pools for employees of a single industrial plant or business enterprise are a good possibility for rural public transport. School-bus-sized operations with fixed-route service from each passenger's home to a single place of employment might work if enough employees could be persuaded to ride. These are even more useful models for effective transport of the elderly and handicapped in rural areas.

It is noted that more data is available on car ownership by elderly persons than on the needs of handicapped persons. The relative transport disadvantage of elderly households is compounded by the high incidence of such households in rural areas. Local social service and welfare agency data can provide details of handicapped persons without access to automobiles. Data on hospitals, clinics, and senior citizens offer information on the physical, economic, and other characteristics of their clients. In addition to addresses and other information from these organizations, supplementary data can be obtained from direct surveys. Information obtained from stage highway and transport departments could be used in conjunction with the other sources to identify the primary target groups. Rural inhabitants who are neither elderly nor handicapped and who would desire public transport may also be identified.

13 FALCOCCHIO, J.C. and CANTILLI, E.J. (1974) *Transportation and the Disadvantaged*, Farnborough: Lexington.

This book is about the transport problems faced by the disadvantaged: the poor, the young, the aged, and the handicapped. These groups are transport–disadvantaged primarily because they number amongst them the greatest incidence of autoless individuals. Their transport problems are identified and analysed within the context of a car-oriented society. The purpose of this book is to bring together the body of knowledge relative to the transport problems of the disadvantaged. The consequences of a lack of transport are examined relative to their effects on the groups affected. Transport improvements are evaluated in terms of measurable impacts on specific goals and planning objectives. For the poor, an analytical model has been developed which permits the evaluation of economic benefits and costs of transport improvements for an important component of this segment of the population. Current transport planning methodology and criteria are reviewed and recommendations for improving the transport planning process at the local level are provided. A central theme explored in the book is the ability to improve employment opportunities through transport planning, so long as a degree of public subsidy is accepted. The authors stress the need to consider the circumstances of specific groups in mobility planning.

3C14 GB, DEPARTMENT OF TRANSPORT (1979) Concessionary fares for elderly, blind and disabled people, Cmnd 7475, London: HMSO.

3C15 GLOVER, JG. (1978) Concessionary fares on public transport in England and Wales. Paper presented at the International Conference on Transport for the Elderly and Handicapped, Loughborough University of Technology.

This paper examines the reasons for providing concessionary fares on public transport for the elderly, blind, and disabled, and the advantages and disadvantages of so doing. An objective is suggested. The relevant legislation is examined and this is followed by a description of its effects which have been sufficiently varied in different areas to arouse widespread dissatisfaction. A case study of concessionary fares in Surrey, details the methods and the problems involved in setting up a unified scheme. It is stressed that there are three parties whose requirements have to be met—the local authority, the bus operator, and the concessionaire. The scheme and its results are covered in depth. In conclusion the benefits of a concessionary fares scheme on public transport as a whole are emphasized.

3C16 GLOVER, J.G. (1979) Concessionary bus fares for the elderly. Paper presented to the Conference on Public Transport Planning, Loughborough University of Technology, September, pp. 177–83.

The cost of travel for the elderly is an emotive issue, and much dissatisfaction has been caused by the wide variations in benefits in different parts of the country. This paper traces the history of concessionary fares and the social objectives of providing them. The types of concession are discussed and the financial considerations explored. The transport objective is inextricably entwined with the social objective and a new approach (adopted in Surrey) is outlined whereby fares for the elderly become an integral part of the public transport plan (PTP).

7 HAUSER, E.W., ROOKS, E.H., JOHNSTON, S.A. and McGILLIVRAY, L. (1975) The use of existing facilities for transporting disadvantaged residents of rural areas. Research Triangle Institute, North Carolina, Division of Socio-Economic Studies, 2 Vols.

Volume one emphasizes solutions to the transport problems of the elderly, the handicapped, and the poor people in rural areas. More general treatment has been given to the problems of other transport-disadvantaged groups such as the young and persons in non-car and one-car families. Programmes were investigated that were determined to be sufficiently flexible to promote increased use of privately owned cars, taxis, vans, or buses by the rural disadvantaged groups. Volume two continues the survey of a variety of programmes for improving the mobility of the transport disadvantaged using only locally available resources—public or private vehicles. The vehicles range from small buses to 7–14 passenger vans to private cars. The programmes include volunteer drivers in their own cars, leased personal vehicles, subscription service, transport service by social service agencies, regular fixed-route/fixed-schedule service, and others. The report is a manual for laymen, based on the authors' suggested planning methodology as demonstrated in a south eastern rural area. Ten alternative transport programmes were examined for their potential utility. The Delphi technique translated non-quantifiable goals into quantified data.

8 JONES, T.S.M. (1977) Young children and their school journey: a survey in Oxfordshire. *Transport and Road Research Laboratory*, SR 342.

A survey of 4,209 junior school children at 18 schools in Oxfordshire provided information on the mode of travel for journeys to and from school. The schools surveyed served rural areas, small towns, and urban fringe estates. Explanations were sought in terms of distance travelled, household car ownership, and the age and sex of the respondent. More than two-thirds of the pupils walked to school and nearly one-fifth travelled by car. In the afternoon, car use dropped by one-half and walking increased correspondingly. One quarter of the pupils were accompanied to school by an adult in the morning but only one sixth were escorted home in the afternoon.

Distance had the most significant effect on modal split: four-fifths of the pupils who lived less than 0.8 km from school travelled on foot. Of those pupils living more than 1.6 km from school 94 per cent used the school bus or a car. In those households where there were no cars 3 per cent of children travelled to school by car whilst in those households which had at least two cars, one-third travelled by car. In addition very young children were more likely to travel by car than were the older ones. Other variables had only a limited effect on modal split.

3C19 LATHAM, G.R. and WESSELING, F.W. (1976) Research in special paratransit service for the handicapped. *Transportation Research Record*, 608, pp. 78–80.

This paper discusses the development of the Disabled Adult Transportation System in Edmonton, focusing on the user from two points of view: research and marketing. Three research techniques were used to determine and identify the user—incidence levels, civic census, and a registration system. Each technique is defined and described with a review of its advantages and disadvantages. The underlying philosophy of the marketing programme was to involve disabled persons. This was achieved by information meetings, public meetings, and an Advisory Council that included disabled persons. The Advisory Council has met on a regular basis throughout the development and operational stages of the system and is considered to be central to the system.

3C20 LOMBAERS, J. (1982) Adaptation of rural public transport with the standard bus to users of wheelchairs, Delft University of Technology, Monograph.

This research was carried out on the modification required in the design of a bus for public transport in rural areas for better accessibility to users of wheelchairs. It contains studies of wheelchair users' needs and the policies of bus companies before presenting a morphologic scheme and a package of research requirements. Proposals for adaptation of the existing public transport fleet are made, and ideas for such innovations as lift equipment are discussed, and the report ends with an evaluation of the alternatives (in Dutch).

3C21 MOSELEY, M.J. (1978) The mobility and accessibility problems of the rural elderly: some evidence from Norfolk and possible policies, in Garden, J. (ed) *Solving the Transport Problems of the Elderly: The Use of Resources*, Beth Johnson Foundation, Keele, pp. 51–62.

22 McKELVEY, D.J. and DUEKER, K.J. (1974) Transportation planning: the urban rural interface and transit needs of the rural elderly. Iowa University, Institute of Urban and Regional Research, Report 26.

The three objectives of the report are: to identify and assess rural transport problems, especially those affecting the elderly; to identify specific problems and actions taken during the planning and implementation phases of a seven county rural transport system in south eastern Iowa; and to suggest research questions that could be addressed to evolve more comprehensive and effective transport planning programmes. The following are observations emphasized by the authors: Planning needs should be as coordinated and comprehensive as possible at the regional (rural-urban) scale; Planning may not require extensive surveys to initiate a satisfactory system; Door-to-door service is required for most elderly; The process should involve users, transport operators, political leaders, and social agencies; Promotion of the system is critical and should emphasize identity with and use of the system through memberships, reasonable fares, and availability of all trip types for both elderly and nonelderly; Some level of continued funds from state, county, or federal sources should be assured prior to implementation; and Extensive monitoring and evaluation of demonstration systems need to be undertaken to facilitate planning of future systems.

23 NOTESS, C.B. (1978) Rural elderly transit markets. *Journal of the American Institute of Planners*, **44** (3), pp. 328-34.

In rural areas a significant proportion of elderly people are isolated from social service and recreation centres. Yet special transit vehicles serving the elderly carry only a small percentage of all elderly people. This article sheds light on this apparent discrepancy. An approach to disaggregating the transit demand is described, and is used to derive upper bounds for demand for a comparison of urban and rural travel data. Special emphasis is placed on how the attractiveness of social services affects travel demand. Interagency panels are proposed as a feasible means for including service attractiveness in demand predictions.

24 NOTESS, C.B. *et al.* (1975) Transportation of elderly to rural social services. Virginia Polytechnic Institute and State University, Virginia, College of Architecture.

In an effort to organize a systematic approach to the development of guidelines for public agencies estimating the need for, and use of, special transit systems, and to enable them to design cost-effective systems in terms of vehicle size and number, routing, scheduling, and general operating procedures, this report summarizes the current status of the rural transport problem for the elderly and discusses a methodology for designing and implementing a rural transport system. Detailed information from surveys in south western Virginia and other sources were used and a variety of travel variables were inter-related to develop an approximate image of travel activity of the rural elderly, showing effects of residential density, income and living situation on frequency, and mode of travel. The nature of social services and currently available travel services are detailed. Although less than 3 per cent of all elderly use special services, at least 10 per cent would prefer such services. Questions concerning the findings substantiate the need for a broad systems perspective. A broad formulation for studying the effects of attractiveness of transport services is proposed. Analysis of alternative operating configurations for typical rural transport systems revealed that significant operational cost savings could be realized by coordinating the provision of rides to a variety of social services. It was concluded that a systematic and comprehensive definition of rural transport problems is essential to the development of a successful rural transport programme; it cannot be assumed that simple rules and approximations to transport system design are applicable to all possible rural service delivery scenarios; and demand estimates may be generated through existing, but approximate methods. Data from existing systems must be monitored, collected, and utilized in planning future systems.

3C25 NUTLEY, S.D. (1980) Accessibility, mobility and transport-related welfare, the case of rural Wales. *Geoforum:* 11, pp. 335–52.

3C26 NUTLEY, S.D. (1983) *Transport Policy Appraisal and Personal Accessiblity in Rural Wales*, Norwich: Geo Books.

This book attempts to analyse accessibility from a consumer/welfare orientation using a time space geographical framework and procedure to articulate the problems of the individual. Details of the framework are used to evaluate the Rural Transport Experiments

(RUTEX) carried out in Dinefior [4C30]. Data are presented for accessibility before and after the implementation of the experiment for both car users and non-car users, for social groups and for individual districts. Improvements to the methodology include weighting of accessibility, recognition of multi-purpose trips, and the setting of standards for school and medical trips. The changes which have taken place in the study area are outlined as is a household survey of travel behaviour and accessibility, and the methodology is then applied to a further five case studies in rural Wales.

327 PATTEN, C.U. (1975) Age grouping and travel in rural areas. *Rural Sociology*, **40** (1), pp. 55–63.

Travel characteristics and transport needs of older rural residents remain limited. This study follows the progress of a trial minibus system and evaluates its impact. Travel purposes seem to correspond to those of a younger age and the nature of demand suggests small scale specific applications. But unless the system is relatively inexpensive, the general poverty of rural areas may preclude serving the needs of the rural older persons.

328 PATTON, C.V., LIENESCH, W.C. and ANDERSON, J.R. (1975) Busing the rural elderly. *Traffic Quarterly*, **29** (1), pp. 81–98.

The rural exodus, the growth of industrial society, and expansion of urban areas has left the countryside in US and many other countries in a critical position. The decline of the family farm and migration of youth has meant a generation problem for rural areas. This study reports on new ideas of rural infrastructure and in particular on a plan to provide cheap, efficient transport to remote rural areas in order to serve the needs of elderly farm families otherwise cut off from amenities.

329 POPPER, R.J., NOTESS, C.B. and ZAPATA, R.N. (1976) Demand for special transit systems to serve the rural elderly. *Transportation Research Record*, 618, pp. 1–6.

Regional planning agencies have become increasingly aware of the transport needs of the rural elderly. A promising solution to some of these problems has been the development of a rural special service transit system that gives elderly persons who lack means of transport access to crucial social services. A preliminary, important step in planning such systems is estimating demands; unfortunately little demand information is available to aid in making such decisions as selection of vehicles, routing, and scheduling. This paper examines the demand for transport services for the elderly and presents techniques for approximating travel demands. Methods based on attitudinal surveys, comparative trip rates, and participation frequencies illustrate that the best estimates currently possible are based on average travel behaviour. Further, such methods only approximate the many factors affecting demand. Data monitoring to formulate an economic demand model, which would account for the significant variations of behaviour, is suggested by this study as a relevant future research activity.

3C30   RIGBY, J.P. (1976) Journeys to school. *Proceedings of the Institution of Civil Engineers*, **60,** pp. 179–82.

A survey conducted by the Transport and Road Research Laboratory into the travel patterns of secondary school children in Berkshire is described. The travel modes considered were bike, car, bus and school coach, and making the journey on foot. It was concluded that the quality of the school journey was inadequate, and was caused in part by educational reorganization, leading to larger schools. The need for such large schools was questioned.

3C31   RIGBY, J.P. (1979) A review of research on school travel patterns and problems. *Transport and Road Research Laboratory*, SR 460.

Increasing concern over the cost and safety of school journeys, allied to an interest in how pupils use the transport system, has led to a number of studies of school travel, which are summarized in this report. Attention is restricted to journeys to primary and secondary schools. Considerable differences are found between journeys to the two types of school which reflect the age and capabilities of the pupil, and the size and location of the schools. Journeys to primary schools are usually short and about four-fifths are made on foot. Secondary school pupils travel longer distances and are more likely to use motorized transport. The main influences on travel mode are journey length, school type and location, and household car ownership. Although cycle ownership amongst young people is common, few cycles are used for the school journey. Reference is made to findings of research concerned with safety, congestion both at school entrances and more generally in the transport system, to methods of reducing the cost of school travel to local authorities, and to the potential for reducing the demand for motorized travel.

232 ROBSON, P. (1982) Patterns of activity and mobility among the eld- erly, in Warnes, A.M. (ed) *Geographical Perspectives on the Elderly*, London: Wiley, pp. 265–80.

Presents a description of the day-to-day activity that old people are engaged in and the travel that this involves. Reviews the concepts of mobility and accessibility in the context of activities but does not have a particular focus on rural areas. The argument revolves around the case for an interdisciplinary approach to the problem.

233 SAHAJ, L. (1979) Using taxis to serve the elderly and handicapped. *Transportation Research Record*, 696, pp. 85–7.

Three user-side subsidy demonstration projects funded by the Urban Mass Transportation Administration are described, along with an evaluation of six locally sponsored subsidized taxi programmes in the San Francisco Bay area. Although these programmes are not located in rural areas, the techniques and methods employed are applicable to the provision of services to the elderly and handi- capped living in rural and small-town communities. The study con- cluded, for example, that subsidized taxi service is especially well suited to low-volume, scattered demand as in smaller communities; that taxi operators are willing to participate in subsidized pro- grammes to transport the elderly and handicapped; and that user- subsidized taxi service is a workable, economically viable transport mode for the elderly and handicapped.

234 SKELTON, N. (1982) Transport policies and the elderly, in Warnes, A.M. (ed) *Geographical Perspectives on the Elderly*, London: Wiley, pp. 303–21.

An interesting case is presented on how particular transport policies have benefited the elderly. The section on the rural transport prob- lem and the elderly questions whether suitable policies can ever be created given the high costs involved and the nature of the bus.

Perhaps the impact of social services and voluntary transport schemes is likely to be more effective.

3C35 TICE, R.K. and FAIN, R.T. (1983) Volunteers in a rural specialised transportation program: the OATS' experience. *Specialized Transportation Planning and Practice*, **2** (3), pp. 225-35.

The Older Adults Transportation Service (OATS) is a multi-county specialized transport programme currently operating 145 vehicles and serving 88 largely rural counties in Missouri. Initiated in 1971 by a small group of volunteers, OATS had its origins in the consumer cooperative movement, and has never abandoned either its cooperative roots or its strong reliance on volunteers. OATS serves a broad constituency and continues to rely heavily on its 1000 locally based volunteers who assist the paid staff in both policy level decisions and operational features of the system.

3C36 WACHS, M. and BLANCHARD, R.D. (1976) Life-styles and transportation needs of the elderly in the future. *Transportation Research Record*, 618, pp. 19-24.

Several common views of the transport requirements of elderly Americans are reviewed, and conclusions are reached regarding the older population of the next two decades. While the elderly of today are relatively dependent on public transport, live at higher densities, have lower incomes, and travel relatively little compared with other groups, there are indications that the elderly of the future may not be similar. Planners wrongly assume that a decline in mobility occurs with ageing because of the ageing process itself. Rather, people bring certain long-established life-styles into their old age. The mobility patterns of today's elderly reflect life-styles that were developed decades ago, when mobility was limited for all citizens, regardless of age. By contrast, the elderly of the next 20 years will include many suburbanites, many drivers, and many who travel a great deal. Planning and forecasting methods for the future transport needs of the elderly should not be based on the transport patterns and needs of those who are currently elderly, but should focus more on those who are now in their thirties and forties and will become the elderly of the future.

3C37 WALTON, C.M. (1971) A strategy for increased mobility of specific rural socio-economic groups: a rationale for transportation decision making for small communities. Unpublished Ph.D. Thesis, Department of Civil Engineering, North Carolina State University, Raleigh.

3D Activities and telecommunications

)1 ANON (1977) Telekommunikationer, Transporter, Energi, Transportforskiningsdelegationen, Monograph 1977:6 (in Swedish). (Telecommunications, transport, energy)

This report deals with the state of present documentary evidence concerning the potential impact on the transport sector and its energy consumption of telecommunications and similar technologies. The main focus has been an analysis of the interchangeability of physical transport and various types of telecommunications. The report also includes documentation of the indirect effect of telecommunications on transport needs, as well as studies of the significance of teletechnology for the future efficiency of transport production.

)2 BUTCHER, H., COLE, I. and GLEN, A. (1976) Information and action services for rural areas: a case study in West Cumbria. University of York, Department of Social Administration and Social Work, Papers in Community Studies 4.

This report can be viewed as a case study and it forms a critical examination of how the problems of reaching some small communities in West Cumbria with information and advocacy services was approached by using a mobile 'information and action' van. Successive sections deal with the mobile unit, take-up of the van's services, service delivery and operation of the van, the social context and conclusions.

)3 CHRISTIE, B. and ELTON, M. (1979) Research on the differences between telecommunications and face-to-face communication in business and government, in GB, Departments of the Environment and Transport, Impacts of Telecommunications on Planning and Transport, Research Report 24, London: HMSO, pp. 55–84.

Many business functions can take place effectively without any face to face contact and video conferencing may also fill the gap where visual impact is important. The implications on location of companies and the scale of interactions are also highlighted.

3D4 CLARK, D. (1979) The spatial impact of telecommunications, in GB. Departments of the Environment and Transport, Impacts of Tele- communications on Planning and Transport, Research Report 24, London: HMSO, pp. 85-128.

In rural areas, telecommunications have facilitated the centraliza- tion of service functions in towns, thereby creating difficulties of access. Some of these problems could be overcome through access to the telephone and if service provision was more oriented toward telecommunications. This might be achieved through rural infor- mation centres and by combining transport and communication through an integrated policy to upgrade rural communications.

3D5 CLARK, D. (1981) Telecommunications and rural accessibility: perspectives on the 1980's, in Banister, D.J. and Hall, P.G. (eds) *Transport and Public Policy Planning*, London: Mansell, pp. 135-47.

The case is argued that with the development of new telecommun- ications systems many of the exchanges in rural areas could take place by non-physical means. By overcoming distance and time barriers to interaction, telecommunications could offset or compen- sate for difficulties of physical movement in rural areas. What is required is a rural accessibility policy that embraces both physical and non-physical movement, with telecommunications being given equal weight to the car, the bus, and the train.

3D6 CLARK, D. and UNWIN, K.I. (1977) Information needs and infor- mation provision in rural areas: a pilot survey. Lanchester Polytech- nic, Department of Geography and Department of Urban and Re- gional Planning, January.

This paper reports the results of a pilot survey of information needs and information provision in rural areas, undertaken for the De- partment of the Environment as part of an exploratory programme examining the socio-economic impacts of telecommunications. The study area is in East Lindsey, Lincolnshire. The overall objective of the rural communication project is to assess the extent to which new telecommunications technologies could improve community infor- mation provision in rural areas, and hence to assess the need for rural planning policies to encompass and consider such develop- ments. The more limited objective of the pilot study, which is reported in this paper, is to prove and evaluate a methodology for evaluating information needs and assessing its potential for meeting the overall objective in a larger, but similar, exercise.

07 CLARK, D. and UNWIN, K. (1979) Community information in rural areas: an evaluation of alternative systems of delivery, in Shaw, J.M. (ed) *Rural Deprivation and Planning*, Norwich: Geo Abstracts, pp. 147–65.

08 CLARK, D. and UNWIN, K. (1980) *Information Services in Rural Areas: Prospects for Telecommunications Access*, Norwich: Geo Books.

09 CLARK, D. and UNWIN, K. (1981) Telecommunications and travel: potential impact in rural areas. *Regional Studies*, **15** (1), pp. 47–56.

This paper examines the implications of telecommunications for non-work travel in rural areas. Contact diary data are used to identify the individual components of daily travel, and the possible effects upon these of developments in telecommunications are discussed. Some substitution of journeys to information and advice agencies is possible, but the increased penetration and use of the telephone is likely to raise the level of visiting for social purposes. An overall increase in the demand for rural travel seems likely. The implications of any stimulus effect for rural transport provision and policy are considered.

10 COWAN, P.D. (1973) Moving information instead of mass: transportation versus communication, in Gerbner, G., Gross, L.P. and Melody, W.H. (eds) *Communications, Technology and Social Policy*, New York: Wiley, pp. 339–52.

Concludes that transport and communications are mutually reinforcing.

11 DHILLON, H.S., DOERMANN, A.C. and WALCOFF, P. (1978) Telemedicine and rural primary health care: an analysis of the impact of telecommunications technology. *Socio-Economic Planning Sciences*, **12** (1), pp. 37–48.

12 EDWARDS, M. (1979) Service provision via local communication centres, in GB Departments of the Environment and Transport,

Impacts of Telecommunications on Planning and Transport, Research Report 24, London: HMSO, pp. 245-66.

Nine service areas are considered in terms of their present and prospective uses of local communication centres. They do not depend on large investment programmes but before any firm conclusions can be drawn, further work is required on shared facilities, implementation and monitoring of schemes, and the design of the facilities.

3D13 EDWARDS, S.L. and DENNIS, S.J. (1976) Long distance day tripping in Great Britain. *Journal of Transport Economics and Policy*, **10** (3), pp. 237-56.

The purpose of this paper is mainly to examine long-distance recreational trips, ie those of more than 25 miles each way. Reference is also made to shorter distance trips where this is relevant or unavoidable. Existing sources of data on day tripping are investigated and the information they give extracted. This is then used first to build up the national pattern of long-distance day tripping; average journey length, mode of transport, number of trips made per annum, etc, and the influence of such variables as car ownership, income and age on the propensity to make a day trip. Second, though it is not possible to examine recreational flows for the whole country, it is possible to do so for the South West Region of England. Models are constructed for various destination areas in that region, from which assessments are made of the effect on day tripping of, on the one hand, road improvements affecting the Region and, on the other, increases in the price of petrol in recent years.

3D14 EUROPEAN CONFERENCE OF MINISTERS OF TRANSPORT (1983) Transport and telecommunications. Economic Research Centre, Round Table 59.

The use of telecommunications in transport systems has led in recent years to considerable advances in system operation, ie their regulation, control, and management. This has clearly marked the place of telecommunications both as a technology for the organization and management of transport and also, the complementarity, especially on the technological side, between transport and telecommunications. Two new fields for application stand out on the operations side: paratransit and freight transport. The notion that telecommunications could substitute completely for transport has to be ruled out, as a static notion, blind to both the parallel growth of transport and telecommunications over recent years and to the structural changes affecting relationships between the two. The need to examine transport/telecommunications relationships within a dynamic perspective has naturally prompted analysts to forge the concept of relative substitution within the overall communications continuum. The potential really lies in changes in commuting patterns, some substitution for inter-city business travel and the use of electronic mail.

Finally, the nature and magnitude of changes in economic structures and in land use that might be induced by telecommunications has yet to be assessed. Telecommunications may act as an incentive to decentralization, but in reality the effects may be ambiguous. This may be the case in rural areas.

5 GB DEPARTMENTS OF THE ENVIRONMENT AND TRANSPORT (1979) Impacts of Telecommunications on Planning and Transport, Research Report 24, London: HMSO.

See Christie and Elton [3D3], Clark [3D4], Edward [3D12], Short [3D32] and Tyler [3D36].

6 HAYNES, R.M. and BENTHAM, C.G. (1979) Community Hospitals and Rural Accessibility, Farnborough: Saxon House.

A review is presented of accessibility problems associated with the rationalization of an important part of the health service. Surveys of hospital patients, visitors and staff in a large part of rural Norfolk reveal some of the hidden costs—human as well as financial—of the 'big is efficient' paradigm. Again, a more all-embracing process of decision making is recommended.

7 HOWIE, M.R. and HANNA, K. (1976) Effects of communication and transportation on utilization of agency services by rural poor people in South Carolina. Orangeburg, South Carolina State College Research Bulletin 5.

8 HUDSON, H.E. and PARKER, E.B. (1975) Telecommunications planning for rural development. IEEE Transactions on Communications, 23 (10), pp. 177–85.

The major premise of this paper is that telecommunication services can play important roles in rural development. The authors argue that the implementation of a telecommunication infrastructure should be a high priority for development planners. An analysis is presented of the application of telecommunications in rural economic development, sociopolitical organization, and the extension of basic social services. The authors cite examples of applications of two-way audio communication and conference-circuits for remote areas. The advantages of satellites for providing telecommunication services to rural settlements are presented, and communication policy options for developing regions are outlined.

3D19 KRAEMER, K.L. (1982) Telecommunications—transportation substitution and energy conservation. *Telecommunications Policy*, **6** (1), pp. 39–59.

The substitution of telecommunications for transport is held to have major potential for increasing energy conservation within the USA, other developed nations, and even developing nations. This article examines the substitution hypothesis based on research and experience of the past decade, and focuses on the theoretical potential of telecommunications/transport substitution for energy conservation and reviews recent research on public attitudes and on some substitution experiments in organizations.

3D20 MILLER, C.E. (1980) Telecommunications transportation substitution: some empirical findings. *Socio Economic Planning Sciences*, **14** (4), pp. 163–6.

The subsidized provision of telephones is discussed in the context of the substitution of transport by telecommunications. A study of substitution within the patterns of communication between geographically dispersed members of extended family groups is described. Data on the communication patterns of a sample of New Town families are presented. In this case, no evidence of a substitution effect is apparent: the policy implications of this result are discussed.

3D21 MITCHELL, C.G.B. and TOWN, S.W. (1979) Access to recreational activity. *Transport and Road Research Laboratory*, SR 468.

This report summarizes the findings of a research project which examined the relationship between transport availability and participation in sports and active informal recreation; it focused on local facilities. The report used data from the National Travel Survey and existing research to examine levels of participation in various activities and looked at the main influences on these levels. Factors found to be important, particularly for participation in sport, were age, sex, income, socio-economic group and the level of car ownership. The mode of transport used to reach a facility was found to vary with the size and location of the facility and the user's personal characteristics. In general cars were most commonly used to reach sports facilities, although in the case of children (the most frequent participants), non-motorized transport was more important; bus use was not great. Walking was more common for informal recreation. Distance travelled to reach a facility varied with the mode of transport used. Since some sections of the population have limited access to cars, it is suggested that a single measure of catchment based on car travel time or distance is unsatisfactory, and it would be more appropriate to define separate catchments for the users of different transport modes.

22 MOSELEY, M.J. and PACKMAN, J. (1982) Mobile services in rural areas, First Interim Report, University of East Anglia, Norwich, July.

This is the first of a series of discussion documents that are related to a research project. The research is designed to clarify the range and nature of mobile and delivery services in rural areas, to assess their ability to alleviate the social problems of such areas and to investigate the scope for increasing their potential. The report summarizes the services available in Britain from a review of secondary sources.

23 MOSELEY, M.J. and SPENCER, M.B. (1978) Access to shops: the situation in rural Norfolk. In Moseley, M.J. (ed) *Social Issues in Rural Norfolk*, Norwich: Centre of East Anglian Studies, pp. 33-44.

Considerable concern has been expressed in recent years about the social implications of the demise of the village shop. Related to this are policy questions concerning the possibility of bolstering up these shops or strengthening the key settlement policy. Transport issues are clearly influential, whether the demise of public transport accentuates the problems of rural residents and whether the growth in car ownership can alleviate all the access problems. This study examines residents in two rural areas in Norfolk to determine present and likely future levels of access to shops.

3D24 NATIONAL COUNCIL FOR VOLUNTARY ORGANISATIONS (1981) Alternative rural services: a community initiative manual, Bedford Square Press, London.

This manual has been compiled to advise and assist rural residents how to retain their services and, where they have been removed, how communities can help themselves. Each of nine basic services are considered separately; the causes for their decline being outlined, as well as suggestions as to how they could be sustained in different circumstances.

3D25 NATIONAL COUNCIL FOR VOLUNTARY ORGANISATIONS (1981) The future of telephone and telecommunication services in rural areas, Rural Briefing.

3D26 O'CINNEIDE, D. and BREEN, W.G. (1982) Transport and telecommunications: the Cork business community study. *Irish Journal of Environmental Science*, **2** (1), pp. 25-31.

Reductions in fuel resources and urban traffic congestion suggest future limitations on mobility. It is possible that new telecommunications technology will carry an increasing share of future communications. This paper examines the feasibility of rerouting business information flows to advanced telecommunications media.

3D27 OREGON DEPARTMENT OF TRANSPORTATION (1975) Telecommunications: the state of the art and planning implications. Oregon Department of Transportation, Planning Section, Salem, Oregon.

This overview of the science of telecommunications and some of its possible implications focuses on the possibility of using telecommunication as a substitute for travel. Various combinations of four subsystems (2-way audio, 2-way audio-visual facsimile transmission, and remote computer services) are currently used in diverse fields through the country. Although many operational systems are limited geographically, they are already substituting for travel. The development of telecommunication science has been directed toward the improvement of communications and the bringing of social services within reach of the disadvantaged. Studies indicate that about 24 per cent of all work trips and about 50 per cent of all shopping trips could be replaced by telecom methods. There is a real possibility that substitution of telecommunications for travel will lead to changes in urban form and to decentralization. A possible consequence of such decentralization is the decline of CBD office growth, and the concomitant impacts on mass-transit—especially rapid rail. The social and psychological implications are also considered. The acceptability of a mechanical form of communication and a possible 'information overkill' are discussed.

28 PLASSARD, F. (1982) The substitution between transportation and telecommunications, Paper presented at the PTRC Annual Summer Conference, Warwick, July.

The development of new technologies of communication and the continuation of the economic crisis provoked a whole discourse predicting that the solution for the problems of transport lies in those new technologies.

This belief in an absolute substitution between transport and telecommunication is based on a very tiny experiment. So, it seems more promising to abandon the approach using the concept of absolute substitution for another one using the concept of relative substitution.

To try to assess this substitutability between the communication practices, 120 households have been surveyed in Lyons. The results show that the content of phone exchanges is rather poor, and 75 per cent are only simple exchanges of family news. Nevertheless, it is possible to point out that the calls to the family or the friends lead to a journey only in 15 per cent of the cases, against 40 per cent for the calls linked to purchases or appointments.

29 RIGBY, J.P. (1978) Access to hospitals: a literature review. *Transport and Road Research Laboratory*, LR 853.

Literature has been examined from the fields of transport, town planning, and medical care, to determine the current pattern of hospital accessibility and the expected trends in hospital access and location. Staff and visitors comprise more than two-thirds of all those who travel to hospitals. Car and bus are the modes most often used for the hospital journey. The relative numbers of different users and the modal split vary according to the size and type of hospital and its catchment area.

Inhabitants of rural areas experience travel difficulties because of long distances to hospital and poor public transport. Large hospitals which serve large catchment populations are likely to aggravate such difficulties. Other access problems are long journey times and high costs, where users do not have a car available; this deters some people (particularly visitors) from travelling.

The future change in the hospital stock is likely to be limited: the potential for improvements in hospital access therefore lies in transport provision rather than in locational changes. Points suggested in the literature for further attention include the use of wider criteria for deciding hospital transport provision, improved coordination of existing public and hospital transport, and additional subsidy for certain travellers, when resources permit.

3D30 SCHNEIDER, J.B. and SYMONS, J.G. (1971) Regional health facility system planning: an access opportunity approach. *Regional Science Research Institute Discussion Paper Series*, 48.

Regional comprehensive health planning agencies (CHPA's) are charged with the responsibility of improving the delivery of health care in our large metropolitan areas. In this paper, a model is developed to assist these agencies in the performance of this task. The philosophy of the approach utilized is that CHP's should seek to encourage changes in the health care delivery system within a region that will increase the amount of access opportunity available to consumers in all parts of the region, improve the equity of the geographic distribution of access opportunity within the region, and reduce the number of populated areas in which the access opportunity to the medical care system is below an areawide minimum standard. The major concept on which the model is based is that of access opportunity. This term refers to the ease with which the health care services in the region can be reached and obtained by a resident of the region. Two applications of the model to physicians' offices and nursing homes are discussed, as are other potential applications of the model.

)31 SHANNON, G.W., SPURLOCK, C.W., GLADIN, S.T. and SKINER, J.L. (1975) A method for evaluating the geographic accessibility of health services. *Professional Geographer*, **27** (1), pp. 30-6.

Functional rather than physical measures of distance are more sensitive to the effort involved in travel for medical services. Travel time, for example, often varies by time of day and mode of transport. Geographic space has a substantial impact upon recognition of illness and utilization of health and hospital services. Measurement of geographic accessibility is also integral to the development of a more comprehensive index that incorporates socio-economic, attitudinal, and other functional measures of separation. The methodology demonstrated provides one procedure for the computation, graphic display, and statistical comparison of accessibility appropriate for both immediate use by health planners and research to provide a more comprehensive index of accessibility.

)32 SHORT, J. (1979) Residential telecommunication applications: a general review, in GB, Departments of the Environment and Transport, Impacts of Telecommunications on Planning and Transport, Research Report 24, London: HMSO, pp. 23-53.

A discussion is made of the social and economic impacts of advanced residential telecommunications services that are likely to come in use in the next thirty years. Remote education, remote shopping, and applications in the field of social services seem likely to have the most significant effects, particularly in rural areas where telephone ownership will be nearly universal.

)33 SPROUNCER, S.M. (1977) Accessibility to shopping opportunities in rural areas: the role of mobile shops, Cranfield Institute of Technology, MSc Thesis.

)34 TAYLOR, C. and EMERSON, D. (1981) Rural post office: retaining a vital service. Report by the National Council for Voluntary Organisations for the Development Commission.

)35 TAYLOR, D.H. (1975) An examination of mobile shop operation in rural areas, Unpublished MSc Thesis, Cranfield Institute of Technology, Centre for Transport Studies.

Activity relocation is an alternative to the provision of transport. Rural areas suffering from a lack of facilities relative to towns and cities have been regarded traditionally as in need of transport in order to improve access to urban activity centres. Rural transport is always expensive and not always convenient and it may be therefore that in some cases activity relocation, (that is, taking activities to people) is preferable to transporting people to activities. This thesis considers one activity, shopping, and one method of relocation, mobile shops. This work shows that the cost of mobile shop operation is not prohibitive but problems arise due to the fact that the type of service offered by a mobile shop is not particularly well suited to modern shopping demands. Furthermore, the profitability of operation in rural areas is restricted by insufficient time available for trading due to time-consuming travel between settlements. It is apparent however that if mobile shopping facilities were given some form of financial encouragement certain sections of the rural community would benefit.

3D36 TYLER, M. (1979) Implications for transport, in GB Departments of Environment and Transport, Impacts of Telecommunications on Planning and Transport, Research Report 24, London: HMSO, pp. 129-68.

The focus is on the impacts that are likely to occur in the next ten years. Included here would be reductions in the growth rates of business travel, the restructuring of work patterns with highly decentralized arrangements (working from home) and office dispersal to neighbourhood work centres.

3D37 WEEKLEY, I.G. (1977) Lateral interdependence as an aspect of rural service provision: a Northamptonshire case study. *East Midland Geographer*, **6** (8), pp. 361-74.

The impact of the private car on the countryside has been significant not only in encouraging the growth of population in accessible villages but also in modifying the spatial patterns of rural service provision. Services were once provided on a largely segregated basis, but now there is a distinct hierarchy with the dominance of neighbouring urban centres. This system may in turn be superseded by the lateral interdependence of rural communities so that the wide range of service needs can be met.

38 WELLS, M. and TOLLE, J.E. (1976) The significance of telecommunications as a partial substitute for transportation. Urban Mass Transportation Administration, Final Report UMTA-PA-11-0013-78-1.

The major objective of this research is to determine the feasibility of
using existing communications technology to prevent the need for
many of the Central Business District (CBD) inter-office business
trips made in the Pittsburgh, Pennsylvania area. The effect these
technologies may exercise on future urban form and travel patterns
is also examined, as various types of communication systems, their
use, cost-effectiveness, advantages/disadvantages, and short and
long-term forecasting as to present and future changes are discussed.
The work trip offers the greatest potential for relieving congestion
and associated costs, and since two out of five trips within the urban
area (world-wide) are home to work and work to home, the possibilities of reducing peak hour congestion, delays, accidents, and pollution are immense. There are indications that in the future offices
may provide suburban branches for the convenience of employees
who can work together effectively with picture phones and time-
sharing computers. However, although work trips may decrease, the
additional time and ability to travel may result in dramatic increases
in transport for pleasure. The report addresses the Contact Record
Surveys which were developed to present existing trip-making based
on a sample of Pittsburgh CBD centres. Results of the questionnaires
are analysed and implications for substitution are formulated. The
results of the survey tend to support the hypothesis of this thesis that
sophisticated telecommunications could substitute for many inter-
office business trips originating in Central Business Districts. The
results, based on limited data, underscore the need for further research in this area.

39 WELSH COUNCIL (1973) Hospital location and accessibility in Wales,
Welsh Council, Cardiff.

The purpose of this study is to examine problems of accessibility as
they affect hospitals in Wales, in the context of the development of
the idea of the district general hospital (DGH) and of the smaller
hospitals which complement its services. The concept of the DGH
in the 1962 hospital plan is outlined and the pattern of main hospitals in Wales described together with the important role that the
small hospitals play. Financial assistance is provided to some patients

travelling to hospitals and to some visitors. Two general hospitals are then analysed in detail from the perspective of accessibility to them, and these studies are complemented by analyses of a long-stay hospital for the mentally handicapped and two closely linked geriatric hospitals.

3D40 WHEELER, M. (1972) Hospitals, accessibility and public policy. *The Hospital and Health Services Review*, March, pp. 82–5.

In this article, the accessibility of a district general hospital in a low-density rural area of eastern England is considered. The findings of a survey of out-patient transport use are reported, and certain policy implications are discussed.

3D41 WILKS, D.F. (1981) The substitution of telecommunications for travel, Symposium on computer control of transport, Sydney, February, pp. 56–61.

3D42 WOOLLETT, S. (1981) Alternative Rural Services: a Community Initiatives Manual. NCVO, Bedford Square Press.

This manual provides the answers to questions about how rural communities can support, retain, or even provide services that are threatened with closure or have never existed. A wide range of rural services are included with garages and public transport featuring prominently—community buses, car sharing schemes, social car schemes, postbuses, school buses, and hired village buses. For each service, the manual explains how it is financed and organized, how it can be supported and improved by the community, and gives advice on alternative methods of organization where conventional forms of provision are impracticable. In addition, there are sections on how to obtain information and support, the potential of village halls and other premises, appropriate organizational structures and frameworks, the role of parish, district, and county councils, and the support available from rural community councils and women's institutes.

4 Transport modes

4A Conventional public transport—the bus

Up until the last twenty years public transport almost everywhere enjoyed increased patronage and was able to break even financially whilst still providing the benefits of cheap travel. Since that time the commercial role of public transport has conflicted with the need to provide an adequate service to those without access to a car. Governments and operators have become increasingly concerned by the problem of maintaining public transport's share of the travel market and by the necessity to provide ever increasing levels of public support for transport operations (Webster and Bly [4A78]). Most recently the concern has been over whether investment decisions and revenue support do in fact give value for money (Hibbs [2A34]). These problems are apparent in many countries, not just Britain (Oldfield *et al.* [4A56]), and extensive reviews and surveys have been carried out; for example in the United States (Burkhardt [4A7]), US Department of Transportation [2B46], [4A77]), Germany (Heinze [2C8]), and Sweden (Wiberg [4A82]).

The conventional bus runs to a fixed timetable on fixed routes and is suitable for carrying large numbers of people along well defined corridors of demand. Unfortunately, demand patterns in rural areas are dispersed and small in number; it has been recently suggested (Banister [3A2]) that the role of the conventional bus may be limited. Nevertheless many studies have examined the economics of bus operation in rural areas (e.g. Kidder [4A40], Nash [1B5]), the role of public transport (e.g. Larson [4A43], Martin and Warman [4A47]) and the users of public transport (e.g. Mitchell [4A51]). The conclusions reached are similar in that the operator has the dilemma of trying to maintain services on a reduced level of revenue support (Tyson [4A73], Williams [4A83]). The possibility of cross subsidization of services is limited with the financial performance of profitable urban services deteriorating and the present trend towards deregulation with each route being competed for on an individual basis.

Results.

There are several alternative strategies that could be adopted by the operator. The first is to raise fares so that any shortfall in revenue over cost can be reduced; in the last ten years fares have risen significantly in real terms. However, it now seems that elasticity of demand with respect to fares is increasing towards unity. The extra revenue gained from increasing fares is outweighed by the loss in

But

patronage (Bly [4A4], Collura *et al.* [4A13], Neely [4A55]). Reductions in service frequencies could result in cost savings with the withdrawal of peak service vehicles (Tyson [4A73]), but in rural areas with existing frequencies already at very low levels this alternative may result in no service. Route rationalization has usually been carried out in conjunction with the previous option. The Market Analysis Project (MAP) of the National Bus Company is one kind of selective service planning tool (Barrett and Buchanan [4A3], Brooks and Kilsby [4A6]). MAP looks at the entire network in and around a town or an area within a county with a particular view to the reduction in the peak vehicle requirement (Bursey *et al.* [4A11]). The outcome has been to match service provision more closely with expressed demand, with changes being introduced in routes and frequencies so that most of the demand could be met either by substituting one route for two or through rescheduling of services (Jelley [4A39]). Service withdrawal can lead to inconvenience and in some cases hardship, but this has only been found in extreme cases (Oxley [4A58]).

Other solutions

Improved coordination of bus services and interchanges with other modes so that duplication can be reduced are other ways in which cost savings can be made (Greenbie [4A27], Tebb [4A65], Thelan *et al.* [4A66]). Similarly, many rural people have a poor

difficult

image of the quality of the bus service and there may be some scope for improving the information available (Soot and Stenson [4A62]). Other research has suggested that rural bus services could be run more efficiently by small scale private operators as their unit costs tend to be lower (Gilmour [4A25], Jackson and Martin [4A37], Tunbridge and Jackson [4A71]). The arguments here are not clear as private operators are not committed to supply extensive stage carriage networks and are dependent upon schools or works contracts for their primary source of income (Fausch [4A21], Hutton [4A34], Jackson and Martin [4A37]).

4B Conventional public transport—rail

Rural railways in many Western countries have also been in decline over the last twenty years. Several studies have examined both the effects of Government policy—Nash [4B21] on European railways and Warren [4B31] on the American inter-city network—and the social consequences of closure (Hillman and Whalley [4B16]). Most discussion has concentrated on the financial and commercial issues such as levels of subsidy and fares (e.g. Sunden [4B29] on the Swedish railways), elasticities of demand (e.g. Oldfield and Tyler [4B22] on British railways), and the economic issues raised in investment appraisal—Sammon [4B24] on the American system and Starkie [4B27] on the British system.

Different policies have been pursued to ensure that an integrated public transport system is available in rural areas. Some argue (e.g. Barrett and MacBriar [4B2]) that replacement buses could provide a better service than infrequent rural trains and this view has recently been supported by the Serpell Committee on British railways' finances [1B3]. In many European countries the railways already run the rural bus services and timetables are fully integrated (e.g. Heinze [2C9] in Germany and Eckmann [2C5] in the Netherlands). The railways are naturally resistant to any extensive closure of rural railways and have been examining ways of reducing operating costs through cheaper rolling stock (e.g. the railbus) and unmanned railway stations. More radical proposals such as the conversion of railways into busways have also been extensively debated (Hall and Smith [4B13], Cooper and Spaven [4B6]). The future for the rural railway is indeed uncertain.

4C Unconventional public transport

Paratransit or unconventional transport modes are those forms of transport between the private car on the one extreme and conventional public transport on the other. The most comprehensive study has been carried out in the USA and centred on the urban field (Britton [4C19], Kirby et al. [4C50]), but other reviews have also been made (eg Abkowitz and Ott [4C1], Bovy and Krayenbuhl [4C17], Rimmer [4C74] and the US Department of Transportation [4C90]). In most cases the focus is on the urban situation, but the summary in table 4.1 concentrates on the rural situation where possible and gives examples of relevant work. The basic character-

Table 4·1 Unconventional Rural Transport—The State of the Art

Service	Research	Comments
Minibus	Greening and Jackson [4C39], Scottish RUTEX Working Group [4C77].	Cost savings over conventional bus limited as nearly 70 per cent of costs relate to wages.
Postbus and Dual Purpose Vehicles	Adams [4C2], Fleishman and Burns [4C35], Lugton]4C56], Scottish RUTEX Working Group [4C79], Turnock [4C88], Watts et al. [4C93].	Multiple purpose transport. One vehicle and driver to perform a number of apparently distinct functions.
Community Bus	Balcombe and Dredge [4C12], Banister [4C13], Devon RUTEX Working Group [4C26], Kropman and Peters [4C53], Gubbins [4C41], Smith [4C82], Vanoon [4C91].	Relies on volunteers, hence significant savings in costs.
Subscription Bus	Bautz [4C15], Kirby and Bhatt [4C49], LGORU [4C55], Ward [4C92].	Usually used for work journeys or access to stations, health care centres.
School Bus	Dinefwr RUTEX Working Group [4C30], Fausch [4A21], Hutton [4A34].	Attempts to make use of spare capacity or to use a bus for a greater part of the day.
Diverting Bus	Breur and Verdonck [4C18], North Yorkshire RUTEX Working Group [4C67].	Often no fixed schedule or route and destinations reached without transfer.
Dial-a-Bus	Aex [4C3], Balcombe [4C10], Dirkse [4C31], Hoey [4C45], Oxley [4C72].	Mainly been applied in the urban situation.
Jitney	Fouracre [6D16], Howe [6D23], Jacobs and Fouracre [6C24], Silcock [4C81].	Illegal in most Western countries but widespread in the developing world.
Taxi	Froysadal [4C36], Karash [4C46], Teal et al. [4C83].	Sometimes used for particular groups such as the handicapped.
Car Sharing and Pooling	Davis et al. [4C25], Devon RUTEX Working Group [4C27], US Department of Transportation [4C89], Wood [4C97].	Some doubts over whether formalized car sharing works better than informal schemes in rural areas.
Shared Car Hire	Balcombe [4C9], Devon RUTEX Working Group [4C28], [4C29], North Yorkshire RUTEX Working Group [4C68], [4C69], [4C70], Scottish	Has been used for hospital services.

Table 4·2 Temporal and Spatial Characteristics of Some Conventional and Unconventional Transport Modes in Rural Areas

Space	Time		
	Fixed		*Variable*
Fixed	Railway Postbus Conventional Bus		Jitney
		Route Deviation Rural Drop-me-off	
Variable	Community Bus Car Pool Subscription Bus School Bus	Time Deviation Dial-a-Bus	Private Car Rental Car Taxi Private Car Hire

istics of the unconventional modes in terms of temporal and spatial constraints are summarized in table 4.2.

In Britain, sixteen rural transport experiments (RUTEX) have been established in Devon, North Yorkshire, South Ayrshire, and Dinefwr (in Dyfed). The locations selected were all 'deep' rural areas where conventional services were never likely to be viable and the purpose of the experiments was to test a range of service innovations. The experiments included flexible route services, organized transport services by private car, hospital services, an emergency car service, postbus services, shared hired cars, and community bus and car services (Balcombe [4C10], [4C11] and table 4.1). None of these services operate without a subsidy, but at the lowest levels of demand, voluntary car services seem to provide the best value for money as there are no direct wage costs to pay. Where demand is higher, the postbus, the community bus, and the shared hire car services can provide a public transport service at roughly equivalent levels of subsidy. All experiments are now completed but ten services are still in operation with financial support from local authorities (Coe and Fairhead [4C21]).

One problem with paratransit is that of evaluation. Given a particular situation, which of the unconventional modes is most suitable? An experiment assesses one or two alternatives in a specific location and often only over a short period of time. As a result of the rural transport experiments, some appropriate evaluation procedures have been developed (Martin [4C58], [4C59], Tunbridge [4C85], and Tunbridge and Hale [4C86]).

The voluntary sector has become more involved in organizing and running community transport services. There are the small scale voluntary car schemes and the more organized bus schemes. In Britain about fifteen community bus schemes are operating in rural areas and some cover their total costs (Banister [4C13]). In the Netherlands, however, the community bus concept has been taken much further and the 'buurtbus' is operated in over fifty locations with frequent services that are fully integrated with the conventional public transport services (Vanoon [4C91]). Revenue-cost ratios are much lower than the British counterparts, but in both cases a crucial role is played by the volunteer; the long term success of these schemes depends on the continued interest and support of key individuals within the local community.

As compared with the institutionalized and closely regulated forms of conventional transport, these unconventional alternatives provide an increasingly important addition to the available options for rural transport operators. Indeed, where demand levels are low, they may provide the only option as their flexibility in routing and timings allows a better adaptation to the dispersed demand levels in rural areas. Experience in developing countries may be particularly useful, and some examples have been given in table 4.1 (e.g. Fouracre [6D16]), but here again most experience comes from the urban situation (ECMT [4C33]).

4D The private car

In many ways the car is ideally suited for a transport mode in rural areas. Its convenience and flexibility give significant advantages over public transport, and even on cost criteria the differences can be marginal where bus patronage levels are low. The important consideration becomes whether the best use is being made of the private car. It may take on an explicitly social function with the introduction of shared car ownership and the village car, or there may be considerable scope for car pooling or sharing schemes (Kurth [4D11], Watts [4D20]). Taxis are also suited for rural areas with the quality of flexibility (Gallagher [4D7], National Swedish Road and Traffic Research Institute [4D16] and Weiner [4D21]); some experiments in Germany (Heinze [2C8]) have suggested that taxis can be used almost as a 'paratransit' mode running along specific routes or operating in small areas with an explicit social function. Finally, there has been the growth of cycling in rural areas, particularly for young people and for recreational activities (Countryside Commission [4D1], GB, Department of Transport [4D9] and Katteler and Kropman [4D10]). The problem facing the rural planner is one of awareness of the alternative modes that could be used to alleviate inaccessibility in particular locations. A broad perspective must be adopted that considers both conventional and unconventional public transport as well as the private car and taxi before coming to a decision (Banister [3A2]). The package is likely to be mixed as each mode will be specific to part of the market and will complement each other. It is not a case of competition between modes in the classic sense as many rural residents do not have a choice.

4E Waterways and freight

There are two main transport uses to which the inland waterways can be put, namely recreation and freight. In Britain, recreational use is increasing (British Waterways Board [4E2], Harrison and Stabler [4E8]) but the commercial potential for freight is low due to the capacity constraints in existing waterways and the extensive use of coastal shipping (Baldwin [4E1]). The great river systems on continental Europe offer a much greater potential (ECMT [4E4], Korompai [4E9] and Noortman]4E11]).

Little research has been carried out on freight transport in rural areas as most problems have been perceived as urban based (Corcoran and Christie [4E3]). The principal issue has been that of lorry routes where certain sized vehicles are restricted in access to particular rural routes (GB, Department of Transport [4E5]). Although rural counties are required to prepare lorry route plans, the response has not been enthusiastic (Self and Hewitt [4E15]).

4A Conventional public transport—the bus

1 ARIO, O. and ETSCHBERGER, K. (1977) Verkehrsbedienung duennbesiedelter räume durch linienoder bedarfsbus. *Nahrverkehrspraxis*, **25** (3), pp. 86–91 (in German). (Serving sparsely developed areas by means of a scheduled bus system or demand responsive bus system.)

4A2 Asp, K. and Lundin, O. (1980) Kollektivtrafiken i bilsamhaellet. VTI Rapport 166, Statens Vaeg-och Trafikinstitut, Linkoeping, Sweden (in Swedish). (Public transport in the car society.)

4A3 Barrett, B. and Buchanan, M. (1979) The National Bus Company 'MAP' Market Analysis Project. *Traffic Engineering and Control*, **20** (10), pp. 471-74.

The NBC's Market Analysis Project has been designed to rationalize the operation of NBC's 18,000 buses, to provide a cheaper and more effective service for passengers, and to ensure that NBC's subsidiary companies are market oriented. The project involves passenger surveys and the computer analysis of data, leading to a report on service reorganization.

4A4 Bly, P.H. (1976) The effects of fares on bus patronage. *Transport and Road Research Laboratory*, LR 733.

This report reviews the information available on the elasticity of bus patronage with respect to the fares charged, both in the UK and in other countries. Estimates of overall fares elasticity obtained across individual fares changes, from time-series analysis and from cross-sectional data, are all consistent with a typical mean value of -0.3 in a range from -0.1 to -0.6. These values appear to be much the same in the different countries from which the data were obtained, and they have been stable over time. Elasticities at off-peak travel times seem to be about twice those in the peak, short-distance elasticities are larger than those for long journeys, demand from 'non-captive' passengers may be twice as elastic as that from 'captive' passengers, and urban rail travel is found to be only half as elastic as bus travel.

4A5 Bonney, R.S.P. (1969) Transportation in rural areas. Proceedings of the Town and Country Planning Summer School held at the University of Nottingham, 10th-12th September, pp. 64-9.

4A6 Brookes, T. and Kilsby, D. (1979) The National Bus Company 'MAP' Market Analysis Project: 2. Collecting and presenting the demand information. *Traffic Engineering and Control*, **20** (11), pp. 541-5.

Examines the extensive data collection exercise and the conversion of those data to usable information.

.7 BURKHARDT, J.E. (1978) Overview of problems and prospects in rural passenger transportation. *Transportation Research Record*, 696, pp. 3-6.

This overview of the state of the art in rural passenger transport focuses on lessons that have and have not been learned during the past decade. Significant progress has been made on certain technical issues such as planning techniques, resource requirements, and performance standards. At the same time, very little progress is evident in some nontechnical areas—particularly in the areas of political leadership and financial stability. Future developments in rural passenger transport will vary significantly.

.8 BURKHARDT, J.E. (1981) Replanning existing rural public transportation systems. *Transportation Research Record*, 831, pp. 37-43.

A commitment to provide accountable, effective, and responsive transport services can best be supported by hard factual data concerning effectiveness and efficiency measures. Based on an analysis of system goals versus current performance, a transit system manager can preserve, enhance, alter, or terminate system operations. Methods of improving effectiveness and efficiency are discussed along with methods of handling six common problems: lower ridership than expected, low vehicle use, low revenues, basic changes required, cash flow, and use of incorrect or inappropriate types of vehicles.

.9 BURKHARDT, J.E. and MILLAR, W.W. (1976) Estimating costs of providing rural transportation services. *Transportation Research Record*, 578, pp. 8-15.

The issue of rural transport has attracted the attention of public policymakers. Now that the general need has been recognized, decision makers want to move to the important questions of demand and cost. Despite the existence of hundreds of small-scale transport systems, many of which are rural, very little research on demand is available to guide the would-be designer of a rural transport system. This paper reports work done by the Governor's Rural Transportation Task Force in Pennsylvania. Among the task force objectives was estimating demand for and cost of transport in all rural areas of Pennsylvania. Based on what little documentation of demand for

public transport systems in rural areas is available, a range of demand estimates is produced. Alternative service options are introduced to show their influence on final costs. These two factors—level
of demand and level of service—appear to be the most significant
determinants of the cost of rural transport systems.

4A10 BURKHARDT, J.E., GARLAND, A.D., GARRITY, R., KAYE, I. and
SALTZMAN, A. (1978) Rural Public Transportation. Transportation
Research Board, Washington, DC.

4A11 BURSEY, M., McCALLUM, D., MacBRIAR, I. and MILLS, K. (1979)
The National Bus Company 'MAP' Market Analysis Project: 3.
System Design. *Traffic Engineering and Control*, **20** (12), pp. 575-82.

Final stage of MAP where revisions to the existing bus services are
produced and implemented—some examples are given.

4A12 CASEY, R. (1979) Overview of accessible bus services. *Transportation
Research Record*, 718, pp. 47-52.

By December 1978, the number of transit authorities that operated
fixed-route, wheelchair-accessible bus services totalled five. This
paper is intended to disseminate information about these initial efforts. The majority of the operational data and results are from the
experience of the St Louis metropolitan area with accessible bus
service, which was operated by the Bi-State Development Agency.
Very few persons who use wheelchairs have used the fixed-route
accessible bus services to date. Ridership has averaged only a few
trips per day. However, the reliability of the services has been poor
and some wheelchair boardings have been denied due to unavaila-
bility or malfunctioning of lift equipment. Consequently, judgment
of the effectiveness of accessible bus services based on this early
experience is premature. Accessible bus operations can have a substantial economic impact. In addition to the capital cost of the lift
equipment, operating costs have increased due to the heavy lift
maintenance and repair workload and, to some extent, to the
changes in operational procedures that partial accessibility may
necessitate. Due to the low number of riders who are wheelchair
users, the overall mobility of this population group would seem to
be little changed.

3 COLLURA, J. CANNER, L., COPE, D. and GORDON, S. (1981) Guidelines for allocating public transportation costs among towns in nonurbanized areas. *Transportation Research Record*, 817, pp. 41–8.

A crucial question affecting the long-term viability of public transport programmes in nonurbanized areas concerns the allocation of deficit costs among towns receiving service. An evaluation is presented of alternative cost-allocation procedures that include one or more of the following variables: population, property valuation, passenger trips, passenger miles, vehicle miles, and vehicle hours. The procedures are evaluated based on several criteria, including simplicity, data requirements, cost of use, and equity (or perceived fairness) of the allocations. The evaluation brings into perspective the need to make trade-offs among these criteria. Sensitivity analysis is therefore conducted to determine the relative differences in allocations depending on the procedure, the data sampling method, and the cost assignment policy. Population, ridership, and cost data on two public transport programmes in nonurbanized areas of Massachusetts are used to conduct the evaluation. One service, operated in Barnstable County, is offered on a prearranged demand-responsive basis. The other provides fixed-route, fixed-schedule service to nine towns in Franklin County.

4 COLLURA, J., NKONGE, J.H., COPE, D.F. and MOBOLURIN, A. (1981) Charging human service agencies for public transportation services in rural areas. *Transportation Research Record*, 830, pp. 15–21.

Seven procedures that could be used to charge human service agencies for public transport services in rural areas are presented and evaluated. These procedures consist of two general types: population based and use based. A population-based procedure charges each agency on the basis of the number of clients, whereas use-based procedures charge agencies according to the amount of service consumed in terms of passenger trips, passenger miles, vehicle hours, and/or vehicle miles. The procedures are evaluated in terms of their ability to satisfy objectives of simplicity, cost, efficiency, and equity as well as their applicability to different types of public transportation services (ie shared-ride versus exclusive-ride services). In addition, the constraints of funding sources, the demands of accountability, and costing methods are examined. This presentation of the procedures will be of importance to public transport providers and administrators of human service agencies who are negotiating contracts for the provision of public transport services to agency clients. The evaluation of the procedures will be useful in determining the most appropriate procedure for use in particular circumstances. Finally, it is expected that the presentation and evaluation of procedures will aid in the task of simplifying and standardizing accounting, reporting, and billing methods for use in rural public transport programmes.

4A15 COUNTRYSIDE COMMISSION (1978) Recreational public transport. A guide to organizing and operating services in the countryside. Countryside Commission Advisory Series 5, Cheltenham.

4A16 DEHAMPERS, J.M. and VAN AMPERS, J.M. (1976) Het voorzieningsnivean van streetbuslijnen. *Verkeerskunde*, **27** (2), pp. 108–11 (in Dutch). (Service levels for regional and country bus services.)

The study has two aspects: first, the assessment of frequencies offered, planned, or potentially viable for regular public bus services other than local town routes; second, the prediction of effects that alterations in frequency of service, scheduled trip time, and routing, will have on passenger volumes, including that forecast of passenger volumes for new routes. Frequencies will be judged against either measured or forecast passenger volumes. The aim is a normative system in which the passenger volume is the decisive factor for the frequency to be offered on the route under consideration. For forecasting passenger volumes on proposed routes, a methodology is being developed which leads to a formula which is in between a polar formula and the gravity model. Consequently information required can be produced quickly and at low cost. Moreover the procedure remains a clear one. A methodology of this type is essential for a proper assessment of the effect that any reduction or improvement of frequency will have on passenger volumes.

4A17 DOBBS, B. (1979) Rural public transport: the economic stranglehold, in Halsall, D.A. and Turton, B.J. (eds) *Rural Transport Problems in Great Britain—Papers and Discussion*, Institute of British Geographers, Transport Geography Study Group, pp. 23–33.

There are two parts to the question of the economic stranglehold. The first set relate to economic, social, and political forces which affect all aspects of life; these forces only indirectly affect public transport but are no less significant for this. The second group affect the immediate provision of service through operational and efficiency criteria with the concern to provide maximum mobility at a reasonable cost in the face of uneven demand in time and space. These issues are discussed with respect to Gwynedd and the future seems bleak.

18 ENNOR, P.D. (1976) Public transport in rural areas: an overview. Symposium on Unconventional Bus Services, Transport and Road Research Laboratory, Crowthorne.

A thorough review of change in the provision of public transport services in rural areas is presented. The conclusion reached is that the future for the bus is bleak and that county councils ought to face the inevitable decline of services. New ideas should be encouraged and not rejected because of beliefs that are now not relevant.

19 ERIKSSON, M. (1977) Kollektivtrafik i glesbygd, Trafiktecknik, LTH. Lund, Sweden. (in Swedish) (Public transport in rural areas.)

20 EXECUTIVE OFFICE OF THE PRESIDENT (1979) Rural Development Initiatives: Improving transportation in Rural America, Statement, June.

The report outlines ways in which transport in rural America can be improved. Items discussed include social service and public transport, commuter air service, railroad branchline rehabilitation, and ridesharing. These improvements in rural transport are designed to help rural and small town residents overcome the problems of isolation, gain full access to essential human services, and meet the transport requirements of healthy, growing economies.

21 FAUSCH, P.A. (1981) Integration of public and schools transportation: Hohenlohe, Germany, Case Study. *Transportation Research Record*, 831, pp. 56-8.

The ongoing rural public transport demonstration in Hohenlohekreis in the Federal Republic of Germany is described. Hohenlohekreis is roughly the equivalent of a small county in the United

States. It contains an area of 775 km² (300 miles²) and is essentially
rural. The demonstration in Hoehenlohe appears to be a unique
effort in that it integrates public school traffic into public transport
to achieve the goals of reducing the overall cost and making transit
more useful and attractive to users. What has been accomplished is
the coordination of all rural public transit (regular-route transit,
school bus, intercity bus and rail, and elderly and handicapped
services) into one geographic area under one coordinated organizational strategy. The demonstration will not end until August 1982,
but it shows that integration of rural public transport and school
transport works in the physical sense; that cooperation of school
officials is essential; that planning for this type of service takes a lot
of time, is very difficult, and involves considerable planning at the
tactical level; that coordination of rural public transport services can
only be realized if there is an institution to provide for the coordination; and that there is significant room for more innovation at the
planning level in paratransit services, both in Europe and in the
United States.

4A22 GALLOP, K.R. (1975) Potential for selective diversion of conventional bus services. Proceedings of a Seminar on Rural Public Transport, Polytechnic of Central London.

It appears that demand-responsive systems have a potentially useful
role to play in the rural field. There are many cases of villages
without any form of bus service, or with only one journey a week
into the market town, where considerable hardship is caused to
people living there without access to private transport. Some villages
lost their bus service as a result of economies by the bus operators.
Other villages situated near a main road were served by an inter-
urban service following a circuitous route, but are now isolated
where the service has been modified to follow the most direct route.
This latter type of situation has been investigated, to examine the
role of a demand-responsive service, by a case study of an area in
south east Dorset. The author concludes that the proposals put forward here are practical and capable of implementation. The opportunity to divert an inter-urban bus service on demand to serve
villages off the main route may exist not only in south east Dorset,
but in many parts of rural Britain. It would be possible to improve
the public transport facilities for a number of villages with very little
extra cost to the bus company concerned and without any significant

increase in journey time. Concurrently, fuel and vehicle costs would be saved by the bus operator by scheduling the bus service direct when there are no requests from villagers.

23 GANSER, K. (1974) Offentlicher nahverkehr Ausserhalb der Verdichtungsraume. *Raumforschung und Raumordnung*, **32** (6), pp. 229–70 (in German). (Public transport outside the population centres.)

A series of seven related articles on public transport. The contrast of city environment to country is brought out with the latter's dependency on private cars. The idea of traffic discrimination is mentioned since many country people cannot afford a car. The view is put forward that on social grounds public transport should now be encouraged in the country areas as it has been in the towns.

24 GB, MINISTRY OF TRANSPORT (1965) Rural bus services: report of local enquiries, London: HMSO.

Following the report of the Jack Committee, 1961, local enquiries were arranged in four rural areas in England and Wales. Three of these were the areas in Lincolnshire, Montgomeryshire, and Westmorland which were the subject of surveys in 1963 and the fourth was an area in Northamptonshire north of Brackley. An enquiry team was appointed by the Minister in each area, comprising an independent Chairman and representatives of local authorities, bus operators, and appropriate local voluntary organizations with the following terms of reference: 'To enquire into possible remedies for the passenger transport problems arising in the area and to make recommendations to the Minister as to the most appropriate practical solution.' The investigations made and experiments mounted are described together with the conclusions reached by the teams. All the additional or modified bus services described, including school buses carrying fare-paying passengers, were operated with the appropriate licences or approval from the Traffic Commissioners.

25 GILMOUR, P. (1974) The economics of private bus services in Australia. *Traffic Quarterly*, **28** (3), pp. 437–52.

Many anomolies exist within the Australian passenger transport system, principally caused by government regulation of the private sector and the provision of subsidies to cover the deficits of the public sector. Private enterprise buses receive no direct government subsidies and yet it makes efficient use of the road network—this paper discusses why this is so.

4A26 GIRNAN, G. and MULLER, K.W. (1980) Success of investment in local public transport in Germany. *Transport Policy and Decision Making*, **1** (2/3), pp. 253–65.

Since 1967, substantial public funds have been made available by federal and state governments for construction work to improve local public transport in towns and cities. This has made it possible to implement large-scale projects—such as underground and commuter railway systems—and a large number of smaller schemes designed to improve urban traffic conditions. The present article describes the initial situation as well as the statutory bases for improving traffic conditions in towns and cities, and presents a survey of the investment and construction work being done in local public transport. This is followed by an analysis of the transport improvements achieved so far as well as the consequences for urban planning and public policy in the social and labour market fields.

4A27 GREENBIE, B.B. (1970) Interchange planning in a rural area. *Traffic Quarterly*, **24** (2), pp. 265–78.

The effect of controlled access roads on areas of low density population is significant as a series of high access nodes are created at the interchange points. High land values are realized when the decision is made on a particular development.

4A28 HALL, C. (1975) Rural transport: a poor relation? *Built Environment*, **1** (3), pp. 119–20.

Although experimental schemes for the promotion of public transport in rural areas are in operation, it is thought that financial and conservation considerations are likely to bring about further reductions in rural services. Even in rural areas where 70–80 per cent of households have the use of a car, the young and old remain relatively immobile for much of the time. This situation is likely to get worse with rising petrol costs. Possible solutions to this problem have led to such developments as the post bus and dial-a-bus. Now that subsidies for such socially justifiable rural services are accepted, it is concluded that the loading of rural bus services must be improved by restraints on rural car use designed to boost bus services.

29 HARMAN, R.G. (1978) Rural public transport—who pays, who benefits? Proceedings of the PTRC Conference, University of Warwick, July.

Presents a study of the importance of transport to users in a distinctly rural area. The aims were twofold: to establish the feasibility of analysing the relative proportions of income spent by households of different income levels on the basis of inexpensive data sources, and to examine the rural situation and its policy implications. Much less is spent per household on public transport in rural areas than the national average, and this amount is greatest among middle-income groups. Car ownership is correspondingly much higher for all but the poorest households. This suggests that car ownership is a strain on those incomes, especially the lower incomes. Revenue support in the study area was progressive with lower and middle income groups receiving a net benefit but there was no even progression of proportional benefit. It is concluded that the village bus needs a large input of developed expertise and funds if it is to survive.

30 HARMAN, R.G. (1978) Rural public transport—Revenue support for rural bus services. Conservation Society, Transport WP 4, Sheffield.

The author gives the background to rural bus services and the decline in their patronage. The latter is attributed to the 1972 Local Government Act whereby county councils were given the duty to control and develop their local public transport system within the county and to a decline in coverage due to a reduction in the number of local facilities and increasing centralization. According to a survey carried out in two areas of Norfolk in 1975, rural families spend approximately one-third the amount on local bus travel that urban ones do and make one-ninth the number of trips (the average trip length being considerably greater). Mention is made of innovative schemes (minibus, car sharing, post buses, bus clubs). It is suggested that policies should be improved in two respects: more real work should be put into thoroughly understanding and developing rural public transport and there is a need for increasing revenue support for operators.

4A31 HEWITT, J.R.A. (1975) An examination of bus route costing methods and their application in rural areas. Unpublished MSc Thesis, Centre for Transport Studies, Cranfield.

This thesis examines the costing models that have been developed in recent years for allocating costs of bus operation to routes and considers their relevance to rural routes in particular. The problems of operating public transport in rural areas are considered and the growth of official recognition of these problems which led to the inclusion of a provision for subsidies in the 1968 Transport Act. The establishment of subsidies provided a spur to the development of more accurate costing models in the bus industry. Three models are considered—those developed by the National Bus Company; by a firm of consultants for the Transport and Road Research Laboratory; and by a firm of consultants for the West Yorkshire Passenger Transport Authority. The provisions of the three models are compared with the needs of rural areas and weaknesses are identified. The costs of operating bus services in Bedfordshire are then examined and comparison made between the costs of provision of urban and rural services, and in particular different types of rural service. Some conclusions are drawn about the relative costs of different types of rural service and an exploration is made of the implications for transport planning in rural areas.

4A32 HIGGINSON, M. (1980) On the buses: Municipal bus operation under contrasting policies. Polytechnic of Central London, Transport Studies Group Discussion Paper No 9.

Sets out to monitor the progress of a sample of British urban bus operators through the 1970s by comparing their performance with that predicted by a standardized elasticity model. Operators selected include Southampton City Transport, Northampton Transport, and Reading Transport.

4A33 HOARE, A.G. (1975) Some aspects of the rural transport problem: an experimental survey. *Journal of Transport Economics and Policy*, **9** (2), pp. 141-53.

The geographical and sociological aspects of the rural transport problem are assessed as they relate to the individual. It then considers the extent to which the perception of rural transport inadequacies inter-relates with other problems perceived in the local area and its relative importance. These findings are placed within the context of public policy formation.

34 HUTTON, J. (1978) The economics of school transport. *Social and Economic Administration*, **10,** pp. 51–8.

In recent years expenditure on the transport of children to and from school has increased considerably, and at a time of cuts this item has come under scrutiny. An economic approach would have much to contribute to decision making in the field of school transport. This paper reviews the economic aspects of the issue, discusses the present system, and proposes changes in the light of these economic factors.

35 JACKSON, A.F. and McKELVEY, D.J. (1978) Transit problems in small cities and non-urbanized areas: inventory of transportation services in places less than ten thousand population outside of urbanized areas. North Carolina Agricultural and Technical State University, Transportation Institute, Greensboro, North Carolina.

36 JACKSON, R.L. and JOHNSTON, I. (1979) Financially viable works bus services. *Transport and Road Research Laboratory*, SR 511.

A study of a number of works bus and coach services operating with little or no financial support from employers is reported. All operated over routes more than 8 km in length. Fares were less than those charged in many conventional stage carriage services and, in terms of pence per km, decreased as route length increased. When route lengths were greater than 12 km, fares were lower than the perceived costs of motoring, taken to be petrol costs of 2p per km (1978 prices). Generally vehicle loads were 40 or more. Overall the group of services exhibited features which an earlier economic study had predicted would be necessary for break-even operation. The work indicated that female workers were generally prepared to tolerate higher fare levels, which meant that services for women could operate over shorter distances on a break-even basis. It also suggested that break-even services for women could be operated to smaller work units. In a speculative section the advantages, disadvantages, and potential of works bus operation are discussed.

37 JACKSON, R.L. and MARTIN, P.H. (1979) The organisation and role

of private bus and coach companies. *Transport and Road Research Laboratory*, SR 485.

A study of the organization and operating methods of privately owned bus and coach companies is reported. It shows that the industry is a growing one dominated by relatively small companies which plays a significant role in providing local road passenger transport. Notable features of private bus and coach companies are their apparently low overheads, the flexibility of their full-time staff, and the extent of use of part-time drivers. Peak school contracts form the main basis of their work and many have all their vehicles committed to at least one such contract during peak periods. This peak work is supplemented by a smaller number of works contracts. Off-peak work is more limited and varied, consisting of a mix of other school services, transport of shift workers, Social Services work, licensed road service operation, various one-off contracts, and, in the case of minibus operators, parcel and school meals deliveries. At the weekends and during the summer holidays many operators run day outings or licensed services to the coast or other places of entertainment and interest. Their costing methods lead many private operators to charge comparable prices for both peak and off-peak work. Such methods contrast with that used by many publicly-owned companies which lead to a much higher level of pricing in the peak.

4A38 JACKSON, R.L. and MARTIN, P.H. (1979) The economics of contract bus services. *Transport and Road Research Laboratory*, LR 899.

An analysis is made of the prices charged by privately owned bus and coach companies for works and school contract services in a particular area. A regression equation is obtained which relates the contract price to the type of contract (works or school), vehicle size, and distance run. This equation is used to compute the fare required for a works contract service to break-even at varying loads and journey lengths. This shows that it is unlikely that, because of their low capacity, break-even services could be operated with minibuses. In order to break-even at stage bus fares, a contract coach service would need to attract about 25 passengers. Increased loads would result in proportionally lower fares. To become financially attractive to car drivers a service would need to carry 40 passengers for an average journey length of at least 10 km. It is shown that, on average, each vehicle earned about £150 per week from its peak hour contracts. Standard costing indicates that an equivalent period of stage-carriage operation would cost at least £200 per week.

9 JELLEY, C.A.B. (1980) The National Bus Company 'MAP' Market Analysis Project: 4 Examples of study bus system design. *Traffic Engineering and Control*, **21** (1), pp. 14–20.

This, the fourth and final article of the series, contains examples of the use of MAP data in several examples covering the design of both peak and off-peak services for several rural and urban areas and an off-peak inter-urban service. The effect of traffic management measures is also considered in one case. Analysis of the demand in Yeovil, a small Somerset town, by half-hourly periods emphasized the differences in the pattern of passenger movement from fine-zone origins to coarse-zone destinations throughout the morning peak. Exact destinations and origins of passengers were used to modify the rural peak service between Evesham and Pershore in Worcester. Average hourly off-peak passenger movements from the outer housing estate to the centre of Andover in Hampshire were monitored. It is estimated that the full Andover study could reduce running costs by 20 per cent, with a revenue loss of between 3 and 9 per cent. The rural off-peak study proposed an increased service between Abergavenny and Raglan in South Wales; reduced journey times and a more frequent service are proposed for the off-peak inter-urban links between Birmingham and Stourbridge. Time savings and a more frequent and reliable service are the result of a traffic management scheme in the Midland town of Tamworth.

10 KIDDER, A.E. (1976) Economics of rural public transportation programs. *Transportation Research Record*, 578, pp. 1–7.

Rural transit systems cannot be expected to be self-supporting. Revenue rarely comes close to the 7 cents/mile (4.4 cents/km) that is typical of the costs of the system. Costs are high because low population density and the great number of destinations in most rural areas cause high per-passenger cost for driver salaries and management. Ridership on subsidized systems that have been set up under the Office of Economic Opportunity and similar auspices tends to be a small fraction of the general population and even the disadvantaged population. Competition from car alternatives (car pooling and ride sharing) dimishes the effective demand for transit solutions.

Getting programmatic consensus on destinations is difficult because of conflicting alternatives; therefore, ridership is low. A subsidy large enough to provide minimum service levels to all the disadvantaged in a region is beyond what appears to be the fiscal capacity of local governments in rural areas. Few of the original Office of Economic Opportunity experiments have been picked up for sustained local funding. In light of these findings, restricting new expenditures of money for rural transport demonstration programmes to low-cost innovations such as systematized car pooling, transport vouchers for specific target populations, or consolidating social-service transport and service delivery programmes may be useful.

4A41 KIHLMAN, B. (1982) Transportförsörjningen för billösa i glesbygd (Transportation for the carless in rural areas), Statens väg-och trafikinstitut (VTI), Linköping, Sweden, Report 283.

This report is a literature survey of the provision of bus routes and paratransit in rural areas. The focus is on current schemes in Sweden and the legal aspects involved in setting up a paratransit system are included. Foreign paratransit experiments in rural areas are also covered and the lessons for Sweden are drawn.

4A42 KILVINGTON, R.P. (1979) Problems of public transport—retrospect and prospect. Paper presented at the Conference on Public Transport Planning, Loughborough University of Technology, September.

This paper reviews the changes that have taken place in travel patterns over the last twenty years. The rise in car ownership has been matched by the fall in public transport patronage. More recently there has been the emergence of the problems of public transport in rural areas, a willingness to experiment, the plethora of transport documents, increased Government control, and the social objectives of policy.

4A43 LARSON, T.D. and LIMA, P.M. (1975) Rural public transportation. *Traffic Quarterly*, **29** (3), pp. 369–84.

Rural public transport demonstration funds are authorized by the federal-aid Highway Act of 1973. To determine rural public transport needs and evaluate parameters of service, the Pennsylvania

Department of Agriculture operates such a demonstration project. Essentially a dial-a-ride minibus service, the system has recently been expanded to serve 21 counties and has the following objectives: to collect relevant cost data, to determine efficiency measures, including optimum procedures for scheduling and dispatching, and to enhance the effectiveness of inter-agency co-ordination of transport alternatives. The ultimate goal is to develop a state-wide rural transport network. In a discussion of rural transport system needs, alternative systems, administrative and legislative developments, and future models are considered.

4 LEWIS, A.D. (1978) Role of the intercity bus in rural public transportation. *Transportation Research Record*, 696, pp. 79–81.

In the US, there has been a rebellion against the costly ineffective public policy of large scale investment in prestigious transport schemes. The intercity bus on the other hand is a low cost mode that has in the past had an important role to play in rural transport. It still provides over 14,000 communities with their only form of public transport.

5 LIPPOY, R. (1978) Standard i kollektiv glesbygdstrafik, Stockholms Universitet, Kulturgeografiska Institutionen, Stockholm (in Swedish). (Standards in public transport in thinly populated areas.)

6 LOCAL GOVERNMENT OPERATIONAL RESEARCH UNIT (1977) Problems and solutions in rural transport. LGORU, Manchester.

A review that deals with the rationalization of existing bus services, the co-ordination of different types of service, and experimentation with new forms of service.

7 MARTIN, B.V. and WARMAN, P. (1979) Rural public transport. *Highway Engineer*, **26** (8/9), pp. 8–17.

This paper describes a methodology for planning public transport on a county-wide basis where the principal concern is the needs of villages, small communities, and small towns. The paper describes the relationship between the needs of small communities and the provision of transport. It highlights the complex social relationships that exist between the long-term character of a rural area and the supply of transport services. Having provided the context for public transport, the methodology developed by the authors in various studies over five years is described in terms of the data, the technical procedures developed, and typical results obtained.

4A48 MARTIN, P.H. (1978) Bus services in small towns. *Transport and Road Research Laboratory*, LR 848.

A study is made of fixed route bus services operating in towns with populations in the range 5000 to 30,000. Analysis of eight such services is carried out to identify and, where possible, quantify those factors which favour their operation. The study was undertaken to assess the potential for and advisability of extending this type of operation to other small towns. Quantitative assessment of the study services is based on the assumed objective of maximizing the number of bus passengers, subject to financial constraint. The implications of this objective are analysed and it is thought to be compatible with the corporate aim of a public transport undertaking and the social aim of a local authority. It is concluded that, although in general such services are not profitable, their provision can be well justified provided that the selection of the town and the service design take sufficient account of the factors discussed.

4A49 MAURO, G.T. (1978) Public transportation planning for the suburbs. *Transportation Research Record*, 661, pp. 37-9.

Due to the demographic characteristics of suburban areas and the unusual transport problems they present, effective public transport planning demands flexible and innovative approaches. This paper describes a unique procedure used in a recent planning assignment for Camden and Burlington Counties, the New Jersey suburbs of Philadelphia. They typify the diversified geographic, socio-economic, and population attributes and limited planning resources of such areas across the country. The essence of the planning methodology was a 'prototype' approach which entailed: formulating a list of the bi-county transportation problems which was then condensed to a shorter list of 'model problems'; selecting a 'prototype' for each particular problem within the general categories of: transit user groups, geographic areas, and major trip attractors/generators; developing a unique solution for each problem; analysing each prototype solution for adaptability to other similar problems within the same group; using this mechanism as the primary tool for public transport planning for suburban areas, it maximizes the impact of available resources by concentrating upon solving specific problems while concurrently establishing the basis for wide application of results and recommendations.

50 MINISTERE DES TRANSPORTS (1979) Les transports collectifs interurbains: table ronde des 26 et 27 avril 1979, Paris, (in French). (Inter urban public transport: round table conference.)

51 MITCHELL, C.G.B. (1980) The use of local bus services. *Transport and Road Research Laboratory*, LR 923.

Patronage of local bus services has been falling since at least 1952. This report uses the national travel surveys of 1965, 1972/73, and 1975/76 to examine how the use of local bus services has changed since 1965. A declining proportion of bus trips are made to and from work, and an increasing proportion for shopping. Characteristics of bus users with respect to age, sex, area of residence, car ownership, income, and the socio-economic group of the user's household are studied. Variation of bus use with time of day and with season is shown. It is found that demand for bus travel by adults has become less peaked, and that by 1975/76 most of the additional peak demand was due to children.

52 MUNTON, R.J.C. and CLOUT, H. (1971) The problem bus. *Town and Country Planning*, **39** (2), pp. 112–16.

Whilst rates of car ownership are higher in rural areas of England than in the towns, there are some sections of rural society (retired people on fixed incomes, and the poorly paid agricultural workers) which do not share in this trend towards increased personal mobility. The reduction of rural bus services may well cause hardship to such people. This article considers the detailed aspects of local mobility for inhabitants of five parishes in northern Norfolk. In the long term the whole *raison d'être* of rural bus services will have to be rethought, primarily with a view to providing a service for the poor and the elderly. Minibus services, possibly connected with the collection of mail, might provide a realistic escape route for a cost-conscious society from a continued contraction in services. Enormous problems associated with the volume and source of subsidies for rural services remain.

4A53 NATIONAL COUNCIL OF SOCIAL SERVICE (1976) Rural transport: information from Rural Community Councils. What is the alternative? National Council of Social Service, London.

The purpose of this document is to disseminate information about new ideas, experiments, schemes, etc., concerning public transport in rural areas. Examples of schemes being tried are postbuses, school buses, minibus, car schemes, works buses carrying fare-paying passengers, railway re-openings, etc. The report is arranged alphabetically by rural community council, and for each such council, brief details are given of type of transport scheme, where it is operating, by whom, and with what success. Also briefly mentioned are any surveys conducted in the rural communities which have helped to establish a new transport scheme or project.

4A54 NATIONAL SWEDISH ROAD AND TRAFFIC RESEARCH INSTITUTE (1979) Planering foer kollektiv landsbygdstrafik, Transportnaemnden, Monograph (in Swedish). (The planning of rural public transport.)

This report is a study on the structure of commuter traffic in Uppsala County. Its purpose is to obtain material to be used as a basis for effective planning of bus-tours for commuter traffic to and from work, the connecting of an area and a working place through bus connections, and commuter traffic during energy crisis. A densely populated area was used as a basis for the study, and its connections with densely and sparsely populated areas as well as the connections within the areas themselves are described in the form of maps and tables. Also, the material is classified according to the commuters' branches of industry and their choices of transportation. In November 1975, of 18,000 commuters only 12 per cent used public transport. The explanation is thought to be that most bus schedules were not adapted to the commuter traffic, and the bus fares were too high. Thus, by using employers' enquiries the time of this traffic to and from work was mapped in order to determine bus-tours according to the commuters' need. By re-arranging the bus schedules the traffic output in Uppsala county increased by 35 per cent. Through co-ordination this improvement could be obtained by only 5 per cent increase of the resources in the form of buses and drivers. Preliminary estimations show that the total number of rural bus-tours has increased 50 per cent during one year. If only commuter traffic is taken into account, the increase is even greater.

5 NEELY, G. (1978) Financing the rural bus, in Cresswell, R. (ed) *Rural Transport and Country Planning*, London: Leonard Hill, pp. 61–73.

This paper reviews the complex question of how much service ought to be provided, the costs of the service, the fares charged and any forms of concessionary fares. If the services have to be subsidized then a further set of questions are raised as to who should pay. What seems to be required is some commitment and long term planning.

6 OLDFIELD, R.H., BLY, P.H. and WEBSTER, F.V. (1981) Predicting the use of stage service buses in Great Britain. *Transport and Road Research Laboratory*, LR 1000.

Bus patronage has been declining in Great Britain at about 4 per cent per year from 1960 to 1979. In order to see how the future trend is likely to be affected by the level of subsidy provided and by different assumptions regarding the economic climate in which public transport operates (including future trends in car ownership and the price of fuel), a simple bus patronage prediction model has been constructed and used to predict the number of bus journeys up to the end of the century.

Two versions of the model have been developed: one which categorizes trips by purpose and type of traveller, and another which combines all these trip types but deals separately with different regions of the country. In both types households are categorized by car ownership (no car, one car, and two or more) and their trip rates calibrated using National Travel Survey data.

Future bus travel was found to be sensitive to the level of economic growth assumed for the economy and to the amount of bus subsidy provided. It is estimated that by the end of the century bus patronage will have fallen by about 42 per cent relative to the 1979 base year if subsidy is kept constant in real terms and the economy grows at 2 per cent per year. If the subsidy is phased out (though still keeping the concessions for the elderly and school children), patronage is likely to fall by 51 per cent of its 1979 value, while on the other hand patronage could be held constant if subsidy grew in real terms at about $8\frac{1}{2}$ per cent per year.

Lower growth rates of the economy are likely to result in a smaller loss of patronage; similarly increasing fuel prices are also likely to favour public transport but it would require dramatic rises in fuel

costs between now and the end of the century (with the real price
of fuel rising to probably $3\frac{1}{2}$ times the present price) for patronage
to retain its 1979 value, assuming subsidy remains constant.

4A57 OSTENFELD, T. (1976) Planlaeggbubg av kollektivtrafik i landsdis-
trikter, Köbenhauns Universitet, Rapport 4, (in Danish). (Planning
of public transport in rural areas.)

4A58 OXLEY, P.R. (1982) The effects of the withdrawal and reduction of
rural bus services. *Transport and Road Research Laboratory*, SR 719.

This report analyses the effects of reductions in stage carriage bus
services in three rural areas as determined by before and after surveys. In one area, the effects on mobility and modal choice were
slight, despite bus service changes which improved the ratio of re-
venue/cost. In the second area, modal changes were recorded, but
again without any significant loss of mobility to the former bus users.
The third area, where the bus reductions were comparatively more
severe, produced both modal change and a fall in mobility. This fall
mainly occurred in journeys for social and shopping purposes. Estimates were made of the personal travel costs before and after the
service changes in the second and third areas. The problem of plac-
ing a value on trips no longer made and trips made by non-vehicular
means is discussed but it is concluded that, unless an unrealistically
high price is placed on such journeys, the net savings achieved by
the operating bus companies well outweigh the aggregate increase
in personal costs borne by the former bus passengers. However,
while the savings from the service reductions were spread throughout
the community, the costs fell on relatively few individuals. Although
inconvenience is the best description of the effect of the bus reductions on most individuals, a minority were found who suffered real
hardship.

4A59 PAULHUS, N.G. and DAWSON, T.C. (1979) *Providing Transportation for
Rural Americans*, US Department of Transportation, Office of Intergovernmental Affairs, May.

4A60 PEDERSEN, P.O. (1976) Rural public transport in Denmark—its past
and its future development. Paper presented to the Polytechnic of
Central London Conference, December.

61 PFLUG, W. (1981) The bus and coach industry of West Germany. *Omnibus*, Jan/Feb, pp. 1–10.

A general review of the bus and coach industry in Germany: the number of buses and coaches relative to the population is lower than in Britain, but the much greater role of the railways, rapid transit, and tramways result in a greater overall use of public transport.

62 SOOT, S. and STENSON, H.H. (1980) Cognitive aspects of transit use in areas of high and low travel density. Illinois University, Chicago, Urban Mass Transportation Administration, Final Report UMTA-IL-11-0028-81-1, December.

The report addresses several questions regarding the manner in which information on transit systems should be prepared and disseminated. The report is divided into six chapters, ranging in topics from the fundamental broad-based questions of how well urban residents understand their city and the transit system, to specific questions of what to include on a transit map. The report identifies the numerous steps a transit planner needs to consider in preparing a comprehensive information dissemination (marketing) programme. In this report, the six studies of cognitive factors in mass transit use are reported, namely: interviewers posing as lost travellers gathered route information from fellow travellers; business establishments were telephoned and asked for route information/direction to their places of business; bus riders were surveyed to determine whether route names or route numbers were preferred; distance perception and 'mental maps' of Chicago were studied in a sample of respondents; three varieties of transit route maps were tested for their utility to users; and a literature survey of cognitive factors in transport use was performed. All studies point out problems existing in the proper form and usage of transit route information by the public.

63 SPREITER, H. (1974) Busnetzplanung für ländliche regionen. Institute für Orts-Regional-und Landesplanung, Informationen Dise 28, April, 22–24 (in German). (The planning of bus networks for rural regions.)

Provides a survey of the problems inherent in the planning of bus networks for rural areas as stated in present literature and practice. Theories are examined regarding regional traffic systems and the tasks of regional traffic planning. Planning practice in.Switzerland is specifically examined.

4A64 TAYLOR, J. (1978) Cheaper National for rural rides. *Coaching Journal and Bus Review*, **46** (6), pp. 35–6.

4A65 TEBB, R.G.P. (1978) Traffic characteristics of a network of co-ordinated rural bus services. *Transport and Road Research Laboratory*, SR 367.

A survey of the traffic patterns on an interconnected group of stage-carriage bus services in South and West Yorkshire is presented. Their value as inter-urban, urban-rural, and purely rural services is considered, together with the amount of traffic passing through the rural locations at which connections take place. The degree of bus-bus transfer traffic is also considered.

Although the services as a whole show only marginal gains in traffic or revenue as a result of the provision of rural connecting services, it is shown that the interchange facilities were used by over eight per cent of the passengers at the sites, and that they were therefore of significant value to the rural community. It is suggested that local authorities elsewhere may find, in areas where bus services remain reasonably frequent, that the low support costs of providing rural connecting facilities are preferable to a financial commitment to the creation and operation of other kinds of rural bus schemes.

4A66 THELEN, K.M., CHATTERJEE, A. and WEGMANN, F. J. (1980) Evaluation of alternative transit routing configurations in a hypo-thetical low density area. *Transportation Research Record*, 761, pp. 53–6.

The provision of fixed-route transit services in low-density suburban areas poses significant problems for urban communities. Tradi-tionally, fixed-route bus service has been provided to these areas as an extension of the radial system in the core city. However, little information exists that would guide the selection of a certain pattern under a given set of conditions. As energy continues to be in short supply, the question of extensions of fixed-route service to low-density areas may become more pressing. This paper discusses the intrinsic service characteristics of six alternative routing patterns in a hypothetical low-density area. Costs (determined from vehicle miles travelled), coverage area, passenger travel time, and competitiveness with the walk mode are the performance measures used to evaluate each routing pattern. The results indicate that different types of routing configurations do have different implications with respect to these performance measures. No single pattern was found to satisfy all service objectives equally well. Threfore, it is necessary for decision makers to assign priorities to different service characteristics and then to make the necessary trade-offs between those characteristics to arrive at a decision that meets community objectives.

67 TOPHAM, N. (1968) Road passenger transport in unremunerative areas. *Yorkshire Bulletin of Economic and Social Research*, **1**, pp. 28–40.

This paper provides an examination of the structure, the viability, and the prospects of road passenger transport in non-urban areas. The structure of the bus industry and the basis of cross-subsidization, which supports it is outlined together with factors that since 1950 have tended to maintain aggregated vehicle miles and passenger journeys. The notion of adequacy and the reasons for modal choice in the trade-off between public transport and private transport are covered, and a summary of the various reports and suggestions that have been put forward to maintain and support non-urban services is made in which the arguments for reorganization are presented.

68 TRANSPORTATION SYSTEMS CENTER (1976) Rural passenger transportation state-of-the-art overview. Report for the US Department of Transportation Technology Sharing Program, October.

69 TRANSPORTATION SYSTEMS CENTER (1977) Rural passenger transportation primer. Report for the US Department of Transportation Technology Sharing Program, January.

70 TRENCH, S. (1975) Economic criteria and transport subsidies, in Wilmers, P.H.M. and Moseley, M.J. (eds) Rural Public Transport and Planning. Regional Studies Association, Discussion Paper 4.

It is argued that the present arrangements for relating the utility and social opportunity cost of trips in public and private transport lead to a signifcant bias in favour of the latter. Bus operating subsidies tend only to be granted after specific evidence of consumer hardship is produced, in marked contrast to measures to improve the lot of the private motorist.

4A71 TUNBRIDGE, R.J. and JACKSON, R.L. (1980) The economics of stage carriage operation by private bus and coach companies. *Transport and Road Research Laboratory*, LR 952.

This report considers the economics of stage carriage operation by private bus and coach companies. A fares comparison carried out in two Traffic Areas showed that in 1973 the mean fare charged on rural and inter-urban stage services run by private operators was 25 per cent less than that charged on similar services provided by public operators for a wide range of journey lengths. Given comparable levels of revenue support the difference might have been 30-40 per cent. Between 1974 and 1978 the fare gap between the two types of operator appeared to have been widening. Other economic analysis indicated that private operators' lower fares stemmed largely from lower unit costs, rather than higher loadings or other possible sources. Past TRRL work suggests that at least some of these lower unit costs are likely to derive specifically from the nature of private companies, namely small working units without commitment to supply extensive stage networks [4A37, 4A38].

4A72 TURNS, K.L. (1974) *The Independent Bus*, Newton Abbot: David and Charles.

It is the author's primary aim to dispel some of the myths that have developed over the last fifty years creating a misleading picture of the small operator as a vicious, anti-passenger, 'pirate'—as equally fallacious as the romanticized view. A further function of this work, however, is the recording and preservation of an important aspect of social history now in danger of disappearing from sight. Also, in a region by region review of the breadth and scope of the independent bus services still operating today, the author shows his concern to reveal both the good and the bad, to display the essentially uncomplicated nature of bus operation, and to encourage the public users to assert their rights by participating in the planning of their own services.

4A73 TYSON, W.J. (1972) A critique of road passenger transport subsidy policies. *Manchester School of Economic and Social Studies Bulletin*, **4,** pp. 397-417.

In rural areas it is doubted whether the resource allocation argu-

ment for subsidies could be maintained in view of the present relationship between marginal social costs and price for private transport. In such areas the grounds for subsidy become much wider and
hinge essentially on considerations of the benefits to be derived from
land use. It is questionable whether subsidies to public transport are
the best means of obtaining these benefits.

74 TYSON, W.J. (1972) An economist's view of public transport subsidies. Polytechnic of Central London, Rural Transport Seminar,
November, pp. 3-21.

This theoretical paper makes the three points that benefits to the
community of local public transport services are not truly reflected
in revenue from users; operating costs are not necessarily equivalent
to either private or social opportunity costs; and since subsidies were
(at the time of writing) allocated only on revenue and operating
costs data, then the subsidies were not necessarily as cost-effective as
they might have been.

75 TYSON, W.J. (1977) Measuring bus passenger miles. Paper presented
at the Sixth Annual Seminar on Rural Public Transport, Polytechnic of Central London, November.

It is argued that passenger mileage could be a useful supplement to
the other statistics collected by bus operators (passenger numbers
and receipts), but it is no substitute for them. Some difficulties are
outlined and the results of one such study are presented with a
particular focus on how some of the problems can be overcome.
These are particularly acute with the tickets that allow the traveller
unlimited access to the bus at any time.

76 UGOLIK, W.R. and KNIGHTON, R.C. (1979) Estimating the effects
of alternative levels of service on rural transit ridership. *Transportation
Research Record*, 718, pp. 34-9, (also available as New York Department of Transportation PRR 144).

This paper deals with the need to assess public response to alternative levels of service and travel flexibility on proposed rural transport
systems. A public opinion survey was conducted in rural Otsego
County, New York, among 254 households, 30 of which had no
telephones. The survey presented three public transport options
(fixed route, dial-a-bus, and mobility club) and asked questions

about possible use of such services at different fare and service levels. The survey questionnaire was designed to minimize noncommitment bias and responses were separated on the basis of car availability. Estimates of potential ridership were made for each transit option at different fare levels, service levels, and travel-flexibility levels. Although it is not suggested that the demand estimates developed for Otsego County are transferable to other areas, the relative changes in demand resulting from changing fare, service, and travel-flexibility levels should be generally useful.

4A77 US DEPARTMENT OF TRANSPORTATION (1979) *Proceedings of the Fourth National Conference on Rural Public Transportation.* Transportation Research Board, DOT-1-79-19, September.

4A78 WEBSTER, F.V. and BLY, P.H. (1981 and 1982) The demand for public transport. *Transport Reviews*, **1** (4), pp. 323-52, and **2** (1), pp. 23-46.

These papers and the original report attempt to synthesize the very large literature available on the different factors which affect the demand for public transport, and to draw conclusions which have a direct applicability to transport planning and to draw inferences between countries. This review is in two parts. The first looks at the objectives of transport policy, describes past trends in patronage, costs, reviews the various techniques used to predict demand, and examines the likely impacts of the main background factors such as changing affluence, car ownership and land use. The second part deals with the more direct demand factors such as fares and quality of service and the introduction of various traffic and transport measures (traffic restraint, bus priority, etc). It outlines methodology on costing public transport services and draws the supply and demand sides together in a consideration of particular strategies which are at the disposal of the operator, the planner and the policy maker.

4A79 WEISS, D.L. and NEVEU, A.J. (1978) Attitudes toward transit service in small urban areas. *Transportation Research Record*, 661, pp. 32-6.

An analysis of the attitudes of residents of several small urban areas toward transit improvement was conducted in an attempt to identify groups with similar preferences. The groups were described by several demographic characteristics: age, sex, cars owned. Two methods were used: a comparison of the preference rankings of each group across the cities; and discriminant analysis to identify groups with similar attitudes. The results indicate that there is some similarity within certain demographic groups, across the cities. However, respondents as a whole exhibited great similarity of preferred choices, irrespective of demographics or city. The two most preferred improvements were special vehicles for the handicapped and reduced fares for the elderly and handicapped. It is concluded that there exists some similarity in the attitudes towards transit improvement among the cities, but the development of any distinct groups proved impossible with the limited set of demographics available for use in this study.

WHITE, P.R. (1976) *Planning for Public Transport*, London: Hutchinson.

This basic textbook on public transport planning takes the British system as its context. There are a series of general chapters on organization and control, the role of public transport, and bus, coach and rail systems. The focus switches to the urban context, but there is a general review of some of the specific problems of rural transport which deals with the existing network, the opportunities for improvement, regulation and licensing and cooperative organization.

WHITE, P.R. (1978) Potential for public transport in rural areas. Proceedings of a Conference on the Future of Transport in Rural Areas, Department of Town Planning, Oxford Polytechnic, November 1977, pp. 1–9.

This review paper begins by dispelling certain myths about rural public transport, such as the inevitable decline and the levels of support required to maintain services. It then goes on to discuss present patterns of demand in rural areas and the implications of these changes for the transport operator. The conclusion suggests that the role for the volunteer could be expanded and that better use could be made of taxi and school bus, works buses and post bus services.

WIBERG, U. (1976) Traficservice i glesbygd (Traffic services in rural areas), Umea University, Report 4, Department of Geography, Umea, Sweden (in Swedish).

4A83 WILLIAMS, M. (1981) The economic justification for local bus transport subsidies. *International Journal of Transport Economics*, **8** (1), pp. 79–88.

Firstly this paper deals with aspects of federal, stage and local intervention through subsidy payments to local bus transport systems in Illinois. Then it reviews the main economic and social arguments for subsidies and discusses a special subsidy programme instituted in Illinois to help small urban communities, and finally it provides empirical results so that the justification for subsidies can be evaluated.

4A84 WILLIS, E. (1974) A system of route costing for the bus industry. *Traffic Administrator*, **8** (10), pp. 10–14.

Within rural areas increased car ownership has reduced the demand for rural bus services, many of which were relatively marginal in profitability even in the peak demand years of the 1930s and early 1950s. The 1968 Transport Act allows local authorities to subsidize loss making but socially necessary services, with a large amount of additional support being provided by central government funds. The present route costing system has a number of faults which result in costs being relatively arbitrarily allocated. This means that profit or loss on routes may be over or under estimated. The costing system described here works on a depot basis, but may be adjusted to cope with areas where the interworking of vehicles between depots is common. The methods of calculation used are explained in some detail. For ten selected rural bus routes in Wales the profit or loss was obtained using this improved method. They differ considerably from the figures obtained using the National Bus Company formula. The accounting system outlined would provide a more accurate picture of the profitability of bus routes.

4A85 WILLIS, K.G. (1974) Transport in rural areas, in Whitby, M.C., Robbins, D.L.J., Tansey, A.W. and Willis, K.G. (eds) *Rural Resource Development*, London, Methuen, pp. 177–97.

4B Conventional public transport—the railway

4B1 APPLETON, J.H. (1970) Disused railways in the countryside in England and Wales, London: HMSO.

This report, initiated by the Countryside Commission, is a study of disused railways and a set of proposals about alternative uses to which they might be put. The focus is on recreational use. Two important conclusions suggest that the present system for disposing of disused railways does not ensure that the land is put to the most advantageous use in the public interest. Second, that it is wrong for British Rail to determine where the public interest lies; local planning atuhorities appear to be the bodies best equipped to perform this duty.

2 BARRETT, B.M. and MacBRIAR, I.D. (1982) In place of trains. Paper presented at the PTRC Annual Summer Conference, Warwick, July.

The history of rail replacement bus services in the 1960s is a very good example of how not to achieve integration of public transport services. All too often a rail service from a small town (A) to the main railway line at an obscure junction (B) was in competition with a bus service from A to a market town at C. The bus service, running directly to C and passing through the centres of the intermediate villages, tended to carry all of the local traffic; the train only carried the limited number of through passengers who wanted the change on to a mainline train at B. When the inevitable proposal was made to close the branch, this was only allowed to proceed on condition that a rail replacement bus service continued to operate from A to B, serving the inconvenient station sites in between. No attempt was made to integrate the two bus services—for example by running a service via an alternative mainline station. It was not surprising then that after a year or two, the replacement bus service was carrying very few passengers and not earning any money for the bus company. Amidst much self-righteous complaining from rail users who were now driving to C to board the trains, the rail replacement service was withdrawn.

With this sort of scenario in mind, it is not surprising that the public are somewhat unconvinced by suggestions of bus services to replace railway lines. If a service is going to be provided where a railway closes, then it will have to be provided on better terms than those that applied in the 1960s. The authors examine this problem from a marketing viewpoint so as to show how successful services could be introduced in the future.

4B3 BAYLISS, B. (1981) *Planning and Control in the Transport Sector*, Farn-
     borough: Gower, pp. 124–65.

     Chapter 5 of this collection of papers covers railways and subsidy
     policy in three countries (West Germany, Netherlands and Sweden).
     The differences in policy are outlined from the system with the
     highest subsidy level, to that which has an operating profit and that
     which has recently introduced a significant increase in the levels of
     subsidy. The argument is stated that policy objectives could perhaps
     be more effectively achieved through other means and that the cost
     effectiveness of rail subsidies should be assessed.

4B4 CENTRAL TRANSPORT CONSULTATIVE COMMITTEE (1979) Rural rail-
     ways. A report on British Rail's other provincial services, CTCC,
     London.

     This report documents the tenuous existence of the 85 railway ser-
     vices outside the south-east, inter-city and Passenger Transport Exe-
     cutive networks. British Rail policy is roundly criticized and for the
     more rural routes, 'rail-bus' services on the continental pattern, with
     minimal capital expenditure, are proposed.

4B5 CLAYTON, G. and REES, J.H. (1967) *The Economic Problems of Rural
     Transport in Wales*, Cardiff: University of Wales Press.

4B6 COOPER, J.C. and SPAVEN, D.L. (1977) Railways into busways
     won't go: A re-examination of two case studies, Polytechnic of Cen-
     tral London, Transport Studies Group, Discussion Paper 6, March.

     Assesses the validity of the assumptions and costings used by Hall
     and Smith [4B13]. Tests this on two of the six case studies.

4B7 COUNTRYSIDE COMMISSION (1979) Dales Rail—A report of an experi-
     mental programme in the Yorkshire Dales National Park, Report
     CCP 120.

     Reports on a successful experimental project in the Yorkshire Dales
     National Park. The Commission, BR and the National Bus Com-
     pany have combined to work from a basic resource (the Leeds-
     Carlisle spine railway) to provide an integrated public transport
     system which gives access to the Park for recreationists, and access
     to the towns for local residents.

8 DODGSON, J.S. (1977) Cost-benefit analysis, government policy and the British Railway network. *Transportation*, **6** (2), pp. 149-70.

Outlines briefly the history of attempts to deal with the question of the optimal size of the rail passenger network. Considers the social cost benefit case for reducing the present size of the network in Britain and the quantifiable benefits from such a reduction.

9 EVANS, R.D. (1972) Fare revenue and cost-benefit analysis. *Journal of Transport Economics and Policy*, **6** (3), pp. 321-3.

This paper suggests that the Cambrian Coast Line Study ought to have included as a benefit of the line the saving of goods bought with their fare money by people who no longer travel.

0 GB DEPARTMENT OF TRANSPORT (1977) The role of British Rail in public transport, London: HMSO.

The government's response to the first report from the Select Committee on Nationalized Industries, Session 1976-77.

1 GB DEPARTMENT OF TRANSPORT (1982) Study of disused railways in England and Wales—Potential cycle routes, London: HMSO.

The study surveyed nearly 1500 kms of possible routes and has prepared outline notes in 33 separately published annexes on about 1100 kms of practical and potentially useful route. All users are considered as are the costs involved and the necessary conditions for successful implementation.

2 GRIGG, A.O. and HUDDART, L. (1979) An opinion survey of the Yorkshire Dales rail service in 1977. *Transport and Road Research Laboratory*, LR 906.

In order to supplement and compare the information obtained from surveys carried out in 1975, the Laboratory in 1977 monitored the use of 'Dales Rail', a countryside transport and recreation experiment undertaken by the Yorkshire Dales National Park Committee. The experiment involved, for the third year in succession, the re-opening during the summer months of stations on the Settle-Carlisle line for charter rail services, and connecting buses. Questionnaire surveys were carried out amongst rail passengers and motorists during the August weekend when the charter service was running, to obtain people's opinions of the service. The survey showed that for most passengers, Dales Rail provided an opportunity of a trip to the Dales which would not have been made had the charter service not been running, and for two-thirds of its passengers Dales Rail provided their only possible transport to the place they were visiting that day. The preferred mode of transport to the station was private car, although many motorists chose to leave their cars at home and travel to the station by bus. Although Dales Rail does provide the possibility of a modal switch by motorists, it is unlikely to attract large numbers of them or significantly reduce traffic congestion.

4B13 HALL, P. and SMITH, E. (1976) Better use of railways. University of Reading, Department of Geography, Geographical Paper 43.

This study examines the main engineering and economic considerations affecting the conversion of a railway to a road, and the replacement of trains with buses and lorries. The findings are then used to evaluate the conversion of two minor urban lines, three minor rural lines, and one major mainline system. It is found that the return on investment is 30 per cent to 60 per cent yearly for converting the rural services, and at least 210 per cent yearly for converting the urban and mainline routes.

4B14 HARTLEY, J.M. and NASH, C.A. (1980) Management objectives for local rail services. University of Leeds Institute for Transport Studies, Working Paper 132, October.

4B15 HEELS, P. and WHITE, P.R. (1977) Fare elasticities on inter-urban and rural bus services. Polytechnic of Central London, Monograph No. 4, February.

The principal aim of this study was to establish a series of values for fare elasticity for different types of bus service outside major urban areas. A selection of routes were sampled and surveys are described in the Sheffield-Doncaster area and the Morpeth area. The routes were chosen to include inter-urban, rural and small town services, to determine the short and medium term effects of a fare increase. The study was to examine not only the number of journeys, but also the changes in journey length and purpose.

6 HILLMAN, M. and WHALLEY, A. (1980) The Social Consequences of Rail Closures, PSI Report 587, London.

This study provides an examination of the impact on former rail travellers of the withdrawal of rail services in ten areas. A strong sense of grievance and evidence of hardship is revealed, but the study was clearly only a partial one: economic data are scanty and it would have been useful to have information on 'control' areas which retained or never had rail services. The ten case studies were chosen from a list of 47 rural lines closed since 1968. Documentary and statistical information on these lines was classified to ensure that the ten lines finally selected were broadly representative of the different characteristics of rural lines. Factors taken into account were: whether or not the route was seasonal, the year of closure, the length of line, whether or not it served a mainly local purpose or functioned primarily as a feeder onto the rest of the network, whether it linked two existing sections of the network or was literally a branch of the network, the number of stations closed, the national and, within England, regional location; the population served, and the nature of alternative transport existing and proposed at the time of closure.

7 HOLT, S.R. and WHITE, P.R. (1981) Modelling of interurban passenger demand on the Southern Region. Polytechnic of Central London, Transport Studies Group Research Report 5, March.

The final report prepared for the British Railways Board that aims to develop mathematical models that will replicate passenger flows on cross country rail services.

8 KEEN, P.A. (1978) Rural rail services, in Cresswell, R. (ed) *Rural Transport and Country Planning*, London: Leonard Hill, pp. 139-46.

The future of the train in rural areas is discussed both from a historical perspective and from an economic perspective. The process of contraction should be planned for in conjunction with adequate replacement bus services. The two modes should be viewed in conjunction with the bus being considered as an extension of the rail service.

9 KINSTLINGER, J. (1976) Rail planning: a state viewpoint. *Transportation Research Record*, 582, pp. 50-60.

The purposes and objectives of the Regional Rail Reorganization Act of 1972; its planning requirements; and the planning efforts of the Pennsylvania Department of Transportation, other northeastern and midwestern states, and various federal agencies in response to that legislation are described. Also included are a description and criticism of the report of 1 February 1974, by the US Department of Transportation in response to the rail reorganization act. Attention is focused on the 17-state Conference of States on Regional Rail Reorganization, its formation and purposes, and its adopted resolutions and positions on rail reorganization planning by the US Railway Association. This paper concludes that federal rail planning is defective because it places undue emphasis on abandonment of excess trackage as the solution to the railroad problem and uses fully allocated system cost rather than avoidable costs for evaluation of branch-line viability. The paper points out that federal rail planning has given insufficient consideration to future potential of the rail mode in moving persons and goods and to energy, environmental, and social needs of communities for continued rail service. Attention is focused on the harmful effects on competition and efficiency that may arise if federal rail reorganization efforts lead to one large single reorganized entity serving the entire northeast-midwest region.

4B20 MILLER, J.J., BAUMEL, C.P. and DRINKA, T.P. (1977) Impact of rail abandonment upon grain elevator and rural community performance measures. *American Journal of Agricultural Economics*, 59, pp. 745-9.

The results of this research indicate that cooperatives located on abandoned rail lines do not die but continue to grow. These findings were justified both from data and statistical analysis, and from a series of case studies. The impact of rail abandonment on rural communities in America is negligible.

4B21 NASH, C.A. (1981) Government policy and rail transport in Western Europe. *Transport Reviews*, **1** (3), pp. 225-50.

This paper presents evidence showing that the performance of Western European railways in terms of market share, traffic trends and support requirements varies greatly, and seeks to discover how far such differences may be accounted for by government policies. It is found that in the passenger sector, the prices charged and the mix of services operated are very influential in determining both market share and support requirements, and that these decisions are almost entirely conditioned by government policy. Performance in the freight sector, which is much more commercially oriented, is more readily explained in terms of geographical differences, which result in some countries having far more suitable traffic for rail transport than others.

22 OLDFIELD, R.H. and TYLER, E. (1981) The elasticity of medium-distance rail travel. *Transport and Road Research Laboratory*, LR 993.

This Report describes further analysis of British Rail's 'National Passenger Accounting and Analysis System' data to estimate demand elasticities with respect to rail fares, following a preliminary report of results obtained from a study of passenger flows between 60 towns and central London termini, over distances up to 120 kilometres. A fresh analysis of an enlarged data base (consisting of the original 60 flows plus a further 80 flows) using a modified form of analysis has estimated mean fare elasticities for season, cheap-day and full-fare, tickets of -0.50 ± 0.07, -0.65 ± 0.06 and -0.20 ± 0.04 respectively, although the errors on the means probably overstate the accuracy of these estimates because systematic errors may well be present. The latest analyses showed that the estimated elasticities were independent of the size of the passenger flow and of distance from London, except in the case of cheap-day trips where the greater the distance travelled the more elastic the journeys. Journey-time elasticities were estimated for two stations in the Western region served by the High Speed Train; both values were found to be about -0.7 ± 0.3 for off-peak travel. The reduction in mean journey time during the peak, however, was too small to enable elasticities to be estimated. A service frequency elasticity of 0.6 ± 0.3 was obtained for season ticket travel from just one of the stations.

23 RICHARDS, K. (1972) The economics of the Cambrian coastline. *Journal of Transport Economics and Policy*, **6** (3), pp. 308-20.

This paper is a critical analysis of the cost-benefit study by the Ministry of Transport of the Cambrian Coast Line. The Report on that study was published in 1969. It is important in the development of cost-benefit analysis of railways in rural areas, since it may be taken as a model for subsequent analyses of loss-making rural train services. It ought to be accurate, both conceptually and statistically, since any mistakes may lead to possible closure of other railways where society would benefit from their retention, and vice versa. In fact the Minister announced in December 1970 that the subsidy to the line was to be withdrawn, and a closure proposal followed soon after.

There are reasons to believe that the Report does in fact contain both conceptual and statistical errors. In this paper only one part of the analysis is considered: the case in which the line would be retained for ten years. The criticisms apply, however, to the other two cases considered in the official study: retention of the line indefinitely, and retention of only the Machynlleth/Barmouth section for a period of ten years.

4B24 SAMMON, JP. (1979) Life without the railroad: economic effect of rail abandonment on the community. *Transportation Research News*, 85, pp. 5–6.

This paper reviews an assessment, made by the Staff Studies Group of the Association of American Railroads, (AAR), of the economic impact on those communities that may lose rail service because deregulation might make easier the abandonment of light-density lines that serve them. Rather than depend on projections that may be biased by assumptions, the method used was to examine the impacts on communities in which rail service had already been abandoned. Several case studies were examined of various communities between 1920 and 1975. It was concluded that there is little adverse community impact attributable to the loss of rail service. The studies have found many instances in which the postabandonment community impacts were positive. Findings show that branch lines are seldom an important part of community economic activity and that other economic factors are more responsible than rail branch-line service for shaping the future of a local economy. Many branch-line abandonments simply marked the end of a series of unfavourable local economic events. The shock of abandonment often forced local communities into the realization that long-standing adverse economic trends had to be reversed if they were to prosper. Shippers often found that switching to other transport required a reorganization of their distribution patterns—a change that resulted in reduction in their total operating costs. Local trucking also provided added local employment and purchases of fuel, meals, and supplies that did more to stimulate the local economy than had the former rail branch-line operation.

25 SIGALOV, M.R. (1980) Railroads as a base for the economic development of sparsely populated regions. *Soviet Geography*, **21** (1), pp. 1–14.

The role of railroads in northern development is cast in a conceptual framework and illustrated with reference to Siberia and the Canadian North. It is suggested that railroads work in conjunction with several types of base cities in fostering northern development. Rear support bases, advanced support bases and local bases are distinguished, and their functions described. The territorial organization of development bases changes over time as transport construction proceeds. As new east-west railroad main lines arise, the rear support functions once exercised by base cities on a more southerly line may be transferred to new base cities on a more northerly east-west line. An example in Siberia would be the transfer of rear support functions from the Trans-Siberian railway to the BAM railway.

26 SMITH, E. (1978) Better use of railways—comments and rejoinders. University of Reading, Department of Geography, Geographical Paper 62.

27 STARKIE, D.N.M. (1979) Allocation of investment to inter-urban road and rail. *Regional Studies*, **13** (3), pp. 323–36.

Returns on marginal projects influence the allocation of resources in the UK between trunk roads and inter-city rail. However, the basis of these returns is not consistent and their use is unlikely to result in an efficient allocation. A review of pricing policies for the two trunk modes suggests both a similarity of basic structure and an opportunity for extending in general terms the allocation principles of rail to the comparable road sector. Broad calculations are derived comparing avoidable costs and revenues for inter-urban road and rail in 1975. Changes in public expenditure patterns since the mid-70s indicate an efficient allocation might be achieved by the turn of the decade. Comments and rejoinders to this paper are made by Button and Nash in Volumes 14 (4), pp. 333–9 and 15 (2), pp. 143–6.

4B28 STEER, J.K. and HOLLINGS, D. (1982) The Mid Wales rail and air transport study. Paper presented at the PTRC Annual Summer Conference, Warwick, July.

Mid Wales is a relatively inaccessible area of Britian where transport costs are a substantial factor in determining the economic and social well-being of the area. The study of the region's non-road based transport system was undertaken in 1981 on behalf of the Development Board for Rural Wales and the Councils of the Counties and one District in the region.

The aims of the study are described: they were orientated towards establishing how the role of the railways serving the region could be enhanced and whether there was a case for developing aviation facilities. Surveys were undertaken in the region, and the findings are presented. The fieldwork comprised a programme of depth interviews with senior management in commercial, industrial and academic institutions in the region, and surveys of travel habits and attitudes amongst key client groups in Aberystwyth and Newtown.

The development from these research results towards a cohesive rail and air transport strategy for the region is described with reference to the technical options available, in respect of low passenger volume aviation services and secondary railway routes. The strategy was advanced both as an investment plan and as a marketing programme. Aspects of the inter-relationship between the provision of improved public transport services and regional development were explored and the implications for provision of tourist plant are described.

4B29 SUNDEN, E. (1981) Low fares experiment pushes capacity to the limit. *Railway Gazette International*, May, pp. 383-6.

In the first year of the Swedish State Railway's low fares policy, it attracted 25 per cent more passengers and an increase of 30 per cent in passenger-kms. The passenger fleet will be increased by 15 per cent (1979-84) to cope with the increased demand and the low fares policy will be maintained until the late 1980s. New changes in travel patterns are expected with the introduction of the high speed train.

4B30 TURNOCK, D. (1979) Legacy of Beeching. *Geographical Magazine*, January, pp. 265-7.

The closure of unprofitable railways has made available vast areas of land and many redundant buildings throughout the country. A study of derelict railways is presented with a focus on the current and possible future uses of these facilities.

31 WARREN, W.D. (1982) Changes in American intercity rail transportation: 1950–1980. *Transportation Quarterly*, **36** (1), pp. 145–60.

The assessment and evaluation of modal split in the intercity passenger market is the basic objective of this study. Important elements of the quality of service are the speed, convenience and prices charged, and these are discussed, with a focus on the speed element. There are serious problems facing Amtrak and the energy question, as yet unresolved, may provide the only hope for salvation.

32 WHITE, P.R. and WILLIAMS, S.R. (1976) Modelling of cross-country rail passenger trips. Proceedings of the PTRC Summer Annual Meeting, Warwick, July.

This paper is concerned with passenger-flows between smaller urban areas, generally over cross-country lines that are peripheral to the Inter-City network. These routes are generally heavily subsidized and often there has been a lack of investment in them over recent years at the expense of the major trunk routes, so that their quality is often inferior to that of Inter-City services. It is these lines that are perhaps likely to be closed first should there be a decision to cut down the size of the BR network. The main objective of this modelling work is to establish demand elasticities for such variables as journey time and frequency, as well as the derivation of interchange penalties, and then to go on to suggest the policy implications of the results.

4C Unconventional public transport

C1 ABKOWITZ, M.D. and OTT, M.T. (1980) Review of recent demonstration experiences with paratransit services. *Transportation Research Record*, 778, pp. 13–18.

Findings from a review of recent paratransit projects sponsored by the Service and Methods Demonstration programme of the Urban Mass Transportation Administration are summarized to identify lessons that have been learned and that may be transferable to other communities that are considering establishing paratransit services. Paratransit activities are reviewed according to three service concepts: demand-responsive transport, brokerage, and ride-sharing. Based on a comparative analysis of project results, several operational and institutional findings are reported. The subject areas include quality of service, user response, operating costs, service substitution, agency role, participation of the private provider, fleet purchase, maintenance policies, and regulatory and institutional barriers to implementation. The major implications of the research effort are summarized, and transferable lessons that may be of interest to communities considering paratransit implementation are identified. Because the discussion is limited to government-sponsored projects, it may not be completely representative of all paratransit operations that currently exist in the United States.

4C2 ADAMS, D.E. (1981) Post-bus for rural passenger transportation and rural mail delivery: an idea whose time has come. *Transportation Research Record*, 797, pp. 76–9.

Rural areas have a growing need for public transport, but service is declining due to high costs and diminishing subsidies. The US Postal Service faces similar problems with its rural service. A number of European countries faced similar problems and have solved them, to some extent, by combining public transport with mail deliveries. Several studies have shown that this approach may be successful in this country. The possibility of reducing the cost of providing both services by combining them demands experimentation.

4C3 AEX, R.P. (1975) Demand responsive transit and the integration of D/R systems with traditional transit. *Transportation*, **4** (4), pp. 419–28.

This paper provides a background of the development of demand-responsive transit in small communities in the USA. It also backgrounds traditional transit in metropolitan areas of the United States and outlines its deficiencies in terms of today's urban sprawl and in terms of today's society in metropolitan areas. Urban sprawl has developed city-like areas around big cities, but with lower population densities, highways and roads were built, and cars were mass-produced. These new populations have never had an alternative to the private car.

Today's society includes an ever-increasing number of senior citizens and handicapped persons; senior citizens find it difficult to get to fixed-route bus stops, handicapped persons have difficulty in boarding regular buses and wheelchair persons cannot even get on board. Particular emphasis is placed upon the examination of the development of demand-responsive transit in metropolitan Rochester, USA, and a Demonstration Project, sponsored by the Urban Mass Transportation Administration of the United States Department of Transportation. The paper also examines and makes reference to the results of integrated transit in Regina, Saskatchewan, Canada.

The Demonstration Project has several key objectives, the principal one of which is the integration of demand-responsive transit with the fixed-route element of traditional transit. Other important objectives of the demonstration are the balancing of peak and off-peak service so as to improve the overall utilization of resources, increase transit coverage, regular (not special) service for the elderly and the handicapped, the utilization of a computer in dispatching, digital communications, and marketing and promotional techniques.

C4 AEX, R.P., ZIEGLER, E.W. and BOYNTON, C.H. (1974) State of the art of demand-responsive transportation. *Transportation Research Board*, SR 154, pp. 3–8.

This group of short papers discusses demand-responsive services and the techniques used to provide them. Particular systems are described for illustrative purposes.

C5 ALTSHULER, A. (1976) The Federal Government and paratransit. *Transportation Research Board*, SR 164, pp. 89–104.

The recent upsurge of interest in paratransit has raised a number of important federal policy issues and seems likely to raise a great many more in the years immediately ahead. This paper is an exploratory effort to identify several of the most important of these issues and to review significant experience to date. It is organized into six sections: definitions, current federal activity, taxis and paratransit, paratransit and conventional transit, labour protection, and summary and conclusion.

4C6 BAILEY, J.M. (1979) Tertiary public transport and public transport
planning. Transport Studies Unit, Oxford University.

The components discussed are the ambulance services, social service
transport, education transport and voluntary transport (works' buses
are excluded). The paper shows that tertiary public transport is a
small, but significant part of public transport, investigates planning
methodology and discusses the practical role of tertiary services in
county public transport plans. Although the relative number of trips
by tertiary public transport is low, it attracts high levels of public
expenditure and can offer large benefits to people who have no
alternative means of transport. The author suggests that its efficiency
could be improved, and that better integration and coordination
with public transport as a whole could be achieved. Results from
several experimental schemes are examined, and suggestions are
made for future research.

4C7 BAILEY, J. and GARDEN, J. (1979) Making the most of community
transport. *Surveyor*, **154** (4557), pp. 15-16.

Reviews the conference on community transport and examines the
success of the new initiatives under a variety of headings. These
include the differences between the urban and the rural situation,
the efficient use of limited resources, cooperation between various
organizations and the institutional barriers that may operate. It was
concluded that if some form of public transport were to continue in
rural areas then a broad and flexible planning approach is required.

4C8 BALCOMBE, R.J. (1979) The rural transport experiments: a mid term
review. *Transport and Road Research Laboratory*, SR 492.

This report describes the background to the government's programme of rural transport experiments (RUTEX) and its organization. There were fifteen experiments, in Devon, North Yorkshire,
Dyfed and Strathclyde, each of which incorporated at least one of
five unconventional features: community transport; small vehicles;
demand-responsive operation; dual-purpose services, and feeder services. The experiments are described in detail, together with results
obtained by the end of 1978. A number of tentative conclusions are
presented, and the future research programme is outlined.

Fifteen experiments were run and included community transport, small vehicles, demand-response, dual-purpose services and feeder services. The objectives of the experiments were to evaluate: the scope for solving rural transport problems within the existing legislative framework; the usefulness of forms of transport outside that framework; the modifications to the licensing system to permit such forms of transport; the effect on existing transport networks. Special legislation, the Passenger Vehicles (Experimental Areas) Act, 1977 was introduced to allow the experiments to take place. It allowed small vehicles to operate similarly to buses without Public Service Vehicle licences, Road Service licences or section 30 permits.

A Steering Committee for the whole project was formed. Four areas were designated with a working group responsible for detailed arrangements within each. Areas for experiment were centred on places that had no transport facilities or that had suffered recent cuts or that were about to face cuts.

Five different operational features can be identified: voluntary effort by local residents in organizing and operating community transport services; using small vehicles where demand is small and/or roads are narrow; arranging routes (and in some cases schedules) according to pre-booked demand; carrying passengers on vehicles making regular journeys for other purposes; linking remote areas to the main public transport network with feeder services.

Where transport services have been poor or non-existent for a long time people adapt and accept. Most people have the use of a car even if only as a passenger so it is unlikely that bus services will be introduced. Where buses are withdrawn there is usually a demand for them but where the service is increased the take-up is small. Demand-responsive services are fairly easy to operate because the demand is not very high.

9 BALCOMBE, R.J. (1980) Rural transport experiments: the Northallerton Hospital Transport Service. *Transport and Road Research Laboratory*, SR 552.

The Northallerton Hospital Transport Service was part of the Government's programme of Rural Transport Experiments (RUTEX). It was a demand responsive shared hire-car service to hospital from two areas containing some 10,000 households. The provisions of the Passenger Vehicles (Experimental Areas) Act 1977 were used to authorize drivers to collect separate fares from passengers. The service operated in the morning and afternoon from Monday to Friday and in the evening from Monday to Thursday. On average 10 return vehicle journeys were made each week and 15 passengers made return journeys, but more than one half of vehicle journeys were made with a single passenger. Without the service 16 per cent of the passengers would have foregone the journey, a further 8 per cent did not know how they would have travelled; the remaining passengers could have made other arrangements. The average passenger spent 80 minutes at the hospital and travelled 31 miles; the average vehicle journey length was 48 miles. Twenty-two per cent of costs were met from revenue, the remainder (£4.50 per passenger journey) by the Department of Transport. The County Council and the Women's Royal Voluntary Service attempted to organize a self financing social car service to be introduced at the end of the experiment but so far (December 1979) not enough drivers have been recruited.

4C10 BALCOMBE, R.J. (1980) Summary and Conclusions. The Rural Transport Experiments. Proceedings of a symposium held at the Transport and Road Research Laboratory, Crowthorne, SR 584, pp. 94–103.

The RUTEX programme consisted of some fifteen experiments each of which is the subject of a detailed report. Each of the previous papers in this symposium has been concerned with some particular aspect of rural transport, and is based on material drawn together from various experiments across the country. The purpose of this paper is to emphazise the points already made and to combine them so as to show what the research as a whole has revealed about the problems of rural transport and their solution. But it is slightly more than a distillation and blending of the previous papers: a few facts and thoughts which did not fit conveniently into any of them have also been added.

It was recognized from the beginning that the experiments would be of little use, even as demonstration projects, unless the problems they were designed to solve were clearly understood. Major surveys were therefore undertaken to discover how people travelled about in rural areas, and what difficulties they encountered. In this respect RUTEX followed several previous studies, but it differed from them in one very important way: the surveys were followed by experi-

mental public transport services designed to help with local problems. As well as yielding valuable operational and financial information, these services, or rather the use made of them, were complementary to the surveys. In many cases the experimental services
provided opportunities for far more journeys than were actually
made, but this ensured that anyone who really wanted to use the
services could do so. The journeys actually made are therefore a
much better guide to what people want or need than can be inferred
from hypothetical questions asked in a survey.

1 BALCOMBE, R.J. (1980) Demand responsive bus services in rural
areas. Proceedings of a symposium held at the Transport and Road
Research Laboratory, Crowthorne, SR 584, pp. 40–60.

Most of the experimental services of the RUTEX programme have
been operated to a greater or lesser extent in a demand responsive
manner—that is routes and possibly schedules have been adjusted
from day to day in accordance with the requirements of individual
passengers. There are two main reasons for operating public transport in this way: to make services accessible to a wider section of the
public than that living near fixed routes; and to make more efficient
use of vehicles by increasing loadings and reducing dead mileage.
    The simplest and the best known example of demand responsive
transport is the taxi, but in recent years buses operating in a taxi-
like manner—commonly known as dial-a-ride—have received considerable attention. In urban areas, while taxi services continue to
prosper, dial-a-ride has been gradually abandoned: the cost of system control heavily outweighs the advantages, if any, of flexible
routing. But in rural areas conditions are different: generally those
without private transport can ill afford taxi fares; and the bus frequencies are such that it is possible to organize pre-booked dial-a-
ride services without elaborate control systems. This paper concentrates on demand responsive bus services, although occasional reference is made to car services to illustrate extreme cases.

2 BALCOMBE, R.J. and DREDGE, A.S. (1980) Community transport.
Proceedings of a symposium held at the Transport and Road Research Laboratory, Crowthorne, SR 584, pp. 61–78.

Reviews the concept of community transport as it relates to the
Rural Transport Experiments. Several car schemes are outlined to-

gether with the Exe Valley Market Bus and a preliminary assessment
is made of their respective costs and benefits. It concludes that community car schemes have greater scope than community bus
schemes.

4C13 BANISTER, D.J. (1983) Community transport for rural areas—panacea or palliative? *Built Environment*, **8** (3), pp. 184–89.

The development of the community concept has provided one possible lifeline to rural areas without bus services. This paper concentrates on the community bus and outlines the institutional and organizational environment within which initiatives can be taken.
Examples are selected of the limited cases in rural Britain and these
are juxtapositioned with the extensive network of Buurtbuses in the
Netherlands. The approach adopted is more systematic and the
community bus is seen as an integral part of the rural transport
scene not an adjunct to it. Questions are raised as to whether the
community concept which relies on extensive use of volunteer labour
is a long term alternative to the public provision of transport services, or whether it is a further stage in the demise of rural public
transport.

4C14 BARKER, W.G. (1979) An analysis of transit and paratransit options
for the elderly and the handicapped. North Central Texas Council
of Governments, January.

4C15 BAUTZ, J.W. (1975) Subscription service in the United States. *Transportation*, **4** (4), pp. 387–402.

In recent years impressive, and sometimes spectacular, results have
been achieved in attracting peak period commuters to reliable and
convenient express bus service. This paper deals with special subsets
of express commuter service, the subscription bus and subscription
van. Subscription service is extremely popular in places where it has
been attempted for commuter trips over 10 miles in length or to
suburban work locations. The service works well in areas that do
not have sufficient density for fixed route, fixed schedule transit.
Most subscription services are organized by private groups often in
the face of restrictive regulatory, legal and institutional constraints.
The fact that they have been successful indicates a huge potential

for commuter subscription services if they were offered as part of the transportation system for an urban area.

The paper describes several types of subscription bus and subscription van services. Where possible cost and revenue data are presented for comparison purposes and recommendations are made to improve the climate for the growth of subscription service. Although the role of subscription service will be to complement and supplement other transit services, it can have a significant impact on commuter travel and should be seriously considered as part of any urban transport system.

6 BLUNT, J. (1976) Do-it-yourself village bus. *Countryman*, **81,** Summer, pp. 86–90.

Describes a scheme in operation in Norfolk in which the National Bus Company supplies the bus, the local community supplies the volunteer drivers and the county council supplies a grant. Apart from this bus service, access to shops, doctors, work and so on is impossible for anyone without a car. Despite this fact the scheme has not received much support and special shopping, theatre and other excursions have been organized to encourage support.

7 BOVY, P.H. and KRAYENBUHL, V. (1978) Introductory report in Paratransit. Report of the 14th Round Table on Transport Economics, European Conference of Ministers of Transport, Paris. See ECMT [4C33].

8 BREUR, M.W.K.A. and VERDONCK, W. (1978) Rufbus, Retax and Bustaxi: three European systems of demand-actuated public transport. *Traffic Engineering and Control*, **19** (6), pp. 287–91.

The article describes three European systems, Rufbus, Retax and Bustaxi, of demand-actuated public transport. The Rufbus system developed by Dormer is intended for rural areas and offers transport between bus-stops in the area of Friedrichshafen. There is no schedule or fixed route and the destination is always reached without passenger transfer. A trip request can be made either by telephone or by a trip selector at the bus stop. The vehicles used are 20-seater Mercedes 0303D buses in which route information is displayed on a terminal in front of the driver. The Retax system developed by MBB is designed for urban areas and also offers transport between bus stops, the route being determined by trip requests from microprocessor-controlled trip selector units. Although initial trials were carried out using the Steyr Citybus, the network now uses a Volkswagen bus with a capacity of 20 passengers. This system features a display showing the next stop as well as the number of passengers to be picked up. The Retax system is controlled by a PDP 11/70 computer. The demand-actuated bustaxi system developed at Delft University of Technology uses selectors connected to the control centre by leased telephone lines. Bus drivers are informed of the route to be followed by digital mobilophone transmission. The system is designed to handle trip requests in urban areas of up to 1500 requests/h. The most important difference between the Bustaxi and the two West German systems is the algorithm used to allot passengers to the vehicles. The differences in the algorithms and operating systems are discussed.

4C19 BRITTON, F. (1977) *Paratransit: An International Survey of Innovative Bus, Taxi and Automotive Transit Arrangements*, Paris: Ecoplan.

4C20 CANADIAN DEPARTMENT OF TRANSPORT (1978) Feasibility study of the mobility club concept in rural and small urban areas. Department of Transport, TP 1489.

This report documents a feasibility study of the Mobility Club concept as applied to a small city and a rural area. The purpose of this overview is to examine the concept in a slightly broader perspective so that results of the study can be interpreted in the context of other geographic areas. The Mobility Club was conceived as a means of providing door to door, demand responsive transport to the handicapped at low cost. The Mobility Club has two distinctly separate driver and user groups, and can handle many trip patterns for a variety of purposes. Because of its flexibility, the club can be tailored to incorporate features that make it adaptable to the needs of a particular locality and/or particular groups. Having examined the Mobility Club concept within an urban and rural environment, it was decided that the rural application looked more attractive at the present time. A cost estimate for the rural application showed that potential yearly deficits were within the range of local funding. Key elements of the implementation plan for the local demonstration project include the establishment of intergovernmental and community responsibilities; clearance of relevant licensing or insurance constraints; planning of organizational infrastructure; establishing a tentative start-up data and service period; administration of a monitoring programme; and evaluating the system following the end of the service demonstration period.

21 COE, G.A. and FAIRHEAD, R.D. (1980) Rural travel and the market for public transport in RUTEX areas. The Rural Transport Experiments, Proceedings of a symposium held at the Transport and Road Research Laboratory, SR 548, pp. 3–18.

The rural transport experiments (RUTEX) were set up to test ways of dealing with transport problems in rural areas where demand for public transport is too small to be served by conventional bus services. Before the experiments were introduced a comprehensive household and travel survey was made; this identified the nature and scale of the problem in each experimental area, provided information about the travel patterns of different groups in the community and made it possible properly to assess the effects of the experimental services on these rural communities. This paper provides background information to the experimental services. The nature of the experimental areas is described, the main findings of the survey are given and compared with similar statistics for the whole of the United Kingdom reported in the National Travel Survey (NTS), and the effect of age, social factors and car and licence ownership on trip making in the RUTEX areas is examined. Finally the rural transport problem and the market for any additional public transport in the RUTEX areas is considered.

22 COOK, A.R. (1979) Paratransit resource guide. Oklahoma University, School of Civil Engineering and Environmental Science, Oklahoma.

23 COOK, A.R. and BARB, C.E.J. (1979) Paratransit case studies: overview. Oklahoma University, Urban Mass Transportation Administration Summary Report.

The report is one element of a set of curriculum materials to support university class and professional short course training in local paratransit planning. In an attempt to capture some of the diverse elements of paratransit and move toward a synthesis of paratransit development, the authors have developed five case studies of local paratransit organizations which have successfully implemented paratransit services. They encompass a broad range of modes, market applications, and institutional structures. Each case study was developed around a common analysis framework, and all facets of service development were investigated. The purpose of this overview is principally to introduce the analysis framework for these case studies and provide pertinent historical background information. It also summarizes the case study experiences, and comments on technology transfer in paratransit service development. In addition, the case study experiences are compared with national statistics and experiences.

4C24 CUTLER, M. (1981) Procurement of small transit vehicles. *Transportation Research Record*, 831, pp. 48-55.

Two aspects of the procurement process for small transit vehicles are described: financing and the bid process. The following financing sources are discussed: federal transport programmes, the Farmers Home Administration, leasing, private financing, non-transport-specific federal programmes, and coordination of vehicles secured from different sources. Although all potential sources of federal funds are generally becoming increasingly limited, there are a number of alternatives to federal transport programmes. In addition, new creative financing methods are being developed in the private sector. Given today's funding realities, coordination of existing programmes and vehicles is essential. Federal procurement requirements are described, and the bid process is followed through from advertisement, preparation of bid documents, and prebid conference to evaluation of bids. Suggestions for contract provisions in such areas as warranty, delivery, inspection, life-cycle costing, and the timing of the process are provided.

4C25 DAVIS, C.F., GROFE, W.H. and STEAHR, T.E. (1981) An analysis of the potential for dynamic ridesharing in a low-density area. Connecticut University, Storrs, Urban Mass Transportation Administration, Final Report UMTA-CT-11-0001-81-1, June.

This report reflects the view that there is a significant reserve of capacity in the highway private car system that could be tapped through ridesharing. The authors suggest that, within limits, not only can the transport system adapt to travel patterns, but travel patterns can be adapted to the transport system and this adaptation can take place within the constraints established by patterns of our daily activities. It is also suggested that implementation of a ride-sharing programme such as described in this report would be simple and relatively risk-free. This research deals with activity patterns and their relation to travel needs in a rural area in eastern Connecticut (10-town Windham Planning Region). Of specific interest is the commonality of trip-making and the flexibility of activity patterns in both spatial and temporal terms. After identifying activity patterns, the research examines the inherent flexibility of these patterns and the potential for ridesharing is quantified using a series of scenarios defined by a set of assumptions regarding such items as participation rate, period of simulation and operational characteristics. The simulation using either the status quo occupancy or 4-person carpools reveals a broad range between a minimal reduction in vehicle miles of travel (3 to 4 per cent) given in existing attitudes and the maximum reduction in vehicle miles of travel (40 per cent). The results suggest that it would be reasonable to expect reductions between 12 and 25 per cent given the degree of willingness to participate evidenced in the questionnaire response.

26 DEVON RUTEX WORKING GROUP (1978) Rural transport experiments: the Exe Valley market bus. *Transport and Road Research Laboratory*, SR 427.

The Exe Valley Market Bus serves an area to the north-west of Tiverton in Devon, where two conventional bus services were withdrawn because they were too uneconomic for local authority support. It is a 'community minibus service', organized and driven by local volunteers (trained to the necessary standard for PSV drivers' licences), operated on a demand responsive basis. The route taken by the bus on any day depends entirely on the passenger list which is made up from casual bookings (made the previous evening) and regular passengers; it has proved possible to estimate passenger pick-up times with an accuracy of ±5 minutes.

In the first half year of operation, the bus carried an average of 81 (one-way) passengers per week; double the number carried on the previous conventional bus services. Some 40 per cent of the passengers lived at least one kilometre from the previous bus routes. Revenue has covered operating costs, but made only a small contribution to the initial costs of vehicle purchase and driver training; some additional income may be raised from private hire and excursions.

4C27 DEVON RUTEX WORKING GROUP (1979) Rural transport experiments: the Mid-Devon lift giving scheme. *Transport and Road Research Laboratory*, SR 525.

The Mid-Devon Lift-Giving scheme permitted motorists to accept payments from passengers in private cars in a designated area, in advance of the general car sharing provisions contained in the Transport Act 1978. It was the only such 'General Authorization' in the Government's programme of Rural Transport Experiments (RUTEX). An assessment of the scheme is presented. The designated area contained only limited conventional public transport facilities, and lift giving was already prevalent. Few residents felt themselves to be experiencing important transport difficulties, either before or after implementation of the scheme. The Authorization had little effect on car-sharing habits in the area; few lift givers wanted payments, and few residents had been inhibited by the previous legislation. Some difficulties were identified concerning the matching of potential lift receivers with possible lift givers; those needing lifts were reluctant to ask for help, but car drivers had difficulty knowing when lifts were required. The relevant provisions of the Transport Act 1978 are likely to have been similarly ineffective in comparable areas elsewhere; organized car schemes may offer a better way of improving rural mobility.

4C28 DEVON RUTEX WORKING PARTY (1980) Rural transport experiments: the Taw valley car scheme. *Transport and Road Research Laboratory*, SR 570.

The Taw Valley Car Service was a commercially operated shared hire car scheme designed to fill gaps within an existing public transport network. It offered residents an improved choice of destinations and of days of travel by making feeder connections with existing services, and it offered a local facility. The area was large, and was divided into separate operating zones. Operators were found to be in limited supply, and the scheme was not established in the whole of the designated area. The service operated reliably, but patronage was low. Lifts and direct conventional buses catered for most requirements at the site, leaving only residual scattered demands. Many of the car journeys were for important purposes, such as medical appointments, but most trips would have been made somehow in the absence of the service, and only about one-fifth of trips resulted in an extra bus or train journey. The low demand resulted in little car sharing, poor vehicle utilization, and consequently poor financial performance. During the second phase of the scheme direct revenue covered 13 per cent of total costs, with indirect generated revenue on other services equivalent to roughly a further 6 per cent of costs.

29 DEVON RUTEX WORKING GROUP (1980) Rural transport experiments: South Exmoor car service. *Transport and Road Research Laboratory*, SR 579.

The South Exmoor Car Service was a voluntary car service with unpaid local volunteers arranging lifts with volunteer drivers. Lifts were permitted anywhere within the area and to a limited number of destinations outside it, some only for medical purposes. No journeys were allowed which competed with the limited existing public transport. Drivers were paid at two different mileage rates; one for journeys they would have made anyway and a higher rate for special journeys. An average of about eleven one-way trips were made each week at a cost of just over £2 in subsidy. All the active volunteers were residents of two of the five parishes in the area as were all but three of the 53 users. The main reason for this localization of the services is considered to be the lack of suitable organizers in the non-participating parishes. Lift giving was the most common form of transport for those without cars before the experiment, which effectively extended lift opportunities by providing a booking system. Demand for additional public transport was so small and dispersed that only a voluntary car service could satisfy it at reasonable cost.

30 DINEFWR RUTEX WORKING GROUP (1979) Rural transport experiments: the Welsh schemes. *Transport and Road Research Laboratory*, SR 507.

Three public transport experiments were conducted in Wales as part of the RUTEX programme, all based on Llandovery in Dyfed. This report describes the planning, operational and financial aspects of the experiments. The three schemes complemented each other and existing services, and had the objective of improving transport provision by means of low-cost options making efficient use of existing resources. The three services were as follows: a postbus served two routes, and operated in typical fashion, providing a service most suitable for shopping and personal business trips. The experimental provision of a two-way Saturday service attracted very little patronage. Secondly spare capacity on four schoolbus routes was made available to the public. These routes were only available during term-time, and attracted only a small group of users, but they were able to cater for certain work journeys, and were provided at very low cost. Finally a voluntary car service was provided over the whole designated area, organized and operated by the Women's Royal Voluntary Service. The service was free to passengers, but available only for 'essential' purposes. Despite some uncertainty about permissible purposes, the scheme provided a valuable service, and coped economically with dispersed and unpredictable demands.

4C31 DIRKSE, G.J. (1980) De bustaxi voor landelijke gebieden, een oproepgestuurd openbaar vervoersysteem. Symposium computer en openbaar vervoer, Delft, May (in Dutch). (The bustaxi for rural areas, a dial-a-ride public transport system.)

4C32 DOHERTY, M.J. and SPARROW, F.T. (1983) The mobility enterprise: a new concept in personal transportation, *Journal of Advanced Transportation*, **17** (3), pp. 279–300.

A Mobility Enterprise is a new transporation concept aimed at increasing the productivity of the automobile through use of mini-micro automobiles in conjunction with a shared fleet of intermediate and full-sized vehicles. The main objective of the Enterprise is to provide a better matching of vehicle attributes to trip requirements and still maintain the personal freedom that seems to be so highly valued by the American driver. While this concept was presented in detail at the 1982 Transportation Research Board Meetings, this updated report provides a view of the progress that has been made in taking the Mobility Enterprise from an innovative concept to an actual experiment. The majority of the information presented in this paper deals with methods for observing consumer attitudes, design-

ing the actual Mobility Enterprise, and methods for measuring mini/
micro automobile performance.

33 EUROPEAN CONFERENCE OF MINISTERS OF TRANSPORT (1978) Paratransit. ECMT Round Table 40, Paris.

A comparison with the rural situation as this report has deliberately
confined its comments to the urban situation. However it does cover
the general definitions and typology together with an extensive bibliography.

34 EWING, R.H. (1979) Demand responsive transit: shifting gears.
Traffic Quarterly, **38** (1), pp. 83–98.

Demand responsive services provide a basic service for the general
public at a reasonable cost and this paper describes how this can be
achieved without a loss in service quality. It draws on a survey of
16 demand responsive systems in four states—most of the examples
are from the urban context but conclusions can also be applied to
rural innovations.

35 FLEISHMAN, D. and BURNS, I. (1981) Can the postal bus play a role
in providing rural transportation? *Transportation Research Record*, 831,
pp. 90–6.

In the search for new approaches to solving the rural transport
problem, one approach that has been proposed and investigated in
the United States, and has seen widespread application in Europe,
is the 'postal bus'. The postal bus concept basically involves the
transporting of passengers in vehicles that are also engaged in the
distribution and collection of mail along designated routes. The
feasibility of the concept in terms of the nature of operational and
institutional requirements and potential barriers is examined. The
overall conclusion is that the integration of mail and passenger transport appears to be a feasible approach to providing passenger service
where none currently exists and/or for achieving greater efficiencies
in the provision of both types of service.

36 FRØYSADAL, E. (1976) Drosjebuss i eidskog. Institute of Transport
Economics Report, Oslo, April (in Norwegian).

Description of a dial-a-ride demand responsive transportation system (using taxicabs) in a rural area with 1000 inhabitants. The results of a year's trial operation are summarized in which each of the six operational areas was served by taxi once a week.

4C37 GB House of Commons (1978) Innovations in rural bus services. A House of Commons Select Committee report on nationalized industries, HC Paper 635, London: HMSO.

Evidence was collected in the summer of 1978. The Committee examined: the type of vehicle used, community buses, the role of County Councils, the Market Analysis Project (MAP), pricing and regulation, financial structure, the role of the Department of Transport, and the general performance of the NBC. The Committee made seven recommendations, most of which concerned co-operation between the various bodies involved. It was felt that more radical proposals should await the findings of the Rutex schemes which had only just started and the overall tone of the report was aimed at reducing costs rather than providing an extended service.

4C38 Glassborow, D.W. (1978) Rural bus services—an assessment of current experiments, in Cresswell, R. (ed) *Rural Transport and Country Planning*, London: Leonard Hill, pp. 161–68.

This paper looks at the wide range of alternative public transport systems that are available for use in rural areas—from the conventional bus, the minibus, the midibus, the post bus, the school bus to the community bus.

4C39 Greening, P.A.K. and Jackson, R.L. (1982) Minibus pooling in Great Britain: legal and economic aspects. *Transport and Road Research Laboratory*, SR 726.

Minibus pooling involves a group of workers getting together to use a minibus to get to and from a common place of work, and sharing its running costs (including depreciation and insurance) between them. The study is based on a review of US experience and a consideration of the potential for application in the UK. It seems to be an attractive alternative for long distance journeys (over about 15 miles) but there are not many of these in the UK.

4C40 Grimmer, M. (1978) Dial-a-Ride systems in Great Britain, in Paratransit, 14th Round Table on Transport Economics, European Conference of Ministers of Transport, Paris, pp. 65-86. See ECMT [4C33].

41 GUBBINS, E. (1979) A guide to community transport. Paper presented at the Conference on Public Transport Planning, Loughborough University of Technology, September.

The HMSO publication with the same title is outlined both in terms of what it sets out to achieve and the means by which community transport schemes can be established [2A22].

42 GUNNARSON, S.O. and OLSSON, L. (1981) Transport service with minibuses: the village bus at Ingarad, Chalmers University of Technology, Sweden, Monograph (in Swedish).

Low density areas in suburbs or in the countryside are missing sufficient base for a satisfactory support of public transport. Most of the inhabitants are therefore bound to use their own cars. With regard to energy saving it is important to find solutions to this type of transport problem. The objective is to test how minibuses (maximum 8 passengers, normal driving licence) can be used for local transport service. This demonstration project started in October 1980, at Ingared, (180 households, 40 km north east of Goeteborg). The service includes commuting to/from the railway station. The drivers are recruited voluntarily by a traffic committee and one-third of the households are more or less involved in this transportation cooperative. The number of commuters is about 15 per day and about 75 children are transported per week. The energy saving has been estimated as 1000 litres/month for this area. The community bus is, from March 1981, integrated in the Goeteborg region transport and its monthly passports and tickets are valid for both local and regional trips.

43 GURIN, D.B. (1976) Paratransit in small communities and non-urbanised areas. *Transportation Research Board*, SR 164, pp. 154-6.

This overview which focuses on the inter-relation of urban mass transportation administration (UMTA) policies that promote paratransit and that foster mobility improvements in small towns and rural areas, contrasts various federal programmes with one another and with non-federal efforts. Federal guidelines that are currently being formulated for a new small-town assistance program are introduced. Legislation is being considered to permit UMTA to provide operating assistance in non-urbanised areas having fewer than 50,000 residents. Precedents for waiving costly labour protection agreements have been established, especially those pertaining to paratransit programmes involving non-profit organizations. The proposed guidelines for UMTA's small-community programme, relate to funds, the apportionment of resources, the administration of the funds, the availability of capital funds, and the requirements for eligibility. Questions that arose during the development of the preliminary guidelines are listed.

4C44 HAWKER, M.E. (1977) Social transport, in Symposium on Unconventional Bus Services, Summaries of Papers and Discussions. *Transport and Road Research Laboratory*, SR 336, pp. 29–30.

Rural social transport schemes have been formed in rural areas by groups of owner drivers under Local Authority auspices. The services (organized by the Women's Royal Voluntary Service) are available for visits to doctors, dentists, opticians or health centres, for visits to friends in care or hospital and for the collection of prescriptions and medical supplies. Some schemes also provide a feeder bus service and a social function. It is a requirement that there is no alternative transport available or that the trip cannot be made at some other time. Drivers are paid a mileage rate for the service offered.

4C45 HOEY, W.F. (1976) Dial-a-ride in the context of demand responsive transportation: a critical appraisal. *Transportation Research Record*, 608, pp. 26–31.

Dial-a-ride service has become one of a number of possible demand-responsive small-bus transport systems. A comparison of several systems suggests that a well-marketed fixed-route bus system can be far more cost effective than dial-a-ride in low-density areas. The concept of demand-responsive public transport should be broadened to include well-planned fixed-route transit. Dial-a-ride appears to have greater value for special-need groups (eg elderly, handicapped) and at times when fixed-route transit would be uneconomical. Better integration with fixed-route elements is essential.

46 KARASH, K.H. (1976) Analysis of a taxi-operated transportation service for the handicapped. *Transportation Research Record*, 618, pp. 25-9.

This paper analyses the demand for and cost of a taxi-operated special transport service for the handicapped. Gross hourly cost is found to be $6.74 for regular taxi service and $8.62 for lift-equipped vans. About 1.5 per cent of the population would need the special service and about one-fifth of the handicapped need the special vans. Demand for this service would take years to develop but after approximately five years, demands of 1.4 trips/week/eligible person could be expected. The net cost of such a service for a standard metropolitan statistical area of 3 million people would be approximately $11 million/year. The net cost of service is very sensitive to the fares charged, to limitations on trip purposes served, and to the advance notice requirement.

47 KEITH, R.A. and SKINNER, R.E. (1977) Paratransit prospects—filling a gap. *High Speed Ground Transportation Journal*, **11** (3), pp. 245-59.

Paratransit is shared riding and it consists of many forms of transport service between conventional public services and the private car. Disappointments with early dial a ride services should not confuse the main issue, namely that paratransit has the potential for growth in the next 20 years whilst conventional services may not.

48 KIRBY, R.F. (1975) Paratransit: a state of the art overview. *Transportation Research Board*, SR 164, pp. 37-45.

This overview summarizes a study of paratransit undertaken by the Urban Institute of the UMTA and FHWA. It pointed out that the different forms of paratransit cannot be distinguished simply by the different types of vehicles involved. Rather, the paratransit forms are differentiated by the type of transport services the vehicles provide. The same vehicle can provide dissimilar services under different operating arrangements. Buses, for example, are most commonly used for line-haul service with fixed routes and schedules. But the same vehicles might just as easily be driven by a designated passenger who picks up fellow workers and delivers them by express from outlying areas to a plant or office parking lot. Similarly, a regular vehicle might function as a rental car or be used with a driver to provide demand-responsive, jitney, or exclusive-ride taxicab services. The more critical distinction is not the physical features but rather the use of the vehicles under certain terms and arrangements.

The study grouped the various paratransit forms according to their major service characteristics: those in which travellers hire or rent a vehicle on a daily or short-term basis and operate it themselves; those in which a traveller calls or hails a vehicle such as a taxicab, demand-responsive bus, or jitney; and those in which travellers prearrange ride sharing such as car pools and subscription vans and buses.

4C49 KIRBY, R.F. and BHATT, K.U. (1975) An analysis of subscription bus experience. *Traffic Quarterly*, **29** (3), pp. 403–26.

The term subscription has been applied to a variety of specialized bus services tailored to serve urban travellers for the journey to work. They can be provided by all types of vehicles, from taxicabs to large buses. Although most experience has come from the urban situation their flexibility may also make this form of unconventional transport suitable for application in suburban and rural areas.

4C50 KIRBY, R.F., BHATT, K.U., KEMP, M.A., McGILLIVRAY, R.G. and WOHL, M. (1974) *Paratransit—Neglected Options for Urban Mobility*, The Urban Institute, Washington, DC.

4C51 KOCUR, G., ZAELKE, D. and NEUMANN, L. (1977) Feasibility study of shared-ride auto transit, Cambridge Systematics Inc and Department of Transportation, Washington, DC.

4C52 KROGH, F., PEDERSEN, P.O., and ULSTRUP JOHANSEN, C. (1979) Kollektiv trafik i tyndt befolkede omrader: udvikling, struktur og planlaeggning. Suc, Esbjerg, Denmark (in Danish).

4C53 KROPMAN, JA. and PETERS, H.A.J. (1982) De buurtbus: bijdrage aan de leefbaarheid in kleine kernen, Instituut voor Toegepaste Sociologie, Nijmegen (in Dutch). (The buurtbus: contribution to the liveability in small villages. A basic report and a summary were published.)

4 KUTTER, E. and MENTZ, H.J. (1979) Verkehrliche auswirkungen der einfuehring eines bedarfsgesteuerten bussystems. *Strassenverkehrstechnik*, **23** (1), pp. 10–15 (in German). (Impact on traffic of the introduction of a dial-a-ride system.)

5 LOCAL GOVERNMENT OPERATIONAL RESEARCH UNIT (1976) The subscriber bus: a new way of financing rural transport, LGORU, Manchester, November.

This report deals with the principle of a subscriber bus. It gives a fictitious example, dealing with the announcement of service cuts, correspondence between the county council and bus company, the public meeting, setting up the association and first-year results.

6 LUGTON, J. (1980) Dual purpose transport. Proceedings of a symposium on the Rural Transport Experiments held at the Transport and Road Research Laboratory, SR 584, pp. 79–93.

Four schemes involving the use of dual purpose transport were included in the RUTEX programme. This paper summarizes their performance and assesses the scope for future developments. The findings from the four experiments are examined in the first part of the paper, followed by a consideration of how the dual purpose mode would have performed at the other Scottish 'RUTEX' sites. The third section considers selected operational aspects of these services which the experiments showed were important and finally, the scope for the introduction of such services elsewhere is considered.

7 MARIN, R.L. and OPPERMANN, M.C. (1976) Rural public transportation: Alternative systems. *Transportation Research Record*, 619, pp. 5–7.

Alternative transport systems for rural areas which use either existing vehicles or the purchase of new vehicles with a wide range of operating and capital costs are examined. Systems requiring new equipment include: A demand responsive system; fixed route system; feeder system; subscription service system; rural family transport system; and institutional commuter vans. Systems using existing vehicles include: Neighbour compensation system (the owner of a vehicle shares rides with a neighbour who does not have access to a vehicle); volunteer driver and vehicle system; leased personal vehicles; social service provider system; group trips (charger service); intercity bus system (would provide transport on a fixed-route and fixed-schedule basis within a rural regional setting); and a combined school bus system. The authors conclude that having some form of public transport available, people who were previously restricted in their travel opportunities would be able to make trips to obtain education and employment to increase their income, and would have more freedom to travel because they would no longer be dependent on other individuals for transport.

4C58 MARTIN, P.H. (1978) Comparative assessment of unconventional bus services. *Transport and Road Research Laboratory*, SR 387.

The report discusses the analytical assessment of unconventional bus systems and its role in the planning and operating of public transport. Quantitative assessment criteria are considered with particular emphasis on their financial and social implications. An example is presented of the use of the fare as a method of achieving these different objectives and is used to indicate a modification to cost benefit analysis to take some account of the incidence of the costs. The influence which the costing method and the vehicle size have on the assessment are discussed and the results of the analysis are applied to indicate the general applicability of various unconventional forms of operation, such as dial-a-bus, minibus, jitneys and subscription services.

4C59 MARTIN, P.H. (1978) Costs of operating dial-a-bus, minibus and conventional bus services. *Transport and Road Research Laboratory*, SR 409.

A comparison is made of the costs of operating dial-a-bus, minibus and conventional bus services. The costs are based on the standard NBC costing of the experimental dial-a-bus service in Harlow and the fixed route services which succeeded it, but are analysed in such a way as to pertain to the general question of whether to operate minibuses or conventional buses. It is concluded that, although a minibus fleet can be operated at about 80 per cent of the cost of a fleet of conventional buses, small vehicles generally cannot be employed during the peak hours. Thus even an off-peak minibus service must bear the full standing costs of the vehicles. This effect more than offsets the lower unit cost of the small vehicles for the operation of off-peak services. Because of their small capacity, it is unlikely that minibuses could achieve sufficient productivity to cover their operating costs from revenue. The necessary provision of spare vehicles was found to represent a high standing cost for the operation of small minibus fleets. In addition, the control costs for a small dial-a-bus service resulted in costs of between 25 and 65 per cent more than an equivalent minibus service. In all cases, the resource costs of operating a bus service were found to be greater than the operator's costs.

60 MILEFANTI, D.C. (1978) Government rural transport experiments, in Cresswell, R. (ed) *Rural Transport and Country Planning*, London: Leonard Hill, pp. 169–78.

Sets out the reasons behind the RUTEX experiments and outlines the actual areas that have been selected, together with the administrative arrangements.

61 MISNER, J. and WAKSMAN, R. (1976) Service and cost characteristics of small-community transit: a tentative overview of operational results. *Transportation Research Board*, SR 164, pp. 143–53.

This report is divided into four sections: the first covers the range of goals that may motivate the initiation of transit service in a small community and the service characteristics that can usually be achieved and this is followed by a summary of the factors that determine operating costs and those that are subject to management and control. Fare structures, fare collection procedures, subsidy levels, and the relation between ridership and revenue collection are outlined in the third section and a brief summary of the main conclusions is made.

62 McANGE, T.R. and BOWEN, S.P. (1981) Transportation survey and rideshare matching model for rural communities. *Transportation Planning and Technology*, **7** (1), pp. 67–72.

A simple and flexible low technology rideshare matching model was developed for a rural area. A brief survey form provided information on distance to work, fuel consumption and currently used transport mode in conjunction with information on employment location and work schedule. The model developed used a computerized system for proximity matching of potential ride shares and an existing computer program with detailed modifications was used for data analysis. Unlike other rideshare matching programmes, this model relies on grouping by community names to match riders.

4C63 McKELVEY, D.J. and WATT, R.S. (1978) Innovative approaches to rural transportation. *Transportation Research Record*, 661, pp. 1–6.

This paper identifies innovative approaches to rural public transport at federal, regional, state and local levels, but there is no attempt to evaluate them. Examples include federal and regional task forces; state assistance with planning, management, funding and cash-flow, coordination, and insurance; and local level approaches to service provision, cost savings, revenue sources, coordination, user side subsidies, maintenance, and promotion.

4C64 NATIONAL CONSUMER COUNCIL (1978) Rural rides. Experiments in rural public transport—a consumer view, National Consumer Council, London, December.

This report contains a fairly comprehensive review and analysis of the various experimental and unconventional services introduced in recent years in rural areas with poor or non-existent public transport. Sufficient services now exist to make it possible for the National Consumer Council to assess their role, relative merits, costs and effectiveness from which it makes specific recommendations on aspects of policy and operation. The report also discusses current accessibility problems and the results of a survey of areas where unconventional schemes are in operation; it also examines the legal, administrative and technical details of operation. Types of service included are postbuses, works and school buses, community buses, social car schemes, commercial mini-buses and hired village buses, all of which the authors emphasize, are seen as a supplement, and not as a substitute, to normal bus services.

Analysis of accessibility problems reveals that it is the pensioners, housewives and those with low incomes who suffer most, and continuation and extension of services will be necessary for these people who are unlikely to benefit from any rise in car ownership. Examination of the legal and administrative aspects reveals the need for considerable voluntary effort and time, as well as the specialist skills needed to operate services such as community buses—so far only eight of these exist. The report shows that both postbuses and community buses can be economic and provide an appropriate service. But the viability of further services of both kinds depends on the continuation of the New Bus Grant, due to be phased out in the early 1980s. A strong plea is therefore made for its retention. This is but one example of how a combination of legal, administrative and financial factors can affect the viability of a particular service; the provisions of the 1978 transport Act, which changed the law on payment for lifts and brought in Public Transport Plans, may modify relative costs and improve co-ordination. All the services reviewed have some potential in appropriate situations; the Council strongly recommends that assessment should not be based solely on costs, but on 'a method of evaluation that is both consumer-oriented and related to the cost of provision' thus taking into account the needs of those using the service.

5 NATIONAL COUNCIL OF SOCIAL SERVICES (1977) Rural transport: new developments in rural transport provision.

This new edition attempts to give both current information and details of the progress of the schemes covered in the first report and new schemes that have been developed in the intervening period. It does not claim to be comprehensive, but it does give an indication of the numbers and variety of conventional and unconventional transport initiatives in rural areas.

6 NORMAN, A.J. (1978) The role of voluntary transport, Paper presented at the International Conference on Transport for the Elderly and the Handicapped, Loughborough University of Technology, pp. 164–70.

The paper briefly describes the various forms of supplementary transport which may be available to elderly and handicapped people and goes on to discuss the disparity of levels of provision in different parts of the country and the practical problems which arise if vehicles are shared. It is suggested that vehicle sharing and driver recruitment needs to be patiently built up by an organizer attached to a Council of Social Service or other nonspecialized voluntary body and that this is a role which demands considerable initiative and ability. Another approach is to publish an annually updated list of the supplementary transport resources available in an area (examples are given). Actual and possible changes in the law under which supplementary services operate are described and it is suggested that these may have an important effect on the supplementary transport scene. Other major changes may be set in motion by the reappraisal of the organization of social services transport which many local authorities are now undertaking and experience has shown that one factor in this reappraisal is a radical review of the proper relationship between public, statutory and voluntary transport. The paper concludes by suggesting that there is an urgent need to appoint experienced and able people (perhaps recently retired professionals working on a part-time basis) to investigate these matters and to promote the co-ordination of voluntary transport resources at District and County level.

4C67 NORTH YORKSHIRE RUTEX WORKING GROUP (1979) Rural transport experiments: the Ripon flexibus. *Transport and Road Research Laboratory*, SR 491.

The Ripon Flexibus served an area to the west of Ripon in North Yorkshire where it replaced three bus routes. It was operated by a National Bus Company subsidiary using a standard bus which made specified diversions from a circular route on demand. A high level of service was offered initially. During the first phase of the experiment the level of service in the areas as a whole was nearly doubled. However, the improved service carried virtually no more passengers and after seven months the level of service was reduced to a similar level to that offered before the service began, but with the diversions retained. The reorganization had little effect on patronage (on average 160 trips per week), and the diversions were little used and did cause some problems with timekeeping, even though the booking of detours caused few problems. If this phase of the experiment had been operated for a full year, the revenue would have covered 28 per cent of the costs, and the corresponding proportion for the second phase would have been 53 per cent, compared with 45 per cent for the original bus service.

4C68 NORTH YORKSHIRE RUTEX WORKING GROUP (1980) Rural transport experiments: the Northallerton hospital transport service. *Transport and Road Research Laboratory*, SR 552.

The Northallerton hospital transport service was a demand responsive shared hire-car service to hospital from two areas containing some 10,000 households. The provisions of the Passenger Vehicles (Experimental Areas) Act 1977 were used to authorize drivers to collect separate fares from passengers. The service operated in the morning and afternoon from Monday to Friday and in the evening from Monday to Thursday. On average 10 return vehicle journeys were made each week and 15 passengers made return journeys, but more than one half of vehicle journeys were made with a single passenger. Without the service 16 per cent of the passengers would have foregone the journey, a further 8 per cent did not know how they would have travelled; the remaining passengers could have made other arrangements. The average passenger spent 80 minutes at the hospital and travelled 31 miles; the average vehicle journey length was 48 miles. Twenty-two per cent of costs were met from revenue, the remainder (£4.50 per passenger journey) by the Department of Transport.

9 NORTH YORKSHIRE RUTEX WORKING GROUP (1980) Rural transport experiments: Colsterdale car service. *Transport and Road Research Laboratory*, SR 589.

The Colsterdale Car Service was a commercially-operated shared hire car scheme. Part of the experimental area had a weekly bus to Ripon, but it did not conveniently serve Masham, the nearby town. The car service offered all the residents of the area a daily connection with a Ripon bus in Masham. During the second phase of the scheme a connection with the weekly Bedale bus and a daily additional departure from Masham were offered. The service operated reliably, but patronage was low. During the second phase it doubled to, on average, five one way trips per week. Car ownership was high and lifts catered for most requirements at the site, leaving only a scattered residual demand. Many of the car journeys were for shopping and social visits and most would have been made somehow in the absence of the service, and only about one-tenth of trips resulted in an extra bus journey. The low demand resulted in little car sharing, poor vehicle utilization, and consequently poor financial performance. During the second phase of the scheme direct revenue covered 20 per cent of total costs, with indirect generated revenue on the connecting bus service equivalent to roughly a further 8 per cent of costs.

4C70 NORTH YORKSHIRE RUTEX WORKING GROUP (1980) Rural transport experiments: Hackforth and district car sharing service. *Transport and Road Research Laboratory*, SR 594.

The Hackforth and District Car Sharing Service was set up in North Yorkshire in October 1978 as part of the Government's programme of rural transport experiments (RUTEX). Lifts were permitted anywhere within the experimental area (which consisted of three neighbouring parishes) and to a limited number of destinations outside it, which were chosen so that the service did not compete with bus services in the district. Drivers were paid at two different mileage rates, one for journeys they would have made anyway and a higher rate for special journeys. An average of three one-way trips were made each week of which over a third were to provide connection with a bus service. The demand was small compared with the existing level of lifts obtained in non-household cars of about 340 trips per week. The cost of running the service in the first nine months of operation was £5.61. The small demand makes it clear that only a voluntary car scheme could satisfy it economically. Users who were interviewed after one year of operation were pleased with the service offered which reflects the hard work and enthusiasm of the local volunteer co-ordinator and committee.

4C71 ORSKI, C.K. (1975) Paratransit: the coming of age of a transportation concept. *Transportation*, **4** (4), pp. 329–34.

Paratransit is a transport concept whose time has come. Well over 100 paratransit services in the United States and Canada testify to the popularity of this concept. Thanks to paratransit many citizens of small communities are enjoying for the first time the benefits of economical public transport service. In larger cities paratransit has placed flexible, personalised transit service within the reach of many persons who earlier had to rely on infrequent and inconvenient bus services.

What precisely is paratransit? What accounts for its growing popularity? And what lies ahead for this form of transport? In this brief overview we can attempt only brief answers to these questions. To gain a deeper understanding of the nature and potential of paratransit the reader is invited to examine the remainder of this special issue, whose purpose is to provide a comprehensive appraisal of this innovative transport concept [4C3, 4C15, 4C75, 4D21].

72 OXLEY, P. (1980) Dial-a-ride: a review. *Transportation Planning and Technology*, **6** (3), pp. 141-8.

Although as originally conceived demand responsive transport (DRT) systems offered a many-to-many capability with complex computerized control, more recent developments have offered simpler, manually controlled, systems. From the introduction of the first UK DRT systems in 1972 it is possible to observe three broad categories of DRT: first generation small-scale services operated without central control; second generation services providing more intensive coverage and with central control; and, third generation services based on the first generation services but operated in rural areas. Tables indicate the periods of operation of such UK systems from 1972-1979 as well as passenger loading and cost/revenue data. The article evaluates the reasons for a number of the systems ceasing operation, as other DRT systems have, once developed, been replaced by conventional stage carriage operations. The continuance of DRT in the UK is seen as one useful adjunct to conventional services as well as the provision of services for particular groups.

73 PERLOFF, H.S. and CONNELL, K.M. (1975) Subsidiary transportation—its role in regional planning. *Journal of the American Institute of Planners*, **41** (3), pp. 170-83.

Improvements in transport development can arise from applications on a broad scale of experiments already under way that are demonstrating some effective new arrangements for transit. This article describes subsidiary transport services, how they can be integrated into existing services and the information requirements.

74 RIMMER, P.J. (1980) Paratransit: a commentary. *Environment and Planning A*, **12** (8), pp. 937-44.

Paratransit services are now seen as a linchpin of unconventional wisdom which also involves trimming conventional transit to the more densely populated corridors and improving the management of the private car. A certain amount of financial support has been invested in these modes. This paper reviews the ECMT paper on paratransit [4C33] and contrasts the different services in both developed and developing countries [6D27]. It concludes with speculation on a possible reciprocal transfer of organizations and technology.

4C75 Roos, D. and Alschuler, D. (1975) Paratransit—existing issues and
      future directions. *Transportation*, **4** (4), pp. 335–50.

Paratransit services bridge the gap between static fixed route transit
and the flexible automobile travel. Paratransit services provide personalized public transport by responding to the needs of individual
markets and users. Unfortunately, fragmentation of the paratransit
sector and institutional and regulatory constraints have prevented
or complicated realization of paratransit's full potential.

The orientation in this paper is not primarily to identify promising
paratransit applications. Rather, it is to examine basic characteristics of paratransit services, fundamental issues unique to paratransit,
existing problems that are constraining paratransit development,
and ways to overcome or minimize existing difficulties. A taxonomy
of paratransit services is proposed so that these systems can be better
related to each other. The institutional environment of paratransit
is examined from the viewpoints of planning, operations and regulation. A primary focus is on integration of various paratransit services and of paratransit and conventional fixed route services. Several proposals are made relating to improvements in existing
services, new service concepts, new institutional arrangements and
service integration.

4C76 Saltzman, A. (1976) Role of paratransit in rural transportation.
      Transportation Research Board, SR 164, pp. 137–42.

Rural travel characteristics are briefly discussed and comments are
made on the growth of public transport in such areas. The economic
efficiency and consolidation of resources related to rural transport
are described. The need for effective managers with entrepreneurial
skills is indicated, and the question of whether to focus on special
services for subgroups of the population or to provide a variety of
services for the general public is considered. Small, person-person-
alized systems providing door-to-door service were first developed in
rural areas by community action agencies. Although the cost per
passenger trip is high (very long trips are being serviced; and the
average load factors are more than 65 per cent) for rural transit,
two important factors indicate that these systems are being operated
at reasonable cost and are quite efficient. The greatest impact on
transport in rural areas will come from finding ways to more efficiently use equipment and labour that various agencies currently

use to provide paratransit services. Regulations that do not allow flexibility in the use of currently available transport funds must be changed. The need is indicated for an academic option at universities that would train students in planning and managing specialized transport services.

77 SCOTTISH RUTEX WORKING GROUP (1979) Rural transport experiments: Blackmount services. *Transport and Road Research Laboratory*, SR 446.

Detailed information about the design, implementation and operation of the Government's first rural transport experiment in Scotland is reported. The experiment comprises an integrated service operated by a 17 seater minubus (the Medwyn Gypsy) and two postbuses. Parts of the minibus route are served on a demand responsive basis. Results of surveys carried out prior to the introduction of the experiment and since its commencement are recorded. Costs of the experimental service are compared with the costs of the conventional bus services which were previously operating in the area. Patronage on the experimental services consists mainly of women and pensioners who do not have a private vehicle belonging to their household. Most trips are for shopping and social purposes.

78 SCOTTISH RUTEX WORKING GROUP (1980) Rural transport experiments: Stair service. *Transport and Road Research Laboratory*, SR 618.

Detailed information about the planning, design and operation of the Stair shared hire car service, one of the Government's rural transport experiments in Scotland, is reported. The experiment involved a shared hire car (a 5-seater saloon), running on Tuesdays and Thursdays as a demand-responsive feeder service. Bus connections were possible from three villages to which the shared hire car ran. Results of surveys carried out prior to the introduction of the experiment and during its operation are recorded. No other services operated in this area and attention is paid to the new demand and revenue generated on existing public transport by passengers who previously travelled by other modes. Most passengers were women, half of whom did not have a private vehicle available during the day. Shopping dominated trip purposes.

4C79 SCOTTISH RUTEX WORKING GROUP (1981) Rural transport experiments: Ruralink service. *Transport and Road Research Laboratory*, SR 665.

Ruralink provided a bus service bwtween Dalmellington and the Cumnock/New Cumnock area, including Ballochmyle Hospital, all in the Cumnock and Doon Valley District in the Strathclyde Region. The service was operated by Western SMT Ltd, using a 14-year-old 27-seat bus, from 11 April 1978 to 30 June 1979. It provided return journeys between Dalmellington, Cumnock and Ballochmyle on Tuesdays, Wednesdays, Thursdays and Sundays. A postbus service was originally planned for the experiment, but when this proved impracticable, Western SMT were contracted to provide the service. At the same time the scope of the experiment was enlarged by tailoring the service more to the requirements of hospital visitors. The service was unconventional in that there were three optional diversions from the regular route, which were made on request; this arrangement was used about three times a week, and worked well. Although the service was well suited to the needs of people without cars making hospital or social visits, overall demand averaged only 210 passengers per week, and revenue covered less than 20 per cent of costs.

4C80 SCOTTISH RUTEX WORKING GROUP (1981) Rural transport experiments: South Ayrshire hospital transport service. *Transport and Road Research Laboratory*, SR 666.

The South Ayrshire Hospital Transport Service was part of the Government's programme of Rural Transport Experiments (RUTEX). It was a voluntary car scheme designed to take patients and visitors from the villages of Crosshill, Kirkmichael and Straiton to hospitals and other medical facilities in Ayr and further afield. It was run by volunteer organizers, who made arrangements for people (who could not conveniently travel by bus) to be taken by one of a pool of volunteer drivers. The drivers were private motorists, who were paid an allowance of 8p per mile; passengers paid fares to the organizers.

During the experimental period (10 July 1978–30 June 1979) the service provided 33 single and 33 return trips. Most of the passengers were elderly, and few had access to private transport. Although the scheme catered for only a small minority of hospital trips in the area, it was appreciated as a valuable aid to those who used it, and the total cost of the service was £90, about one-third of which was recovered from fares. Such schemes, where they can be organized, appear to be the most economical way of catering for the low, sporadic demand for hospital trips in rural areas.

1 SILCOCK, D.T. (1979) Paratransit—the answer. *Journal of the Chartered Institute of Transport*, **38** (13), pp. 417–20.

Transport planners have shown increasing interest in the application of 'unconventional' or paratransit forms of public transport services in situations where conventional rail or stage carriage bus services are not practical. Various experimental bus services have been introduced as exemplified by the UK RUTEX programme. Many developing countries have such transport systems which have developed over a long period rather than as a result of sophisticated transport planning. Mostly privately owned, these systems perform satisfactorily with respect to local conditions and needs. The article describes a number of these minibus and shared-taxi systems and examines their operating characteristics.

2 SMITH, R.L. (1979) Analysis of volunteer drivers systems in rural public transportation. *Transportation Research Record*, 718, pp. 39–42.

The purpose of this study is to evaluate the potential for continuing, and even expanding, volunteer driver systems in rural areas. Case studies of volunteer driver systems in two Wisconsin counties are used to test the hypothesis that volunteer driver systems can be a cost-effective, feasible means of providing high-quality, specialized transport service in rural areas. In addition, the role of volunteer driver systems in relation to paid driver systems that use vans or buses is examined in terms of an optimum mix of service types. Finally, the implications for public policy in the implementation of the rural public transport operating assistance programme (Section 18 of the Surface Transportation Assistance Act of 1978) are examined.

3 TEAL, R.F., FIELDING, G.J., GIULIANO, G., MARKS, J.V. and GOODHUE, R.E. (1980) Shared ride taxi services as community public transit, California University, Irvine, Urban Mass Transportation Administration, Final Report, CA-11-0017-1, March.

This report examines the use of taxi firms as the providers of publicly supported demand responsive transit. These subsidized shared ride taxi (SRT) systems have become the predominant form of general public DRT in California, with 29 such systems now in operation. Based on California's experiences with subsidized SRT, this study presents case reviews of SRT implementation and operation, analyses the issues associated with the development of taxi-based transit services, and evaluates the peformance of subsidized SRT. The major issues concern: service provision, including the institutional reasons for contracting, competition for contracts, and contractual arrangements and their effects; and the consequences for taxi forms of becoming public transit providers, including legal implications, operational changes, labour-management relations, the impact of subsidization, and future plans. SRT performance is evaluated in terms of cost-efficiency and effectiveness and also compared to that achieved by other forms of community level transit.

4C84 TRANSPORT AND ROAD RESEARCH LABORATORY (1977) Symposium on Unconventional Bus Services: Summaries of Papers and Discussions. *Transport and Road Research Laboratory*, SR 336.

This volume contains summaries of the papers and discussion at a symposium which was intended to bring together a wide cross section of those directly involved in dealing with bus service problems, particularly in rural areas (e.g. Ennor [4A18], Hawker [4C44], Carpenter [6A10], Wilkes [6A54]).

4C85 TUNBRIDGE, R.J. (1980) A comparison of optimal minibus, dial-a-bus and conventional bus services. *Transport and Road Research Laboratory*, LR 928.

An assessment has been made of the comparative performance of minibus, dial-a-bus and conventional bus services when operated at their optimal fare and frequency and in the absence of competing stage carriage services. This was effected using previously developed computer models. The three types of service were assessed individually over the same off-peak operating hours at frequencies from two to six buses an hour and the performances of the services at that profit maximizing and net benefit maximizing fares were examined. It was concluded that, when operated at the same frequency, all three services were equally attractive to passengers. The dial-a-bus service, was, however, found to be less efficient and more expensive to operate. None of the services could be operated at a net profit, although the conventional bus approximately covered its costs at a frequency of two buses an hour whilst generating a positive net social benefit. Comparison with an earlier study, where all services were constrained to operate at the same fare and in the presence of competing stage carriage services, showed that the relative performance and efficiency of the optimal services were unchanged; the optimal services however performed better from both financial and social points of view than those to which the constraints applied.

86 TUNBRIDGE, R.J. and HALE, D.M.J. (1978) Comparative assessment of demand responsive and fixed route bus services. *Transport and Road Research Laboratory*, LR 847.

The operation of dial-a-bus, fixed route minibus and conventional bus services in Old Harlow was monitored; details of their operating characteristics, ridership and user characteristics are presented. A quantitative assessment of the services was made by comparing them when operated for the same hours, at the same fares and when costed on the same basis. The fares were normalized using a previously developed demand model. Pair-wise comparisons were made between dial-a-bus and minibus and between minibus and conventional bus. From these it was possible to isolate the influence of service type and frequency respectively, and it was concluded that when operated at the same frequency, the demand actuated and fixed route services were equally attractive to passengers. However, the dial-a-bus service was found to be more expensive to operate, not only because of the cost of control but also because of the higher vehicle requirement which resulted from its lower operating efficiency. The comparative assessment of the fixed route services favoured the low frequency service using conventional vehicles. This was the only one which generated approximately enough social benefit to cover its resourse cost of operation.

87 TUNBRIDGE, R.J. and MITCHELL, C.G.B. (1977) The preliminary design of many to few dial-a-bus services. *Transport and Road Research Laboratory*, LR 789.

Dial-a-bus is a term used to describe a form of demand activated road-based public transport. A common type of dial-a-bus service is one which links a service area to a few major trip attractors. This is known as a 'many-to-few' type of operation and such an operation normally has no fixed routes, bus stops or timetables.

In order to design such a service to operate without fixed stops, a method is required for estimating the time required to collect or set-down given numbers of passengers in a particular service area. This report provides estimates of the distances to be travelled to connect different numbers of collection or set-down points in service areas of different sizes and shapes. This information allows the round-trip time, the required vehicle capacity and hence the productivity of the dial-a-bus service to be estimated for an assumed level of demand. Mean tour distances, and standard deviations have been calculated for three different operating strategies for service areas of a number of sizes and shapes.

4C88 TURNOCK, D. (1977) The Postbus: a new development in Britain's rural transport pattern. *Geography*, **62** (2), pp. 112–8.

The decline of the rural bus service has been one of several controversial themes in the post-war evolution of the public transport system. The introduction of postbus services on the other hand has been increasing at a rate of some 25 operations per year (1972–1975). This paper outlines the background and the dominance of Scotland which has nearly 75 per cent of services, before describing the different types of service. Other features include the ways in which postbuses have been integrated with conventional services and the future. Scottish services alone carry over 100,000 passengers per annum and the conclusion is one of optimism with two strong caveats. First the post office has a primary duty to run a postal service not a public transport service, and secondly success is dependent upon continued financial support.

4C89 US DEPARTMENT OF TRANSPORTATION (1979) Vanpool research: state of the art review. US Department of Transportation Report UMTA-MA-06-0049-79-5, Washington DC.

4C90 US DEPARTMENT OF TRANSPORTATION (1981) Paratransit: technology sharing state of the art review, Washington, DC, 95 pp.

4C91 VANOON, C.C. (1982) The community bus: a double evaluation. *Verkeerskunde*, **33** (4), pp. 187–9 (in Dutch).

After five years experience two reports (one by the Dutch ministry of transport, the other by the co-operating provinces) throw some light on the community bus. This is a minibus system run by volunteers and serving low density areas. There are well-advertised timetables. About 50 projects serve 120,000 people, resulting in 550,000 person trips per year. Some problems: relief buses in peak periods and paid man-power are required by the operating bus companies. Driving proficiency of the volunteers and their overall profile are still unknown.

92 WARD, D.E. (1975) A theoretical comparison of fixed route bus and flexible route subscription bus feeder service in low density areas. Transportation Systems Centre, Cambridge, Massachussetts.

A parametric model was used to test the variation of demand density on the service level and cost of two alternatives systems for providing low density feeder service. Supply models for fixed route and flexible route service were developed and applied to determine ranges of relative efficiency. It was found that flexible route bus exhibited a lower sensitivity of cost to level of service provided than did fixed route bus. Flexible route bus can provide better service at the same or higher level of productivity at all demand levels below about 100 passengers per square mile per hour, except when minimal service only is to be provided.

93 WATTS, P.F., STARK, D.C. and HAWTHORNE, I.H. (1978) British postbuses—service details. *Transport and Road Research Laboratory*, SR 366.

Detailed information about the numbers, types, and characteristics of British postbus services is reported. Postbus operations are varied in character, but services can be categorized according to a limited number of basic types. The results of surveys of examples of the different forms of operation are recorded, and the work of some other researchers is reviewed. It is found that postbuses can, in general, provide practical passenger services which are acceptable to their particular patronage and that patronage consists mainly of women, and pensioners, with no alternative transport, making local trips for basic purposes (such as shopping or visits to doctors). The type of operation most appropriate to this patronage is discussed.

4C94 WATTS, P.F., STARK, D.C. and HAWTHORNE, I.H. (1978) British postbuses—a review. *Transport and Road Research Laboratory*, LR 840.

The recent expansion of postbus services in Britain is discussed, in the light of institutional factors which have affected the development of this form of public transport. Growth of services has so far been patchy, at least partly due to the Post Office's ill-defined role in this sphere. The services which have emerged are varied in detailed character, but some basic types of operation are identified, and the results of user and of operational surveys of examples of the main types are summarized. Services are found to be capable of providing practical and reliable passenger transport, acceptable to those dependent on public transport, without disrupting mail services. The economic aspects of postbus operation are assessed: the total costs of services, and of certain possible alternatives, are investigated, and the financial performance of some existing Scottish routes is analysed. Postbuses rely heavily on subsidies from central government, and may require additional local support, but nevertheless can provide a relatively low cost service, particularly on long routes.

4C95 WHITE, P.R. (1975) A review of alternative forms of rural public transport, in Wilmers, P.H.M. and Moseley, M.J. (eds) Rural Public Transport and Planning, Regional Studies Association, Discussion Paper 4.

This survey of the various forms of rural public transport relates provision to the pattern of demand for rural public transport. The major differences in traffic levels, it is argued, are associated not so much with average population density as with time of day and week. Nonetheless it is considered important to heed the distinct requirements of deeply rural areas (where a partially demand-actuated service may be best), and those of small towns (both for inter-urban links and for local services).

4C96 WHITE, P.R. (1979) An independent review of alternative transport schemes to date. Paper presented at the Conference on Public Transport Plans, Loughborough University of Technology, September.

This paper covers a wide range of alternatives but the focus is on lift giving and small vehicles where the geographical coverage extends over rural and other non-metropolitan counties. The conclusions suggest that alternative public transport services do provide a supplementary service for specific purposes (eg hospital trips) but that they do not offer a replacement for conventional buses.

97 WOOD, K. (1979) Car pooling—Travel to work at an isolated site. *Transport and Road Research Laboratory*, SR 462.

As part of a study of the use of cars in peak periods, staff at an isolated rural workplace were surveyed to determine how they travelled to work. The survey concentrated on the choice between driving alone and car-pooling in which two or more people travel together, taking it in turns to drive their own car and give a lift to the other(s). Information was obtained in two ways: a questionnaire (90 per cent response), and a follow-up telephone survey of car-poolers. Car-poolers came predominantly from urban areas and travelled medium distances (5–25 km) to work, for short journeys the inconvenience of car-pooling is greater than the saving, and at long distances people are unlikely to live close enough together to form a convenient car-pool. The survey results were modelled using a logit model to try to quantify the factors involved. This showed that diverting 1 km was perceived to be about as undesirable as driving an extra 5 km. However, all the model results should be treated with caution as they are subject to large errors and based on data from only one site.

98 YUKUBOUSKY, R. and FICHTER, D. (1974) Mobility club: a grass roots rural and small town transport concept. *New York State Department of Transportation*, PRR 69.

The dispersion of relatively small numbers of people in rural environments is a substantial barrier to collective means of travel, such as conventional bus service or demand-responsive transit. Accordingly, this paper proposes and analyses an approach based on ride-sharing in private cars that might provide significant relief for the problems of rural immobility. This solution, termed Mobility Club, can be implemented within the manpower and financial resources of most small towns and rural communities. Trip desires of carless individuals are matched to the trip-making intentions of persons with cars, by the Mobility Club telephone dispatcher or ride-broker. A companion feature is the method proposed for increasing the number of 'travel friends', ie the number of persons who are well enough acquainted to trust travelling together. This paper discusses the operational, administrative, and institutional aspects of the Mobility Club concept. A case example is presented to illustrate the magnitude of the potential driver-member supply and tripmaking desires of autoless residents in a sample rural and small town environment. Operating expenses, fare structures, and subsidy considerations are outlined. Finally, the paper lists some simple steps to assist individuals who may wish to start a Mobility Club.

4C99 ZIEGLER, E. (1977) Integrating transit and paratransit. *Transportation Research Record*, 660, pp. 66-9.

The declining fit of radially oriented transit to today's more dispersed travel, the recognition of the role of taxis, and the growth of paratransit have led to strong interest in integrating conventional transit and paratransit. This interest has been based on the expectation that, by and large, these services complement each other—particularly that paratransit can serve markets for which conventional service is either unequipped or overly expensive. Policy statements by the Urban Mass Transportation Administration (UMTA), the American Public Transit Association, and the International Taxicab Association support service integration.

However, the emergence of paratransit has raised more options and issues than can be dealt with by using current information. For example, there are a bewildering variety of service options—choices between public and private operators, labour questions, regulatory changes, insurance issues, high costs, and requirements for special services, to name just a few. Moreover, although UMTA activities for specific modes, primarily dial-a-ride and its variations, have been in progress for over five years, research and demonstrations addressing the integration of paratransit and transit only began within the past three years. The Rochester, New York, demonstration began in April 1975; the UMTA areawide demand-responsive transportation projects are just now being started. Definitive results are not yet available, but the lessons from previous experience and research point toward several general conclusions. This paper highlights such tentative results.

4D Private transport

D1 COUNTRYSIDE COMMISSION (1976) Cyclehire: a practical guide. Countryside Commission, Cheltenham.

This guide is designed to help people wishing to set up a cycle hire scheme. It is also a first attempt to summarize the practical findings from the Commission's hire experiments at Clumber Park, near Worksop, and Parsley Hay, in the Peak District National Park.

D2 COUNTRYSIDE COMMISSION (1977) Routes for people, an experiment in rural transport planning. Countryside Commission: Cheltenham.

Describes an experiment carried out in the Peak District National Park which was intended to provide for lorries, recreational motorists and walkers, cyclists and horseriders.

D3 COUNTRYSIDE COMMISSION (1980) Cycle Hire. Countryside Commission, Advisory Series 6.

The experimental cycle hire schemes run in Clumber Park and Parsley Hay since the mid 1970's have found that cycle hire was popular with nearly all age groups. Accordingly in this booklet, the Commission outlines a number of cycle hire schemes which could have any of the following five objectives: first, to provide an attractive recreational activity, second, to transport visitors from other forms of transport to more distant places, third, to ease congestion, fourth, to encourage people to use cycles for recreation, and fifth, to enable those not owning cycles to cycle in attractive countryside.

D4 COUNTRYSIDE COMMISSION (1980) Recreational Cycling. Countryside Commission, Advisory Series 8.

A research programme for the Commission has shown that there are considerable opportunities for further recreational cycling. The booklet lists and describes four design options: making better use of the existing system; adopting the existing system; using other resources; and, purpose built provision.

D5 DONALD, R.G. (1980) Modal split models based on car availability: The application of such models in studies of medium sized towns. *Transportation Planning and Technology*, **6** (3), pp. 149-58.

The paper examines the difficulties of applying a modal split model based on car availability in transport studies of medium sized towns. The urban populations are generally less than 100,000 and represent areas where there are no serious deterrents to car use. These modelling difficulties are illustrated by analysing data from two transport studies carried out in Kent. The awareness of the deficiencies described in the traditional car ownership modal split models has led to the adoption of car availability models.

4D6 EDWARDS, D.A. (1977) Spatial variations in car ownership in rural settlements. Unpublished MSc Thesis, Centre for Transport Studies, Cranfield.

4D7 GALLAGHER, R.W. (1978) Taxis and subsidized programmes in rural areas. *Transportation Research Record*, 696, pp. 82–4.

The taxi industry in rural communities is undergoing scrutiny, especially as it relates to the transport of special groups within a community—the elderly, handicapped, and others who do not have access to cars or to public transit. A major concern of the taxi operators is the survival of small taxi operations of ten vehicles or fewer in communities with populations of 25,000 or less. This paper describes ongoing small-taxi programmes in Lancaster County, Pennsylvania; Houston, Texas; and Indianapolis, Indiana. Possible solutions to the problems of the taxi operator in rural areas, such as direct subsidies, mergers with a centrally located operation, and support through social service agency transport contracts are examined.

4D8 GB DEPARTMENT OF THE ENVIRONMENT (1974) The availability of cars in 1971 with special reference to rural areas in England, PRP 3, London, October.

The study, based on the 1971 Census of Population volume on the Availability of Cars in England and Wales (published in April 1974), was confined to inter-regional comparisons and to intra-regional differences in car availability. The latter part of the study consisted of calculating the percentage rates of car availability in each Rural District in England. The results for households with no car and with two or more cars available were then mapped. An indication of the differences in car availability between urban and rural areas, as a whole, was also obtained and related to the figures for England and Wales.

9 GB Department of Transport (1981) Cycling: A consultation paper. London: HMSO, May.

Outlines the main issues in which the Government can play a role in improving facilities for cyclists. Discusses a number of activities in which the Government is engaged and several new initiatives which it has recently taken or is considering such as the study of disused railway lines to identify which could be made into safe cycle routes.

10 Katteler, H.A. and Kropman, J.A. (1980) Aanbod van fietsgelegenheden en fietsgebruik, Instituut voor Toegepaste Sociologie, Nijmegen (in Dutch). (The relationship between cycling facilities and the use of the bicycle.)

11 Kurth, S.B. and Hood, T.C. (1977) Car-pooling programmes: Solution to a problem? *Transportation Research Record*, 660, pp. 48–53.

Information from 26 car-pool programmes is reported that suggests that appeals to self-interest made through work organizations are more effective than other means of encouraging car pooling because employees of work organizations form a known population with a common destination and, typically, a similar work schedule. It is proposed that such appeals should focus on the benefits of car pooling for the individual rather than on general values such as patriotism. Interviews of selected long-term car-pool participants (two or more years) indicated that work organizations provide a setting in which personal information about potential participants can be obtained and that this information facilitates the formation of car pools. These interviews further suggested that the intimacy of the private car may limit the size of car pools as well as the willingness of some individuals to participate in them. Ride-sharing programmes that present alternative transport modes may be more effective than car-pool matching programmes in changing current patterns of work travel.

12 Lucarotti, P.S.K. (1977) Car availability—the fundamental modal split. *Transportation Planning and Technology*, **3** (4), pp. 203–13.

This paper questions a tacit assumption which underlies the very structure of the concept of generalized cost. The traveller cannot make a choice about travelling by car unless there is a car available to him. It is argued that a large proportion of the observed modal split variability can be deterministically accounted for by this variable.

4D13 MAROTEL, G. and TARRIUS, A. (1979) Expériences de transports collectifs en voiture individuelle en mileu rural. Institute de Recherche des Transports, Paris.

4D14 MITCHELL, C.G.B. (1981) The influence of the car on personal travel. *Transport and Road Research Laboratory*, SR 681.

In virtually every country the number of cars is increasing, although in many the rate of increase has slowed since 1974. Much of this growth must reflect the advantages the car offers its owners, including greater access to activities, and, in some cases, cheaper travel. People who have cars available to them tend to make longer journeys to essential activities, such as work, than do people without cars, and they also make more journeys to discretionary activities such as recreation or social events. There is some evidence that once a person obtains the use of a car, he or she uses the opportunity it provides to develop a way of life that depends upon continuing to have a car available. In a similar way, the increasing availability of cars has allowed the development of towns and the locations of activities in ways that would not otherwise have been practicable. Because of the popularity of the car as a means of transport it is necessary to recognize the difficulties of those without cars as well as problems such as accidents and pollution that cars cause. Some groups of people, such as children, will never have the direct use of a car however many cars there are, and many people cannot afford one. The developing pattern of land use and activities that the use of the car has encouraged is often more suitable to those with cars available to them and can be difficult to serve by public transport. In some countries taxes on car fuel are used to support public transport systems which provide mobility for those without cars. In rural areas which are not suitable for conventional public transport, mobility can be provided by car sharing, lifts and car hire services. It is likely that for elderly and handicapped people the most effective aid to mobility is the motor car, though at present relatively few old or handicapped people do have cars available to them.

5 McCOOMB, L.A. and STEUART, G.N. (1981) The automobile passenger—a forgotten mode. *Transportation Research*, **15A** (3), pp. 257-63.

Current practices in urban transport planning tend to neglect the car passenger. This study shows that a large number of urban trips are made as a car passenger and that the general characteristics of these passengers are similar to transit passengers rather than car drivers. The significance of these findings are discussed in terms of modelling the use of various urban travel modes.

6 NATIONAL SWEDISH ROAD AND TRAFFIC RESEARCH INSTITUTE (1979) Taxi, krav och utvecklings-moejligheter, Kommunikationsdepartmentet, Monograph DSK 1979: 4 (in Swedish). (Taxi requirements and development possibilities.)

The traditional use of taxi is mainly the transport of people to and from railway stations and airports, and transport of people to and from different public places (e.g. places of entertainment, hospitals, etc). The use of taxi as a means of transport in areas such as school children transport, and substitution for time scheduled collective traffic, expecially in rural areas, has lately increased considerably. The dominating business form of taxi transport is one licence one owner, and the owner then has drivers in his employment. Presently there are approximately 9000 licences for taxi traffic in Sweden and only 400 to 500 taxi companies have more than one licence. The taxi companies often run a co-operative local calling station and this organization can effectively cope to a small extent with the fluctuating demands especially in densely populated areas. In the report the author describes alternative company organizations such as: the big company, which would own and control all its taxi cabs and licences, the association of licence holders, and competing taxi companies. The author describes the development of the utilization of taxi cabs in the collective transport, along with the distribution of taxi licences. The possibilities of a collective taxi transport (e.g. jitney services) is discussed along with the simplification of the construction of the taxi fare.

17 PAASWELL, R.E. (1973) Problems of the carless in the United Kingdom and the United States. *Transportation*, **2** (4), pp. 351-72.

An examination of current population statistics shows that in the US more than half of the population is without immediate access to a car, and in the UK more than three-fifths of the population is without access to a car. This phenomenon has been accentuated by national investment in both counties in major highway programmes. The term carless refers to more than just households that own no cars. It extends, in household with cars, to those without licences (old and young), the handicapped, and even the licensed drivers who have no access to the family car when it is in use elsewhere (eg at work). The most severely affected are those in urban areas and especially the urban poor. Transport expenses are limited for the poor when other family expenditures (food, shelter) take a high priority. Once the work trip has been satisfied, money for other trips, for the poor, is not always available. One solution to cost-free travel is pedestrianism (walking), but this too is difficult in urban areas where the pedestrian has been overlooked in favour of the car. Solutions to problems of the carless include dial-a-ride, better public transit, and better design of urban form.

4D18 RHYS, D.G. and BUXTON, M.J. (1974) The rural transport problem: a possible solution. *Town and Country Planning*, **42** (12), pp. 555-8.

In certain rural areas traffic is so sparse and losses so great that subsidies for bus services are not forthcoming. In such areas the social use of the private car, either subsidized or not subsidized, provides the best way to save the public transport network. The social car service in Clwyd is described together with the implications for wider use of such schemes.

4D19 RIIPINEN, M. (1981) Behaviour of pedestrians and drivers on some rural pedestrian crossings. Central Organization for Traffic Safety, Mnograph 42, January (in Finnish).

The report deals with the mutual actions between drivers and pedestrians near and on pedestrian crossings. Children under ten years and the aged had more difficulties in crossing the road. A pedestrian's decision to wait before crossing the road was influenced more by the speed of approaching vehicles than the number of them. The drivers slowed up more often when there was a group of pedestrians crossing, women were more careful on crossing than were men and

young boys between 10–20 years were the most inclined to cross the
road outside pedestrian crossings.

20 WATTS, P.F. (1980) Rural shared hire-cars: a comparative assessment of their potential. The Rural Transport Experiments, Proceedings of a Symposium held at the Transport and Road Research
Laboratory, SR 584, pp. 19–39.

The RUTEX programme included four schemes employing hire cars
provided by commercial operators. This paper reviews the performance of these services, and considers the potential for this mode of
operation at other rural sites. The paper is divided into four main
parts. Firstly, the mode of operation, and its financial aspects, are
described, and secondly, the performance of the four experimental
schemes is summarized. Thirdly, the lessons learnt from the experiments are reviewed and in the final section the potential capability
of shared hire cars for dealing with the different demand patterns at
a number of other rural sites is considered theoretically.

21 WEINER, E. (1975) The characteristics, uses and potentials of taxicab
transportation. *Transportation*, **4** (4), pp. 351–67.

Taxicab transport is a significant segment of urban transport. Taxicabs, along with other 'paratransit' type systems, provide service
with charactistics between the car and mass transport. Consequently, they are well suited to a number of special purposes, and
taxicabs currently serve a wide range of trip purposes by travellers
with varied socio-economic characteristics. Taxicab transport is most
attractive for serving lower density area and off-peak travel particularly where there is only minimal mass transit service. In this
regard, taxicabs are a supplement to conventional mass transit. The
use of taxicabs for collection and distribution functions for both
passengers and freight is gradually being realized and the multiple
use of taxicabs offers advantages of increasing taxicab productivity
and reducing individual trip costs. Many of the problems related to
taxicabs are regulatory and institutional in nature. Unless these
constraints are eased or removed, wider application of taxicab transport, including productivity gains, will be limited.

4E Waterways and freight

4E1 BALDWIN, M. (1980) British freight waterways today and tomorrow, Inland Waterways Association.

Examines freight carried on United Kingdom inland waterways, and suggests that the extent of such transport is underestimated and that government statistics mislead. Certain recommendations are made and the paper also includes discussion on access by sea-going craft to inland waterways, the environmental and economic advantages of using waterways and the role of waterways in European and United States transport systems.

4E2 BRITISH WATERWAYS BOARD (1978) Recreation on inland waterways. BWB Report, Amenity Services Division.

4E3 CORCORAN, P.J. and CHRISTIE, A.A. (1978) Review of the results of lorry planning studies. *Transport and Road Research Laboratory*, SR 381.

The purpose of the review is to bring together the main findings of the lorry planning studies carried out on behalf of the Department of the Environment and the Department of Transport, and to present some general conclusions of assistance to transport planners. The first part of the review summarizes the general conclusions drawn from the studies on lorry planning methods and covers surveys, traffic modelling, evaluation and consultation. The second part discusses the results of a number of studies and draws general conclusions relevant to plans for small and medium towns and conurbations, non-urban lorry route networks, the enforcement of controls and long-term lorry planning measures.

4E4 EUROPEAN CONFERENCE OF MINISTERS OF TRANSPORT (1980) Competitive position and future of inland waterway transport. ECMT Round Table 49, Paris, January.

There is a concern over the fact that the use of economic regulating instruments at the national level has not been as effective as hoped, so that a satisfactory economic situation for inland waterway transport has not been brought about.

The debate in and about inland shipping is now at its height, amongst other things as a result of the following: approaching completion of the Europa Waterway (linking the Rhine and the Danube); profit situation of inland shipping; the infrastructure cost issue; trends in freight rates; amendment of the Mannheim Acts (Supplementary Protocol No 2); and the firm commitment of the European Community in the field of waterway transport. The report summarizes the main arguments on each of these points with particular attention being paid to the Danube-Rhine link.

5 GB DEPARTMENT OF THE ENVIRONMENT (1976) Rural Lorry Uses Study. DoE Research Report 12.

A study of the costs of restrictions on the use of heavy goods vehicles in rural areas, with particular emphasis on re-routing and the use of small vehicles. The analysis is broken down by commodity and the results suggest that certain types of freight are most susceptible— where high volumes are required, where transport costs are high with respect to delivered costs and where there are economies with large vehicles.

6 GB DEPARTMENT OF TRANSPORT (1980) Report of the Inquiry into Lorries, People and the Environment (Chairman A. Armitage). London: HMSO, December.

Considers the cause and growth in the movement of freight by road and of the impact on people and the environment. Reports on how best to ensure that future development services the public interest.

7 GB DEPARTMENT OF TRANSPORT (1981) Lorries, People and the Environment. London: HMSO, Cmnd 8439.

This report examines the environmental and social problems caused by lorries and gives the central conclusion in the Armitage report, which is that the public interest would best be served by maintaining and developing the economic benefit from heavy lorries and at the same time reducing their adverse effects. This white paper sets out the measures with which the government now proposes to initiate this change and describes the government's attitude towards: the trunk road programme (priority to bypasses and motorways) and local roads, routes for lorries, competition between the railways and the roads, noise, vibration and pollution, safer lorries, lorry weights and dimensions, assessment of environmental effects, operators' licensing, enforcement, and speed limits.

4E8 HARRISON, A.J.M. and STABLER, M.J. (1981) An analysis of journeys for canal-based recreation. *Regional Studies*, **15** (5), pp. 345–58.

This paper analyses data from a survey of the amenity use of canals for boating, angling and informal activities; its main purpose is to consider the impact of income on visitors' journeys to the canal. The distribution of visitors between different travel modes is considered; for motorists and pedestrians the distributions of journey distance and time are analysed for each activity. A new model is developed, assuming a rectangular catchment area and a log-normal probability distribution of visitors' leisure expenditure, and it is shown to fit the distance distributions well for all activities. A major conclusion is that Clawson's assumption of indifference between travel expenditure and other costs is not valid.

4E9 KOROMPAI, G. (1975) Inland waterways of the Danube as reflected by using international comparisons. *Acta Geographica Debrecina*, 14–15, pp. 61–79.

The completion of the Europa canal linking the Danube with the Rhenish region will be of considerable importance to countries such as Hungary. Having reviewed the experience of inland waterways in America and Europe the general characteristics of Danubian ports are outlined.

4E10 NATIONAL WATERWAYS TRANSPORT ASSOCIATION (1981) The role of waterways in regional and local planning. NWTA, Planning Paper No. 3.

Reviews transport costs, industrial location, international transport, environmental improvements in respect of noise and vibration, visual intrusion, pollution and safety, and non-transport benefits of water transport.

4E11 NOORTMAN, H.J. (1973) Inland waterways—Their role and significance in European transport. *Transportation Planning and Technology*, **2** (2), pp. 129–44.

This paper begins by describing the waterways in Western Europe and identifies that part of the network which has potential for modern freight transport. Similarly the present stock of barges is summarized, and the two facets are put together to give a total picture of the present volume of trade as in the Netherlands this amounts to ninety percent of all tonne-kilometres transported by inland water road. The Mannheim Act is significant in overall transport policy in Western Europe and its main sections are itemized. Finally some trends are highlighted and break-even point analysis is carried out to determine what distances and volumes it is economic to use inland supply for. The possibilities seem to be good, particularly if further large scale investment takes place.

2 OGDEN, K.W. (1980) Licensing and environmental controls on road freight transport. University of Newcastle upon Tyne, Transport Operations Research Group, Research Report No. 32.

A review and summary of the existing situation in Britain. Examines the historical development of licensing and in particular the introduction of the Operator's licence in the Transport Act 1968, and then reviews the Foster Committee's report (1978) on operators' licences and the recommendations that are made.

3 PRUDHOE, J. and CHRISTIE, A.W. (1981) Effects of a lorry control covering a rural area of Hertfordshire. *Transport and Road Research Laboratory*, SR 679.

A lorry control has been applied, for environmental reasons, to the roads within a rural area of Hertfordshire lying between Hatfield and Hertford. During a 9-hour working day about 140 HGVs (heavy goods vehicles over 3 tons weight unladen), most of them concerned with aggregates extraction or refuse tipping, have been diverted from the roads inside the control area to surrounding main roads. The violation rate is about 30 per cent for HGVs with two axles but virtually zero for vehicles with more than two axles. Although the diverted vehicles now pass more dwellings than formerly it is estimated that there was a net reduction in lorry nuisance to households because of the effect of the higher traffic flows on the busier A-class roads to which the diverted vehicles have transferred. The diverted vehicles now travel an extra 5 km at an extra cost of about £1 on the average one-way trip. The total cost to operators is about £45,000 per annum at September 1980 prices; with full compliance it would be about £53,000.

4 RESKE, D. (1980) Der Rhein-Rhone-Kanal ans regionaler und uber-

regionaler Sicht. *Frankfurter Wirtschafts und Sozialgeographische Schriften*, 33 (in German). (The Rhine-Rhone canal from the regional and extra-regional point of view.)

Discusses in detail the significance of a large capacity canal link between the Rhine and Rhone suggesting that while the link might not be strictly profitable it would have great importance nationally and internationally. This monograph is divided into ten extended sections.

4E15 SELF, G.F. and HEWITT, J. (1979) Design and evaluation of lorry route plans. *Highway Engineer*, **26** (7), pp. 9–14.

Since the 1973 Dykes Act introduced the requirement for county authorities in the United Kingdom to prepare lorry route plans, a number of different approaches have been adopted. This paper describes some techniques developed for the design and evaluation of different lorry route plans at metropolitan county scale, and looks at the possible applications of these techniques elsewhere. Two main aspects are outlined. The first is concerned with ways of objectively defining the 'lorry problem' in terms of social impact, as an aid to quantifying lorry impact and thereby providing a sound basis for developing possible lorry routes. The second aspect is the application of mathematical modelling techniques to the testing and evaluation of different lorry route systems. The paper describes some of the ways necessary to adapt conventional transport models, and discusses the advantages and disadvantages of employing these techniques, with comments on their general applicability.

5   Methods and evaluation

5A Transport and regional development

Traditional views suggest that transport is a prerequisite to regional development and that the infrastructure investment has to take place before growth (Rostow [5A17]). This orthodoxy has been challenged; in his classic paper on the American railways, Fogel [5A5] argued that the gains from the railways were small, that many were premature and uneconomic and that they were only a constituent part of the process of industrialization. The debate continues despite some agreement of the fact that there is an overall correlation between measures of transport investment and development. Some (e.g. Brewell and Richards [5A2]) put the case for mutual support, whilst others (e.g. Botham [5A1] and Parkinson [5A15]) argue about thresholds of accessibility. Transport only assumes a prime importance if the levels of accessibility are low, otherwise factors such as government incentives and policy, and labour availability are more crucial in location decisions.

Perhaps it is difficult to be categorical as transport cannot cause development, but it can act as a constraint on growth. Studies should be specific to examining the evolution of the transport network (e.g. Judge and Button in Britain [5A13] or Irwin [5A12] in the USA), prior to a detailed investigation of the links between transport and development. Some progress has been made here in both developed countries—for example in Austria (Ebner [5A4]), Canada (Wilson *et al.* [5A22]), Finland (Halla [5A10]) and France (Grandjean and Henry [5A8])—and in developing countries—for example in Bangladesh (Tarrant [5A20]) and Ethiopia (Rayner [5A16]).

5B Analysis methods

Most analysis methods for transport have been developed for the urban situation and specific rural transport analyses are mainly applications of these methodologies (Skorpa et al [5B38]). In the United States, a rural highway planning system has been devised (Litz [5B24], Litz *et al.* [5B25] and National Technical Information Service [5B29]). Concerns over the absence of a suitable planning process have resulted in the development of a series of manuals and associated computer programs so that guidelines can be established. These methods cover the collection and updating of road inventory data, adequacy rating manuals and the collection of road traffic information.

A second theme in the application of methodologies has been for large scale land use transport models and accessibility studies. Kau [5B19] has attempted to relate employment location and household density to changes in transport costs through regression analysis and the construction of accessibility indices. Parkinson et al [5B33] have used a before and after analysis to examine the changes in accessibility brought about by the construction of a section of motorway (M25) around London. Other analyses have attempted to discuss rural planning methodology with particular reference to the role and organization of transport (e.g. Lucchini [5B26]), the impact of energy on transport (Newell and Esch [5B32]), and a focus on forecasting methods (Stephanedes and Adler [5B39]).

These macro-based studies have been complemented by a series of specific analyses that cover particular components of the conventional transport planning process. It should be remembered that in rural areas one is concerned with the individual, household or village and not with zones that generate or attract large numbers of trips. So methodology should be capable of adaptation to cope with small numbers and extremely disparate patterns of demand. Particular methods to estimate demand for rural public transport have been developed by Pedersen [5B34], [5B35], Gamble [5B12] and Burkhardt and Lago [5B6]. More traditional methods such as gravity models for trip distribution (e.g. Baxter and Ewing [5B2]) and multiflow assignment methods (e.g. Brooks and Harris [5B4]) have been used in the rural context, as well as the engineering approaches based on traffic counts and flows (e.g. Kaesehagen et al [5B18]). Other researchers have developed novel methods for rural applications based either on attitudinal methods (e.g. Banister [5B1]) or activities (e.g. Jones [5B17]). Probabilistic and simulation analyses also seem to offer some opportunities, particularly where unconventional modes such as dial-a-ride (Gerrard [5B14]) are being assessed. Overall, however, it seems that specific rural transport analysis methods have not been widely researched and that where analysis has taken place, it has been descriptive in nature or it has taken well-tried methods from the urban context.

The possible exception to this observation has been in recreational analysis. A wide range of methods have been applied for short trips (e.g. Huddart [5B16]) and even long distance day trips (e.g. Greening and Miles [5B15]). Estimations have been made of both the levels of demand (Miles and Smith [5B28]) and the actual flows along rural roads (Duffield [5B9]). These types of analyses have been made possible by the availability of traffic information from roadside counts and household surveys.

5C Investment appraisal and evaluation

One of the principal difficulties in any analysis of policy alternatives in rural areas is that of evaluation and the dilemma is one of providing maximum accessibility at an acceptable cost. There is a conflict between the efficiency criteria used in cost benefit analysis, and the social and equity issues. Cost benefit analysis has been extensively used for road evaluation for both trunk routes and bypass schemes (GB Department of Transport Assessments Policy and Methods Division [5C25], Davies and Hunjan [5C17], and Mills [5C48]). Low volume roads provide a slightly different problem as the concern is not primarily with the quantification of user savings but design standards that meet specific levels of traffic (Berger [5C5], Carnemark et al. [5C12] and Koch et al. [5C40]).

The exclusion of the distributional impacts can be overcome through the use of matrix techniques. The two best known are the Planning Balance Sheet (Lichfield [5C44] and Lichfield et al. [5C45]) and the Goals Achievement Matrix (Hill [5C34] and Sager [5C57]). Those items which are not quantifiable can be explicitly treated by weighing the net monetary costs or benefits against the spectrum of other impacts, and their distribution across social groups. So the decision maker is able to choose a 'best' decision alternative judgmentally, but the technique does not show how a decision should be made. The most recent addition to the matrix approaches has been the Leitch Framework (GB Department of Transport [5C21], [5C23]) for trunk road assessment. Here the widest possible framework is used to quantify costs and benefits for each scheme across all groups; monetary values are preferred but otherwise suitable descriptions are made. As with the other matrix approaches more information is presented but it does not follow that investment decisions are made (Beesley and Kettle [5C2] and Yass [5C73]).

Public transport evaluation has been carried out on a financial basis usually on a single route basis through a minimum revenue/cost ratio. No consideration is taken of the system-wide effects, although the Market Analysis Project has attempted to include the whole of the bus network around a town in its evaluation (Bursey *et al.* [4A11], G.B. Department of Transport [2A23]). More recently the emphasis of rural transport planning has switched to the needs of residents and minimum service levels with the implicit assumption that each community should be above this threshold for transport provision (Banister [3B5]). Evaluation of public transport should be part of the wider accessibility question. Individuals or groups who do not come up to the accessibility standards can be identified and the impact of changes assessed. Both the financial and the accessibility implications of any change can be calculated and set against the present costed levels of provision together with the maximum support costs. Various forms of this type of approach have been tested (e.g. Moseley [1A34] and National Consumer Council [4C64]), but two main limitations still remain, namely the willingness to pay on the part of the individual and the degree of accessibility, as one is assumed to be either accessible or not accessible.

Other evaluation issues have also become important within the rural context. These include land acquisition costs and community severance (Bell *et al.* [5C3]), social impacts (Taggart *et al.* [5C67]), environmental issues (Bridle [5C7] and Jefferson [5C38]), conservation (Taitz and Harman [5C68]) and participation in the transport planning process (Bruton [5C8] and Levin [5C42]). Evaluation is itself a vast research area and the references included here are by necessity selective.

In developing countries the World Bank has been instrumental in devising suitable appraisal methods for rural roads (Beenhakker and Chammari [5C1]). As well as design standards for low volume roads and economic analysis, the timing of road improvements and construction, the maintenance of roads and investments in other complementary sectors are all important considerations when resources are limited and interest rates are high (Bulman and Robinson [5C10], Guha [5C27], Ministry of Overseas Development [5C49] and Smith [5C61]). Approaches are required that link transport with other development issues, particularly agriculture (Bovill [5C6] and Hine [5C37]).

5D Energy

Transport is the only sector where there has been an increase in energy consumption and its present share of UK petroleum products is now 40 per cent (Banister and Banister [5D2] and Maltby *et al.* [5D12]). In other countries, consumption levels may have decreased as efficiency has improved (Hartgen [5D10]), but overall levels of travel have increased. Increases in oil prices may lead to short term reductions in demand, but trends quickly reestablish themselves (Mogridge [5D13]). Government policy on energy conservation has not been effective in the transport sector partly because transport is a premium user of oil based products and partly because of the contribution that charges on the road system and vehicles (taxes) make to exchequer revenue (Banister [5D3]).

In rural areas journey distances are greater than their urban counterparts, but as there is less stop-start driving better economy can be achieved and so fuel consumption rates tend to be much the same (Potter and Riekic [5D18]). Perhaps more important is the demise of the rural petrol station as low profit margins and turnover mean that the oil companies are not prepared to support them. Prices are typically some fifteen per cent higher in rural areas and the only means by which many petrol stations survive is that they are multifunctional; for example they operate as a local shop and a petrol station. Recreational travel may be affected in the short term by increases in petrol prices. The evidence here is conflicting, but the general conclusion suggests that more local facilities may be used (Shucksmith [5D20]) for day trips, whilst the holiday traffic going for longer periods is little affected (Sullivan and Picha [5D22]). It is the latter type of travel that provides the greatest income for rural areas.

Research has also focused on future energy consumption as it relates to spatial structure. Energy investment is required in both infrastructure and operations. The energy requirements for space heating, transport, industrial processes and maintenance are considerable. Planning policies could have a significant influence on rural energy requirements (Owens [5D15], [5D16]). Selective concentration which is acceptable in planning terms performs well in energy terms as does concentrated development (Owens and Rickaby [5D17]). Transport and energy are important research issues in rural areas and an agenda is required (Murdock and Leistritz [5D14]) to complement the growing literature on the urban context (e.g. Allen [5D1], European Conference of Ministers of Transport [5D6] and Waters [5D23]).

5E Environment and safety

Environmental considerations are very important in rural areas and manuals have been produced (e.g. De Hamel [5E3]). Decisions have to balance the benefits that accrue to one group against other interests. This is particularly true of rural bypass schemes that benefit residents along the old route in the town at the expense of rural residents who are adjacent to the new road (Mackie and Davies [5E12]). Visual amenity and noise seem to be the two principal issues of concern in rural areas (Clamp [5E2], Harland [5E7] and Huddart [5E8]).

Limited analysis has also been carried out on rural safety, for particular users such as pedestrians (Hale *et al.* [5E6]) or for particular types of rural roads (Glennan [5E5] and Radwan and Sinha [5E14]). The methods used have included simulation studies and multivariate analysis. Improvements in safety are a universal concern and analyses have been made of particular countries. For example Janssens [5E10] in Holland, Jacobs and Sayer [5E9] in Kenya, and Loutzenheiser [5E11] in Kansas (USA).

5F Engineering

Manuals also exist for the design and layout of roads in rural areas. For Britain there is an advisory manual (G.B. Ministry of Transport [5F16]) plus comments (Llewelyn and Butler [5F22]). For the USA there are national guidelines for the design of low-volume rural roads (Glennon [5F19]), and similar programmes have been produced for developing countries such as the rural access roads programme in Kenya (Simpson [5E29]). Engineering studies had been made of traffic flows in rural areas (e.g. a series of papers by Ackroyd and others [5F1], [5F3], [5F4], and Taylor *et al.* [5F31]), as well as speed analyses and speed/flow relationships (Farthing [5F13] and Galin [5F15], and estimations on road capacities (Fletcher [5F14] and O'Flaherty and Coombe [5F26]). Many of these are based on extensive empirical surveys together with a range of mathematical modelling techniques; some have been reviewed by Allsop [5F7]. Other studies have focused on particular aspects of rural roads such as carriageway markings (Bennett [5F9]), signposting (Wootton [5F34]), junctions and interchanges (Constantine [5F12] and Lyles [5F23]), road surfaces (Peters [5F28] and Visser *et al.* [5F32]), and the requirements for road maintenance (Organisation for Economic Cooperation and Development [5F27]).

As with many of the references in this section on methods and evaluation, most research and publications have been on the urban context. To some extent the methods are directly transferable between the urban and rural situations, but most of the references quoted here relate exclusively to the rural applications. So a specific guide has been presented here, and the reader interested in the more general aspects should refer to the relevant bibliographies listed in Section 7.

5A Transport and regional development

.1 BOTHAM, R. W. (1980) The regional development effects of road investment. *Transportation Planning and Technology*, **6** (2), pp. 97–108.

From analyses of the British road building programme, it is concluded that the regional development effects of highway construction are small. Legislative influences (e.g driving hour limitations and taxation measures) may have a significant effect. The roads programme has had a centralizing effect on the distribution of employment.

.2 BREWELL, K. A. and RICHARDS, R. O. (1976) Regional transport development and economic growth. *ASCE Journal of Transportation Engineering*, **102** (TE2), pp. 271–90.

Transport plans and economic development plans for regional development are postulated with the presumption that the resulting pattern of land uses and activities resulting therefrom are mutually supportive. A study of rural regions in Iowa relating urban development goals to transport policy and programmes had resulted in a method of quantifying the regional distribution of transport accessibility and the regional distribution of economic activity. Comparing the distribution of manufacturing activity with the distribution of retail activity provides a socioeconomic structuring of rural regions. This structuring of regions can then be compared to the distribution of transport accessibility within regions and among regions to assess the consistency of the respective development planning. The analysis methodology has implied application beyond the study locations.

5A3 BRIGGS, R. (1981) Interstate highway system and development in nonmetropolitan areas. *Transportation Research Record*, 812, pp. 9-12.

The current revival of development in small urban and rural communities is one of the more dramatic changes in socioeconomic trends in this century. Since other writers have suggested that the Interstate Highway System played a key role, this paper empirically examines the relationship between the location of freeways and migration and employment change between 1950 and 1975 in all nonmetropolitan counties in the United States by using both descriptive statistics and regression models. The results show that, while counties with freeways as a group have higher average growth rates, even after confounding factors such as proximity to metropolitan areas and presence of urban population concentrations are controlled, the presence of a limited access highway is far from an assurance of development for an individual county. Tourist services are the industry most closely associated with Interstates but, contrary to common conceptions, manufacturing and wholesaling are not clearly associated. The Interstate system was less able to explain the spatial pattern of development than nontransport factors. Its role appears to have been to raise accessibility levels throughout the nonmetropolitan United States, which has benefited many communities, not just those adjacent to Interstates.

5A4 EBNER, J. (1979) Transport and regional policy in Austria, in Blonk, W.A.B. (ed) *Transport and Regional Development: an International Handbook*, Farnborough: Saxon House, pp. 81-93.

Due to its topography and geographical boundaries, regional policy has an important role to play in Austria. The attraction of the towns has facilitated a rural exodus and so policies such as in transport have been initiated to ensure that the remote areas offer more opportunities.

A5 FOGEL, R.W. (1964) *Railroads and American Economic Growth: Essays in Econometric History*, Baltimore: Johns Hopkins.

A6 GARRISON, W.L. (1955) The spatial impact of transport media: Studies of rural roads. *Papers and Proceedings Regional Science Association*, **1** (2), pp. 211-25.

The paper examines the interrelationship between the concepts of location and those of interaction with a special focus on rural roads. The preliminary results are reported on the relationships between road quality and quantity, and land values.

A7 GAUTHIER, H.L. (1973) The Appalchian development highway system: Development for whom? *Economic Geography*, **49,** pp. 103-8.

This paper reviews progress since the passing of the Appalchian Regional Development Act and concludes that there has been a failure to design and execute a regional plan. Regional priorities have been neglected in favour of local benefits, and the benefits have gone to urban not low income and rural areas.

A8 GRANDJEAN, A. and HENRY, C. (1984) Economic rationality in the development of a motorway network. *Transport Reviews*, **4** (2), pp. 143-56.

This paper describes two complementary aspects of the French motorway programme: on the one hand, the emergence of the network within French society from 1955 to 1980, and on the other, the choice of specific routes for the arcs of the network. In addition, certain comparisons between the British and the French situations are made.

There is an explanation of how the global network was conceived by the French road administration and how, in overcoming varied opposition, it came to be a goal of national policy. There follows a description of how the building of the network was financed, with one means always (to date) succeeding another just in time.

Naturally, as in Britain or any other country, the specific choice of a route in France provokes conflicts. The Ministry of Transport has recently experimented with an original and interesting method of negotiation—on the segment between Bourges and Clermont-Ferrand—which successively determines the line of the road within a wide band (anywhere from 5 to 20 kilometres wide depending on the local physical constraints) previously specified by the administration. Some conclusions are drawn from this experience by comparing it with the more traditional 'preferred route' approach.

5A9 HALL, P. (1967) New techniques in regional planning—experience of transportation studies. *Regional Studies*, **1** (1), pp. 17–21.

A systematic methodology now exists for the metropolitan area transport study, but problems remain in predicting land uses and the economic and social patterns behind them. Evaluative models consider the social value of alternative patterns of land use and transport. There are difficult problems of providing rational explanations for the working of the model; the level of explanation will be improved by close communication among professionals expert in different aspects of urban growth and change.

5A10 HALLA, N. (1977) Vaegprojektens invertan paa samhaellenas ekonomiska utveckling. Paper presented at the Nordiska Vaegtekniska Foerbundets Congress, Finland (in Swedish), The influence of road projects on the economic development of society.

Major investment in a road project is generally considered to stimulate economic growth and development in the affected area. Consideration of cumulative effects may produce different priorities from user benefit estimates, for instance when there are large regional differences in employment. Investigation of cumulative effects was made in Finland to find the income distribution effects of planned road projects. Income effects in a region result from investments made from outside, while capacity effects are due to increases in fixed capital and production capacity owing to the investment. Six improvement schemes in six municipalities were examined using statistics and postal enquiries to companies and local authorities. The attitude of a company to a road project was found to depend on its position relative to the road. Location of industrial companies depends mainly on supply and skill of labour, while the most important factor for service firms is nearness of the market. Access to main routes is very important for all companies. Turnover and labour in industrial companies rose faster nearer the road than elsewhere, while for commercial companies this was the fastest in town centres. Cumulative effects are very small, being 3-4 per cent of annual turnover of industrial companies.

11 HILEWICK, C.L., DEAK, E. and HEINZ, E.E. (1980) Rural development: a simulation of communications and transportation investments. *Growth and Change*, **11** (3), pp. 26-38.

This article assesses the relative effectiveness of alternative programmes aimed at achieving certain development goals, namely the concept of subnational economic development, and the resolution of the problems of rural Americans, and their need for equity in the receipt of services and equality of opportunity for socio-economic development. The article attempts to identify the relative sizes and types of changes as well as the extent and sequence of linkages to other sectors that transport and communications investments might cause within typical rural communities. Attention is focused upon a comparison of the rural growth impacts that investment in communications as opposed to transport networks might stimulate. Current views on investment impacts are discussed as are also policy choices and the Harris simulation model which is a multiregional, multidisciplinary forecasting tool. Empirical results from the model are described and observations are made regarding investment impacts. The simulation results demonstrate the advantage of investing in communications, rather than transport, in order to stimulate rural development.

12 IRWIN, L.H. (1977) Transportation problems and research needs in the rural sector. *Transportation Research Circular*, 187, pp. 19-22.

Recommendations regarding research needs on social economic and environmental aspects of rural transport are presented, the evolution of the rural transport is described, and problem areas in the system are itemised. The rural transport system has evolved into an uncoordinated, multimodal transport network in which one mode or another is overbuilt in some regions of the country. The particular situation with regard to highways, railroads, and bridges is noted. Research in the following areas is suggested: optimal use of the present transport system, optimizing the extent of the present system, optimizing the organization of the transport system, optimum land use, and standards.

5A13 JUDGE, E.J. and BUTTON, K.J. (1974) Inter-urban roads in Great Britain: Perspectives and prospects. *Transportation Planning and Technology*, **2** (3), pp. 185–94.

In the light of recent ministerial statements and increasing public discussion on such topics as the role of the nationalized transport industries and the current fuel shortages, it would seem that transport policy is once again a subject for debate. The last reappraisal of public expenditure commitments some time prior to the current energy crisis saw only relatively minor amendments to the inter-urban roads programme. The wide publicity and public interest given to the development of inter-urban roads suggests that it may be timely to examine the way in which the trunk route network has developed in recent years and to assess the nature of recent policy and planning decisions in a slightly wider context.

The purpose of this paper is, therefore, to examine the nature of the growth in the national inter-urban road network since the war and to assess the prospects for its future development. This will involve an appraisal of the way the network has developed, a consideration of the administrative and analytical procedures involved, and an evaluation of this process. Finally, a number of comments are made on possible modifications and improvements in the future planning of inter-urban roads.

5A14 LINEHAM, R. and WALTON, C.M. (1976) Interurban transportation networks and rural economic development. *Transportation Research Record*, 617, pp. 29–41.

This research attempts to develop an understanding of how policies that alter the characteristics of interurban transport systems are likely to influence the growth and development of potential rural communities. Three stages of research into economic development and the influence of transport on that development are covered here. In the first stage, a case study of several industries that located in the rural town of Sealy, Texas, was used to determine both objective and subjective influences on location choice. In the second stage a multivariate analysis was made of the towns in the rural region through which a recently upgraded interurban highway passed, to determine the statistical correspondences between location in the regional infrastructure and the export-base growth. In the third stage an examination was made of the trends in industrial typology in relation to location in the regional infrastructure. The findings of the studies verify the need to provide basic and essential guidelines for use by residents of small rural communities and by professional planners who plan the major interurban transport systems.

15 PARKINSON, M. (1981) The effect of road investment on economic development in the UK. Department of Transport, Government Economic Service, Working Paper 43.

A review of theory and empirical evidence of the relationship between road investment and general economic theory is presented. It is concluded that general statements on the possible development effects of particular schemes should be given much weight in the evaluation of a road scheme. Studies should concentrate on the particular facts of each individual scheme.

16 RAYNER, N. (1980) Rural roads and economic development in Ethiopia. *Logistics and Transportation Review*, **16**, (4), pp. 313-24.

Using equations (developed by Howe [6D21]) fitted to data on the area, population and rural road length in 14 Ethiopian provinces, the author argues that Ethiopia has an excessive provision of rural roads and that the relative position of rural accessibility is much greater in the South than the North. The policy implications are difficult to determine but a very careful evaluation of any new project is essential.

17 ROSTOW, W.W. (1960) *The Stages of Economic Growth*, Cambridge, Mass.: M.I.T.

18 SHARP, C. (1980) Transport and regional development with special reference to Britain. *Transport Policy and Decision Making*, **1** (1), pp. 1-11.

Transport investment alone does not encourage regional growth in the less prosperous regions of developed countries. A simple model is calibrated that shows how the market area of low-cost producers is expanded when transport costs fall. The industries most likely to develop in less prosperous areas as a result of transport investment are those where production costs do not vary with location and where transport costs form a relatively high proportion of total costs.

5A19 SIMMONS, J.M. and BADEN, A. (1982) The impact of the M25 on planning in the London Region. Paper presented to the PTRC Annual Summer Conference, Warwick, July.

This paper draws on work undertaken by the Regional Monitoring Group of the Standing Conference on London and South East Regional Planning (SCLSERP) in 1981. The M25 orbital motorway around the metropolitan area of Greater London has hitherto been considered mainly as a transport matter. Now that its construction is advancing, there is growing concern and interest over the impact the motorway may have on regional planning policies, as regards both the Metropolitan Green Belt and the regeneration of inner London. The paper sets out the findings of regional monitoring work, relating current planning policies in the London region to changes in accessibility which the motorway is likely to create and the effect on development pressures which is likely to result. Conclusions are drawn concerning the expected impact of the new route, both on economic development and environmental policies and on the value of the wider type of impact assessment.

5A20 TARRANT, J. (1979) Rural transport and development in Bangladesh. *Bangladesh Development Studies*, **7,** (4), pp. 109-20.

Analyses the role of transport in rural development arguing that the lack of roads and the small number of farmers owning boats ensures that the first level of marketing is local with inevitable implications for the level and fluctuations of prices. But small farmers buy, as well as sell, rice which suggests that investment in on-farm storage might be more beneficial in terms of income distribution than investment in rural transport. Improvements in transport should concentrate on the supply of social and productive services to rural areas.

5A21 WATERS, W.G. (1979) Transportation and regional development: The persistent myth. *Logistics and Transportation Review*, **15** (4), pp. 527-46.

The persistent myth is to believe that transport is a dominant factor in determining economic growth. It is of course a mixture of some fact and much fiction. Regional development plans are reviewed in relation to the role of transport and the relationships which sustained the myth are noted.

22 WILSON, F.R., BRANDER, J.R. and ROGERS, G. (1979) Transportation and regional economic development—Some empirical evidence from the Atlantic region of Canada. *Transportation Research Forum Proceedings*, **20** (1), pp. 9–16.

The results are presented of two years of an on-going research project to quantify a relationship between transport and regional economic development. Data were obtained on two specific aspects: the determination of the importance of transport as a locational factor, and the cost of transport as a percentage of input cost or factory gate price depending on which side of the market the transaction occurred. Analysis of location factors revealed the importance of owner/managers residence on the plant location decision. Statistics demonstrate the importance of noneconomic factors in industrial location decisions relative to the Atlantic Provinces. The significance of these non-economic factors must be considered in regional planning and policy-making. It is also concluded that improvements in transport infrastructure especially the highway strengthening programme should be designed to assist the established industrial base rather than to attempt to alter the relative attractiveness of the region for new industry.

5B Analysis methods

B1 BANNISTER, D.J. (1979) A method for investigating consumer preferences for certain transport policy alternatives, in Goodall, B and Kirby, A. (eds) *Resources and Planning*, Pergamon International Library, pp. 325–41.

This paper reports certain results of the trade off analysis which was applied to testing consumer preferences to certain rural policy alternatives. Problems and advantages of the technique are discussed within the empirical framework of the study and it is concluded that attitudinal or psychometric methods have much to offer transport research, particularly where there is little evidence of the impact of policy innovations.

5B2 BAXTER, M. and EWING, G. (1981) Models of recreational trip distribution. *Regional Studies*, **15** (5), pp. 327–44.

Singly constrained gravity models for recreational trip distribution are investigated with different subsets of data, measures of distance travelled, deterrence functions and levels of zonal aggregation. Estimates, and their interpretation, exhibit some consistency for the most disaggregate system, however the data is treated; for more aggregated systems there is much variation in the results obtained. Models that allow for the effect of barriers to travel are developed, and a multi-stop model incorporating features peculiar to recreational trips is proposed and calibrated. Some unresolved problems associated with the use of this model are indicated.

5B3 BERTHOUD, R. (1972) Rural Travel Survey: Methodological Report. Social and Community Planning Research Report, August.

This document describes the survey methods used in a home interview survey of travel behaviour in the area to the west of the West Midlands Conurbation. The brief for the survey was to establish an inventory of weekday travel undertaken by public and private transport by persons resident in the survey area. Descriptions are given of the sampling selection, interviewing and fieldwork, and data preparation procedures. Appendices provide further details of the coding, editing and computer edit check specifications and also include copies of the questionnaires and other survey documents.

5B4 BROOKS, J. A. and HARRIS, M. R. (1972) The application of multiflow assignment to major traffic studies in a rural area. *Traffic Engineering and Control*, **14** (7), pp. 330–2.

The multiflow assignment technique has been used on a number of major traffic studies which covered areas up to 2000 mile^2 and with up to 1000 links in the system. Two descriptions are used to demonstrate the flexibility of the approach both for the base year situation and for a posed solution. Assignment processes have to be carefully tested and understood before a solution is recommended.

5 BURKHARDT, J.E. and LAGO, A.M. (1976) Methods of predicting rural transit demand. Pennsylvania Department of Transportation, Harrisburg, Final Report RR101, April.

The Pennsylvania Department of Transportation, under Executive Order from the Governor, is responsible for developing a plan for a comprehensive rural transport system for Pennsylvania. The research and methodology included in this report is a crucial part of the development of a comprehensive rural transport programme. There is a pressing need for public transit systems in rural areas. In order to operate such systems efficiently and effectively, local planners must have accurate projections of the number of riders that will demand service. Using data from 100 existing rural transport systems, simulation models of factors influencing the number of riders were developed. The Report provides demand estimation models for both total system-wide and route specific transit systems, and separate models are developed for fixed routes and demand responsive systems. The report also includes guidelines necessary to properly utilize these models.

6 BURKHARDT, J.E. and LAGO, A.M. (1978) Predicting demand for rural transit systems. *Traffic Quarterly*, **32** (1), pp. 105-29.

The object of this research report is to present a simpler method of predicting the patronage of rural public transport systems. Previous methods of estimating the need or demand for rural public transport are discussed; these methods include subjective gap analysis, surveys, per capita aggregate estimates, and simulation of demand functions. Using data from approximately 100 existing rural transport systems, simulation models of factors influencing the number of riders were developed. It was found that reliable estimates of demand could be produced by using a small number of variables that described characteristics of the area and people served, and attributes to the transport system. The elements affecting the ridership of rural demand-responsive transit systems are similar to those affecting the demand for rural fixed-route transit systems, but there are significant differences in the definition of area served, trip generation, and measurement of service responsiveness. The following factors were identified as having a major influence on the number of persons that can be expected to ride a given rural transit system: monthly bus miles, availability of services, population served, other public transport systems, distance, and fares. The greatest benefit of the demand equations is that they provide a rough estimate of how many people might use a system according to specific rural and transit system conditions.

5B7 CLARKE, M., VAN KNIPPENBERG, C., and SPLINTER, T. (1983) Analysing the effects of rural bus service reductions on life styles, Paper presented at the PRTC Annual Conference, Sussex.

When bus services are reduced, the former passengers are forced to adapt their behaviour by one of a number of reactions ranging from retiming their trip, through changing modes or destinations, to abandoning the activity which had previously been the motive for the journey. Such effects are difficult to analyse or model unless consideration is taken of at least some aspects of the interaction between travel and activity patterns.

This paper describes the analytical techniques which are being employed and presents some findings. The project involves collection of activity diaries from bus users in a small village which is currently well served by public transport, analysis of these diaries under various assumptions about future changes to the bus schedule, and follow-up interviews with respondents to discuss their own views of likely effects. The analytical techniques to be discussed include the use of an activity scheduling model to predict and evaluate the interactions between bus services and lifestyles.

5B8 DEAN, C.L. (1982) A service strategy model for estimating trunkline intercity bus service to rural communities. *Transportation Research Forum*, **23** (1), pp. 608-15.

This paper presents the developments of multiple linear regression models useful for estimating the frequency of intercity bus service to small rural communities along trunkline routes. Models of carriers in California are based upon levels of service and supplier strategies. Frequency of intercity bus service to rural intermediate points is shown to be represented by variables that quantify community attractiveness, station density, highway quality, network focus and total corridor bus traffic. The objective of this paper is to gain a better understanding of intercity bus service to rural service points along trunkline routes. To accomplish this purpose, a mathematical model has been developed that will generate estimates of service for intermediate points in the bus network, knowing a few facts about the empirical domain and the trunkline traffic level. The frequency of bus departures has been selected as the dependent variable of interest because it represents the smallest bus supply unit that is responsive to carrier strategies. In addition, 'frequency' is an expression clearly recognized and understood by the communities being served.

9 DUFFIELD, B.S. (1976) A method for estimating recreational traffic flows. *Transport and Road Research Laboratory*, SR 247.

A technique for estimating volumes of seasonal recreational traffic on rural roads has been developed using data from a 50-point traffic census. Harmonic analysis was used to develop a model which gives a prediction of total daily flow for each day of the year. The model is calibrated on data consisting of automatic traffic counts for the road in question taken during two fortnight periods, one in winter, one in summer. Methods were developed to predict the likely mean error in using the model to estimate volumes of daily traffic, based on the estimated or observed flow characteristics for the road.

From the forecasts of total traffic, the seasonal recreational and holiday traffic component can be estimated by applying the 'surplus traffic' hypothesis. This states that levels of non-summer traffic represent mainly 'utility' traffic which can be expected to maintain a relatively constant level throughout the year. Subtracting an estimate of utility traffic from the total traffic flow yields the seasonal recreational component. Evidence supporting this hypothesis, modified to allow for winter recreational flows, is presented. The final traffic 'mix' model was tested using data from two Scottish border roads. Results were satisfactory, but further testing would be appropriate when suitable data becomes available.

10 ENGLISHER, L.S. and SOBEL, K.L. (1977) Methodology for the analysis of local paratransit options. *Transportation Research Record*, 660, pp. 8–24.

A system of models has been developed that is capable of predicting the performance characteristics of transit service for the purpose of analysing a wide range of local transit-service alternatives. Patronage and demand forecasting issues are treated parametrically. Local transit is designed to serve access and egress trips bound to and from a regionally oriented line-haul transit system as well as shorter local circulation trips. The model system presented is capable of treating a wide range of modes that can offer such local transit service. In addition to conventional transit and jitney services, which follow fixed routes, point-deviation and checkpoint route-deviation transit can be investigated. More flexible modes, such as checkpoint subscription bus, doorstep subscription bus, and doorstep, many-to-many, dynamically routed transit (dial-a-ride), can also be examined. Comparisons can be made both between alternatives and between operating policies (such as vehicle size and route spacing) within any single alternative. The model system has been designed to predict four important consequences of implementing local transit service: user level of service, operator cost, pollutant emissions, and energy (fuel) consumption. Results from a sample model application are presented. Use of the system would allow a wide range of alternatives to be tested before significant demonstration and experimentation efforts or implementation funds are committed. Such tests can be integrated with corridor and regional analyses on both policy and planning levels of detail.

5B11 EVANS, A.W. (1984) Economic benefit and economic equity in grant-related expenditure assessments for public transport, School for Advanced Urban Studies, Bristol, Report for the Department of the Environment, January.

Local authorities in England receive two main central government grants for local public transport: Rate Support Grant (RSG), which is a large general grant for all services, and Transport Supplementary Grant (TSG). The allocation of these grants to county areas requires assessments to be made of the relative spending needs or claims of each area. The principles underlying these assessments may be different.

The key principle governing the distribution of RSG is 'equalization'—this is, RSG should be distributed in such a way that it is possible for each authority to provide a common level of service for the same local tax rate. The estimated cost of the common level of service, taking into account the circumstances of each area, is called the 'grant related expenditure'.

A key principle increasingly advocated for the assessment of 'accepted expenditure' for TSG purposes, and also for public transport expenditure guidelines, is efficiency—that is, public spending and grant should be distributed so as to maximize net social benefit from public transport. For example, the Bus and Coach Council have recently advocated this, and the Transport Act 1983 mentions that user benefits are to be taken into account in plan-making for public transport.

This paper explores the use of measure of economic benefit in equalization criteria for grant-related expenditure for public transport revenue support. The arguments on economic equity are developed and these related to the economic benefit as a measure of the output of a service, and the principles to the Metropolitan and Shire Counties in England.

B12 GAMBLE, P. (1978) Manual methods of estimating public transportation needs in small urban and rural areas. Washington State Department of Transportation, Public Transportation and Planning Division, Washington D.C.

This report provides manual analytical techniques assigned to assist small urban and rural technicians in analysing public transport options. It is intended for use primarily by planners, engineers and others in communities with less than 50,000 residents. Outside assistance, including computer analysis, should not be required if this manual is used. Two approaches using ten techniques are considered in this manual, and include a rate making and budgeting 'How To Do' discussion.

B13 GB, MINISTRY OF TRANSPORT (1963) Rural Transport Surveys, London: HMSO.

B14 GERRARD M.J. (1974) Comparison of taxi and dial-a-bus services. *Transportation Science*, **8** (2), pp. 83-101.

A probablistic model of a conventional taxi service is formulated and analysed. This model also applies to other queueing systems in which the servers must travel to the customers. The main assumptions are that demand is homogeneous and that the street network is uniform in a certain sense. Computer simulations incorporating these assumptions were made of both the taxi service and a many-to-many dial-a-bus system. It was found that small dial-a-bus vehicles (capacity 6-8) can serve 50 per cent more people than taxis with only a slight increase in travel-time. An attempt to carry more passengers leads to steadily greater travel-times. However, dial-a-bus is generally less affected by changes in demand than taxis. The size of the region served has a pronounced effect on the efficiency of both dial-a-bus and taxi services.

5B15   GREENING, P.A.K. and MILES, J.C. (1979) Modelling the demand for long distance day trips in the Lake District. *Transport and Road Research Laboratory*, LR 881.

In this report a comparison of long-distance day trip making to the Lake District is made using data from surveys conducted in 1966 and 1974. The effect on the growth in the number of day trips by changes in car ownership levels, new motorways and increased fuel costs are discussed. The trip attraction models derived from the 1966 data contain some deficiencies and these are described, and a new model is derived from the improved data base of the 1974 survey. Finally methods of forecasting future trips are proposed based on general cost formulae, changes in travel time and car ownership.

5B16   HUDDART, L. (1981) Response to a bus service for countryside re-creation: A home interview survey. *Transport and Road Research Laboratory*, LR 976.

A programme of research has been carried out at TRRL to assess the demand for public transport services for recreational trips into the countryside. This has involved a study centred on the town of Newport, Gwent which included a first home interview survey to assess the likely demand for possible new services, the introduction of four new experimental bus services, and a second home interview survey to assess the impact of the new services and establish people's reasons for not using the services.

Support for the new bus services was disappointing, and only seventeen (less than 2 per cent) of those interviewed in the second home interview survey had actually used the services. About half of those interviewed had heard of the new services, the most effective forms of publicity being local press advertisements and posters. The main reasons for not using the service were the availability of a car and lack of free time, rather than dissatisfaction with the service provided.

7 Jones, P.M. (1976) Forecasting family response to changes in school hours: an exploratory study using HATS. Oxford University, Transport Studies Unit.

The paper describes the results of an exploratory study conducted among families with children attending Burford secondary school, Oxfordshire, where school hours and school bus schedules were substantially altered from the start of the 1976 Autumn term. The study has two objectives: firstly, to examine the variety of ways in which families might be affected by the change; and secondly, to evaluate a new gaming procedure called 'HATS' (Household Activity-Travel Simulator), which is being developed to explore household response to policy changes. Using the gaming equipment, family members set out a typical term-time day (indicating what they were doing, when and where) on individual boards, and subsequently physically rearranging the activity and travel patterns depicted, as necessary, to take account both of school induced changes and any secondary repercussions (e.g. changes in family meal times). Interviews were conducted during Summer 1976, prior to the introduction of the change, and households were subsequently recontacted to establish what adaptations they actually made. Results indicate that the new arrangements considerably affected some families, and that the gaming procedures led to a much greater realism in response than simply asking for verbal reactions (even though the families have had considerable warning of the change, and a chance to consider its likely effects at some length).

8 Kaesehagen, R.L., Moser, B. and Fischer, J.F. (1979) A rural road traffic flow simulation model. *Australian Road Research Board Conference Proceedings*, **9** (6), pp. 153–69.

This paper describes the development and a proposed methodology for calibration of a simulation model for estimating, at the micro level, operating speed and fuel consumption for all levels of traffic flow on a section of two-lane rural road of any complex horizontal and vertical alignment. Some observations of the results of model runs using default values of free speed, acceleration and deceleration are made. The primary use of the model is to develop an operating speed and fuel consumption relationship with road geometry, surface type and road roughness for use in a highway planning model being developed by Brazil's Ministry of Transportation that will define the inter-relationships between the three components affecting road transportation cost: construction, maintenance and utilization.

5B19 KAU, J.B. (1977) A transportation land use model for rural areas. *Annals of Regional Science*, **11** (2), pp. 41–54.

The spatial distribution of employment and population is complicated by many factors such as accessibility income variance, prices, geographical characteristics, and government intervention. This analysis attempts through two stage least squares regression analysis to isolate the impact on employment and household density of changing transport costs as measured by accessibility. This proved to be a sensitive barometer of changes in the transport system and it was used to forecast particular impacts of these changes.

5B20 KING, R.L., YOUNG, S.L. and CHUDLEIGH, P.D. (1982)
Vol 1 Data collection procedures and data assembly
Vol 2 Traffic generation from rural land use
Vol 3 An assessment of the effect of the Road User Charges Act.
Road Research Unit, National Road Boards, New Zealand, Bulletin 59.

The first volume introduces the two projects, their objectives and the methods used to collect the appropriate data, and it also presents the form of the data bases generated. The second volume presents results on land use and rural traffic generation patterns, and it includes information on both freight and personal trip generation by type of land use, size of farm, location of farm and enterprise type. The third volume presents information relevant to the Road User Charges Act and makes an evaluation of how the new distance tax may affect transport costs and total costs for farmers of different types located in different areas.

5B21 KLEIN, D.H. (1979) A recreation needs assessment process—an origin destination approach. *Transportation Planning and Technology*, **5** (3), pp. 169–82.

Presented here is a process that communities can use to plan improvements in their recreation system which are responsive to the expressed needs of their residents. It is particularly useful for demonstrating the optimum locations for urban parks to maximize energy conservation and social service return on capital investment. Central to the process is a comparison of projected recreation needs and desires, based on an attitude survey, with the capacity of the existing local park systems, to identify future deficiency problems. The process employed a regional origin-destination travel model to distribute demand. A citizens' advisory committee to the planning programme, along with the parks and recreation commission, reviewed and made recommendations for each task in the process.

22 KUHN, H.A.J. (1968) Factors influencing traffic generation at rural highway service areas. *Highway Research Board*, 240, pp. 1-10.

There are a number of factors influencing the volume of traffic a highway service facility generates. A better understanding, not only of the degree of influence but also of how various influences interact with one another, may allow the development of a predictive generation model for highway services and this paper highlights some of the basic principles of such an approach.

23 KURTH, D.L., SCHNEIDER, M. and GUR, Y. (1979) Small-area trip distribution model. *Transportation Research Record*, 728, pp. 35-40.

A model for predicting trip tables for small areas based on the access and land development travel function is described along with the results of an initial test of the model. The model provides trip tables required for subregional analyses without the need for windowing into a regional data set. The model requires minimum-path friction skim trees and trip-end data for the small area as input. Trip-end data can be derived from ground counts on links that enter the small area or from the results of an assignment of a regional trip table. Test results from a small area in Hudson County, New Jersey, suggest the validity of the model, but the need for further refinements to the model is the main conclusion.

24 LITZ, L.E. (1979) Rural highway planning system. Federal Highway Administration, Washington.

The author describes a basic 'Rural Highway Planning System' developed by the Federal Highway Administration over the past four years, which uses the concept of collecting the minimum basic information needed to plan and operate an efficient highway transport programme. The programme makes maximum use of the computer. A series of manuals of instructions and 40 computer programs have been developed, and these will be furnished by the Federal Highway Administation to any country wishing to install the system for its own planning programme [Litz *et al.* 5B25].

5B25 LITZ, L.E., CUTRELL, J. and CENTENO, K. (1977) Rural Highway Planning System. Computer Program Users' Manual, Volume 1. Federal Highway Administration.

An effective highway transport planning process is the basis for, and is a necessary continuous part of, efficient highway transport management. A series of manuals and accompanying computer programs were developed to provide guidelines for establishing a system and the basic data collection programs and analysis that are a necessary beginning for accomplishing such a planning process. The object of the manual is to assist with the development of efficient procedures for analysing the road inventory data beginning with the receipt of the completed field forms. It includes a suggested organization for office operations and documentation to assist with the installation and use of the computer programs that were developed for the system.

Volume 2 is concerned with the updating of the road inventory data and for analysing adequacy rating data beginning with the receipt of the completed field forms.

Volume 3 is concerned with the updating of the road traffic data (volume, classification and weight).

5B26 LUCCHINI, S.F. (1981) A planning methodology for the organization of rural areas. *Vie e Trasporti*, **50**, (475), pp. 109–22 (in Italian).

This article discusses rural planning methodology with particular reference to the role and organization of transport. The author points out that continuity between the work zone and the rural habitat can only be maintained by the improvement of transport modes and territorial mobility, and an increased speed in the internal network. A territorial socio-economic analysis shows that rural areas can no longer be regarded as the residue from other land use selections, and that since planning and development processes are often irreversible rural areas must be regarded as an increasingly scarce resource.

5B27 MARCHE, R. (1980) La modelisation de la demande multimodale en transport interregional de voyageurs. Proceedings of the World Conference on Transport Research, London, April, Volume 2, pp. 1159–74 (in French).

This paper describes a multimodal model for regional travel and outlines the objectives of the project, the conceptual framework and the preliminary applications. As a conclusion some comments are made on the possible developments both in the short and long term.

28 MILES, J.C. and SMITH, N. (1977) Models of recreational traffic in rural areas. *Transport and Road Research Laboratory*, SR 301.

Congestion on roads leading to and within popular scenic areas has prompted research into mathematical models of recreational traffic. These techniques are intended to provide better information for the design of road improvements, traffic management schemes and facilites for outdoor recreation. In this report existing modelling techniques which conform to the established structure of trip generation, trip distribution and traffic assignment are reviewed. Direct demand modelling and systems simulation are also explored as alternatives. Discussion of the alternative structures for a recreational traffic model and recommendations for further research are given in the concluding section.

29 NATIONAL TECHNICAL INFORMATION SERVICE (1980). The rural transportation planning system, NTIS.

An effective highway transport planning process is the basis for, and is a necessary continuous part of, efficient highway transport management. A series of manuals and accompanying computer programs were developed to provide guidelines for establishing a system and the basic data collection programs and analysis that are a necessary beginning for accomplishing such a planning process.

30 NEUMANN, E.S. and BYRNE, B.F. (1978) A poisson model of rural transit ridership. *Transportation Research Record*, 661, pp. 21–7.

A Poisson Model for ridership on rural public transport routes is developed and the models are tested on data collected previously in the research, and some modifications made. Illustrated is a technique of using analysis of variance on ridership rates to determine those which are significantly different, so as to form categories for cross-classifications which are not arbitrary.

5B31 NEVEU, A.J. (1982) Quick response procedures to forecast rural traffic: background document. *New York State Department of Transportation*, Transportation Analysis Report 3, June.

This study developed a quick response method to forecast traffic volumes at project sites located on the rural highway network. Using data from the State's rural continuous count stations, and various State, County and Town level demographic data, a set of elasticity based models were derived. These models forecast future year annual average daily traffic as a function of base year traffic modified by various demographic factors. These models were estimated based on the type of service the roadway carries: interurban, urban to rural, and rural-to-rural. Nomographs and a user's manual describing the simple six-step process to use the model were developed and distributed to the regional offices.

5B32 NEWELL, J. and ESCH, R.E. (1979) Impact of population and energy on transportation needs: multimodal approach. *Transportation Research Record*, 710, pp. 19–26.

This paper documents a computer process developed to explore the potential diversion of automobile trips by purpose and length for various population growths and energy futures and the impact this diversion will have on transport needs. The technique is a straightforward method of using the existing statewide transport model to generate statewide highway trip tables for each possible future. There tables are split by trip purpose based on analysis of actual statewide origin-destination data and then split into modes based on trip purpose and length information gained in the survey of air, rail, and bus travel characteristics. Information on the modal split in other mass transit corridors in the United States is also used as a guide. The variables in this process are easily understood and thus may be quickly adjusted to reevaluate transport needs and to reflect various planning policies. Once the modal trip tables are generated, they are assigned to a statewide air, rail or bus network based on station accessibility; the remaining trips are assigned to the highway network. The end product is a computer plot that shows the potential travel volumes by mode and the probable impact of each population growth and energy future on state highway needs. This technique is being appied in rural portions of 13 of Michigan's 14 planning regions.

3 PARKINSON, M., EASTMAN, R. and BROWN, W.M.M. (1982) Before and after study on the M25. Paper presented to the PTRC Annual Summer Conference, Warwick, July.

The Godstone to Sevenoaks section of the M25 was opened in November 1979. The Department of Transport commissioned consultants to carry out a before and after study on this new road, with particular emphasis on some of the relationships used in the economic appraisal of trunk road schemes.

A large amount of data has been collected on speeds and journey times, vehicle fuel costs and accident rates. These data relate to predicted and actual performance on the M25 itself as well as on the A25 route affected by this new route. The paper considers the accuracy of the predictions for this particular investment with respect to the identified characteristics, and the extent to which such results might be regarded as typical.

34 PEDERSEN, P.O. (1980). A demand model for public transport in rural areas. *International Journal of Transport Economics*, **7** (3), pp. 345-58.

In the literature on rural public transport, it seems to be generally agreed that the traditional urban transport demand and modal split models cannot be used to forecast rural demand for public transport. First, because a rural model must be based on individual behaviour rather than on household behaviour; secondly, rural public transport trips are not the result of a modal choice between car and bus, as the potential car driver and bus passenger are not generally the same person; thirdly the service quality of public transport must play a larger role than it does in the urban models; and fourthly, the number of passengers in each zone is so small that the macrostatistical methods cannot be used.

However, few attempts have been made to develop alternative demand models; rather it is argued that rural demand for public transport cannot be forecasted but must be estimated on the basis of practical experiments. Instead most work has been focused on the development of measures of individual car availability and public transport. This paper reports on an attempt to set up a model of the generation of public transport trips in rural areas. The model is based on simple counts of passengers to and from individual tariff zones in the rural county of Ribe in Denmark in November 1977.

In addition, the results of a passenger count on the urban buses in the town of Esbjerg in September 1976 have been used to compare traffic demand under urban and rural conditions.

5B35 PEDERSEN, P.O. (1981) Planning the structure of public transport networks in low density areas. *Transport Reviews*, **1** (1), pp. 26-43.

One of the important principles of modern transport planning is that transport networks should be hierarchically structured. Thus, public transport networks are often divided into fast national and regional networks between the largest centres and local feeder services, often at different levels.

At higher levels of the hierarchy this has obvious advantages in terms of speed, capacity, economy and/or safety. However, at the lower levels in low density areas the hierarchial principle leads to reduced services and also to increased costs to school buses and social transport. The paper proposes a more integrated network with more direct links between lower level centres than exist in the hierarchical network.

To compare the qualities of a hierarchical and an integrated network, two alternative bus networks were designed for a rural county of Denmark, Ribe in West Jutland. Consequences of the two networks were computed in terms of costs, passengers and accessibility, and it is shown that the integrated network is no more expensive than the hierarchical, but that it is likely to attract more passengers and gives the rural population better access to workplaces, schools and urban services.

As a result, the paper argues that some transport problems in low density areas, which we today try to solve by dial-a-bus and similar expensive experiments, are partly created by the hierarchical network and therefore should rather be solved by restructuring the network.

5B36 PLUMMER, R.W., KING, E. and DESPHANDE, G. (1971) Development of intercity trip generation and trip distribution models for rural communities. *Transportation Research Record*, 638, pp. 32-8.

The object of this study was to analyse intercity trip linkages and to model intercity travel for towns of less than 50,000 population. The travel data used consisted of external travels surveys conducted at 21 cities during 1965 to 1969 and a methodology was developed to update travel surveys. The nature of intercity travel for smaller cities was analysed, and models were developed to forecast travel for these cities.

7 ROBINSON, G.K. (1980) A model for simulating traffic on rural roads. Australian Road Research Board, Technical Manual ATM 10, February.

This manual describes a computer model which simulates traffic flow on a rural road (the model, and the associated computer program, is referred to by the name TRARR). The model allows overtaking prohibitions, auxillary lanes, horizontal and vertical curves, and variable sight distance to be studied. Vehicles may vary in performance and drivers may vary in their behaviour when unimpeded, following other vehicles, overtaking or merging. The detailed coding of the computer program was done with three objectives in mind: the behaviour of vehicles should be able to be varied greatly by changing the data without changing the program, the program should be reasonably efficient, and the program should be modular so that it may be easily modified. TRARR is thus a suite of programs with several subroutines common to all versions. The model is intended for the estimation of travel time costs of possible road alignments. Such costs may be combined with estimates of accident costs, construction costs and fuel consumption obtained in other ways to aid decisions about rural road design. Within its appendices, the report gives samples of input data and corresponding output, and a complete listing of the source code of the program. The detailed logic of the program is described partly in the body of the report and partly in the comments included in the source code.

8 SKORPA, L., DODGE, R., WALTON, C.M. and HUDDLESTON, J. (1974) Transportation impact research: a review of previous studies and a recommended methodology for the study of rural communities. Council for Advanced Transportation Studies, Texas University, Austin.

This report, which is the third in a series describing the research project entitled 'Transportation to fulfil human needs', is presented in an effort to provide both a picture of the state-of-the-art and a summary of specific results, especially those which have a direct bearing on the study of inter-urban transport in rural environments.

The report presents a brief classification and definition of the types
of methodology used in transport impact studies, and summarizes in
detail the findings of previous research according to the type of impact investigated. The report comments on the usefulness and limitations of previous studies and proposes a strategy for future research
appropriate both to the state of the art and to the needs of this
present effort. The need is indicated for a re-evaluation of the methodology of impact studies in general and for the development (from
specific case studies) of a methodology appropriate to transportation
systems impact on small communities. The report covers such aspects as impact of highway improvement, the effects of other transport modes and the modelling of highway impact (models of land
development and land value are reviewed).

5B39 STEPHANEDES, Y.J. and ADLER, T.J. (1979) Forecasting experiments
for rural transit policymakers. *Transportation Reserch Record,* 718, pp.
42–4.

The paper addresses problems faced by transit managers and funding agencies. Such problems have been identified through the interaction of state and federal officials and during a review of rural
transit systems in northern New England performed during the first
part of 1978. Some of the first problems that transit managers face
are in the initial application for funding and making plans based on
socioeconomic and demographic characteristics of the service area.
These problems are further complicated by the urgency with which
funding agencies expect to see results in order to decide about funding continuation and budget approval, which ultimately results in
system delay. The magnitude of this overall system delay depends
on four individual delays, each of which is from four months to one
year long. These delays have been identified during work on case
studies of rural transit systems in northern New England: vehicle
acquisition delay, schedule change delay, subsidy award delay, and
ridership information delay. A simulation technique is used in the
analysis of the effects of different policies on the development of a
rural transit system. Results of policy experiments agree with the
observed behaviour of rural transit systems in northern New England. The technique is useful primarily as a quick turnaround
policy-analysis tool. The technique has potential applications for
policy analysis at two levels: the managerial level to help in project

planning and operation and the fund allocation level to help in decisions about funding approval, funding allocation, and funding renewal.

STEPHANEDES, Y.J. and EAGLE, D.M. (1983) Job search trip distribution in rural areas. *Journal of Advanced Transportation* **17** (2), pp. 183-99.

A job search trip distribution model is developed based on a disaggregate binary logit structure. The proposed model includes a set of economic and transport level-of-service variables, and can aid in evaluating transport and economic policies which seek to improve service area unemployment. Transport and socio-economic data from four Minnesota towns are used for model testing and validation. Travel conditions for the period of expected employment are found to influence destination choice. For all communities studied expected length of employment is the strongest determinant of choice. The proposed specification predicts job search trip distribution up to 76 per cent correctly and is not strongly influenced by location of application.

SULLIVAN, B.E. (1974) An analysis of the demand for and supply of rural public transportation: the case of Alberta. Unpublished PhD Thesis, Stanford University, California.

TOURISM AND RECREATION RESEARCH UNIT (1980) Models of recreation travel, TRRU Research Report 33, University of Edinburgh.

UGOLIK, W. (1980) Patterned demand rural transit system. *New York State Department of Transportation*, PRR 186.

Describes an algorithm to evaluate bus routes in rural areas.

VAN TOL, H. (1979) Is een normerings-systeem voorhet voorzieningsniveau van het streekvervoer toepasbaar? Ministerie van Verkeer en Waterstaat, 's-Gravenhage, Netherlands (in Dutch). (Are standards for rural public transport performance measures applicable?)

WALSH, J.A. (1980) An entropy maximizing analysis of journey to work patterns in County Limerick. *Irish Geography*, **13** (1), pp. 33-53.

5B46 WARREN, R.P. and COLLURA, J. (1978) Data recording recording and evaluation. The Barnstable County experience. *Transportation Research Record*, 696, pp. 58–65.

A mechanism for collecting data on rider and operating character-istics of regionwide public transport services is described. The mech-anism, a serially numbered rider identification pass, is being tested as part of an ongoing demonstration project in Barnstable County, Massachusetts. Service is provided on a prearranged demand-re-sponsive basis by use of ten 12-passenger vehicles. Passengers acquire passes in advance and complete a questionnaire on their socioecon-omic characteristics and physical disabilities. When passholders telephone to schedule a trip, the dispatcher records their pass num-ber, pickup time, trip purpose, and origin and destination. Special attention has been given to minimizing the data to be colleced by the bus driver: the driver records only on and off odometer readings for each trip. By using the passholder questionnaire and the daily driver log forms, socioeconomic and trip data are collected for all riders. These data may be used to evaluate vehicle productivity and efficiency; examine the impacts of local policy decisions; assess the portion of a deficit to be paid by each town; develop user charges and contractual agreements for use by social-services agencies; iden-tify those persons who are eligible for the services of a social-services agency; and describe user characteristics. The uses of the pass in fare collection and marketing are discussed, and capital and operating costs of the pass are estimated.

5B47 WHITE, P.R. (1975) A probabilistic approach to rural network scheduling. Polytechnic of Central London, Rural Public Transport Seminar, November.

The basic premise suggests that in many rural areas, the rigidity of fixed routes and fixed stopping points is becoming wasteful to the operator and irritating to the passenger. Buses make diversions form a potential direct route via nearby villages, but pick up and set down no passengers on lightly-loaded runs; the average bus passen-ger already finds many of the indirect rural routes rather slow, and becomes doubly irritated when diversions serve no purpose. This paper outlines a procedure for determining whether variations in timing and routing are desirable.

48 WYTCONSULT (1977) Rural transport analysis manual. Document 801, June.

The distinction between rural and urban areas is discussed and the zoning system developed to emphasize this distinction is described. The Rural Data Bank is described, and this provides ready access to planning information describing the characteristics of any rural community in the County. The information is stored on a zonal basis and the analysis of these characteristics and the uses of the results are summarized, as is the development of a hierarchy of activity centres in the county.

Public transport in rural areas was studied in detail and the analysis of operating costs and revenue, and the compiling of public transport data bank are described. A major section of the report is devoted to the accessibility analysis in rural areas which uses a specially developed suite of programs, and is based on a sifting of timetable information for public transport to determine whether journeys to particular facilities, or ranges of facilities are possible using schedule services. The hierarchy of facilities is used to classify the facilities available in each zone. and the analysis can also be used to determine the catchment areas of particular facilities. Data compilation, program logic and operating instructions are described in detail. A brief comparison of this method with that employed by the Urban Studies is included.

The final section of the report contains details of the structured surveys conducted during the course of the Studies which have relevance to rural areas, and details of most of the data compiled during the course of the Study is given in the Appendices.

5C Investment appraisal and evaluation

1 BEENHAKKER, H.L. and CHAMMARI, A. (1979) Identification and appraisal of rural roads project. International Bank for Reconstruction and Development Staff Working Paper 362, October.

This paper describes an operational approach to the identification and apprasial of projects consisting of rural roads and complementary investments. The objective for such projects is to prepare and implement a comprehensive, multi-sectoral development programme on the basis of rural roads in their zones of influence. The methodology can, therefore, also be applied to rural development projects. The principal purpose of the identification process is to ascertain the development potential of a rural road's zone of influence. In many instances this may depend on the potential of one or two crops, which, therefore, should be examined with more care. The appraisal methodology determines the appropriate scope and timing for road improvements or construction, their maintenance needs, and the complementary investments in other sectors, without which (in most cases) the road improvements or construction would not be justified. In other words, the project attempts to achieve an optimal development package for each road's zone of influence The linkages between agricultural and transport components are emphasized.

5C2 BEESLEY, M.A. and KETTLE, P.B. (1979) The Leitch Committee's recommendations and the management of the road programme. *Regional Studies*, **13** (6), 513-29.

In response to criticism of the Department's trunk road appraisal procedures, the Committee, in 1977, advocated what it viewed to be a comprehensive appraisal framework (LCAF), including all relevant impacts and groups. The authors argue that LCAF is intended to be operated within a 'managerial' decision model, where there is an aim of making consistent evaluation at all stages of scheme appraisal and in determining priorities between schemes. The likely effects of trying to implement this decision model are examined and it is concluded that at various stages where appraisal now enters, LCAF will be impractical or unsatisfactory, or both.

The authors go on to argue that although LCAF should be developed for particular stages of the decision process, decisions on schemes will still fail to be generally regarded as fair unless basic changes are made to the way conflicts of interest between groups are resolved. To remedy this, a system is recommended in which a lay panel, drawn from the public at large, would determine distributional issues and take the decision on routes, and the LCAF has an important part to play in this. Compensation provision should be extended. Finally, the proposals are contrasted with the recommendations in the recent White Paper on public inquiry conduct and their anticipated effects.

5C3 BELL, M., HEARNE, A.S., VICK, C.M. and VANK, C.M. (1977) Motorway, trunk road development and the farmer. *Transport and Road Research Laboratory*, SR 330.

The report discusses the problems of land severance, for new motorway or road construction purposes, of a farming community. While not intended to take the place of legal expertise, the report attempts to cover the various stages of planning and construction of new roads, how farms may be affected, and what can be done to minimize possible adverse effects. The notes are said to be based on the practical experience of farmers faced with the disruption of farm business for road construction works. Information is presented under the following headings: role of the National Farmers' Union; how new roads are planned—a stage by stage account; planning and design; the public inquiry; the Secretary of State's decision or deferral; land acquisition; and construction of the road.

5C4 BENEDICT, R., PRATO, R. and PARAMO, J.A. (1980) Disenos estructurales economicos de caminos de la red terciaria. Paper presented at the IRF Inter American Regional Meeting, Buenos Aires, May (in Spanish), Economic structural design of local roads.

Rural roads serving the agricultural and cattle-producing areas of Argentina have no fixed maintenance system, and deterioration comes quickly. The authors propose a construction programme featuring structures of low initial cost, all-weather use, and simple and economic maintenance. They propose that the roads should be built with local soils treated with stabilizing agents that provide low cementation, without asphalt surfacing. The resulting roads would be water-resistant and could be maintained with the same infrastructure tht currently exists for the maintenance of earth roads. The study of stabilized mixtures as soil-sand-lime seems to indicate that this is one solution compatible with the proposed method. The report analyses the use of the soil-sand-lime method, with emphasis on the use of sand from the Parana River.

C5 BERGER, L. (1976) Methodology for establishing the economic viability of low-volume roads. *Transportation Research Board*, SR 160, pp. 385-95.

The importance of low-volume or feeder roads to regional economic development is discussed, and a methodology for appraising the economic value of low-volume roads is described. The methodology stresses the integrated role of low-volume roads in a rural, regional, and national framework. This paper discusses the transport planner's approach to evaluating and designing low-cost low-volume roads and gives a detailed list of his tasks.

5C6 BOVILL, D.N. (1978) Rural road appraisal methods for developing countries. *Transport and Road Reserch Laboratory*. SR 395.

This report is concerned with appraisal methods for roads in rural areas of developing countries where existing traffic levels are very low and where benefits to investments in the area will be mainly related to increases in agricultural production and improvements in social welfare. Commonly used appraisal methods are critically reviewed and improved techniques incorporating social and economic objectives are proposed.

5C7 BRIDLE, R.J. (1981) Environmental appraisal of trunk roads. *Proceedings of the Institution of Civil Engineers*, **71** (2), pp. 287–304.

Examines this issue with reference to the groupings identified in the Leitch Report on transport evaluation—travellers, owners and occupiers of adjacent property, the users of facilities accessed from the road, groups indirectly affected by local and national policies and financial authorities.

5C8 BRUTON, M.J. (1980) Public participation, local planning and conflicts of interest. *Policy and Politics*, **8** (4), pp. 423–42.

Argues through a series of case studies that public participation is about conflicts of interest. Some form of distributional bargaining is undertaken as an integral part of the process, although from a position of only partial knowledge.

5C9 BUDHU, G. and HOBEIKA, A.G. (1980) Transportation investment in less-developed countries: The case of Guyana. *Transportation Research Record*, 747, pp. 93–7.

The procedure of incorporating the transport variable in determining the effect of transport investment for low-volume roads is generalized and applied to regions in Guyana where water is the only mode of transport. Several regions in Guyana that have poor means of access are known to have characteristics similar to developed regions of the country that have 'efficient' modes of transport. Yet these regions remain sparsely populated and relatively underdeveloped. Previous studies that have used the traditional approach of quantifying benefits against costs have always concluded that transport investment was infeasible in such regions. The economic activities and constraints of the Berbice-Orealla region of Guyana are formulated into a linear programming model to determine the net economic effect of transport investment in the region. The analysis shows that the benefits of improved transport for the region exceed the costs. Application of the model to other less-developed regions would assist in priority ranking of transport investments in less-developed countries. Various criticisms and attributes of the model are also discussed.

0 BULMAN, J.N. and ROBINSON, R. (1977) A road transport investment model for developing countries, in Visser, E.J. (ed) *Transport Decisions in an Age of Uncertainty*, The Hague: Martinus Nijhoff, pp. 311–18.

The Road Transport Investment Model calculates the sum of the construction costs, the road maintenance costs and the vehicle operating costs over the 'design life' of the project. It enables the designer to minimize total costs as the optimum choice of geometric standard and road type (the surfacing could be earth, gravel or bitumen) can be selected. It has been tested in Kenya and Ethiopia.

1 BURKHARDT, J.E. (1979) Residential dislocation: Costs and consequences. *Transportation Research Record*, 716, pp. 20–7.

This study investigated methods for predicting the dislocation consequences of alternative highway route and design proposals. It also assessed existing compensation practices in light of significant consequences. Data for these purposes were primarily derived from two household surveys before and after relocation. Interviews were conducted at six sites that represented a variety of project characteristics and geographic regions. The study found that specific dislocation consequences of alternative route and design proposals cannot be accurately predicted using data concerning the characteristics of the displaced households, the communities, or the projects. Compensation practices and relocation procedures have more effect on the nature and extent of changes incurred by those relocated than do demographic or geographic characteristics. Thus, current compensation practices, which constitute significant improvements over previous practices, do not discriminate for or against any particular population subgroup. However, the elderly are more likely to be in a worse position after the move than others due to essentially non-compensable factors rather than compensation practices. Therefore, planning procedures to avoid disrupting large concentrations of the elderly are required. The study concluded that, although the relocation process works well for many persons, certain improvements are still required.

5C12 CARNEMARK, C., BIDERMAN, J. and BOVET, D. (1976) *The Economic Analysis of Rural Road Projects*. International Bank for Reconstruction and Development, Working Paper 241, August.

The purpose of this paper is to set forth a general approach for the economic analysis of rural road projects. In this context, the paper discusses the shortcomings of traditional economic analyses of highway projects which have focused on the quantification of road user savings. The paper points out that such an approach is specifically unsuitable for rural roads with low levels of traffic. The authors emphasize the interdependence of transport and agricultural production systems in the rural environment and argue that the analysis should focus on the mechanisms by which transport cost savings are translated into increased agricultural production and income. The critical questions to be answered are: who benefits from the transport cost savings, how will producers respond to these cost savings, and do other constraints exist which may prevent the full developmental impact of a road from materializing?

From an analytical point of view, rural road projects are separated into two categories depending on the current level of economic activity in the area of influence. In areas of low economic activity, a producer surplus-oriented analysis is recommended as a means of quantifying the benefits of increased economic activity induced by the road and any complementary investments. The principles set forth in this paper are gradually being introduced in World Bank operational work, particularly in the context of rural development projects. The work at this time does not, therefore, represent established World Bank policy, but it reflects the direction in which World Bank appraisal practices are evolving.

13 COLLURA, J. and WARREN, R.P. (1979) Regional paratransit services: An evaluation. *Transportation Engineering Journal ASCE*, **105** (TE6), pp. 683-97.

This paper describes a data collection method that was used in a public transport project in Barnstable County, Massachusetts. Each person who uses the bus service acquires a pass in advance and completes a questionnaire regarding socioeconomic characteristics and disability. When the passholder telephones to schedule a trip, the dispatcher records his or her pass number, pickup time, trip purpose, origin and destination. As a result all data is recorded and available for analysis. These data may be used to evaluate vehicle productivity and efficiency; to examine the impacts of local policy decisions; to assess the portion of the deficit to be paid by each town; to develop social service agency user charges and contractuual agreements; to identify social service agency eligibles; and to describe user characteristics.

14 CONRAD, P.E. and THOMPSON, J.M. (1980) Feeder roads and their economic impact on agricultural coordination and transmigration. Paper presented at the 4th IRF African Highway Conference, Nairobi, January.

Feeder roads tied to a penetration road are critical elements in the coordinated settlement of virgin territory with characteristics that make it suitable for agricultural development. The same may be observed for other types of economic developent in a rural setting, but the important aspect is the necessity for evaluation of the proposed roadway network within the context of total development prospects in the area served. The need for an integrated approach requires trade-offs in respect to the level of detail possible within the resources available for project evaluation. The author cites three case studies in The Gambia, Nicaragua, and Bolivia, to indicate how this trade-off on the level of detail has been resolved to meet the needs of the situation under study. The method has identified valuable criteria for evaluating the economic desirability of penetration-feeder roads as a means of promoting the development of areas with agricultural and related potentials.

15 COOPER, T.W. and KANE, A. (1981) Minor rural roads: Finance trends and issues. *Transportation Research Record*, 813, pp. 15-20.

The local rural road problem is primarily one of finance. The purpose of this paper is to examine the sources and trends in local rural highway revenues and expenditures, to identify issues, and to explore solutions. Revenue for local rural roads ($3.1 billion for 1979) is generated equally by the local jurisdictions and by state and federal grants in aid. Local jurisdictions rely almost entirely on property taxes and general revenues for local support for highways. However, road-user charges provide a substantial portion of the local road burden via shared or the user-tax revenue. Because of the role of the local rural road, some claim that this shared financial burden (user and nonuser support) is justified, and others argue that users should cover all highway costs. County roads programmes are oriented towards routine maintenance of conditions. In fact, local road maintenance has increased in real dollars since 1970, whereas capital road improvements have dropped by one-fourth. Consequently, local road conditions are judged to be declining. The conclusions reached are that existing local rural road revenue sources are imperilled by energy conservation and voter demands for fiscal restraint: local road programs are basically maintenance operations and user charges ought to cover the cost; and revenue sources are available. Specifically, local governments should expand road user tax revenues by defining existing taxes as user fees and dedicating them to highway use and by exploring the creation of new user revenue instruments and mechanisms such as a local gasoline tax that piggybacks the state tax. Finally, local governments need to articulate the condition of local roads and what that means in terms of costs to government, local economy, and road user.

5C16 CORNWALL, P.R. and THOMSON, J.M. (1983) The development of priorities for rural roads, in *Highway Investment in Developing Countries*, London: Thomas Telford Ltd, pp. 79–87.

5C17 DAVIES, P.W. and HUNJAN, J.S. (1981) Some comment on the COBA method. *Highway Engineer*, **28** (1), pp. 14–18.

Continuing the theme of cost benefit analysis applied to highway networks, the article concentrates on traffic and constructional cost sections of the COBA methodology. This computer-based technique estimates economic costs incurred by traffic using a road network. The basic elements are concerned with network data, traffic description, economic values of traffic, construction and land use. The elements may be used in the assessment of trunk road schemes with COBA being used as a standard package for most cases. The application of COBA provides assistance in assessing networks by identifying problems and solutions, and also aiding in design. Developments of COBA will add to the realism of the technique and allow more direct treatment of networks and traffic patterns.

18 EDMONDS, G.A. (1983) Rural transport policy in developing countries, in *Highway Investment in Developing Countries*, London: Thomas Telford Ltd, pp. 119–24.

The objectives of rural road transport planning can be, and often are, varied and diverse. In a strict planning sense the objective can be seen as purely to extend the road network, to provide the final link in a chain which is seen to start at the port or a major city. More rationally, rural roads can be planned to meet various development objectives, be they strictly economic or socio-economic. On the other hand, they may be prepared to meet political objectives related to integrating the rural population or strategic/defence objectives. The assumptions regarding rural transport planning are discussed and it is suggested that there are many basic questions to be answered.

19 GALLAGHER, W.E. (1982) The impact of new developments on decision-making for trunk road schemes. Paper presented to the PTRC Annual Summer Conference, Warwick, July.

In 1978, the Department of Transport accepted a recommendation of the Advisory Committee on Trunk Road Assessment that it should give explicit recognition to uncertainty in trunk road appraisal. Accordingly National Road Traffic Forecasts were issued that year and revised in 1980; presented in the form of a range with high and low growth forecasts for each year up to 2010. Regional Officers were required to consider a range of scheme forecasts consistent with the national forecasts and, in choosing between options, to avoid giving special emphasis to any particular forecast within the range.

The paper considers whether this simple yet effective method of dealing with uncertainty is still valid in the light of the recent research findings. It also examines the way in which the principles have been applied over the past three years and explains the changes, if any, which should now be introduced.

The paper also discusses other advances in appraisal techniques which have been made possible by the better understanding of uncertainty, and it describes recent changes in the Department's approach to decision making which arise from other considerations.

5C20 GB DEPARTMENT OF TRANSPORT (1978) Report on the Review of Highway Inquiry Procedures. London: HMSO, Cmnd 7133.

This report looks at the purpose of highway inquiries, the need for the road, where it should be located and the role of the public at the inquiry. The new arrangements are covered and the proposals for further action summarized.

5C21 GB DEPARTMENT OF TRANSPORT (1978) Report of the Advisory Committee on Trunk Road Assessment, (Chairman G. Leitch), London: HMSO.

Examines the Department of Transport's current procedures and methods, mainly in respect of traffic forecasting, traffic modelling, and the economic appraisal of trunk road schemes. It also sets out current practice in Germany, France and the United States, and reports the criticisms of the current methods in Britain and makes suggestions for their improvement.

5C22 GB DEPARTMENT OF TRANSPORT (1980) Policy for roads: England 1980. London: HMSO, Cmnd 7908.

This paper updated the 1978 version (Cmnd 7132) and proposed that spending should be stabilized at the 1978 level, following the halving of expenditure between 1974 and 1978. Within this new context the paper proposed three priorities: 'first, roads which aid economic recovery and development; second, roads which bring environmental benefit; and third, preserving the investment already made'. The resulting policy is thus one of orbital roads around London, Birmingham and Manchester, a network of east-west routes to complement the basically north-south motorway system, and a mass of bypasses around historic towns.

5C23 GB DEPARTMENT OF TRANSPORT (1980) Trunk road proposals: A comprehensive framework for appraisal. London: HMSO.

4 GB DEPARTMENT OF TRANSPORT (1981) Public inquiries into road proposals—what you need to know. London: HMSO, February.

This booklet is intended to explain the arrangements and procedures at public inquiries into road proposals in simple terms. It does not intend to give an authorative interpretation of the law as only the courts can do this.

5 GB DEPARTMENT OF TRANSPORT ASSESSMENTS POLICY AND METHODS DIVISION (1981) COBA 9, Department of Transport, London.

COBA (Cost Benefit Analysis) compares the costs of road schemes with the benefits derived by road users and expresses them in terms of a monetary evaluation. COBA is the fourth version of the program to be used in taking decisions on trunk roads.

26 GONZALEZ, S.M. and JOFRE, F.A. (1982) The economic appraisal of accidents for rural roads projects: The Chilean case. Paper presented at the PTRC Annual Summer Conference, Warwick, July.

This paper presents a methodology to estimate accidents cost/benefit in rural roads project appraisal with an application to the Chilean case. Basically, it is necessary to resolve two main problems. First, to study cause/effect relationships in accident occurrence that allow, through statistical methods, prediction of the reduction in type and quantity of accidents due to the project. Second, it is necessary to apply a price vector, that could be constant or variable through the economic life of the project. It has been customary to adapt, and even to apply directly accident rates reduction and pricing methodologies coming from studies developed in industrialized countries.

This work presents statistical models based on pooled data collected from Chilean rural roads; and accidents are postulated to be, ceteris paribus, a function of geometric characteristics, type of surface and vehicle flow. It was found that accidents involving pedestrians should be treated separately from those involving only vehicles. Road width, horizontal and vertical curvature, number of intersections, population density and vehicle flow are found to be significant explanatory variables for accidents on paved roads. On unpaved roads (gravel and earth) the type of accident presents a great variability and satisfactory macro-statistical relationships were not found: thus, a disaggregate analysis is recommended in this case.

5C27 GUHA, S. (1980) Economic impact of rural roads. *Indian Highways,*
8 (7), pp. 41–7.

A balanced and adequate transport system may be an essential
precondition for the efficiency of the whole economy, but the network in rural India is hopelessly inadequate. In this paper a quantitative study is an attempt to apportion the role of promoted growth
in the rural sector between the pucca road system and other sectors
(e.g. development activities). The purpose is to promote a rational
discussion so that unbiased selection criteria for rural roads can be
established.

5C28 HALE, C.W. and WALTERS, J. (1974) Appalachian regional development and the distribution of highway benefits. *Growth and Change,* **5**
(1), pp. 3–11.

5C29 HARRISON, A. and DRUITT, S. (1982) NESA: A modelling procedure
for the evaluation of trunk road schemes in Scotland. Paper
presented at the PTRC Annual Summer Conference, Warwick,
July.

The evaluation of all Trunk Road Schemes in Scotland costing more
than £1m is being made with the use of NESA—a computer program commissioned by the Scottish Development Department. The
primary objective is to produce a cost benefit analysis, but its unique
structure integrates many stages previously dealt with by separate
programs with the result that the complete highway modelling process is handled by NESA. The program places emphasis on the relief
of congestion at controlled and uncontrolled intersections and is
particularly applicable in medium sized urban situations. In addition to highway assignments and a junction delay analysis, net
present values of test schemes measured against a 'do-minimum'
network are produced.

   Data input and file management are greatly simplified—a NESA
model is self-documenting, all details of parameters and options
being held together with the network description, assignment and
junction details on one physical storage unit. Consequently, both
experienced and inexperienced users will find little difficulty in using
the program which has been applied to a wide range of urban and
rural problems. The authors describe the structure and use of NESA,
and discuss its advantages and limitations.

30 HAUSER, E.W. (1975) The Evaluation of Transportation Programs for the Rural Disadvantaged. Unpublished PhD Thesis, N. Carolina State University, Raleigh, USA.

31 HAYTON, F. and JOHNSTONE, M. (1979) The economic effects of bypasses on local business. Highlands and Islands Development Board, Transport Research Paper 5.

This study evaluates the economic impact on businesses in five communities bypassed by the new M90 and A9 in Tayside Region, Scotland. The communities chosen were Kinross, Milnathort, Bankfoot, Birnam and Dunkeld which vary in size, function and time of bypass. Using a questionnaire, operators of businesses in the accommodation, catering, garage and retail sectors were interviewed, regarding the nature of their business and the impact of the bypass on various aspects of it. Supplementary data on changes in businesses was obtained from valuation rolls. The impact of the bypass is discussed in terms of: pre-bypass attitude; change of operators; changes made in anticipation of and since the bypass; effect on trade and employment; effect on particular sectors of each type of business; and operators' suggestions and comments. These findings are summarized, and a number of factors are identified which influence the economic impact of a bypass on a community.

32 HEARNE, A.S. and VANRNE, A.S.E. (1979) Farming consideration in highway assessment. *Highway Engineer*, **26** (7), pp. 15–20.

Farming is primarily an economic activity; hence the agricultural input to the highway planning framework ought to be given in financial terms. Recognition of the institutional structuring of farm land into individual holdings enables such a predictive financial impact model to be devised. The aggregation of the predicted loss of income upon farm units for a proposed scheme will give the national agricultural resource loss consequent upon the construction of that scheme.

33 HEATHINGTON, K.W. and BROGAN, J.D. (1977) Simplified procedures for preliminary evaluation of public transportation alternatives. *Transportation Research Record*, 638, pp. 1–7.

A simplified approach is proposed to quickly evaluate at a gross level various alternatives for providing public transport services. The alternatives, ranging from very simplified bus-oriented systems to high-speed rail facilities operating on dedicated rights-of-way, are reviewed in terms of meeting specified criteria for public transport services. The sketch-planning procedure reviews and evaluates alternatives without substantial outlays in time or resources. Computer capabilities are not required. At this level of analysis sketch planning enables the planner to differentiate between alternatives that have merit and those that should not be given a more detailed analysis. The data required for sketch planning come from two sources – the socioeconomic and demographic variables enumerated in census reports and origin-and-destination data available from metropolitan area transport studies. Criteria for evaluation should be established for each area under study to provide for differences among urban areas. The planning procedures proposed here are generally more applicable to medium-sized and small urban areas.

5C34   HILL, M. (1968) A goals-achievement matrix for evaluating alternative plannings. *Journal of the American Institute of Planners*, **34** (1), pp. 19–29.

5C35   HILL, M. and WERCZBERGER, E. (1978) Goal programming and the goals achievement matrix. *International Journal of Regional Science Review*, **3** (2), pp. 19–29.

5C36   HINE, J.L. (1975) The appraisal of rural feeder roads in developing countries. Paper presented to the Summer Annual PTRC Conference, Warwick, July.

In recent years it has been recognized that conventional cost benefit criteria which concentrate on transport cost savings appear to give unsatisfactory guide-lines for the evaluation of investment in rural feeder roads within developing countries. This paper is divided into two parts: the first looks at the general economic and social environment in which rural roads must be planned; the second considers some evaluation techniques that have been applied or conceivably could be used.

5C37   HINE, J.L. (1982) Road planning for rural development in developing countries: A review of current practice. *Transport and Road Research Laboratory*, LR1046.

This report is written as a guide to assist with all road planning in rural areas of developing countries, but the focus of attention is on the smaller rural roads. A critical examination is made of the relationship between road investment and rural development. In addition, a variety of economic appraisal techniques are reviewed.

Case study material is used to identify some of the circumstances which will induce a favourable response to road investment. The evidence suggests that this is most likely to occur when road investment brings about a relatively large change in transport costs in an area which has underused land, a skilled mobile workforce and a competitive transport industry. The treatment of benefits accruing to agriculture in the appraisal of rural road projects has generally been poorly carried out. The basis of the forecasts tend to be weak and a failure to consider all the relevant costs of production has meant that on balance it appears that road benefits are often overvalued. Where there is some basis for predicting changes in agricultural output the World Bank's producer surplus approach is cautiously advocated. For road planning within larger development plans, for road maintenance and rehabilitation programmes and in situations where prediction is more difficult a minimum transport cost solution is suggested.

38 JEFFERSON, J.R. (1977) Route location with regard to environmental issues. GB Department of Transport.

Includes the report of an internal working party and the ten discussion papers associated with it. The method of evaluation suggested has after certain modifications been used on an experimental basis.

39 JENSEN, O.H. (1976) Evaluation of public transportation. Institute of Mathematical Statistics and Operations Research, The Technical University of Denmark.

This paper discusses the provision of public transport in rural Denmark and presents an operational research model that can be used to plan these services. An example of the model is given for one Danish county and the four submodels are described: the model of the region; the model of the household; the model of public transport and the model of car ownership. The overall aim of the process is to demonstrate the interactions between the submodels highlighting an integrated approach to evaluation.

5C40 KOCH, J.A., MOAVENZADEH, F. and CHEW, K.S. (1979) A methodology for evaluation of rural roads in the context of development.
Transportation Research Record, 702, pp. 31–8.

Despite a good rate of national growth, rural poverty is on the rise
in many developing countries. Transport, particularly roads, is perceived as an important component of rural development. In an effort
to obtain a more valid basis for selection among investments, an
evaluation framework capable of accounting for the various socio-
economic objectives of the rural development effort in the assessment
of rural transport projects is formulated and preliminarily tested. A
potentially appropriate set of developmental objectives is identified,
and possible measures proposed. Utility assessment techniques are
suggested for developing decision maker's preference functions, and
ultimately scaling project contributions to the criteria. These scaled
measures of the criteria for each project are then incorporated into
a single value structure as a basis for project ranking and thus
decision making. Depending upon the decision maker's access to
information and articulation of his preferences among the criteria,
equal or cardinal weights may be directly assigned to the criteria,
or an ordinal ranking of them may be done, and an upper or lower
bound decision rule used. The ranking of the projects varies with
the approach. The proposed appraisal framework is seen as a simple
but valuable tool in the project selection stage where a decision
maker faces an array of potential projects and needs some means for
evaluating their relative worths. Although a case study has been
carried out, testing under actual field conditions remains to be done.
Moreover, this is a first step effort, and certain refinements are
needed.

5C41 LEMER, A.C. (1979) Analysis in planning and programming non-
urban highway investments: US and UK experience. Paper
presented at the PTRC Annual Summer Conference, Warwick,
July.

Two case studies are taken—*US case*. In September 1975 a research
project was undertaken under the auspices of the National Cooperative Highway Research Program (NCHRP) in the US, to investigate 'Techniques for Evaluating Options in Statewide Transportation Planning/Programming'. The purpose of this project was to
provide techniques for testing and evaluation of state-level planning

options, techniques which are reasonable in their cost, sensitive to the policy issues facing decisionmakers and thus broadly useful to these decisionmakers.

UK case. In February 1977, the Advisory Commission on Trunk Road Assessment was formed to review and comment on the UK Department of Transport (DTp) method of appraising trunk road schemes. With excursions into traffic forecasting and design standards, the Leitch Commission focused on a single analysis technique, a cost benefit method embodied in a computer program called COBA, to which most major trunk road schemes were subjected as part of the decisionmaking process.

One may then conclude that project analysis in the US could usefully be expanded by complete disaggregation of the framework. Such analysis has been undertaken by some UK investigators, particularly in overseas applications. It may then be that the principal differences between the two studies, and between US and UK practice, are related to philosophy of what can be measured and in what terms measurement should be made, and the extent to which the public is likely to argue with the analyst about his conclusions. Many in the US feel that while development of better planning techniques is a useful exercise, real success in planning for decision is likely to be more dependent upon the degree to which the planner/analyst establishes credibility with the decisionmaker and the public.

42 LEVIN, P.H. (1979) Highway inquiries: A study in Governmental responsiveness. *Public Administration*, Spring, pp. 21–49.

Reviews the response of Government to problems raised by the highway inquiry process. It is one area in which the Government and the public come into contact and where the former have attempted to diminish the discretion exercised by officials and inspectors. There is now greater ministerial and parliamentary involvement in formulating proposals and agreeing procedures.

43 LICHFIELD, N. (1970) Evaluation methodology of urban and regional plans. *Regional Studies*, **4** (3), pp. 151–65.

44 LICHFIELD, N. (1971) Cost benefit analysis in planning: a critique of the Roskill Commission. *Regional Studies*, **5** (3), pp. 157–83.

The work on the (Roskill) Commission on the Third London Airport, and also that of its research team, was an outstanding contribution to the practice of decision-making in urban and regional planning. Nevertheless at certain critical stages in their process the Commission was at serious fault. This paper examines those methodological weaknesses, and in particular, the Commission's unsatisfactory use of cost-benefit analysis and its inadequate treatment of issues of regional planning. Had the Commission made better use of cost-benefit analysis as a framework for arriving at its decision, it is possible that an alternative conclusion would have been reached, namely the one subsequently reached by the Government, Foulness.

5C45 LICHFIELD, N., KETTLE, P. and WHITBREAD, M. (1975) *Evaluation in the Planning Process.* Oxford: Pergamon.

5C46 MALE, J.W., COLLURA, J. and SCHUDINER, P.W. (1981) Allocating public transit costs among participants. *Transportation Engineering Journal*, ASCE, 107 (TE2), pp. 213-25.

A methodology was developed to aid in the selection of procedures to allocate regional transit costs among participants. It provides a means for comparing a variety of allocation procedures, based on the equity of the cost allocation and the cost to use the procedure. Data from Barnstable County (Massachusetts) were used to illustrate the procedure in its various forms and these were compared to an allocation based on each participant's individual costs.

5C47 MAYER, W.N. (1982) Evaluation of goods transport investment scheme for developing countries. Paper presented at the PTRC Annual Summer Conference, Warwick, July.

Most developing countries rely heavily upon a few strategic routes for the transport of their imports and exports and any interruption to the smooth flow of traffic can have disastrous economic effects. The situation of land-locked countries is particularly difficult in that they must rely upon the co-operation of neighbouring countries.

Investment in the improvements of existing routes and the development of new links is often financed by loans or grants from international agencies. The success of such schemes is heavily dependent upon careful consideration of the demands upon the resources of the countries concerned required for the long-term operation and maintenance of the new system. This paper discusses some of the important factors involved in making an appropriate scheme evaluation, with particular reference to a recent lake transport study in Africa.

348 MILLS, G. (1977) Economic appraisal and reappraisal of an interurban road in Great Britain. *Journal of Transport Economics and Policy*, **11** (1), pp. 3–23.

The present study chooses for reappraisal one British inter-urban road, for which an unusually thorough investigation was made before the road was built. This particular road is of interest in its own right; but this paper also attempts to draw general conclusions, first on the design and execution of investment appraisal calculations, and secondly on the merit of low-cost, low-standard roads, a category of which this road has turned out to be an important example. Much of the published literature on public sector investment appraisal concentrates on the conceptual aspects, e.g. how to devise an operational measure of consumers' surplus and (in a more applied context) how to value time savings. Also of importance are the practical problems, eg of making measurements and assessing their reliability. In its review of the appraisal procedures for inter-urban roads, the present study focuses attention on these practical tasks, and deliberately shuns many general conceptual issues.

349 MINISTRY OF OVERSEAS DEVELOPMENT (1977) A Guide to the Economic Appraisal of Projects in Developing Countries. London: HMSO.

350 MISHAN, E.J. (1971) *Cost Benefit Analysis*, London: Allen and Unwin.

351 MURPHY, H.W. (1979) Design and maintenance strategies for a rural road system. Paper presented at the PTRC Annual Summer Conference, Warwick, July.

Design and maintenance strategies for the road system controlled by the Main Roads Department, Queensland, Australia, are currently being reviewed. Approximately 60 per cent of roads in the system have been paved and bitumen surfaced and there is now a significant proportion of these roads requiring pavement overlays. By current standards, most of these roads would require widening and some would require improvements to horizontal and vertical alignments.

However, at present there are insufficient funds available to carry out all of this work.

For a number of years it has been Departmental policy to construct or reconstruct roads to high geometric standards but to design pavements with a view to overlaying at a later date—usually for a life of about 10 years. This paper examines the implications of such policies, having particular regard to the financial constraints, the age and condition of the present sealed road system, traffic growth and geometric standards. Alternative strategies are suggested.

5C52 NASH, C., PEARCE, D. and STANLEY, J. (1975) Critieria for evaluating project evaluation techniques. *Journal of the American Institute of Planners*, **41** (2), pp. 83–9.

This article stresses the underlying values implicit in any project evaluation technique. Value bases of conventional benefit-cost and matrix evaluation techniques are considered and their underlying similarity is noted. The article offers four criteria considered vital in choosing a suitable evaluation technique.

5C53 PEARMAN, A.D. (1979) Comparing road and rail investment using a multiple criteria framework: Can the Leitch Committee recommendations be implemented? Paper presented at the PTRC Annual Summer Conference, Warwick, July.

The main recommendations of the recent Leitch Advisory Committee on Trunk Road Assessment deal with matters internal to the road transport sector. However, since a balanced approach to the provision of transport as a whole requires that interdependence between roads and the other transport sectors be properly taken into account, there are likely to be significant implications in its recommendations for assessment procedures within and between other modes. In particular, this paper concentrates on interdependence between the road and rail sectors in the area of investment appraisal, where Recommendation 60 of the Leitch Committee states that 'Strategic or policy studies conducted to compare the rates of return from investment in road and rail should be conducted on the basis of cost benefit analysis, within [a multiple criteria] framework, rather than financial appraisal.' In the short time available to the Committee, it was not in a position to make any detailed suggestions about how this recommendation might be implemented. Since, however, especially in the rail sector, a number of major investment decisions are close at hand (for example, further electrification), it is clearly important to form a judgement about Recommendation 60, and not merely at an abstract level, but as a political and economic practicality.

4 RAHKONEN, O.J., COOK, C. and CARAPETIS, S. (1983) Institutional aspects of rural road projects, in *Highway Investment in Developing Countries*, London: Thomas Telford Ltd, pp. 63–70.

The growth of institutional capacity is a key aspect of the development process and critical in the design of project identification, planning and implementation procedures. In the past, projects have often partly failed because they have not been adequately tailored to a particular institutional and cultural context. Rural roads projects are particularly 'institution-intensive' both because they depend heavily on local human resources for their implementation and because their effectiveness often depends on simultaneous efforts by other agencies involved in the rural development process. Seven major themes emerge in discussions of the institutional aspects of rural roads projects: Centralization vs. decentralization; New vs. existing institutions; Public vs. private sector; Political commitment; Beneficiary participation; Inter-agency coordination; Human resource development. Current knowledge indicates that it is possible to establish only the most important principles and common factors influencing these institutional issues. Therefore, project designs should be tailored to specific local circumstances, with the goal of making the most effective use of resources to serve development objectives.

5 ROBINSON, R. (1976) The Kenya road transport investment model. *Transport Research Board*, SR 160, pp. 336–54.

A model is described that can be used to aid investment decisions regarding roads in developing countries. It calulates the construction cost of a road and predicts its condition as vehicles traverse it. Having predicted the condition of the road, the model estimates road maintenance and vehicle operating costs for each year. All these costs are then discounted back to the base year and summed over the life of the road to obtain the total cost. All estimates are made in terms of physical quantities, and costs are obtained by applying unit rates to these. The model is flexible and can be used to study the economics of varying stage construction alternatives such as upgrading an earth road to a gravel or paved road at any time during the design life. A case study of the application of the model to a paved road in western Kenya is described. Good agreement is obtained between actual and predicted construction costs. With a first year average daily traffic of about 400, vehicle operating costs over 10 years are two and a half times the cost of initial construction. Road maintenance costs are less than one per cent of the total transport cost.

5C56 ROE, M. (1982) Policy evaluation for highway priorities. Paper presented at the PTRC Annual Summer Conference, Warwick, July.

This paper discusses the application of an evaluation methodology developed for allocating priorities between competing highway investments for the annual Transport Policy and Programme document. The importance of policy priorities has been recognised in the development of the technique which has attempted to move away from traditional cost-benefit and goals achievement approaches and their inherent difficulties in application.

The results of applying the new methodology based upon trends and correlations identified within traffic data, are discussed and comparisons made of the priorities allocated to investment using the new technique and the old, existing 'Priority Evaluation' technique. The effect upon distribution of transport expenditure, the practical implications of introducing the new method, its ability to reflect more effectively political priorities, to overcome contentious issues of valuation, measurement and aggregation, and to produce more robust scheme rankings, are discussed. Finally problems still to be overcome are outlined and some of the proposed approaches to solving these problems opened for debate.

5C57 SAGER, T. (1981) The family of goals-achievement matrix methods: respectable enough for citizen participation in planning? *Environment and Planning A*, **13** (9), pp. 1151-61.

A recent survey shows that of the traditional evaluation techniques only modified goals-achievement matrix (GAM) methods are widely used in structure planning. This paper attempts to argue that the economists' critique of GAM is too general, secondly to clarify the links between GAM and other evaluation methods, and finally to discuss how GAM can be structured for use in local participatory planning.

8 SAMUELS, A. (1981) New roads: The assessment of need, usefulness and desirability. *Journal of Planning and Environmental Law*, January pp. 15–25.

Examines the issue of new roads with particular emphasis on current governmental approaches and priorities, the problem of measuring need, traffic forecasting and economic assessment. Attention is given to local factors and specific groups of individuals affected. The Standing Advisory Committee on Trunk Road Appraisal (SAC-TRA) framework for appraising a scheme is also set out.

9 SCHMIDT, R.H. (1980) Freeway impact on agricultural areas. *Natural Resources Journal*, **20** (3), pp. 581–602.

This study identifies and attempts to bring into proper perspective the conflicts, problems, and benefits that occur in rural areas traversed by limited-access highways. While super highways are often responsible for less expensive vehicular transport than surface roads, benefits to farmers, and ranchers are generally minor in comparison with the detrimental effects brought about by freeway construction. It is noted that freeways are permanent structures with permanent consequences, and that there is a need for better overall planning. Adequate consideration must be given to all values that are involved when freeways are constructed in agricultural areas. The article discusses the parcelling and connectivity of agricultural land and notes the problems caused by freeways in changing the number, size and shape of fields and in altering cropping and rotational practices. Some of the other problems attributable to freeway construction are also discussed and include impairment of air drainage, impairment of surface and subsurface drainage, reduced effectiveness of windbreaks, disruption of the overall farm or ranch operation, increased weed danger, air pollution damage, mobility, rural living, and urban encroachment.

50 SLEE, B.J. (1979) Simulating the appearance of rural roads. *Transport and Road Research Laboratory*, SR 426.

This report describes a method for making films to simulate the appearance of new transport systems in rural landscapes. The simulation films are made using the 'travelling matte' process, which is a motion picture special effects technique. Film of an existing road of the correct standard, carrying traffic is combined with film of the background landscape, so producing a simulation film, Two methods are briefly described, one using cine film, the other video.

5C61 SMITH, J.D. (1983) The choice of appraisal techniques when resources are limited—a case study of the rural roads programme in Peninsular Malaysia, in *Highway Investment in Developing Countries*, London: Thomas Telford Ltd, pp. 71–7.

Rural road projects are now seen as representing only one part of a wider development process in rural areas. The developmental role that some rural roads are expected to play has created the need for more realistic and complex models of rural transport behaviour. As a result appraisal techniques relying mainly on cost benefit analysis have been used, particularly where loan agencies have required detailed technical and economic feasibility studies. The trend towards more complicated appraisal methods in developing countries may not be practicable in situations where data and expertise are limited. Further the implementation problems resulting from a road programme in Peninsular Malaysia indicate that the use of several variables in the analysis stage tends to increase the potential errors inherent in forecasting future activities. This paper suggests that in such cases simplified procedures are needed to make the best use of limited resources.

5C62 SMITH, J.D. and WEEKS, N.E. (1975) The problem of route selection in a large rural area. *Traffic Engineering and Control*, **16** (3), pp. 114–17.

The envelope of the M1–A1 study included Leicester, Peterborough, Cambridge, Bedford, and the planned New Town of Milton Keynes, and covered a predominantly rural area of about 40 miles (63.2 km) square. This paper describes how the route selection process prior to evaluation has been approached, and how important variable parameters which were 'external' to the envelope of the study were incorporated. Possible applications of the procedures adopted are also discussed, in particular numerous alternatives appear to satisfy the goal being strived for.

63 Smith, R.L. (1977) Evaluation of rural public transportation demand models that include level of service measures. *Transportation Research Record*, 638, pp. 49–50.

Rural public transport (RPT) demand models that incorporate measures of level of service have recently been developed by Burkhardt and Lago [5B6]. The models provide demand estimates at macro (systemwide) and micro (route) levels for both fixed-route and demand-responsive systems. The primary measure of level of service for the fixed-route models is the frequency of service in terms of round trips per month or per day. Another measure of level of service is bus miles. The measure of level of service for the demand responsive models is the average reservation time in days.

In this paper, Burkhardt and Lago's level-of-service models are evaluated by direct application to estimate the demand for two existing RPT systems and by comparison with a simple trip-rate demand model. In addition, the level-of-service model coefficients are evaluated in terms of the expected elasticities of demand.

64 Smith, R.L. (1978) Record keeping and evaluation. *Transporttion Research Record*, 696, pp. 66–8.

This paper identifies major sources of information, record-keeping issues, and evaluation methodologies. Much is being learned about developing a unified reporting system, and record-keeping needs are addressed in terms of data availability, problems in data collection, and the potential impact of a federal operating subsidy. A systems approach to system evaluation is outlined together with the trade-off or balance sheet evaluation methodology. Service standards are proposed as a means of institutionalizing system evaluation.

65 Smith, R.L. (1979) Evaluation of rural volunteer driver transportation systems in Wisconsin. *Transportation Research*, **13** (5), pp. 309–15.

The purpose of this study is to evaluate the potential for volunteer driver systems in rural areas. Volunteer driver systems in which volunteers are reimbursed for mileage are hypothesized to be a cost-effective means of providing high quality, specialized transport in rural areas. The reason for the growth of volunteer driver systems are outlined in terms of their advantages and disadvantages. Volunteer driver systems are used extensively in Wisconsin to provide specialised transport service for the elderly and handicapped. The potential for expanding the systems exists as the result of a new state operating assistance programme. Two-well-developed volunteer driver systems which serve rural areas in Winsconsin are analysed and compared with paid driver systems using vans, and models are developed to compare the costs of volunteer driver and van systems. The analysis shows that volunteer driver systems provide high quality door-through-door service with lower costs per trip than all but the most productive van systems. With professional direction problems of volunteer recruitment and retention, volunteer reliability, and driver safety can be minimized. Insurance is a problem but has not severely restricted the growth of volunteer systems in Winsconsin. Volunteer systems can best serve high priority trips while van systems are better when extensive grouping of rides is possible. Finally implications of the results for federal operating assistance are discussed.

5C66 STEIN, M. (1977) Social impact assessment techniques and their application to transportation decisions. *Traffic Quarterly*, **31** (2), pp. 297-316.

This paper describes how social factors could be conceptually integrated into the transport planning process. It also outlines how social impact analysis can be used to avoid negative impacts and to promote positive impacts from transport services.

5C67 TAGGART, R.E., WALKER, N.S. and STEIN, M.M. (1979) Estimating socioeconomic impacts of transportation systems. *Transportation Research Record*, 716, pp. 9-20.

This study develops a methodology to estimate the socioeconomic impacts of multimodal transport plans and programs in Maryland. The impacts include government expenditures on plan implementation, socioeconomic impacts of expenditures (i.e. personal income, employment, and population), displacement of businesses and households, and land use, accessibility, safety and socioeconomic impacts of new transport services and facilities. The programmes evaluated include low-capital improvements and operating programmes. The methodology consists of 26 impact-estimating equations, each of which was developed for statewide regional, and county levels of detail.

3 TAITZ, L. and HARMAN, R. (1979) Assessing trunk roads—The conservationist viewpoint. *Long Range Planning*, **12** (1), pp. 56–61.

A methodology is proposed for examining the trunk roads programme from the environmentalist viewpoint. The dichotomy is discussed between the desire for individual mobility and the need to evaluate external costs which are rarely levelled in full upon the beneficiaries.

9 TIPPING, D.G. (1980) Evaluating road improvements in developing countries. Paper presented to the PTRC Annual Summer Conference, Warwick, July.

In appraising projects for road improvements in developing countries, it has long been standard practice for external aid agencies to seek by quantitative means an economic justification, so as to arrive at an estimate for the internal rate of return. The principal category of benefits in these appraisals is normally the saving in vehicle operating costs (VOCs) which road users will enjoy as a result of the road improvement.

This paper re-examines the pre-eminent position which has been given to road user savings, from three points of view:
(i) The accuracy with which it is possible to project VOCs over the life of a road.
(ii) The effect of road improvements on the distribution of income.
(iii) The relevance of road user savings, as compared with the development impact of road investments.

0 TOKERUD, R. (1976) Economical structures for low-volume roads. *Transportation Research Board*, SR 160, pp. 267–77.

Abnormal increases in prices and a concurrent decline in highway revenues have forced a reevaluation of highway projects. A national bridge inventory revealed that 133,000 bridges in the United States are structurally deficient or functionally obsolete, and 117,000 of these are on roads being maintained by counties and other local jurisdictions. The needs on the low-volume roadway system far exceed funds available. It is hoped that the potential economies suggested in this paper will lead to better use of the funds available. This paper investigates the economics for low-volume structures and it explores the total project range for structural economy including planning, design, and construction. Although not primarily addressed to the hydraulics involved in stream crossings, the paper points out some of the hydraulic considerations that should be made. Specifically, a great deal of attention is directed to the actual practice of agencies constructing bridges on low-volume roads, The three principal structural materials of timber, concrete, and steel are discussed, and certain structural details are suggested for economy, as well as structural types.

5C71 UNDERWOOD, W.C. (1981) Planning rural systems: How and why should you start. *Transportation Research Record*, 831, pp. 26-8.

A general overview of major factors that should be taken into consideration when local officials and interest groups begin planning for rural transit systems is presented. Before planning is initiated, a number of key issues must be addressed; these are included in a table titled 'the preliminary rural transit survival test'. After the test has been taken, a score can be calculated to assess the chances of sucessfully planning for and implementing a rural transit system. Certain steps that should be taken before planning commences are suggested, and the need to focus attention on establishing procedures for evaluating transit operating and financial performance is emphasized.

5C72 WELLMAN, B. (1977) Public participation in transportation planning. *Traffic Quarterly*, **31** (4), pp. 639-56.

This article presents a number of sociological considerations for the conduct of participatory planning. Then a number of specific participation techniques are evaluated and it is concluded that there is considerable scope for innovation once certain misconceptions are overcome.

5C73 YASS, I. (1979) The Leitch Report and after. *Highway Engineer*, **26** (6), pp. 34-7.

In considering the report of the Advisory Committee on Trunk Road Assessment (Leitch Report) it is the author's opinion that there are three main lessons on the Leitch Report: that the future is uncertain, that we should not concentrate on what can be measued to the exclusion of what cannot, and that people should be able to understand what is proposed and why. Decisions must not depend on one particular set of figures, but must have a wider backing. The Leitch framework will help people to see how a scheme affects them, but it must avoid the misleading impression that the Department of Transport is not also concerned with the wider public interest. The problems are complex, but in many cases the answers do not require complicated techniques to solve them.

5D Energy

1 ALLEN, W.B. (1980) Research needs in the transportation of energy. *Transportation Research Circular*, 216, pp. 46-7.

A major research task is to assess the demand for energy transport by origin-destination, by energy type, by mode, and by time frame. Another question is the economic regulatory impediments to or economic regulatory protections needed to ensure that energy materials move and are developed at the socially optimal level. A major research task would also be to investigate the economic cost of non-economic regulations (e.g. safety and environment). A need is also felt for an investigation of the appropriate funding base for transporting energy materials. Both a macro and a micro study of optimal modal investment are needed. On a macro basis this relates to such questions as rail versus slurry pipelines. On a micro basis it relates to keeping branch lines open versus highway improvements. Analysis of lowest resource costs is necessary with externalities internalized and the interdependence between modes is also important. Because of economies of density, the possibility exists that diversion of energy traffic from rail may impose higher costs on other rail users. Likewise, the inability of rail to win new energy transport (artificially— through regulatory restrictions) may mean that shippers are deprived of these economies of density.

2 BANISTER, C.E. and BANISTER, D.J. (1983) Transport, travel and energy in the UK: Trend analysis of published statistics. *Energy Policy*, 11 (1), pp. 39-51.

Transport is the only major sector where there has been an increase in energy consumption over the last ten years. This article concentrates on the road and rail sectors and presents an intermodal comparison of the trends on a time-series basis. The underlying reasons are explored and some of the complex interactions between individual factors highlighted. Several options for reducing energy consumption in the transport sector are proposed. Given the efficacy of oil for transport, there is only a limited opportunity for improvements in the existing stock of vehicles (through measures such as increases in car occupancy) and technological improvements offer the best alternative. Energy consumption in transport will continue to increase unless these changes take place and at present there is no evidence of a fall in consumption levels.

5D3 BANISTER, D.J. (1981) Transport Policy and Energy: Perspectives, Options and Scope for Conservation in the Passenger Transport Sector. University College London, Town Planning Discussion Paper 36.

The current situation with respect to energy use in transport is outlined, both at the national level and for different income groups. The evidence is taken primarily from the British experience with a further concentration on the passenger transport sector. Having established the importance of the problem and identified transport as a major oil user, Government policy is outlined. Action on energy conservation in transport only seems to take place if energy priorities coincide with other objectives of transport policy. Certain issues are highlighted, such as the question of public acceptability, response to price rises, distributional impacts and the implications for public transport. In each case, the complexity of apparently simple decisions is discussed in terms of energy savings and secondary effects which may work against the initial savings. In the final section, the arguments are drawn together under two basic alternatives—the do-nothing policy of minimum Government intervention, and a positive interventionist approach that involves energy contingency planning. Examples are taken from overseas. The conclusion reached is that despite certain statements on the importance of energy savings in the transport sector, little change in policy is likely to take place in the short term because of the secondary benefits that accrue to the Government.

4 BENDIXSON, T. (1975) The effects of changes in fuel supply on transport for countryside recreation. *Recreation News Supplement*, 12, pp. 2–5.

The Countryside Commission initiated a study of the impact of energy supply and policy on recreation demand patterns. Using various sources it was estimated that approximately one per cent of national energy consumption was attributable to recreation travel by car. Surveys in the summer of 1974 showed lower petrol sales, traffic flow and new car registrations, and that energy conservation measures were likely to affect recreation motoring before commuting. This leads to an increased demand for large country parks close to urban areas to which public transport services can be profitably run. Other items identified were cycleways, picnic stops near towns, alternative transport within national parks and the use of greenbelts.

5 DARE, C.E. (1981) Transportation energy contingency plans for rural areas and small communities, Missouri University, Rola, Final Report for the Department of Transportation, DOT-I-82-24, December.

Following the petroleum supply disruptions of the 1970s the Federal Government took actions to ensure continuation of transport services during a critical situation. This led to development of state transport energy contingency plans; however, the Missouri transportation Fuels Emergency Plan, like those of many states, does not contain specific recommendations for small communities and rural areas. This investigation was undertaken to determine the most effective transport fuel conservation measures which could be implemented by such areas during energy emergencies. Recommendations are presented concerning strategies to reduce gasoline use in rural areas and the institutional arrangements required for coping with a fuel shortage. It is suggested that the multi-county regional planning commission should become the lead agency in implementing and coordinating fuel conservation measure in rural areas. The existing network of emergency preparedness officers should be utilized to inventory local fuel distribution services, monitor local service station operating practices and to serve motorists who might be stranded.

5D6 EUROPEAN CONFERENCE OF MINISTERS OF TRANSPORT (1980) *Transport and Energy*. Report of the 52nd Round Table on Transport Economics, Paris.

5D7 FEENEY, B.P. (1980) Energy and road transportation—the need for research. An Foras Forbartha, Dublin, November.

This report examines the general pattern of energy use in road transport and identifies deficiencies of data. It is concluded that the major deficiency is the absence of personal travel information and a household survey is proposed. Energy conservation measures are reviewed and research needs identified. A programme of road transport energy research is outlined.

5D8 GB DEPARTMENT OF TRANSPORT (1981) *Review of the UK Transport Energy Outlook and Policy Recommendations*. Advisory Council on Energy Conservation, Energy Paper No. 47, London: HMSO.

5D9 HARTGEN, D.T. (1979) Transportation energy overview: Emphasis on New York State. *Transportation Research Record*, 710, pp. 26-33.

This paper summarizes recent work by the New York State Department of Transportation on transport energy analysis, consumption and conservation. Current uses and sources of American transport energy are reviewed with a particular emphasis on New York. Transport energy (gasoline, diesel, and jet fuel) comes primarily from domestic sources, Africa, and the Middle East, and is used principally for automobiles, commercial vehicles and air travel. New York uses a relatively higher share of transport energy in transit and air travel than does the rest of the United States. The paper also shows gasoline use by trip purpose and location in upstate New York describes baseline transport energy forecasts and the importance of increased automobile fuel efficiency on conservation, and reviews public attitudes toward conservation and change in travel behaviour during the energy crisis of 1973-1974. Possible conservation actions and their potential are also summarized.

5D10 HARTGEN, D.T. (1980) Transportation energy contingencies: A status report on public response and government roles. *Journal of Advanced Transportation*, **14** (1), pp. 47-72.

This paper summarizes recent work at the New York State Department of Transportation to develop transportation energy contingency plans for dealing with energy crises such as experienced in 1973-74 and 1979. Using recent household survey data from New York these two recent crises are described and compared with respect to shortfall, price rises and public response. Shortfalls of 11-13 per cent and price rises of 30-35 per cent were found in both cases. Generally, public responses were similar, focusing on driving slower and cuts in discretionary shop travel, but the 1979 crisis also showed major savings in vacation-related actions and fuel-efficient car purchasing. Responses varied greatly by area and demographic group. Should prices rise further or major shortfalls occur, major actions would be likely to be substituted for smaller actions, particularly driving slower and car tune-up. The impact of the November 1979 Iranian shut-off is estimated to be a shortfall of 4-8 per cent compiled with a price rise of 15-20 per cent by Spring 1980. But, clearer government roles and responsibilites for contingency actions, coupled with current contingency plan development by local governments and recent establishment of state conservation targets, should mean greater effectiveness in dealing with these events and hence generally less impact than in the past. Local governments can initiate numerous transport energy-saving actions in urban areas, thus assisting public response and decreasing the probability of future crises.

1 LEAKE, G.R. (1980) Fuel conservation—is there a case for stricter motorway speed limits? *Traffic Engineering and Control*, **21** (11), pp. 551-3.

This paper uses available evidence to determine the probable order of magnitude of fuel savings accrued from a reduction in speed limits on motorways. It is argued that the main impact of speed restrictions will be felt on rural motorways where traffic is essentially free-flowing. Fuel savings from reduced speeds would occur on cars only because commercial vehicles already have a lower speed limit (60 mile/h on motorways) and a reduction would have less effect. Using data on the distribution of car engine sizes and the speed distribution on motorways, the author is able to estimate the average fuel consumption as a function of speed. Results from a study on the effect of reducing speed limits from 70 mile/h to 50 mile/h are used to predict possible fuel savings. Although 127000 tons of petrol per year would be saved by introducing a 60 mile/h speed limit and 237000 tons would be saved per year by a 50 mile/h speed limit, these savings only represent 0.5 per cent, or 1 per cent of the total fuel consumption of road vehicles. It is concluded that this level of savings is unlikely to balance the additional cost of enforcement.

5D12 MALTBY, D., MONTEATH, I.G. and LAWLER, K.A. (1977) An analysis of energy use by passenger transport in the UK. *Traffic Engineering and Control*, **18** (12), pp. 564-8.

This paper has three main sections. First the relative importance of passenger transport as an end use of energy is assessed. National statistics are used to illustrate the current dependence of passenger transport as a whole on oil as a primary source of energy, and the relative roles of bus, rail, and private transport. Second, the nature of current energy use by passenger transport is examined in greater detail. This is done on the basis of the 1972/73 National Travel Survey data. Obviously changes in passenger transport energy use depend on many factors, a critical one being how individual travellers perceive real increases in the cost of energy, which might be brought about by market forces and/or government intervention. Such changes will vary significantly between different travel purposes, and possibly between different geographical areas because of such factors as spatial size and quality of existing transport infrastructure. Therefore this analysis of current energy use in passenger transport is presented for different geographical areas, for different journey purposes and for different modes of transport. The third and final section discusses some implications of this analysis for passenger transport from the viewpoint of energy related policy imposed by central government.

5D13 MOGRIDGE, M.J.H. (1978) The effect of the oil crisis on the growth in the ownership and use of cars. *Transportation*, **7** (1), pp. 45-67.

Since the oil crisis of 1973, a number of studies have been made in various countries of the effects of the rise in petrol prices on the level of traffic flow, but rather fewer have attempted to delineate the complex chain of reactions within the car market set off by this impulse. This paper attempts to do this, using data from the UK.

   Since 1966 during the prediction stage of the first London Transportation Study it became obvious that low income and high income households had different rates of growth of car ownership, mainly because low income households bought cheap, old cars which vary in quantity and price differently from expensive, new cars. The Greater London Council therefore sponsored a study of car prices by age and size, starting from 1957 annually, and since the oil crisis, evaluated monthly. This has enabled an analysis of the strong change in trend that had occurred, with large cars depreciating 15 per cent per annum more than the smallest. The quantities of cars of each size registered each month are available from national statistics and this means that the previous one per cent per annum increase in car size was arrested, with new cars becoming substantially smaller.

A model of the car market has been developed which relates on the one hand the price distribution of cars by age, and on the other hand the price distribution of the stock of cars owned at each household income level. Via the expenditure on car purchase at each household income level and the distribution of the length of time between purchase and resale of cars, a fully dynamic model has been developed to relate expenditure flows and stock, and the effect of different trends on the dynamic equilibrium in the car market has been tested.

14 MURDOCK, S.H. and LEISTRITZ, F.L. (1979) *Energy Development in the Western United States: Impact on Rural Areas*, New York: Praeger.

This attempt to provide an overview of social economic and demographic impacts of energy development in rural areas in the Western US, identifies major topics related to the impacts and the major spects of these areas, discusses research findings and suggests emerging generalizations. Research issues and priorities requiring additional analyses and emphases are noted. The first chapter discusses questions relating to the scope of energy developments and to the nature of impacts in rural areas, and the second introduces the topic of energy resources and the levels of development projected for the immediate future. The historical, social, demographic, and economic context of energy development in the west is discussed and employment-related issues surrounding energy development are described. The fifth chapter examines the size, distribution, and characteristics of energy-related populations in impacted areas. This is followed by an examination of the effects of energy developments on agriculture and business, the cost and revenue structures, community service structures, and the social impacts of energy development related to social structures organization, values, attitudes, and perceptions. The interrelationships between many of the above factors are outlined and the policy implications and forms of assistance available for managing impacts are summarized.

5D15 OWENS, S.E. (1979) Energy and settlement patterns. *Built Environment*, **5** (4), pp. 282–6.

By seeking land-use patterns which reduce the need for energy and into which energy saving technologies can be introduced, planners can aid energy conservation. But constraints will still exist—physical and, more importantly, social and institutional ones.

5D16 OWENS, S.E. (1981) Energy: Why planners must be involved. *International Journal of Environmental Studies*, **16**, pp. 197–206.

It seems probable that planners will increasingly be involved with all aspects of the energy system. This paper attempts to outline some of the fundamental issues with which they will be concerned. It considers, first, the physical and socio-economic impacts of energy supply facilities and then discusses the ability of the planning system to respond to energy development pressures. It then turns to the less tangible problems of energy efficiency in the built environment and considers the potential for improvement together with some of the many constraints involved.

5D17 OWENS, S.E. and RICKABY, P.E. (1982) Energy and the pattern of human settlements. Paper prepared for the Watt Committee on Energy.

The focus of debate on energy and planning has been on the planning implications of energy supply systems, while much less attention has been given to the fundamental relationship between the spatial organization of society and the way in which energy is used. The relative neglect of the latter subject, and its policy implications, may be attributed in part to a more general bias towards concern with energy supply rather than energy demand, but some more specific factors may also be identified.

Any modifiction of settlement patterns would involve relatively long term policies, and the achievement of 'energy-efficiency', even if new settlements were being planned, would inevitably be limited by innumerable physical, social and institutional constraints, some of which are considered in this paper. The argument here is that in spite of practical constraints, there may be significant opportunities for planners to contribute to the more rational use of energy in the medium to long term. Some consideration is given to 'energy integrated' planning, in the context of both a highly urbanized and an underdeveloped rural area.

As well as the more obvious practical difficulties, however, there are some theoretical problems to be overcome (though some planners have not waited for theory!). Among these are the intrinsic difficulties involved in identifying energy-efficient settlement structures or development patterns.

8 POTTER, S. and RIEKIC, G. (1980) The transport policy implications of corporate financing of motoring. Paper given to the Motoring Costs Conference at the Transport Studies Unit, Oxford, October.

9 RING, S.L., BREWER, K.A. and BUTLER, D.L. (1976) Evaluation of interaction between rural regional transportation and energy availability. *Transportation Research Record*, 561, pp. 12–22.

The energy crisis of 1973 can be considered an indicator of future problems. The impact on personal and goods mobility alone will have far-reaching consequences, not only in the urban areas, but also in the rural regions. In fact, because of the less dense population distribution, rural regions are more sensitive to changes in energy form, cost, and availability. Maintaining the desirability of US rural regions as a place to live is important to the welfare not only of this country but also of other countries of the world who depend on the US food exports for their survival. The wholesale abandonment of unproductive railroad lines imposes limitations on the economic viability of bypassed small cities. It creates constraints in the options for electric power generation and distribution system development and will have a dramatic effect on the economics of grain terminal locations and grain transport. Even the system for providing heat to isolated farm homes and small towns will be inter-related with transport forms of the future. Transport system decisions have far-reaching implications on individual life-styles and the welfare of the nation, and it behoves decision-makers to consider these inter-relationships.

5D20 SHUCKSMITH, D.M. (1980) Petrol prices and rural recreation in the
1980s. *National Westminster Bank Quarterly Review*, February, pp.
52–9.

Rural recreation which is dependent on the availability of petrol
supplies was affected by shortages in the summer of 1979. The evidence suggests a switch to short distance activities around the urban
centres at the expense of recreation in the remoter rural areas.
Holiday makers going for longer periods of time are less likely to be
affected and these provide the greatest revenue for rural areas.

5D21 STOAKES, R. (1979) Oil prices and countryside recreation travel.
Countrysde Commission WP 20, Cheltenham, Gloucestershire.

5D22 SULLIVAN, E.C. and PICHA, K.C. (1982) Recreational travel: gasoline shortages and price increases. *Transportation Engineering Journal*,
ASCE, **108** (TE2), pp. 207–16.

An empirical study utilizes visitation data from a number of recreational attractions in California to estimate the reduction in travel
due to the gasoline price increases that occurred during 1977–79
and the gas shortage in 1979. Differences in the price elasticities and
the impacts of a gas shortage are determined by comparing private
and public recreation sites, located both in urban and rural areas.
Local facilities have suffered from the increases in prices, but national attractions are affected by the gas shortages. Transit may
provide a low cost alternative to local recreation areas.

5D23 WATERS, M.H.L. (1980) Research on energy conservation for cars
and goods vehicles. *Transport and Road Research Laboratory*, SR 591.

This paper describes the research techniques, gives some results and
indicates the practical use that can be made of the research work
relating to energy conservation for cars and goods vehicles. It also
examines briefly the prospects for road transport in the future when
natural oil is so scarce and expensive that substitute fuels will be
needed.

5D24 WAYNE, F. (1978) Energy for future transport. Scottish Association
for Public Transport, Glasgow, 2 volumes.

25 ZANIEWSKI, J.P., MOSER, B.K. and SWAIT, J.D. (1979) Predicting travel time and fuel consumption for vehicles on low-volume roads. *Transportation Research Record*, 702, pp. 335-41.

A major experimental investigation of the effect of roadway characteristics and environmental conditions on traffic behaviour was conducted in Brazil. Empirical relationships were developed for predicting free speeds on positive and negative grades. Free speed was found to be related to vehicle class, grade, surface type, and road roughness. These relationships have been incorporated into a computer program (TAFA) for predicting travel time, free speed, and fuel consumption on low-volume rural roads. Example applications of the model show its usefulness in evaluating operational and road maintenance strategies which are of interest to highway engineers and economic analysts.

5E Environment and safety

E1 BENTS, F.D. and HELDUND, J.H. (1978) Some characteristics of culpable drivers in rural accidents. *Conference Proceedings of the American Association for Auto Medicine*, 2, pp. 293-9.

In 1971 and 1972 the Pennsylvania State Police collected special data on 15,415 automobile accidents in rural Pennsylvania. The data collected included both items routinely obtained by the police and supplemental items selected by the National Highway Traffic Safety Administration. Culpability for each accident was determined by the state police. The data were analysed to investigate the predictive ability of the following driver characteristics on culpability: age, sex, route familiarity, driving experience, and experience or familiarity with the accident vehicle. Iterative fitting methods of multivariate contingency table analysis were used to fit log-linear structural models to the data, to test the fit of these models, and to compare the predictive effect of these variables and their interactions. The results indicate that route familiarity is the strongest predictor, followed by age and driving experience. Driver sex and experience with the accident vehicle have only minimal predictive power. No interactions were significant: the route familiarity, age and driving experience enter independently into the final model. The findings suggest that drivers unfamiliar with their route may be more vulnerable to inadequate controls, poor highway design, information overload or other distractions at the time of the crash.

5E2 CLAMP, P.E. (1976) Evaluation of the impact of roads on the visual amenity of rural areas. Department of the Environment, Research Report 7.

The report presents the findings of a research project into an assessment of the change in visual amenity resulting from the introduction of new roads into a landscape. In the results, two indices are derived with the following characteristics. The first index which would give a measure of the attractiveness of present landscapes that could be expressed on either a numerical or verbal scale, could be used in compiling landscape amenity maps for structure plans. The second index would be used to determine the change in score, on the same scale, caused by the building of motorway, dual carriageway or 3-lane single carriageway roads. The methods of deriving these indices and their application are described.

5E3 DE HAMEL, B. (1976) Roads and the environment. Department of the Environment, London: HMSO.

This manual describes the environmental issues in carrying out the road programme, the principles of route selection, the design of motorways and bridges and the ways in which they can be accommodated in the landscape so that amenity disbenefits are minimized.

5E4 DEOMAS, T.H. (1976) Roads and the environment. London: HMSO.

The author gives an account of recent developments in the design of new roads and adjoining areas. A description is given of the environmental issues involved in carrying out the road programme, the principles of route selection, the design of motorways and bridges, the steps taken to fit them into landscape and to minimize any adverse effects upon amenities in town and country, and the services available to road users. It is pointed out that many new roads may bring a positive improvement to the quality of the environment and emphasis is placed on planting. A series of photographs illustrate the topics covered.

5E5 GLENNON, J.C. (1979) Highway safety requirements for low-volume rural roads. *Transportation Research Record*, 702, pp. 286–94.

This paper summarizes research that was undertaken to reevaluate the safety needs on low-volume rural roads. Based on a series of functional analyses relating safety performance to specific design and operation elements, a set of revised guidelines was developed. The revised guidelines apply to total roadway width, horizontal curvature, roadside design, speed signs, curve warning signs, centreline markings and no-passing stripes. These guidelines are proposed to supplement the existing national policies, with each revised guideline either replacing or clarifying the existing national guideline. The widespread application of the revised guidelines should provide for more consistent design and traffic control of low-volume rural roads consonant with a rational balance between highway investment, highway safety, and traffic service.

E6 HALE, A., BLOMBERG, R.D. and KEARNEY, E.F. (1980) Model regulations and public education for rural-suburban pedestrian safety. Dunlap and Associates Incorporated, Final Report for the National Highway Traffic Safety Administration, DOT-HS-805-639, August.

The objectives of this study were to review the rural suburban pedestrian accident data and determine which accident types were amenable to counter measures development. Countermeasure classes considered were model traffic regulations and public information and education and the results of the analysis indicated that the development of four prototype regulations to serve as legislative models appeared to be promising in reducing the target accident types. A complete discussion of the background data, the countermeasure objectives, content rationale, and the requirements for further development, implementation and testing (where appropriate) is provided for the model regulations and media packages.

E7 HARLAND, D.G. (1978) Rural traffic noise prediction—An approximation. *Transport and Road Research Laboratory*, SR 425.

The noise prediction method described in this paper is an approximation designed to assess in broad terms the changes of noise level following change in a transport network. It gives a fairly accurate prediction of the fractional change of land area exposed to a given noise level but is less reliable as a prediction of the absolute change. An example prediction is given in an appendix.

5E8 HUDDART, L. (1978). An evaluation of the visual impact of rural roads and traffic. *Transport and Road Research Laboratory*, SR 355.

A survey of the visual impact of roads and traffic on the Lake District scenery was made in the summer of 1975. Residents and visitors to the Lake District were asked to assess views on a cine film showing a seven box rating scale. The films showed a number of typical Lake District scenes with roads of differing standards superimposed and carrying different amounts of traffic. Ratings became less favourable as the size of the road construction increased but, contrary to the pilot survey, increases in moving traffic had little effect except in the most picturesque locations. Further research on the impact of moving traffic is to be carried out.

5E9 JACOBS, G.D. and SAYER, I.A. (1976) An analysis of road accidents in Kenya in 1972. *Transport and Road Research Laboratory*, SR 227 UC.

Nairobi Province was found to have the greatest number of accidents and casualties but the rates per million vehicle kilometres were lowest in this province. Fourteen per cent of all casualties were fatal which is a high fatality rate compared with countries in Western Europe and North America. This may be a reflection of the likelihood that in Kenya non-fatal personal injury accidents may not be as well recorded as fatal accidents. The proportion of all casualties that were occupants of commercial vehicles was very much higher in Kenya than in Europe. The number of accidents involving two vehicles was proportionately lower than in Great Britain whereas there were proportionately more vehicle-pedestrian and single-vehicle accidents in Kenya than in Britain. The incidence of single-vehicle accidents was particularly high in rural areas. Accident rates on murram (i.e. gravel surfaced) roads were found to be very high in relation to the volume of traffic carried by these roads.

5E10 JANSSEN, S.T.M.C. (1976) Verkeersveiligheid in Plattelandsgehieden, Institute for Road Safety Research, (in Dutch). (Traffic safety in rural areas.)

The problems of traffic hazards on rural highways are studied in a special area in Holland, in which the number of fatal accidents suddenly doubled. The method of study is described and recommendations are presented for measures to increase safety in this area.

Furthermore, criteria are presented for long range research on the lay-out of rural highways, which could lead to common applicable infrastructural changes for the increase of traffic safety in rural areas.

11 LOUTZENHEISER, R.C. (1979) Improving traffic safety in rural Kansas. *Transportation Research Record*, 709, pp. 13–19.

The traffic engineer's goals are to provide safe, efficient, and convenient movement of persons and goods on streets and highways and to provide adequate modal transition. In larger urban areas and along primary roads, this purpose has been met to varying degrees. However, in rural areas where most cities have populations of less than 5000, there is a lack of proper traffic-control devices and of traffic engineering studies and help. In southwestern Kansas, the population density is less than 4 persons/sq km (10 persons/sq mile), and there were no local traffic engineering personnel in the 41,150 sq km (16,000 sq mile) area. The Greater Southwest Regional Planning Commission created a position of regional traffic engineer in late 1976, which was funded through the Kansas Department of Transportation and the Federal Highway Administration. During the first two years, the engineer has involved 29 of the 45 cities in federally funded traffic-sign-improvement projects, completed or initiated analysis at several high-hazard locations, assisted local units of government to become aware of and obtain state and federal funds, and worked with local government personnel in 18 of the 19 counties in the region to establish some local expertise in traffic safety. The primary benefit of the regional traffic engineer has been that traffic engineering has been brought to southwestern Kansas with a personal touch. The local units of government could not individually afford, and, in fact, would not need a fulltime traffic engineer. Under the commission assistance plan, the engineer is on call to all the local units, is governed by them, and is used by them. A regional traffic engineer is a means of providing expertise to rural areas.

12 MACKIE, A.M. and DAVIES, C.H. (1981) Environmental effects of traffic changes. *Transport and Road Research Laboratory*, LR 1015.

The report describes a study of the environmental effects of traffic and traffic changes in nine towns where changes in traffic flow had occurred due to by-pass construction or traffic management schemes. An assessment of the nuisance caused by particular traffic flows has been made. The study also examined the effects of noise and air pollution on people's sensitivity to traffic. Nuisance was measured by means of personal interview surveys of people at home, pedestrians and people working in shops and offices. Nuisance levels changed considerably when the traffic levels changed. The single traffic variable most strongly correlated with nuisance was the number of lorries over 16 tons GVW, but there was also a high correlation between nuisance and total traffic flow. A multiple regression analysis showed that these two variables could explain 85 per cent of the variance in the nuisance data.

5E13 MACKIE, A.M. and GRIFFIN, L.J. (1978) Environmental effects of traffic: case study at Mere, Wiltshire. *Transport and Road Research Laboratory*, SR 428.

The report gives an assessment of the degree of traffic nuisance in a small town at different levels of traffic flow, before and after the construction of a by-pass. Measurements of traffic characteristics and of public attitudes are given. A nuisance index ranging from 0 to 6 showed a median of 1.7 when trunk road traffic passed through the town. This dropped to 0.3 when the traffic changes due to the by-pass occurred. Such environmental ill-effects as there were, were virtually eliminated by the reduction in flows following the opening of the by-pass. The main disadvantage was considered by some respondents to be a drop in commercial activity in the town. The study is one of a series of case studies where changes in traffic flow have occurred, and from which more general conclusions will be published.

5E14 RADWAN, A.E. and SINHA, K.C. (1980) Countermeasures to improve safety at multilane rural intersections. *Transportation Research Record*, 773, pp. 14–17.

The objective of this study was to apply a computer model to evaluate, design, and control alternatives to improve safety at intersections of multilane major highways with two-lane minor roads. The NETSIM network-flow simulation model was used in this research. Measures of effectiveness considered in evaluating alternatives included average delay per vehicle and number of traffic conflicts. Several modifications were made to the NETSIM model to incorporate the calculations of the measures of effectiveness. Field studies were conducted for gap acceptance, traffic delay, and traffic conflicts, and the results were used to substantiate the model's validity. Different design and operational countermeasures for stop-controlled and for signalized intersections were evaluated by a group of simulation experiments.

5 SHEPHERD, N. and LOWE, S. (1982) Accident model for minor highway improvements. Paper presented at the PTRC Annual Summer Conference, Warwick, July.

The paper describes the development of a set of models which relates the occurrence of non-junction accidents on two-lane rural roads to traffic, geometric and other conditions. The models proved to be robust in validation and using data that are normally available to highway authorities, could be readily implemented to evaluate the likely accident benefits arising from highway improvement schemes. The paper discusses the advantages of these models over current standard procedures for estimating potential accident benefits.

Separate models were derived for four categories of single- and multiple-vehicle accident; they were calibrated from data obtained at over forty widely varying sites throughout England. The paper describes the site selection process and the methods of data collection. The results of some preliminary data-scanning exercises are given.

5F Engineering

1 ACKROYD, L.W. and ABBISS, J.C. (1970) Traffic flow patterns at a rural motorway location. *Traffic Engineering and Control*, **12** (7), pp. 373-5.

This article presents a detailed study of daily, weekly and seasonal variations in traffic flow on the M1 at a particular rural interchange. The location is typical in that it has neither a pronounced daily commuting pattern nor a high seasonal variation due to predominantly recreational traffic.

2 ACKROYD, L.W. and BETTISON, M. (1974) Traffic speeds on steep gradients on rural single-carriageway roads. *Traffic Engineering and Control*, **15** (16/17), pp. 766-7 and 769.

This article describes an investigation into the speeds of heavy vehicles and their influence on traffic on two long steep gradients in Derbyshire, one of which has no crawler lane. The advantages to other vehicles are considerable in reducing time and costs.

5F3 ACKROYD, L.W. and BETTISON, M. (1974) Vehicle speeds on the M1 in Nottinghamshire, 1969-73. *Traffic Engineering and Control*, **15** (9), pp. 440-1.

This short note summarizes changes in vehicle speeds on a straight level section of the M1 in a rural location. Mean speeds of all vehicles seem to be increasing over the 4-year period.

5F4 ACKROYD, L.W. and BETTISON, M. (1979) Vehicle speeds on the M1 motorway in Nottinghamshire—1974-78. *Traffic Engineering and Control*, **20** (5), 254-5.

Updates the previous surveys although the monitoring has been carried out less frequently. Observations were made under the same conditions, but two sets were taken when the speed of the traffic was restricted because of major resurfacing work.

5F5 ACKROYD, L.W. and MADDEN, A.J. (1975) Vehicle speeds and paths at rural diamond roundabout motorway interchanges. *Traffic Engineering and Control*, **16** (5), pp. 215-19.

Two flyunder and one flyover version of this type of interchange were subject to detailed study. With the low convergence angles and long direct tapir acceleration lanes provided, most of the acceleration to merging speed occurred on the slip road, leaving the acceleration lane to provide only the necessary merging distance.

5F6 ACKROYD, L.W., MADDEN, A.J. and ERNEST-JONES, S.R. (1973) A study of vehicle merging behaviour at rural motorway interchanges. *Traffic Engineering and Control*, **15** (4/5), pp. 192-5.

The patterns of gap acceptance and rejection in this 'dynamic' merging situation are extremely complex, with a wide range of driver behaviour. The situation was further complicated by the different geometry at the various locations.

7 ALLSOP, R.E. (1975) Models for rural road traffic. University of Newcastle upon Tyne, Transport Operations Research Group, March.

A review was made of recent work in Britain on the planning and modelling of traffic on rural roads, both inter-urban traffic and traffic having a rural origin or destination. The need was revealed for more satisfactory models of commericial vehicle traffic both over long distance and in its impact on its areas of distribution. It appeared that increasing attention was being given to recreational traffic and to the possibilities of restricting large or heavy vehicles to a limited sub-network of the rural road system.

8 ALLSOP, R.E. and NICHOLL, J.P. (1980) Recommendations regarding a survey of speeds of vehicles at a sample of sites on rural single-carriageway trunk and principal roads in Britain. University College London, Transport Studies Group, Working Paper.

9 BENNETT, G.T. (1973) Carriageway markings for rural transport. *Traffic Engineering and Control*, **15** (3), pp. 137-8.

About two-thirds of all injury accidents at priority junctions on rural roads in the UK involve one turning vehicle and one non-turning vehicle on the main road. This article is concerned with ways in which such accidents might be prevented, and in particular how carriageway markings might be used for this purpose.

10 BRILON, W. (1977) Queueing model of two-lane rural traffic. *Transportation Research*, **11** (2), pp. 95-107.

A mathematical model is presented of the traffic pattern on two-lane highways having no structural obstacles to impede overtaking. The model is based on a queueing analogy of the process of overtaking. Calculations resulted in an indication of the real travel time distribution on a road of this type. This can be used to derive various parameters from which the quality of the traffic pattern can be discerned. The dependence of such parameters on the traffic volume and the fraction of trucks is shown by one example and the agreement of the model with empirical results can be demonstrated at some points. The model proposed in this this work can be used as an aid in setting standards for the capacity of two-lane highways and in estimating the consequence of traffic control policies, e.g. speed limits, on such roads.

5F11 BROGAN, J.D. and MCKELVEY, F.X. (1981) Lightweight accessible buses: Selection maintenance and general care. *Transportation Research Record*, 831, pp. 44–48.

Guidelines have been developed to assist private nonprofit agencies that have little experience in providing transport services in selecting vehicles and related equipment appropriate to their service needs. Emphasis is on lightweight accessible vehicles—that is, lift-equipped vans, modified vans, and small buses. Operating and maintenance experiences of agencies currently using such vehicles are summarized. The information may be used to assist existing or potential operators to understand the applications and limitations of the current state of the art in vehicles and equipment.

5F12 CONSTANTINE, T. (1966) Capital costs and land requirements of interchanges in rural areas. *Traffic Engineering and Control*, **8** (6), pp. 388–92.

Interchanges are custom designed to local site and traffic conditions, but the majority can be broadly grouped into standard types according to their geometric and operational characteristics. The land requirements and capital costs vary considerably, not only with the type of interchange, but also with various designs of the same type. To assess the order of magnitude of these variations the author carried out detailed design studies of several standard types and designs of interchanges with different classes of all purpose roads and motorways. In order to obtain a true comparison it was necessary to eliminate the influence of topography by assuming a level site. In this paper the author summarizes the results in the belief that they give a useful guide to the order of magnitude of the land requirements and costs involved and provide the background information which is so necessary in the preliminary design stages of motorway schemes.

5F13 FARTHING, D.W. (1978) Some factors affecting rural speed/flow relations. *Traffic Engineering and Control*, **18** (1), pp. 12–18.

A study of rural speed/flow relations where a high proportion of heavy vehicles occurs on steep gradients. Designed to supplement the TRRL studies on rural roads throughout the country both on dual and single carriageway roads.

14 FLETCHER, J.H. (1968) Traffic capacity of rural two-lane highways. *Traffic Engineering and Control*, **9** (11), pp. 533-5.

Apart from the motorways, most highway expenditure in Great Britain is directed to maintaining and progressively improving the extensive network of two-lane roads. The purpose of this paper is to highlight the effects of various types of improvement on traffic flow and safety.

15 GALIN, D. (1981) Speeds on two-lane rural roads—a multiple regression analysis. *Traffic Engineering and Control*, **22** (8/9), pp. 453-60.

This paper presents regression equations for the effects of the human factor, the mechanical factor, the traffic factor and the environment on the average journey speed as well as the 85th and 95th speed percentiles. The effects of road geometry were not studied since they have already been extensively examined. Results show that, for light vehicles, the effect of driver's age and sex was significant. Average speeds decreased with increasing age and male drivers travel faster than female drivers. It was also found that there was a substantial influence on the type of land use near the roads on speeds. Speeds in low-density residential areas were lower by at least 10 km/h than those on similar roads in agricultural and wooded areas. Weather also was found to have a significant effect on speed with speeds on a dry roadway in fine weather higher than on a wet surface and on a cloudy day. Results also showed that movements in platoons had a significant effect on reducing speed, but the effect of total flow in either direction was not significant. The proportion of trucks in the observed lane had a significant effect in slowing down speed, as did the proportion of trucks in the opposite lane. Significant reductions in speed occurred with vehicle age, whilst car speeds increased significantly with engine size.

16 GB MINISTRY OF TRANSPORT (1968) Advisory manual layout of roads in rural areas. London: HMSO (reprinted 1974).

17 GB MINISTRY OF TRANSPORT (1968) Advisory manual on traffic prediction for rural roads. London: HMSO.

5F18 GIPPS, P.G. (1976) An abbreviated procedure for estimating equilibrium queue lengths in rural two-lane traffic. *Transportation Science*, **10** (4), pp. 337-47.

On two-lane two-way roads overtaking opportunities are limited by the opposing traffic. For fixed volumes in both directions the opportunites for vehicles in one lane to overtake depend on the mean length of queues in the second lane, so that the mean queue length in the first lane is a function of the mean queue length in the second lane and vice versa. This paper takes an earlier procedure for determining the mean queue lengths in the two lanes at equilibrium and simplifies it by assuming that the distribution of queue lengths is known. The results obtained by assuming that the underlying distribution is Miller, Borel-Tanner, or geometric are then compared by a numerical evaluation.

5F19 GLENNON, J.C. (1979) Design and traffic control guidelines for low-volume rural roads. *NCHRP Report*, 214, October.

Low-volume rural-roads, those carrying 400 vehicles per day or less, constitute two-thirds of the total US highway system. Their key importance to the national transport objective cannot be denied. Not only are they the largest single class of highway, but they are also the vital link of the nation's agricultural economy. National guidelines for the design of low-volume rural roads are contained in the 1971 AASHTO publication 'Geometric Design Guide for Local Roads and Streets'. For traffic control devices, the basic guidelines are presented in the 'Manual of Uniform Traffic Control Devices'. But, because these national guidelines reflect the safety of primary highways, their application to the reconstruction of existing low-volume rural roads is continually being questioned in a time when local highway agencies must spend a majority of their limited funds for highway maintenance. This research was undertaken to reevaluate the safety needs on low-volume rural roads. On the basis of a series of functional analysis relating safety performance to specific design and operational elements, a set of revised guidelines was developed. The revised guidelines apply to total roadway width, horizontal curvature, roadside design, speed signs, curve warning signs, centreline markings, and no-passing stripes. These guidelines are proposed to supplement the existing national policies with each revised guideline either replacing or clarifying the existing national guidelines. The widespread application of the revised guidelines should provide for more consistent design and traffic control of low-volume rural roads consonant with a rational balance between highway investment, highway safety, and traffic service.

F20 KHASNABIS, S. and HEIMBACH, C.L. (1980) Headway distribution models for two-lane rural highways. *Transportation Research Record*, 772, pp. 44–51.

The distribution of vehicle headways on two-lane two-way roadways has been the subject of continuing research for a number of years. The growing interest in headway generation models is related to the increased application of simulation techniques to describe traffic-flow patterns through the use of digital computers. A headway-distribution model developed for varying traffic-volume conditions (80–630 vehicles/h/lane) is described. The model was developed as part of a research project on the feasibility of using simulation techniques for depicting traffic flow on two-lane highways. A total of 18 sets of headway data (2 sets for each site) were collected for nine sites in North Carolina. The process of model development consisted of testing the field data by using a number of existing simple models and progressing with increasing degrees of complexity until an acceptable match between the field data and the model output was obtained. The study showed that none of the existing models (the Negative Exponential, Pearson Type III, and Schuhl models) provided satisfactory results for the wide range of traffic volumes tested. A modified form of the Schuhl model, incorporating parameters developed from the North Carolina data, provided the most reasonable approximation of the arrival patterns noted in the field. Parameters developed in the study are presented, along with a nomograph that can be used by traffic researchers to describe the time spacing between successive arrivals of vehicles on two-lane highways.

F21 LARSEN, M.B. (1980) Liability implications for low volume rural highways. *Transportation Engineering Journal*, ASCE, **106** (TE6), pp. 803–14.

Sovereign immunity of local governments has been diminishing as tort liability plagues local government and imposes heavy financial burdens. Design standards should be set for rural roads so that the engineer is not liable for lawsuits should accidents occur along a particular stretch of road that he has built.

5F22 LLEWELYN, F.J. and BUTLER, D.A. (1969) Layout of roads in rural areas. *Traffic Engineering and Control*, **10** (12), pp. 615–17.

The Ministry of Transport manual on the layout of Roads in Rural Areas is reviewed [5F16]. It seems to reflect the length of time between preparation and publication, and could already be updated.

5F23 LYLES, R.W. (1980) Evaluation of signs for hazardous rural intersections. *Transportation Research Record*, 782, pp. 22–30.

An experiment to evaluate the effectiveness of several different signs (or sign sequences) in informing motorists of an intersection on the road ahead in rural two-lane situations is described. Typically, intersections that would require these treatments would be those where stopping sight distances for prevailing speeds were inadequate. As random motorists approached and passed through two test intersections, they were 'tracked' by means of a data-collection system that collected time intercepts of motorists at 60 m (200 ft) intervals in the vicinity of the intersection. These data were supplemented by manually collected vehicle registration and classification data, and in selected instances, survey data collected from motorists who had passed through the intersections. The results essentially showed that a regulatory speed-zone configuration and lighted warning signs were more effective than more traditional unlighted warning signs in reducing motorists' speeds in the vicinity of the intersection and increasing their awareness of both the signs and conditions at the intersection.

5F24 MORRIS, P.O. (1979) Research on lightly trafficked urban and rural roads. *Australian Road Research Board Region Symposium*, Perth.

A review is made of some ARRB research projects, on road materials and design, which are related to the' behaviour of lightly trafficked urban and rural roads. The projects are those with which the author has been either directly or indirectly involved. For roads in the residential areas surveyed, the subgrade had attained near saturation, and seasonal movements of moisture were shown to be small and to occur only at the real edge. Overall strength measurements as indicated by Benkelman beam testing are proposed for determining maintenance procedures. A survey of the vehicle population provided data on critical dimensions for cross-overs and field testing of gutter inlets led to modifications of earlier recommendations. For roads surveyed in the rural areas subgrades attained an equilibrium moisture condition of generally less than 0.90 of standard optimum moisture content, and on routes along the coastal strip subgrades are likely to become wet of standard optimum moisture content. For these conditions, full width construction is preferred to boxed construction. 'Dry' compaction, of road making is possible, but heavy compaction equipment is necessary for the best results. In the wet tropical areas, significant seasonal subgrade moisture change can occur under the whole of the road.

25 NICHOLL, J.P. (1980) Factors associated with the distribution of vehicle speeds at points on single-carriageway rural A-roads. University College London, Transport Studies Group.

26 O'FLAHERTY, C.A., and COOMBE, R.D. (1971) Speeds on level rural roads: a multivariate approach—1. Background to the study *Traffic Engineering and Control*, **13** (1), pp. 20–1.
2. The modelling processes. *Traffic Engineering and Control*, **13** (2), pp. 68–70.
3. The speed models produced. *Traffic Engineering and Control*, **13** (3), pp. 108–11.

A series of three linked papers that study the effects of the layout of the highway on vehicular speeds, while taking into account the detailed influences of traffic composition, traffic flow characteristics and environmental conditions. Part one discusses the background to the study with part two concentrating on the multiple linear regression modelling procedure. The final part assesses the models produced on the four speed statistics for the four vehicle classes.

27 ORGANISATION FOR ECONOMIC COOPERATION AND DEVELOPMENT (1973) *Maintenance of Rural Roads: Principles of a Road Maintenance Management System*. Paris: OECD.

This report outlines possible approaches for defining maintenance strategies. The data collection and analysis needed for this purpose are discussed. A system of standards for programming maintenance expenditure is developed, and a possible method for the choice of priorities is presented. In order to provide for the best utilization of available resources on the basis of road user needs, it is recommended that a total system of maintenance management be implemented without delay and that the choice of priorities be based on a coherent set of standards.

5F28 PETERS, R.J. (1980) Rural surface recycling. *Transportation Research Record*, 780, pp. 64-7.

Federal state and local agencies are currently faced with a number of very critical problems which include the reduction in available funds due to inflation, a declining tax base, and declining revenue from taxes on fuel. A possible answer to these current problems is the serious consideration to re-use existing inplace materials by recycling for construction and maintenance needs. By recycling, energy and materials (aggregates, binders, guardrail etc) are conserved and the pavement geometrics and environment are also preserved.

5F29 SIMPSON, J.A. (1980) The design, construction and maintenance of low cost roads. Paper presented at the 4th IRF African Highway Conference, Nairobi, January.

The author describes the Rural Access Roads Program, under which it is planned to construct 14,000 kilometres of all weather farm-to-market roads in 25 high-potential agricultural districts in Kenya. This is believed to be the largest labour intensive public works programme being undertaken in Africa today, and is providing daily employment for 12,000 labourers in the rural areas. The programme involves a decentralized management structure with delegation of considerable responsibilities to Field Engineers, each of whom is responsible for the execution of an agreed construction programme. He supervises 2 to 4 construction units, each of which has a labour force of 250 to 300 men, producing 45 kilometres of gravel roads per year. Maintenance is carried out by ex-construction labourers who are each responsible for two kilometres of road. They are provided with tools and paid for working twelve days each month. These methods are claimed to be technically and financially viable, especially when foreign exchange savings are taken into account.

'30 SKINNER, D.N. (1976) The planning and design of rural roads: the implications of landscape and recreation. Scottish Tourist Board, Edinburgh.

'31 TAYLOR, M.A.P., MILLER, A.J. and OGDEN, K.W. (1974) A comparison of some bunching models for rural traffic flow. *Transportation Research*, **8** (1), pp. 1–10.

On two-lane two-way roads overtaking opportunities are often limited by traffic and highway factors so that vehicles may be forced to queue behind slower vehicles before overtaking can take place. To explain this clustering or bunching of traffic several bunching models have been proposed. One such model which has been used is the Borel-Tanner distribution of bunch sizes. The paper examines this model, and others, and çompares them using both experimental and simulated bunch size data. From the comparison it is suggested that a more general model than the Borel-Tanner model is the two-parameter Miller distribution of bunch sizes which can be fitted to a wide range of traffic conditions.

'32 VISSER, A.T., DE QUEIROZ, C.A.V., MOSER, B. and MOSER, L. (1979) A preliminary evaluation of paved and unpaved road performance in Brazil. *Transportation Research Record*, 702, pp. 304–12.

The study of unpaved and paved road performance was a principal part of the 'Research of the Interrelationships of Road Construction, Maintenance and User Costs' conducted in Brazil during the period 1975 to 1979. The paper outines the experimental design methodology and measurement techniques for the pavement and maintenance studies. Preliminary results of the performance of unpaved and paved roads, monitored on 30 unpaved sections and 65 paved sections in Brazil are discussed. Equations predicting roughness, rut depth and gravel loss, are presented for unpaved roads. These performance parameters are a function of average daily traffic, horizontal alignment, vertical geometry, wearing course material type, maintenance and wet or dry season. Preliminary findings on analyses of roughness and rut depth on paved roads are also discussed.

'33 WILLIAMS, E.L. (1979) Why do rural regions need good roads? *Highway Engineer*, **26** (6), pp. 30–3.

The paper discusses characteristics of rural regions and of East

Anglia in particular, with special reference to the present settlement pattern and the road network. The existing network is assessed and progress toward adaptation to modern needs reviewed. The interconnection between central and local government expenditure on highways and the problem of priorities of public expenditure, are mentioned. A realistic solution is put forward and reference made to the importance of a satisfactory standard of highway maintenance to all forms of transport.

5F34 WOOTTON, J.H. (1981) Improved direction signs for the benefits of road users. *Traffic Engineering and Control*, **22,** (5), pp. 264–8.

Recent research suggests that drivers waste significant mileage because of inadequate road signs. Surveys of drivers in Gloucestershire and Avon are reported. They show that the majority of drivers were looking for the shortest route but that although most followed a logically signposted route, only 50 per cent actually achieved their objective. Some conclusions are drawn on how direction signing can be improved to reduce the costs to motorists.

6 Area-based studies

6A Great Britain

Many studies of transport in rural areas have been specific to particular locations. They have been carried out by central government (e.g. GB Department of the Environment [2A16], [2A17]), by local government (e.g. Davies [6A17] in Clwyd), by consumer groups (e.g. Winfield for the Welsh Consumer Council [2A62]), by public transport agencies (e.g. Scottish Association for Public Transport [6A50]), or by universities (e.g. Farrington and Stanley [6A24] in Skye and Lochalsh or Rees and Wragg [6A47] in Wales). In each case the approach has been similar. Transport is perceived as a key problem that requires some form of intervention both for economic and social reasons. However, the concern of the analysis has been with the particular problems of the location and suitable policies have been promoted.

Some studies have moved away from this area wide approach towards particular issues in specific locations, for example extensive accessibility studies have been carried out as part of the West Yorkshire Transport Studies (Cooper et al. [6A12], Martin and Daly [6A38]) in areas that surround some of the large industrial towns in the north of England. Similarly, remote rural areas such as the Highlands of Scotland have also been subjected to accessibility analyses (Forde and Sweetnam [6A25]). Particular journey purposes have raised concerns in certain locations. Commuting studies have been carried out (e.g. in Cardiganshire by Lewis [6A37]) as have journeys to school (e.g. Rigby and Hyde [6A48] in Berkshire and Surrey). Most common has been the work on the elderly in a variety of locations, such as Gregory [6A28] in Scotland and Smith and Gant [6A52] in the Cotswolds, and access to hospitals in rural areas. Haynes et al. [6A30] have provided extensive evidence of the effects of hospital concentration in rural Norfolk, and similar studies have been carried out in Gwent (Joint Working Group of TRRL and Gwent County Council [6A36]).

A third dimension of investigation has been to examine specific modes in a particular rural situation. The best examples are the extensive series of rural transport experiments carried out by the Transport and Road Research Laboratory (Balcombe [4C10]). The conventional bus has provided a focus for some studies (e.g. Clout *et al.* [6A11] in East Anglia and Holding [6A32] in Dyfed and Northumberland), but the unconventional modes seem to offer more opportunities. Secondary transport modes (Baker [6A2]) have been tried in a variety of different locations. Minibus services have extended from lowland areas (Orriss [6A43]) to highland border areas (Millar [6A39]), community buses are in operation in about fifteen locations (Banister [4C13], and Deavin [6A19]), and the postbus is widespread, particularly in Scotland (Carpenter [6A10]). Taxi services and social car schemes have been introduced in some areas (Greening and Jackson [6A26]).

The final part of the picture is provided by the numerous recreational studies that have been carried out by the Countryside Commission [6A13] and others (e.g. Dartington Amenity Research Trust [6A16]). Duffell and Peters [6A21] [6A22] have used the Hertfordshire Countryside survey to analyse short distance recreational travel, whilst Huddart [6A33] has examined the problems of non-car owners gaining access to the countryside in rural Gwent. certain amount of research has examined access to the National Parks via the motorway system (Jackson [6A34]) and movement within the parks for those without access to a car (Davison [6A18]).

6B Europe

The situation in Europe reflects that in Great Britain and much has been learnt from the exchange of information. The effects of road investment on regional development and accessibility have provided one focus for research; for example the work of Barre and Vaudois [6B3] and Grandjean and Henry [5A8] in France, De Lannoy and Van Oudheusden [6B7] in Belgium and Apicella [6B1] in Italy. However, the primary concern has been the demise of the conventional bus in rural areas—what De Boer [6B6] calls 'missing the bus'. Most comparisons have been made between the north European countries of Netherlands, Denmark and Germany (Heinze *et*

al. [2C9], [6B13] and Kilvington [2C10]) where the familiar problems of high car ownership levels have been coupled with declining
public transport patronage levels. The conclusions are similar in
that there must be a commitment to public subsidy for rural transport, preferably through standards (e.g. Dijkhuis and Van der Ree
[6B9] and Krogsaeter [6B18]) and a clear balance between public
and private transport (Asp and Lundin [6B2]). Other work has
concentrated on the wider social role that transport plays in maintaining rural communities (Garden and Hoekert [6B10] and Pedersen [5B35]).

The second principal group of area-based studies have covered
the alternatives to conventional public transport. Again experience
from Britain is paralleled by dial-a-ride schemes and rural taxi services in Norway [Frøysadal [4C36]), by minibus experiments in
France and by cooperation between bus and taxi operators in the
Netherlands (Klinkenburg [6B15]). More adventurous schemes
have also been assessed, such as the extensive use of the postbus in
Switzerland (Genton and Rathey [6B11]) and short take-off and
landing air services in north Norway (Strand [6B22]).

In East Europe the situation is slightly different with lower car
ownership levels and extensive bus and rail networks. Nevertheless
there are signs that similar problems are appearing, and certain
decisions will have to be made on the level of service offered and
the acceptable support costs. Published material includes a series of
essays by 'emigre' researchers on a range of issues (Mieczkowski
[6B19]) as well as a limited number of papers (e.g. Pavlik and Vlcek
on the Prague region of Czechoslovakia [6B21] and Denisyuk and
Chernyuk on the southwest region of the USSR [6B8]). As with all
European publications there are the problems of language and availability of papers.

6C USA, Canada and Australasia

Much of the research in North America is regionally based and
examines particular issues. A limited amount concentrates on transport planning (e.g. Prescott and Lorber [6C18] in Iowa) and highway
planning (e.g. Ruppenthal [6C20] in British Columbia), but most
effort is devoted to public transport. The US Department of Transportation [6C25] has produced a manual for Carolina, and Mayne
and Morrall [6C13] have tackled the Edmonton-Calgary corridor

in Canada. Specific studies financed under the Urban Mass Transportation Administration abound for rural public transport; for example in Virginia (Demetsky et al. [6C5]), in Wisconsin (Knapp et al [6C11]) and in Nebraska (Stringfellow [6C23]). Fritz [6C7] has concentrated on the productivity of services in Iowa and through the consolidation of existing systems has produced streamlined services that have increased output by a third. In each case patronage levels have fallen but operating costs have increased, and the analysis has examined the means by which these trends can be mitigated and efficiency improved.

It has also been recognized that many disadvantaged and elderly people will still depend on public transport (Maggied [6C12]) for their mobility. This social awareness is evident in the research output. Demand responsive and dial-a-bus services have been assessed (e.g. Carlson [6C2] in Santa Clara County and Collura et al. [6C3] in Barnstable County Massachusetts) with a view to providing an integrated rural transport system (Pott and Hesling [6C17]). Other research (e.g. Harman [6C9]) has taken the elderly and the handicapped in rural areas as a deprived group and has compared the approaches adopted in different locations (Public Technology Incorporated [6C19]). Van Sickel and Heathington [6C26] have combined the above groups with the rural poor in Mississippi to determine whether existing transport services fit into their requirements for daily activities. Many options have been considered, but future services depend on several factors such as energy availability and price, alternative public transport, both conventional and unconventional, and different organizational structures (Hoel et al. [6C10]). The overriding constraint is the likely levels of financial support in the future.

6D Developing countries

Transport planning in developing countries is concerned with two main issues. First there is the question of appropriate evaluation methods for the particular situation (Tingle [6D35]) and secondly the relationship between transport and economic development (Bovill et al. [6D9]). Blaikie et al. [6D7] have argued that road construction in Nepal has had little effect on the development of the region, nor has it alleviated the problems of a primarily agricultural economy. Conversely, Hennes and Sachdev [6D18] have suggested that in India scarce resources have been allocated to roads to market centres rather than to local villages. The issue of evaluation is critical. Value of time concepts may not be applicable to developing countries (Howe [6D22]) or to low volume rural roads. Simmersbach [6D30] citing evidence from four countries concludes that a producer surplus-oriented type of analysis may be more suitable, whilst Smith [6D32] advocates the use of simplified project appraisal methods that relate to the wider rural development structure and do not make heavy demands on data sources.

Similarly, engineering standards developed elsewhere may not be suitable for application to low cost, low volume rural roads. The problems of estimating rural traffic flows are considerable (Howe [6D21]), and different approaches have been adopted in particular countries; for example Brademeyer *et al.* [6D10] in Egypt, Conrad and Schoon [6D11] in Gambia, De Veen [6D12] in Kenya and Saddler [6D29] in Zimbabwe. Many different modes of transport have been used in developing countries including non-motorized alternatives (Barwell [6D3], Barwell and Howe [6D4]). The majority of applications relate to urban locations (e.g. Fouracre [6D16] and Jacobs and Fouracre [6D24]), but some research covers the particular requirements for intermediate vehicles in rural areas (e.g. Weightman [6D36]). The questions of evaluation and development are likely to remain as principal issues in developing countries with some priority for the projects that discriminate in favour of low income groups (Squire and Van der Tak [6D33]).

6A United Kingdom

1 ADAMS, L. and RENOLD, J. (1975) A preliminary study of rural transport in West Yorkshire. Local Government Operational Research Unit, Report C210, March.

This report describes the results of a preliminary study into rural transport carried out by the Local Government Operational Research Unit for the Metropolitan County of West Yorkshire, by examining the situation in two representative areas of the county. The study aimed to identify people receiving a relatively poor transport service; to propose ways of improving the service, and to formulate ways of evaluating the improvements. A household survey was undertaken in each area, one near Hebden Bridge in Calderdale

District and the other near Woolley in Wakefield District. The results of the study indicate that transport provision in most parts of both areas is relatively good. The main improvements suggested are a minibus scheme in Hebden Bridge, re-routing of one bus service in Woolley, and the use of a community car service in both areas. A mathematical model for predicting rural transport demand has been formulated and undergone preliminary tests. Proposals are made for investigating transport services in the other rural areas of West Yorkshire.

6A2 BAKER, R. (1977) Report on a study of secondary public transport in Hertfordshire. Advanced Transport Systems Department, Hawker Siddeley Dynamics Ltd.

This study of secondary public transport in Hertfordshire covers private operators, taxis, works-owned buses as well as aspects of carsharing. About 40 per cent of the primary stage carriage sector mileage is accounted for by the secondary transport although it is complementary and serves a different market. Recommendations are made for administrative changes at the District and County level so that this sector comes increasingly into the cognisance of the County Council as part of its public transport coordination duties. In this way a better matching of the public's travel requirements to the total resources available could be made, thus allowing a more effective public transport service.

6A3 BARBOUR, K.M. (1977) Rural road lengths and farm-market distances in North-East Ulster. *Geografiska Annaler*, **59B,** pp. 14-27.

The landscape of NE Ulster comprises a number of fairly evenly spaced market towns and a remarkably dense network of roads which radiate like spokes from the towns in all directions. This paper aims to investigate the efficiency of the road system given the inter-market distances and the mean farm sizes prevailing in the area. The method adopted is to devise a number of geometrical road patterns, which, in a hexagon-based landscape, would minimize total road lengths and total farm-market distances.

6A4 BRANCHER, D.M. (1972) The minor road in Devon—a study of visitors' attitudes. *Regional Studies*, **6** (1), pp. 49-58.

The problem of minor roads is reviewed and the significance of the cognition and attitude of visitors in scenic areas is introduced. A survey is described in which visitors were given unstructured interviews, using photographs as focus material. Sampling problems are discussed, the interview content appraised, and themes extracted. The results are then clustered, together with the respondents' personal data, to generate tentative hypotheses for the future more structured investigations.

5 BRIGHT, M.J., GARRATT, M.G. and KINDER, J.D. (1978) Transportation planning in Berkshire—problems and policies. *Traffic Engineering and Control*, **19** (4), pp. 164-9.

Discusses the use of a model to assess the different policy options available to a Local Authority. The focus is on the economic evaluation which despite its problems does, with careful application, provide a sound analytical base to assist better decision-making.

6 BRITISH ROAD FEDERATION (1979) County road needs in Bedfordshire, Cambridgeshire and Northamptonshire. BRF Monograph.

Government cuts in highway spending over the past five years are described, and their implications for the three counties related to traffic problems associated with the Midlands, the east coast ports and the south east discussed. A series of road maps illustrates that there are 15.5 motorway miles in Bedfordshire, none in Cambridgeshire and 28 in Northamptonshire. Other trunk roads account for 70.2, 208 and 130.3 miles respectively. With county roads, principal roads account for 113.5, 235.4 and 233.2 miles respectively, and other roads 1143.3, 2449.8 and 1808.6 miles respectively. This report outlines the trunk and county road needs in the three counties and shows where additional funds are needed to deal with specific local problems. Data presented include details of proposed county council expenditure for five years to 1983-84, public expenditure on transport at constant 1978 survey prices and major road schemes expected to be completed by 1990.

7 BRYANT, P.W. (1977) Petworth area rural transport study. West Sussex County Council, January.

8 CAMERON, G.R. (1979) MAP works in Warwickshire. *Surveyor*, **153** (4518), pp. 13-15.

Warwickshire County Council and the Midland Red Bus Company (a National Bus Company subsidiary) have cooperated in a Market Analysis Project (MAP) to ensure a viable network which would meet most needs and reduce the amount of revenue support required. The author traces the history of the rationalization studies in Stratford-upon-Avon and Warwick-Leamington. In the MAP study, each area is treated separately and any surplus in one MAP is not normally transferred to another area to increase its size or subsidize its fares. A county-wide travel survey was undertaken to establish minimum needs for travel in urban areas based on village size and facilities. The methods used for conveying school children are important; Warwickshire County Council 'buys' passes on stage buses thereby reducing the revenue support which the County Council would otherwise have to pay to the Bus Company. The author regards it as being unfortunate that, as a result of a more efficient service, the government is reducing its revenue support to Warwickshire.

6A9 CARPENTER, T.C. (1973) Postbuses in Scotland. *Coaching Journal*, **41,** November, pp. 44–7.

6A10 CARPENTER, T.C. (1977) Postbuses in Scotland. Proceedings of a Symposium held at the Transport and Road Research Laboratory. *Transport and Road Research Laboratory*, SR 336, pp. 20–21.

Since 1972, postbus services in Scotland have increased from one to 84 and now carry over 100,000 passengers a year. They serve rural areas in all parts of Scotland, complementing conventional bus services on the main routes. Postbuses are cheap to operate as they are an adjunct to existing post services and are eligible for government grants.

6A11 CLOUT, H.D., HOLLIS, G.E. and MUNTON, R.J.C. (1973) A study of public transport in North Norfolk. Department of Geography, University College London, Occasional Paper 18.

Only one-fifth of the parishes of north Norfolk have a bus service suitable for journey-to-work travel and most of the movement was for weekly shopping in local towns, especially on the market day services to Fakenham. Cluster analysis was used on variables such as schools, various shops, bus services and social clubs, dividing

services provided within the parish from those provided at a distance. There is an account of the decline in the provision and use of
bus services, 1952-1970, and finally analysis of a questionnaire
survey on the travel and journey patterns for work, school and shops
and the relationship between travel behaviour and other socio-economic characteristics of the households. The parishes surveyed were
Branchester, Burnham Market, North Creake, South Creake and
Sculthorpe.

2 COOPER, J.S.L., DALY, P.N. and HEADICAR, P.G. (1979) West
Yorkshire transportation studies—2. Accessibility analysis. *Traffic
Engineering and Control*, **20** (1), pp. 27-31.

A detailed analysis of accessibility is made under four main headings:
personal access—to workplaces and facilities; population catchments
for workplaces and facilities; freight access—to outlets and transport
facilities; access to freight generators and transport facilities from
outlets [6A38].

3 COUNTRYSIDE COMMISSION (1972) The Goyt Valley traffic experiment
1971-1972; a report by J.C. Miles.
(1974) Transport for countryside recreation; a report for the
Countryside Commission by Robert Matthew, Johnson Marshall
& Partners.
(1976) Public transport for countryside recreation; a report for the
Countryside Commission by the Dartington Amenity Research
Trust.

4 COUNTRYSIDE COMMISSION (1978) Routes for people: an experiment
in rural transport planning. A joint report with Derbyshire County
Council and the Peak Park Joint Planning Board, CCP 108.

This report is concerned not with the accessibility problems of rural
residents but with the conflict between different road users in a
scenic area, namely the Peak District National Park. An experiment
is reported in which different types of road users—lorries, recreational motorists, cyclists, walkers, etc.—are steered towards different
elements of a defined route hierarchy, including improved A-class
roads, scenic routes and maintained footpaths. '

5 COUNTRYSIDE COMMISSION (1979) Leisure and the countryside.
Countryside Commission CCP 124, Cheltenham, Gloucestershire.

6A16 DARTINGTON AMENITY RESEARCH TRUST (1976) Public transport for countryside recreation: a report to the Countryside Commission, DART publication, 21.

The growth of demand for countryside recreation and the dominance of the private car as a means of transport for such recreation have led to growing official concern about the relative lack of opportunity for countryside recreation offered to those who do not own, or wish to use, private transport, and congestion caused by private cars at certain popular places. This study emphasizes the need for positive and imaginative steps to be taken to make proper use of public transport in recreational planning so as to remedy the major problems indicated above.

6A17 DAVIES, E.R. (1979) New ways forward, public transport alternatives in Clwyd. Clwyd County Council, Mold.

This booklet outlines schemes introduced by the Clwyd County Council over the last four years, showing how they were put into practice; it also contains a report on the development and progress of the new Air Wales service and outlines the operation of a postbus scheme in an area of very difficult terrain. Details are given of an experiment to determine the effect of a fare reduction on bus usage and revenue. The operation of a voluntary social car service in three districts of Glyndwr is discussed. This service is designed to provide supplementary transport for rural areas ill-served by traditional forms of transport, and the scheme has been expanded to form a voluntary essential car service, aimed at areas where no public transport is available, or where passengers are unable to use public transport through age or infirmity. The development of an experimental community bus scheme in the Cerrigydrudion area is described. Results show that a 50 per cent reduction in off-peak fares produced a passenger gain of 22 per cent and a revenue loss of 28 per cent. The highest increase in passengers occurred where the actual amount of the discount was largest.

6A18 DAVISON, P. (1977) National park buses, in Symposium on Unconventional Bus Services, Summaries of Papers and Discussions. *Transport and Road Research Laboratory*, SR 336, pp. 33-4.

A description of the work that the Countryside Commission is carrying out in the National Parks is presented. Some of the rural transport schemes are outlined and it is suggested that public transport in these areas could be improved both for visitors and for residents.

9 DEAVIN, P. (1976) Community bus experiment. Norfolk County Council, April.

A description of the Community Bus experiment which was set up in six villages in North Norfolk in November 1975 is presented. Demand was measured through small scale public participation and initial reactions seem to indicate that the service can cover its operating costs. The key to its success seems to be the collaboration with the County Council and local bus operator, and the availability of a pool of willing volunteer organizers and drivers.

20 DERBYSHIRE COUNTY COUNCIL (1975) Rural public transport study: report. Derbyshire County Council, Matlock.

This paper presents the findings of a study which comprised firstly an analysis of public transport services available to villages in the rural west and south of Derbyshire and secondly a household interview of six typical villages in an area between Matlock and Buxton. The information obtained from the household survey has given a clearer picture of social need for public transport by showing under what circumstances the absence of public transport creates problems for those who have no alternative means of transport available.

21 DUFFELL, J.R. and PETERS, C.M. (1971) Recreation travel in urban and rural areas—1. *Traffic Engineering and Control*, **12** (12), pp. 616-18.

Recreational travel is one of the most rapid growth areas on the social scene. Some of the factors affecting recreational trip generation are given and comparisons are drawn between some published recreational surveys in rural and urban locations.

22 DUFFELL, J.R. and PETERS, C.M. (1972) Recreational travel in urban and rural areas—2. Hertfordshire Countryside survey. *Traffic Engineering and Control*, **13** (1), pp. 31-5.

The results of the Hertfordshire Countryside survey (1969) are given and these have provided the basis for a tentative mathematical model for predicting 'unsuppressed' car parking demand in rural areas. This paper, published in two parts, draws upon previous experience in the Worcestershire and Staffordshire Recreation Survey (1966). The significance of the recreational trip and its effect on the economic appraisal of highway schemes is evident and this is likely to increase.

6A23 ELLSON, P.B. and TEBB, R.G.P. (1977) Passenger resistance to a bus-bus interchange. *Transport and Road Research Laboratory*, SR 269.

Passenger resistance to the use of a rural bus-bus interchange facility in West Yorkshire has been investigated. When alternate through and transfer journeys were offered at hourly intervals a high proportion of travellers delayed or advanced their desired journey time to avoid the transfer. In the case of the transfer journeys the resistance which travellers displayed to using the interchange facility increased with trip length. For inter-urban trips, when through and transfer journeys were offered simultaneously by different routes, virtually all travellers took the through journey in spite of the fact that there was virtually no difference in journey time or fare.

6A24 FARRINGTON, J.H. and STANLEY, P.A. (1978) An evaluation of public transport in Skye and Lochalsh. Aberdeen, University of Aberdeen, Department of Geography.

A study of Skye looks systematically at the accessibility problems of the carless in this very sparsely populated area, grasps the nettle of defining 'need' and evaluates a range of options using both short-term and longer-term perspectives.

6A25 FORDE, M.C. and SWEETNAM, J.L.G. (1977) Transport in the Scottish Highlands—A comparison between the Outer Hebrides and Caithness. Paper presented at the Universities Transport Study Group Conference, Glasgow, January.

Transport within the Highlands and Islands Development Board area presents many problems, and the Board has advocated that ferry charges should be related to a road equivalent tariff. A small scale survey of industrial transport users has been undertaken in the Outer Hebrides and Caithness. The implications for the cost structures of industry are outlined.

26 GREENING, P.A.K. and JACKSON, R.L. (1982) The Basingstoke taxi and private hire car study. *Transport and Road Research Laboratory*, LR 1062.

A study of the role taxis and private hire cars in and around the provincial town of Basingstoke is reported. For a period of a week towards the end of 1981 the drivers of 29 taxis and 31 private hire cars (almost 90 per cent of the total number operating in the town) helped to carry out a survey which provided information on the number, age and sex of users, the frequencies with which they travelled by various forms of public transport, and the timing, purpose, means of booking, origin and destination of their journeys. Details of approximately 5000 taxi hirings and 2000 private hire car hirings were obtained. The data have been used to investigate the operating methods and markets of the taxi and hire car industries, to compare the role of the taxi trade in Basingstoke with that in Northampton (which had been the subject of an earlier TRRL study), and to consider the importance of taxis and private hire cars in the overall context of public transport provision.

27 GREGORY, P. (1978) Transport of the elderly and handicapped in rural Scotland. Paper presented at the International Conference on Transport for the Elderly and Disabled, Loughborough University of Technology, pp. 251-8.

This paper examines an extensive stretch (4600 square kilometres) of rural Scotland lying between Edinburgh and the English border, and brings into focus the needs and travel habits of the elderly, and to some extent, the disabled. There are facts about the numbers of elderly, their ability to walk, and how their independence is undermined with increasing age and physical handicaps. Facts are drawn from interviews with the elderly, a more general household survey, and surveys of patients visiting hospitals, all held in 1974. The travel habits of the elderly on buses are based on surveys undertaken by the Borders Regional Council in 1975 and 1977. This research in the Scottish Borders, undertaken both before and after the introduction of a half-fare Travel Card for the elderly and handicapped, has shown that high transport costs do suppress travel habits. The resulting lack of social contact and isolation is unfair to the elderly, and to the occasional visitors who try to provide them with their communication with the outside world. Few additional resources were required by the introduction of a half-fare Travel Card scheme, and the paper shows that elderly have responded by spending more and travelling more during off-peak periods. The paper concludes by outlining the next steps being considered to improve rural transport facilities for the elderly and handicapped in the Borders.

6A28 GREGORY, W.R. (1982) Hampshire's approach to public transport. Paper presented at the PTRC Annual Summer Conference, Warwick, July.

A range of activities and interests developed in Hampshire since 1974 is described under three headings, development, co-ordination and works. Development is concerned with expected problems and opportunities, including policies and research. Co-ordination is the nuts and bolts of County involvement. The detail of service networks and their inter-relation with each other, subsidy allocation, survey direction, trials to test demand, consultations and special publicity arrangements are all involved. In 1982/83 Hampshire will spend nearly £3.2m in subsidies to bus and ferry services. In full co-operation with the operators the entire County bus and ferry network has been surveyed comprehensively over the last 2½ years at a total cost of approximately £500,000 of which the County has paid 50 per cent. Co-ordination must include internal transport arrangements especially school transport which should complement the public transport networks. All significant passenger fleets should be administered in a fashion which maximizes their utilization within certain constraints. Unconventional transport has much to offer as conventional networks contract and while the origin of the resources matter little it is important that an overall view of transport is taken which must be a proper role for County Council involvement. Publicity efforts must be sustained to achieve real benefits. Hampshire helps the operator to take initiatives improving on the current arrangements.

Works to assist public transport are the most tangible expression of the County's interest and involvement. Hampshire recognizes that the replacement, renewal and improvement of public transport infrastructure neglected for too long cannot be financed solely by the operators' cash flow if a civilized system is the aim. Averaging just over £250,000 per annum the period since 1974 has seen three £1m projects completed. While progress since 1974 has been respectable there are still areas of very considerable potential. The conventional networks still remain the dominant ones and there is a feeling that not all organizations and authorities are pulling in the common direction. Much remains to be done.

29 HARMAN, R.G. (1982) Rural services—change in north-east Norfolk. *Policy and Politics*, **10** (4), pp. 477–94.

In a study of 23 parishes in a remote rural area, changes in the availability of services were monitored over the period 1975–1981. Scheduled bus services and food shops are the two main services to decline. Access and mobility particularly constrain certain groups of people and planning tends to favour those with high levels of mobility rather than those without. The remedy to this problem is for rural counties to practice what they preach, namely that the effects of expenditure occur primarily at the local level and it is to this level where decisions should be devolved.

30 HAYNES, R.M., BENTHAM, C.G., SPENCER, M.B. and SPRATLEY, J.M. (1978) Community attitudes towards the accessibility of hospitals in West Norfolk, in Moseley, M.J. (ed) *Social Issues in Rural Norfolk*. Centre of East Anglian Studies, University of East Anglia, Norwich, pp. 45–58.

Accessibility to hospitals in rural Norfolk is not good. Facilities have been concentrated and the difficulties of access have increased. It is suggested that inaccessibility might not be evenly distributed between different groups of residents and that inconvenience may be the most important issue not the cost of the services. In order to provide tentative answers to some of these questions a survey of community attitudes was carried out in a number of villages in north-west Norfolk. This formed part of a wider study of the potential role of small hospitals (community hospitals) in the King's Lynn Health District. A sample of the general public in these villages was interviewed in order to collect information on aspects of their use of hospitals and on attitudes to a number of issues relating to hospitals in the area.

31 HISLOP, M. (1975) Improving rural bus services. *Local Council Review*, **26,** pp. 149–52.

Hertfordshire County Council have undertaken a survey of rural transport. As a pilot study, a survey was taken at Kimpton, using volunteer questionnaire distribution with the achievement of a very high return rate. A similar pattern was followed in nineteen other villages. The main conclusions reached were the importance of car availability, bus service reliability and the slowness of transport services in reacting to change.

6A32 HOLDING, D.M. (1979) Levels of rural bus provision and fares policy, in Halsall, D.A. and Turton, B.J. (eds) *Rural Transport Problems in Great Britain—Papers and Discussion*, Institute of British Geographers, Transport Geography Study Group, pp. 59-73.

This paper provides a detailed study of two contrasting rural counties, Dyfed and Northumberland. The question being tested is that the distribution of population within the two counties may affect the level of bus service requested and the economics of providing it. Secondly different pricing policies are considered and the relationships between price and demand are compared together with the necessity for financial support. The results are inconclusive.

6A33 HUDDART, L. (1979) A survey of transport on pleasure trips from Newport, Gwent. *Transport and Road Research Laboratory*, SR 504.

In recent years new experimental public transport schemes have been promoted to improve accessibility of attractive countryside to non-car owners. Until now demonstration schemes have been introduced on an ad hoc basis, and to introduce any further schemes a comprehensive understanding of present patterns of recreational travel is needed. A home interview survey was conducted to provide an assessment of transport needs and demands in Newport, Gwent, by a market based approach, and to identify problems involved in travel by public transport. The survey indicated recreational areas popular with the motorist, but virtually inaccessible to those without their own transport, and identified those places that the transport disadvantaged wished to visit. From the information gained from this survey, experimental transport services were to be planned to run from Newport to surrounding recreational areas.

6A34 JACKSON, R.T. (1970) Motorways and National Parks in Britain. *Area*, **2** (4), pp. 26-9.

Accessibility is probably the most important single factor in use of the National Parks. The motorway system is significant as it will increase access to individual Parks by between 0.8 per cent and 135 per cent overall. However there will be large areas of eastern and southeastern England with little or no access of this sort.

35 JEWELL, M.G. (1976) Lancashire's transport planning. *Coaching Journal*, **44,** April, pp. 38–41.

36 JOINT WORKING GROUP OF TRRL AND GWENT COUNTY COUNCIL (1981) The application of accessibility measures in Gwent; travel to hospitals and shops. *Transport and Road Research Laboratory*, LR 994.

This report describes a technique, developed by Gwent County Council and TRRL, for highlighting areas where there may be need for improved public transport services. The method involves the construction of accessibility contours based on travel time by public transport. These contours enclose areas of the county from which it is possible to reach a given facility in 45 minutes travel by bus, plus up to 15 minutes walking at each end. Travel to hospital outpatient clinics and shopping centres is used to illustrate the technique. The areas which fall outside the contours are then examined to see what problems exist in reaching facilities. Population, car ownership and available public transport are studied. The technique is a simple way of identifying areas where there may be transport problems; one map can be produced for the county overall, for each type of facility. In this way, areas for detailed study are greatly reduced.

37 LEWIS, G.J. (1967) Commuting and the village in mid-Wales: a study in social geography. *Geography*, **52** (3), pp. 294–304.

Cardiganshire, a sparsely populated county suffering from depopulation, was chosen for the study. It is argued that commuting is as important for a sparsely populated region as for a more densely populated one. The basic source of journey to work data was the 1951 Census and the major centre of employment is Aberystwyth. A map illustrates the 'commuter hinterland' of Aberystwyth and isopleths show the percentage of occupied population of the settlements surrounding that town employed there. From the study it was evident that the dependence on Aberystwyth for employment led to dependence on it for social provisions and leisure pursuits, leading to the breaking down of the self-sufficient local economy and to the village's own communal life.

6A38 MARTIN, B.V. and DALY, P.N. (1978) West Yorkshire transportation studies 1—The analytic approach. *Traffic Engineering and Control*, **19** (12), pp. 536-40.

In addition to the main urban centres in West Yorkshire there are over 300 rural communities containing some 10 per cent of the population. This article describes the planning approach adopted in the studies and the county-wide data bank developed for the analytical work. Finally the Community Involvement Programme is outlined [6A12].

6A39 MILLAR, A. (1979) A border trial. *Commercial Motor*, **149** (3814), pp. 78-9.

The article describes a development in rural area transport introduced in the border region of Scotland by the Scottish bus group in conjunction with the Border Health Board. Operated by Eastern Scottish, the border courier minibuses run throughout the region carrying health board and council goods and supplies. They are also routed to cover 110,000 miles per year on services for passengers such as schoolchildren and old people attending day centres. The vehicles used for these services are 13-seat Bedford CF340's fitted with Reebur 17 bodies having 110 cu ft capacity goods compartments. The services will be evaluated over the next two years for possible application in other rural areas with similar transport problems.

6A40 MOYES, A. (undated) Accessibility to general practitioner services in Anglesey: some trip-making implications. Department of Geography, University of Aberystwyth, mimeo.

This paper seeks to explore one major proposition: that some of the time which doctors spend visiting patients at home may be time which could be more productively used in seeing more patients in fixed surgeries. In order to investigate the major proposition, three main lines of enquiry are pursued here: firstly, to establish the pros and cons of home treatment by doctors; secondly, to determine the catchment areas of surgeries in a study area (Anglesey) and devise a measure of accessibility to the surgeries; and thirdly, to simulate a possible pattern of demands on the general practitioner services in one area of low accessibility, and of the resultant trips generated. Findings under these three headings suggest some implications for public transport provision for journeys-to-surgery.

41 OCHOJNA, A.D. (1975) Dial-a-ride in Carterton: a review of residents' travel patterns. Cranfield Institute of Technology, Centre for Transport Studies, Report No. 8.

The assessment of the dial-a-ride service, which started in Carterton (near Oxford), in November 1973, is a joint Transport and Road Research Laboratory/Cranfield programme. The service is used mainly by people from non-car owning households and from the lower income groups. It carries 3.2 per cent of all motorized trips to town.

42 OLNEY, G.P. and KILVINGTON, R.P. (1982) Measuring rural accessibility—A study in the Breckland District of Norfolk. Paper presented at the University Transport Studies Group Annual Conference, Bristol, January.

A description of an accessibility measure is outlined together with its application in the Breckland district of Norfolk. Conclusions highlight the difficulties involved and it is suggested that a less complex method would not be suitable. The matrix method requires disaggregation by activity and its relevance to the person type being considered, the quality of public transport and a series of car availability conditions.

43 ORRISS, H.D. (1976) Multi-purpose minibus. *Local Council Review*, **27** (3), pp. 87-90.

In 1975 a community-run minibus service came into operation in Norfolk. This article describes a rather different experimental minibus service with two full-time drivers in the Peterborough-Cambridge-Huntingdon area. The project is multi-service, seven services in one: London commuter link service; work and school door-step service; shop-and-ride, linking outlying villages to St Ives; dial-a-bus in the Sawtry area; local village service in Sawtry; and surgery dial-a-bus which gives personalized transport to and from the health centre at Yaxley. It is to be hoped that East Anglia's pioneering in community transport will succeed and be copied throughout Britain.

6A44 OWENS, S. (1978) Changing accessibility in two North Norfolk parishes, Trunch and Southrepps, from the 1950s to the 1970s, in Moseley, M.J. (ed) *Social Issues in Rural Norfolk*, Centre for East Anglian Studies, University of East Anglia, Norwich, pp. 13-32.

This paper is the result of a largely subjective in-depth study of two villages carried out in 1975, the aim of which was to discover how, and with what consequences, the accessibility enjoyed by the residents had changed over two decades. Modes of transport and changing needs are identified: in general there has been a decrease in the 'self-containment' of each village, and an increase in both the need and desire to travel further. While accessibility and mobility have improved for many, it has markedly worsened for others resulting in increased differentiation.

6A45 OXFORDSHIRE COUNTY COUNCIL (1976) Local transport in Oxfordshire. Oxfordshire County Council, County Hall, Oxford, November.

Provides background information to promote greater public involvement in local transport. Sections cover public transport, the need for transport, unsubsidized services, school buses, conventional bus services, car-sharing, minibuses, village care, licensing and the Traffic Commissioners, and marketing local services. The handbook will be updated as experience of running local transport grows.

6A46 PHILLIPS, M.H. (1976) New ways forward: Alternatives in public transport in Clwyd. Clwyd County Council, Mold.

Topics covered include existing levels of bus provision and car ownership; development of the Derwen and Maelor social car schemes; the community bus; off-peak bus schemes and reduced fares experiments around Holywell. The social car scheme caters mainly for transport to hospitals and doctors, and a standard letter for insurance purposes has been produced by the county. The Maelor scheme, near Wrexham, accounts for about thirty trips per month, and began in January 1974, while the service around Derwen, Clyffylliog and Clocaenog began in September 1975 and carries somewhat lower numbers. A more widespread 'voluntary essential car service' is planned, but only to be used where public transport is impracticable. Extensive background details of setting up the Cerrigydrudion Community Minibus (a Ford Transit provided by Crosville) are given, with timetables and map. Some six off-peak bus service improvements are described, several of which have reached financial break-even. Details of time-tables, costs and revenue for each are given. Similar detail is given of the Holywell area fares experiment, which was not financially successful, although some traffics were evidently more elastic than the typical −0.3 average.

47 REES, G. and WRAGG, R. (1975) A study of the passenger transport needs of rural Wales. Welsh Council, July.

The report contains the findings of a survey into the problems of providing public transport in the rural areas of Wales and attempts to provide assistance to local authorities in devising future transport plans. The demand for public transport in rural areas is examined and criteria determined for assessing an optimum level of public and private transport in any one area. It is pointed out that maximum benefits are not necessarily achieved by subsidizing present networks when a revised travel pattern may satisfy demand and require a lower level of subsidy. The report evaluates costs of the present railway network, the bus industry and the alternative Post Office bus system. Reasons for a rapid rise in car ownership are also examined and the advantages that it offers such as increased mobility, reduced journey time and cost. A detailed discussion of alternative transport strategies is appended.

48 RIGBY, J.P. and HYDE, P.J. (1977) Journeys to school—a survey of secondary schools in Berkshire and Surrey. *Transport and Road Research Laboratory*, LR 776.

The report describes the background to the study and the design, implementation and findings of a questionnaire survey conducted amongst 2,415 secondary school pupils to obtain information on the basic pattern of school journeys in terms of travel mode, time and distance. Interrelationships between these variables are examined; additional explanatory variables include school type, school location, respondent's family background, and service quality. Walk and bus were the most important modes used, and distance had the most significant effect on modal split. Differences in the quality of pupils' journeys were assessed and bus travel was rated lowest, largely because of poor service quality.

6A49 ROBERTSON, I.M.L. (1976) Accessibility to services in the Argyll district of Strathclyde: a locational model. *Regional Studies*, **10** (1), pp. 89–96.

A model which can determine the optimum locations for facilities in an area of circuitous communications is described. Based on real road distances and population data set out on a square grid mesh, the model is applied to the new district of Argyll, a sparsely populated area where the relationship between real road distance and linear distance can be as great as five. Examples are given of locational problems which can be handled by the technique.

6A50 SCOTTISH ASSOCIATION FOR PUBLIC TRANSPORT (1979) Ticket to ride. A guide to public transport in Scotland. SAPT, September.

The report presents a guide to public transport in Scotland where such services are more essential than is generally appreciated. Only 46 per cent of Scottish families have a car, often only used by one member of the family. The planning emphasis should be on improving and extending forms of public transport not superseding them with expensive facilities needed for individual private transport. The aim of the booklet is to improve public awareness at a time of change in transport policy. With the focus on passenger transport, the intention is to clarify the legal and financial position, to outline government policy and to detail responsibilities of the authorities involved.

6A51 SHAW, J.M. (1979) The tourist and his traffic. *Highway Engineer*, **26** (6), pp. 14–17.

The paper argues that the pattern of holiday development and of countryside recreation in East Anglia is almost entirely attributable to changing modes of transport. With the improved accessibility of the region, a continued increase in car-based pressures on the coast and the countryside is inevitable. Traditional traffic and land-use planning provide inadequate frameworks for coping with the resulting problems. There is a strong case for a process of co-ordinated management which has conservation as its prime objective.

52 SMITH, J. and GANT, R. (1982) The elderly's travel in the Cots-
worlds, in Warnes, A.M. (ed) *Geographical Perspectives on the Elderly*,
London, Wiley, pp. 323-36.

Examines the extent of the rural transport problem and concludes
that solutions for the elderly will only be found at a local scale.
Meeting the demands at a time of financial restraint requires the
cooperation of all agencies concerned with the welfare of the elderly—in the transport sphere this means public agencies, voluntary
organizations and the local community.

53 TURNOCK, D. (1978) Highland transport. *Town and Country Planning*,
46, pp. 510-13.

The Highlands and Islands of Scotland seem to be showing some
promising initiatives in the rural transport scene. This short paper
describes some of these, in particular postbuses, ferries and air services. Public transport is becoming more varied yet integration
seems also to be improving. It all means improved employment and
shopping opportunities for locals and more scope for tourists without
access to a car.

54 WILKES, P.F. (1976) Community bus experiment. Paper presented
to the Symposium on Unconventional Bus Services, Transport and
Road Research Laboratory, Crowthorne.

The paper describes the Community Bus experiment which was set
up in 6 villages in North Norfolk in November 1975. The public
participation that was undertaken to measure the potential demand
and form of services required is discussed together with the problems
that have arisen during the initial period of the experiment. An
assessment of the first few months experience up to the end of the
financial year 1975/76 is given and an appendix shows the financial
return of the same period. A second appendix gives the constitution
and terms of reference of the Village Bus Committee and the Steering Committee.

55 WILMERS, P.H. (1979) Implementing the 1978 Transport Act—A
district council view. Paper presented at the Conference on Public
Transport Planning, Loughborough University of Technology, September.

This paper suggests that the Public Transport Planning process in Norfolk has failed to live up to expectations for two basic reasons. The first is the fact that there are too many agencies involved in transport planning and the second is a lack of political will. Local government seems to be the agent of Central Government carrying out defined duties.

6B Europe

6B1 APICELLA, V. (1978) The evolution of the Italian motorway system. *Review of the Economic Conditions in Italy*, **32** (5/6), pp. 331–47.

Describes the development of the Italian motorway system which now totals some 6000 km and extends the whole length of the country as well as linking in with the European network. Fast development was ensured through the concession system offered, mainly to Autostrade SpA (about 50 per cent) a state controlled company. The concession covers a network so that cross subsidization can ensure that the revenue from heavily used sections can be used to finance losses elsewhere on the system. Overall a profit is made. Most of the rest of the network consists of concessions of individual motorways entrusted to companies in which local authorities have controlling interests.

6B2 ASP, K. and LUNDIN, O. (1981) Public transport in the era of the automobile. Swedish National Road and Traffic Research Institute, Linkoping.

A travel survey in Sweden (1978) is analysed and the main results are structured within a transport policy framework that attempts a balance between public and private transport.

6B3 BARRE, A. and VAUDOIS, J. (1979) Autoroutes et agriculture dans la region Nord-Pas-de-Calais. *Bulletin de l'Assocation des Géographes Français*, **464,** pp. 301–5 (in French), Motorways and farming in the Nord-Pas-de-Calais region.

The dense motorway network in Northern France has been built on mainly agricultural land. This has tended to disorganize regional farming space, particularly in areas of intensive agriculture. The responses to these problems (land regrouping and compensation)

illustrate a wide disparity in the region's agriculture and it is concluded that it accelerates the processes of economic demise.

B4 BLONK, W.A.G. (1981) De organisatie van het interstedelijk open-
bare personenvervoer in Nederland. *Tijdschrift Vervoerswet*, **17** (2),
pp. 111-26 (in Dutch). (The organization of interurban public
transport in the Netherlands.)

B5 BRUGGEMAN, J.M. (1979) Inspraak bij stads—En streekvervoer.
Openbaar Vervoer, **12** (2), pp. 61-6 (in Dutch). (Public participation
in urban and rural public transport.)

Consumer organizations of users of public transport increasingly ask
for participation and want to be consulted on possible improvements
or possible worsening measures of public transport. An inventory is
given regarding public participation in urban and rural public
transport in the Netherlands. Developments are considerable in this
sector of public transport, apart from the sector of railbound transport.

B6 DE BOER, E. (1982) *De Bus Gemist*. Summary report of the project
on the Social Consequences of Decline in Rural Transport, Province
of Groningen, Groningen (in Dutch). (Missing the Bus.)

This report contains the main results of the afterstudy of rural transport withdrawal in two provinces of the Netherlands. Withdrawal
and reduction proved to be problematic for two-thirds of the respondents. Optional bus-users massively changed to car use, while
those dependent on bus transport had to resort to inconvenient
departure times (32 per cent) or even had to accept lower levels of
mobility (16 per cent) especially the (slightly) disabled amongst
them (25 per cent). Regarding the fact that especially the weaker
lines (not meeting the criterion of a one hour service for 14 hours a
day) are declining constantly with severe consequences for their
users, a number of proposals are made for these lines.

B7 DE LANNOY, W. and VAN OUDHEUSDEN, D. (1978) The accessibility
of nodes in the Belgian road network. *Geojournal*, **2** (1), pp. 65-70.

This paper presents an analysis of the accessibility of nodes in the
Belgian road network. The intersections of roads are considered as
the nodes and their connecting roads as edges of a network. By

means of the Dijkstra algorithm accessibility values are computed for each node by summing shortest travel times to a reference system of 158 nodes spread evenly over the Belgian territory. A comparison of the measured actual accessibility with that determined from an optimal situation provides an indication of the quality of directness of the Belgian road system. Accessibility and directness are shown cartographically together with an isochronal map for access to Brussels.

6B7 DENISYUK, L.M. and CHERNYUK, G. (1981) Rural commuting in the southwest region (Ukraine). *Soviet Geography: Review and Translation*, **22** (7), pp. 419–28.

This study shows that 60–80 per cent of all commuters live within a radius of 10 km. As a general rule, commuting rates are likely to be most intensive from small monofunctional places with limited employment opportunities. A set of commuting zones is defined, based on the magnitude and direction of commuting streams.

6B9 DIJKHUIS, H. and VAN DER REE, L. (1979) Openbaar vervoer in kleine kernen. Delft University of Technology, Department of Civil Engineering, Transport and Planning Group (in Dutch). (Public transport in small villages.)

After a general analysis of accessibility problems in (small) villages different standards for levels of service are compared. Then a new standard based upon minimum access (in time and space) to facilities is developed. It is applied to a rural area in the central part of the country and proposals for restructuring the present public transport network are made, taking account of present and potential demand and utilizing both conventional and alternative systems.

6B10 GARDEN, J. and HOEKERT, M. (1981) The importance of public transport to life in small villages: a study in progress. Proceedings of the PTRC Annual Conference, Warwick.

In the rural areas of the Netherlands all villages of 1500 or more have relatively frequent public transport services available. However the quality of services to the smaller communities varies widely with the standards of service set on the basis of utilization criteria. This study attempts to understand whether such levels of service are really appropriate to the needs of those living in rural areas. The preliminary findings of the indepth interviews are reported together with some comparisons from similar studies in Britain.

311 GENTON, D.L. and RATHEY, G. (1981) Swiss postal passenger service. *Transportation Research Record*, 831, pp. 59–62.

Solutions for public transport in less populated regions are considered with respect to region size and topography, the national political structure of the country, and population density and standard of living. The Swiss transport system is characterized by a very wide range of transport opportunities, operational factors, and financial aspects. The postal passenger service is the result of a long-term evolution that attempts to offer a satisfactory response to mail and passenger transport needs in rural resorts. This response emphazises efficiency for both the users and the collectives. The organization of the service, the network structure, service quality, tariffs, and the financial situation of the companies involved are analysed. Long-term experience has resulted in the following measures: adaptation to a diffused demand with the highest possible flexibility and spirit of creativity, integration of the transport operations of all private and public companies in order to take advantage of their common resources, and sharing the responsibility beween regional and local authorities in order to ensure a budgetary balance between the operating companies.

312 HARBOORT, J. (1978) Belgian problems in the area of mobility of elderly and handicapped people. Paper presented at the International Conference on Transport for the Elderly and the Handicapped, Loughborough University of Technology, pp. 33–6.

From 1900 to 1970 the number of elderly individuals in Belgium has tripled and the problems with respect to their mobility have become more severe, certainly if account is taken of the changes in the distribution of the population by age category. Mobility problems differ depending on the family structure in which the elderly person lives; these problems are evidently most severe for persons living alone. One problem which is becoming more and more severe is the purchasing of bread, meat and various foodstuffs. The question is therefore posed whether public powers should be used to increase the mobility of the elderly and the handicapped, or whether they should be used to eliminate the need for mobility. In this short paper, an examination is made of some of the means which have been implemented in Belgium to increase mobility and some of the steps, either taken or contemplated, to eliminate the need for mobility. Emphasis is placed on steps aimed at improving mobile shops and on making telephone use easier for elderly and handicapped people.

6B13 HEINZE, W.G., HERBST, D. and SCHÜHLE, U. (1982) Travel behaviour in rural areas: a German case study. *International Journal of Transport Economics*, **9** (2), pp. 193-203.

The discussion of necessary and possible improvements in the provision of transport in sparsely populated rural areas continues to be characterized mainly by hypotheses which display a broad spectrum of varied ideas. This has severe repercussions on forecasts made and instruments used as well as on their feedback into the process of developing objectives. This problem made itself particularly felt in the preparation of a major study project on the possibilities and limits of improvements in the transport services in sparsely populated rural areas. The authors tried to obtain concrete information on the actual transport services provided by means of primary surveys carried out in selected, representative partial areas in Lower Saxony. More attention should be paid to constitutional and social aspects of supplying marginal groups with public transport.

6B14 HOFSTRA, M. (1982) De Kern van het Streekvervoer. Delft University of Technology, Department of Civil Engineering, Regional Planning Group (in Dutch). (The core of rural transport.)

In this study national and regional policies (in the province of Groningen) with regard to land use planning are compared with public transport planning of the same agencies. These prove to be weak and contradictory: the level of public transport should be maintained but the demographic development required for it is thwarted. The provincial evaluation system for public transport is criticized. A modified system taking better account of accessibility periods is proposed and applied to the south-east region of the province.

6B15 KLINKENBERG, J. (1982) De ondergrens van het streekvervoer. Delft University of Technology, Department of Civil Engineering, Transport and Planning Group (in Dutch). (Marginal rural transport—

part I Rural public transport in East and West Dongeradeel, deteriorating levels of service, and part II Attempts for improvement.)

In part one the changes in public transport in a rural area of approximately 160 km² in the Northern part of the Netherlands (Friesland) are analysed. It proves to be deteriorating since 1975 especially in the evening and at the weekend. Consequences for accessibility of the rural population are analysed in detail. In part two an effort is made to develop a new transport network offering improved access without increasing the level of subsidy. This proves to be possible by combining conventional elements (fixed schedule) with non-conventional ones (dial-a-bus) in one system and by co-operation between bus- and taxi-operators. Essential is a division of labour not so much in space (geographic concessions) but in time: more conventional during rush hour and less at other times, especially in the evening and during the weekend.

816 KNOWLES, R.D. (1972) The rural transport problem: a case study: public road transport in Norway. Institute of British Geographers Transport Symposium.

This paper analyses the basic structure of public road transport in Norway. Despite a very weak traffic potential throughout most of the country and a rapidly increasing private car ownership level, and against the trend in all other north and west European countries except Finland, the use of public road passenger transport continues to increase in the country as a whole and in half of the 18 counties. This can be attributed to two main factors; first, to the combination of different types of traffic within each road transport company and secondly, to the long established government and local authority operating and capital subsidies. Changes in company size, origin of revenue, and private car ownership and seasonal variations in traffic are analysed at the county level.

817 KNOWLES, R.D. (1977) An analysis of transport networks in selected marginal areas with special reference to Norway. Unpublished PhD Thesis, Department of Geography, University of Newcastle upon Tyne.

818 KROGSAETER, K. (1977) Transportstandard i staeder och paa landsbygd, Paper presented to the Nordiska Vaegtekniska Foerbundets

Congress, Finland (in Norwegian). (Transport standards in towns and rural areas.)

Roads are a community resource and they are essential for the maintenance of our living conditions. Public debate pays surprisingly little attention to the importance of road traffic for national production and economy, and concentrates instead on its negative consequences. In most cases, road transport offers the best transport standard. In Norway, over 80 per cent of goods tonnage is transported by road, and 90 per cent of passenger transport is by road. In towns, however, 20 per cent of journeys to work are on foot, and foot traffic is therefore as important as cycle traffic and public transport put together. About 80 per cent of national roads have a paved surface at present; this will be raised to 90 per cent in the next 8 years. Only 10 per cent of roads have permitted axle loads of 10 tonnes; this will be raised to 40 per cent by 1986. A large proportion of the road network is shared by vehicular, cycle and pedestrian traffic, and by local and fast long-distance traffic. To raise transport standards and at the same time reduce the negative consequences of road transport, separation and differentiation are the main tasks. The standard of public transport must be improved, whilst the cost of motorways can be reduced by designing them for a lower speed.

6B19 MIECZKOWSKI, B. (1980) (ed) *East European Transport: Regions and Modes*, The Hague: Martinus Nijhoff.

A series of about 13 essays is presented on particular aspects of transport in East Europe. Rural and regional transport in Poland and Czechoslovakia are covered as is the impact of tourism on road capacity in Yugoslavia. The final group of essays looks at international themes such as integration and the role of the passenger car in transport policy.

6B20 OLANDER, L.-O. and PERSSON, T. (1976) Service and work: geographical studies of the use of time with reference to transportation and accessibility in South West Skane (Sweden). Department of Geography, University of Lund, Sweden.

There is a brief English summary of a model, founded in Swedish time-space geography, which has been used to evaluate patterns of service and transport provision in a rural region of Sweden. Alternative systems are evaluated in terms of the opportunities they give to residents to participate in various activities.

321 PAVLIK, Z. and VLCEK, I. (1967) The mobility of rural population. *Acta Universitatis Carolinae Geographica*, **2** (1), pp. 3–37.

Czechoslovak population is broadly dispersed and it has been evident for some time that, economically, a much greater concentration of residential population would be desirable as a response to greater concentration of economic functions in fewer localities or centres. Already greater technical scale of many productive activities has induced growing commuting of labour to work. This has demanded study of the quality of public transport services in relation to needs, the organization of traffic flows and questionnaires for completion by the populace. A number of traffic surveys have been made of commuting from selected residential areas in the Prague region. Sample questionnaires are described and analysed. Journeys have been classified into four groups as journeys for shopping and services, health, business, and other. Journeys from two centres in the Prague region are compared to assess the relationships between purpose of journey, frequency of transport service, mode of transport, distance, quality of local provision of shopping, service, health and business facilities. Theories derived are useful as a general framework but every case is particular in detail as a reflection of specific local conditions.

322 STRAND, S. (1980) Kortbaneflyrutene i Norge, spesielt i Finnmark: Geografisk og sosialt kraftfelt. Institute of Transport Economics Report, Oslo, March (in Norwegian).

The STOL (Short Take Off Landing) systems impact on North Norway is assessed in terms of the geographic and social effects. The description examines the changes in the transport standards for various areas and demographic groups, and also comments on the competition between the STOL systems and the coastal shipping system.

323 WHITE, P.R. (1974) Rural transport and public policy in Sweden. Institute of British Geographers Transport Symposium.

A study of rural public transport provision in Sweden, looking at: the definition of 'rural', measures of public transport use, the existing network, organization and control, and subsidies and planning policy. The author concludes that there are no radical changes in British rural transport policy which one can recommend from Swedish experience, but it is clear that a fairly intensive rural network can be maintained in conditions of far higher car ownership and lower population density, without excessive subsidies. Techniques contributing to this result include bus-rail co-ordination, very good timetable publicity, and in current experimental work, rationalization of the network into 'trunk' and 'feeder' elements.

6B24 WIKLUND, L., LUNDIN, I. and AXELSSON, B. (1976) Planering av taetartstrafik. Sambordning med Landsbygdstrafik. Research Monograph (in Swedish). (Planning of urban traffic. Coordination with rural traffic.)

The object of this study was to devise a planning method for public transport in towns of 20–50,000 population, and to coordinate urban traffic with traffic in surrounding areas. Nykoping (30,000) was chosen as the subject of study. Statistics were collected concerning the population and workplaces in the town and surrounding areas. The existing routes were studied with regard to interchanges between urban and rural services, as well as travelling standards, travel requirements and service frequencies. Economic aspects were taken into consideration and comparisons were made with other towns of similar size. An analysis of problems showed that existing routes are not altogether appropriate, and that peak loads on urban and rural routes occur at the same time, which precludes sharing of vehicles. In the short term, some improvements in standards are possible by using existing resources; special workmen's buses can be provided and a doubling in service frequency would raise costs by about 30 per cent. In the long term, new services to expansion areas must be provided.

6C USA, Canada, Australasia

6C1 BROWN, N.A. (1973) Rural mass transportation feasibility study. Bluegrass Area Development District, Washington DC and Appalachian Regional Commission, Lexington, Kentucky.

The study report is an examination of transit related problems of the six Appalachian counties within the Bluegrass area development district (Clark, Estill, Garrard, Lincoln, Madison and Powell). It outlines steps for the implementation of a rural mass transit system including cost analysis and forecasted benefits during a four-year phased period.

C2 CARLSON, R.C. (1976) Anatomy of a system's failure: Dial-a-ride in Santa Clara County, California. *Transportation*, **5** (1), pp. 3-16.

The dial-a-ride scheme in Santa Clara was initiated in late 1974, but it had failed by 1975. Each of four main reasons for failure is discussed in turn and recommendations are made. The initial start up period is likely to be the most difficult, particularly if total costs are considered in the evaluation.

C3 COLLURA, J., WARREN, R.P., O'LEARY, D.P. and BOHN, D. (1980) Evaluation of the Barnstable County public transportation demonstration project. *Transportation Research Record*, 761, pp. 58-65.

This paper evaluates the public transport demonstration project in Barnstable County, Massachusetts (population, 130,000; area 100 sq km (389 sq miles); 15 towns). Service was provided with ten 12-passenger vehicles on a prearranged demand-responsive basis. The demonstration project operated for 22 months and was then continued on a permanent basis. The paper addresses various aspects of planning and design, which include preliminary project planning, programme monitoring and evaluation, a rider-identification pass, data collection, user characteristics, system performance, financing, user attitudes, pricing, and simple supply-and-demand relationships. Major results and conclusions are that some form of door-to-door public transport service is necessary to meet the special needs of the elderly and the handicapped in small urban and rural areas; consideration should be given to coordinating any new service of this type with similar existing services; the system performance of such a service may need as much as 15 months to reach a stable condition; the use of a rider-identification pass is a relatively low-cost simple mechanism by which to collect fares, market service, and obtain useful data; attitudinal surveys may be helpful in determining user satisfaction and in identifying desired service changes; consideration should be given to pooling various federal, state, and local funds to finance projects; and any method used to apportion the local share of a deficit among towns may have to include a trip-length variable such as passenger kilometres if the desire of local officials is to base the apportionment on each town's level of use.

6C4 COMIS CORPORATION (1974) Nebraska statewide accessibility study. Wheaton, Maryland.

The accessibility analysis has been structured to measure the transport service to necessary community facilities (hospitals, schools, recreational facilities, etc.) available to different groups of residents (young, old, wealthy, poor, white, non-white, etc.) via alternate modes of travel (auto, public transit). Information generated as a result of this analysis enables the transport planner more completely to evaluate the benefits and disbenefits of both existing and proposed facilities.

6C5 DEMETSKY, M.J., HOEL, L. A., STONE, J.R. (1980) Implementation planning of integrated transit services for a small urban and rural area. Executive summary, Virginia University, Urban Mass Transportation Administration, Final Report, UMTA-VA-11-009-81-1, September.

This research focuses on tasks for taking technically feasible preliminary transit options to a local community and translating these plans into an implementable programme. This planning phase, referred to as implementation planning, addresses the following planning considerations: Financial Planning; Management and Organization; Institutional Roles; Regulatory Reforms; and Citizen Participation. The specific problem addressed concerns an evaluation of the requirements for implementing transit alternatives in a low density area and securing a community consensus. To incorporate the realities of a complex public transport planning process, this research project is tied closely to the current public transport improvement programme of Charlottesville and Albemarle County, Virginia. This study includes two elements that are reported in separate volumes of the final report. Volume I describes the financial planning and organizational structures that are necessary to implement integrated transit services in a small and rural area and Volume II evaluates system alternatives through public participation and group interaction by using a completed preliminary plan to focus community interest in public transit. This study reviews the primary organizational alternatives that are appropriate for delivering comprehensive areawide transport. The long term solution was shown to be the transport district. A description of a prototype district is given that evolves from a planning and administrative body to the total operation. The transit preferences of citizens, elected officials, and transit operators in the community were determined in a workshop and a series of interviews that were related to the characteristics of 18 urban and 25 rural transit route alternatives. The preferences were adjusted to reflect the future effects of a status quo scenario, a scenario favouring transit, and one not favouring transit. The urban and rural transit systems were selected by the evaluation model with respect to technical and financial constraints. The transit system improvements which were specified by the evaluation model compared very favourably with actual transit recommendations made by local officials.

36 FLYNN, E.J. (1978) Transportation planning and implementation in small cities and rural areas. *Transportation Research Record*, 696, pp. 16–20.

The Indiana Mass Transportation Improvement Project is responsible for public transport planning in the small urban and rural areas of Indiana. The goals of the Indiana Public Transportation Advisory Committee emphasize the public transport system. In Indiana a unique working arrangement is established in which the mass transport improvement project serves as the staff for local public transport operators. The project attempts to combine planning and operations into a total management assistance programme. Work currently is being done in nine cities of less than 50,000 population and 26 counties in the state. In rural areas, the transport advisory committee plays a dominant role in local transport planning and evaluation. It addresses the community's total transport needs rather than having local social service agencies think only of their own transport needs.

37 FRITZ, T.L. (1978) Private enterprise techniques improve productivity of rural transit systems in Iowa. *Transportation Research Record*, 696, pp. 34–8.

The primary objective of the Iowa Department of Transportation rural transit programme is increased productivity—to be able to produce more output (passengers carried) while using less input (money). When the department assumed control of rural transit in 1976, it became obvious that traditional methods of developing rural transit would hinder, if not actually negate, progress toward the objective of improved productivity. Consequently, the private enter-prize philosophy of management was implemented. This philosophy dictated the consolidation of the 275 rural transit systems into 16 systems and the elimination of nonproductive systems, provided authority equal to responsibility, holding specific people and agen-cies responsible for results, and implemented management and busi-ness decisions into an area of social work. The results, after 3 years of effort on a statewide basis, show that the output has increased by 33 per cent and the input has decreased by 10 per cent. The impli-cations of these results are that transit in general (urban, rural, or intercity) can benefit from consolidating authority and responsi-bility, managing by objectives, and making decisions that are based on economic and productivity analyses.

6C8 GUENTHER, K.W. (1976) Dial-a-ride in the USA: a case study. Paper presented to the Symposium on Unconventional Bus Services, Transport and Road Research Laboratory, Crowthorne.

Ann Arbor has integrated Dial-A-Ride with line bus service into a coordinated system so that it performs a collection and distribution function. It runs both in the urban area and outside to peripheral communities.

6C9 HARMAN, J.J. (1978) Transportation for human services. Paper presented at the International Conference on Transport for the Eld-erly and the Disabled, Loughborough University of Technology, pp. 259–68.

This paper presents a case study of a private-non-profit corporation (PNP) in a rural county in the Northeastern United States. This PNP, Call-A-Ride of Barnstable County, Inc. (CAR), initiated a demand-responsive transport service for the elderly and handi-capped in April 1976 with four operational mini-buses (converted vans with raised roofs, lowered steps, and hydraulic lifts for wheel-chairs). As of December 31 1977, that effort had expanded to 25 mini-buses of which 15 are equipped to accommodate wheelchairs. This enlarged programme included transport for the elderly and handicapped to health care facilities, congregate meal sites, adult day care activities, special education programmes, and food delivery for a 'meals-on-wheels' programme for the elderly. A county-wide demand-responsive public transport programme aimed at the elderly and handicapped was also initiated and ridership began at 250 trips per month and reached 8849 twenty-one months later. The programme brought together nine sources of federal funds through an array of intermediate agencies, added to local sources of support, in order to provide these transport services for the elderly and handicapped. This paper briefly outlines the history of CAR's development of a varied programme of consolidated transport services in rural Cape Cod, Massachusetts. It explores the problems and opportunities of an integrated programme of financial assistance for these services, many of which relate to the emerging interest in elderly and handicapped transport by the national and state governments and various regional entities. In conclusion, the paper evaluates how some of these developments affect present and future services for transport of the elderly and handicapped in rural areas of the United States.

o HOEL, L.A., DEMETSKY, M.J., MORRIS, D., HARGROVES, B.T., STONE, J.R., COTTRELL, B.H. and GOLDBERG, A. (1979) Transit service and organizational alternatives for a low density suburban-rural area: A study of public transit options for Albemarle County, Virginia. Virginia University, Urban Mass Transportation Administration, Final Report UMTA-VA-11-006-79-1, May.

The intent of this study is to provide planning options for public transport in Albermarle County and the City of Charlottesville, Virginia. The results are intended to provide a range of planning options for community service, but not a comprehensive plan for implementation. The options are intended for review in a future study by citizens and officials of the Charlottesville-Albemarle area to be refined according to local opinion as an aid to developing a plan for implementation. The options cover future transit demand scenarios depending on energy availability and price, alternative transit systems, and alternative organizational formats for coordinating low density rural and suburban transit and paratransit services. Special attention is given to the institutional issues affecting coordinated transit. This study approaches the basic problem of transport in low density areas from the institutional perspective of an operating organization. This approach is reflected in the study objectives which are to define the public transport needs and demand in the Charlottesville-Albemarle area; to design alternative transit and paratransit services for the Charlottesville-Albemarle area; and to define and evaluate alternatives to coordinate transit services. The findings of the study are based on local transit and demographic data, state-of-the-art transit and paratransit information, and Commonwealth of Virginia laws and regulations. In addition, two local surveys were conducted. One survey measured transit behaviour and attitudes in Albermarle County, and the other assessed community preferences for transit coordination. The conclusions of the study are presented corresponding to the three major areas of investigation. Suggestions for community action are presented.

6C11 KNAPP, S.F., WORTHINGTON, H. and BURKHARDT, J.E. (1980) Wisconsin manual to coordinate elderly and handicapped transport services in rural and small urban counties. Ecosometrics Incorporated, Urban Mass Transportation Administration, UMTA-W1-09-8004-81-1, December.

This manual has been prepared for use by local officials and staff to assist in the development of coordinated county-wide transport services for the elderly and handicapped (E&H). It is intended for use in the coordination of both specialized and public transport in the predominantly rural counties of Wisconsin. The manual is a product of the development of coordination plans in three counties in Wisconsin: Chippewa, Eau Claire, and Rock Counties. The manual shows how to prepare a plan for the development of specialized transport services in rural and small urban counties. The process assumes for its starting point the existing services for E&H persons within county-based service areas, and it incorporates an assessment of these services in terms of their efficiency and effectiveness. The assessment of efficiency is based on the measurement of five ratios of operating characteristics which are compared with ratios from similar services throughout the country. Likewise, three measures of effectiveness are compared with appropriate nationwide measures. These assessments help to determine the need for better coordination or more service. The manual describes steps to improve coordination, and it includes methods and guidance for projecting costs and ridership, managing financial affairs, and implementing new or revised services. This report provides a bibliography and appendices with materials used in the assessment of the need for coordination, of alternatives, of developing a financial plan, and of implementing the service.

2 MAGGIED, H.S. (1979) Transportation options for the mobility disadvantaged in rural Georgia. Georgia University, Athens, Georgia, May.

The general relationships between and among mobility, personal income, work activity in rural areas were examined, and the manner in which locations and time intervals impeded access to work and determined personal revenues and expenses was considered. Case studies were made of some counties in rural Georgia and of persons who are economically disadvantaged because their personal mobility limits and excludes locations and time intervals in which work is accessible to them. A series of policy proposals to solve the problems are proposed. The study demonstrated that personal mobility was a limiting factor on personal income and work activity particularly in rural areas and small places. Among the actions that were recommended are the following: an advocacy role should be assumed by economic development administrators and planners to enhance work mobility; the spatial dispersion relating non-worker and other potential employee residences to a proposed industrial or commercial activity should be determined; limitations to 1973 Federal-Aid Highway Act should be recognized; limits of demand-responsive and paratransit should be reviewed prior to implementation; and a personalized automobile grant programme is technically possible for a spatially dispersed population.

3 MAYNE, J.W. and MORRALL, J.F. (1979) The Edmonton-Calgary corridor transportation study. *Canadian Journal of Civil Engineering*, **6** (2), pp. 208-20.

The Edmonton-Calgary corridor transport study is an example of multimodal intercity passenger transport planning in a low density corridor. This paper discusses a number of unique approaches used in the study that were the result of the need to deal with the low-density aspects, the need to consider both regional and inter-city travel, and the inherent design of the study. These include its iterative approach to the analysis, its handling of the demand and cost analysis, its consideration of multimodal impacts, and the emphasis on identifying key issues and resulting strategic choices. The success and drawbacks of these methodologies are reviewed. The paper also reviews the major findings of the study, many of which can be extended to a more general context: a competitive market analysis may be of little interest in low-density regions; new technologies tend to bias even further the imbalance between intercity and regional transport service; the automobile has a key role to play in regional transport; for many transport needs the intercity bus is an economical and efficient mode; and an improved rail service is an uncertain and long-term venture, which could detrimentally affect all intercity bus service in the region.

6C14 MIX, C.V.S. and DICKEY, J.W. (1974) Rural public transportation in Virginia. *Transportation Research Record*, 519, pp. 56–65.

Travel in most rural areas is now confined to one mode, the private automobile. Those who cannot own or operate cars either do not travel or must arrange, sometimes paying high prices, for others to take them where they need to go. Public transport should be made available to those in rural areas. This paper analyses the rural transport problem in Virginia and suggests how public transit systems can be developed and operated in rural areas of the state. A number of projects are reviewed that are in operation or are proposed for rural areas in other states. The study concludes that, although scattered, sufficient resources are available in Virginia for the planning and development of rural public transport systems.

6C15 NAVIN, F.P.D. (1978) Transport for the disabled in Western Canada. Paper presented at the International Conference on Transport for the Elderly and the Disabled, Loughborough University of Technology, pp. 312–19.

The world's largest transit company dedicated to the sole purpose of mobility for the disabled is the British Columbia Lions' Easter Seal Transport Service. The service has in excess of one hundred vehicles to transport both children and adults. The annual budget is $1.5 million to transport half a million students and two hundred thousand adults. Adult transport is becoming more a government social service and less a charity operation. The total trip costs in

Western Canada range from $5.00 to $8.50. The vehicles generally carry between 1 and 2 passengers per hour and 50 per cent of the vehicle time is spent travelling empty. The high usage by wheelchair patrons and time consuming courtesy service to and from buildings yields an 'optimal' passenger rate of 2 passengers per hour. Vehicle productivity and unit costs may be reduced by revising and speeding up access procedures to the vehicle and focusing service on major modes of demand. The service may be made efficient by employing taxis for all other service for non-wheelchair patrons. Vehicle productivity will in future decrease as cities spread over greater areas and trip lengths increase. Expanding public involvement in, and financing of, urban public transit will no doubt increase the pressure to provide transit services for the disabled. Increasing costs make it imperative that public transit and subsidized private taxi services be blended to provide maximum mobility at minimum cost.

6 PFEFER, R.C. and STOPHER, P.R. (1976) Transit planning in a small community: a case study. *Transportation Research Record*, 608, pp. 32–41.

This paper describes strategies for estimating potential markets for transit or paratransit service, developing a potential set of transit system concepts, estimating demand for each of a selected subset of concepts, developing an evaluation process, and selecting an implementation strategy. The case study has shown that there is considerable value in conducting limited, small-scale surveys of specific market segments as well as in developing a wide variety of system concepts in order to permit an effective choice among possible systems. An extensive educational effort is needed for the community participants in the process as well as broad-based community representation throughout the process.

7 POTT, J.T. and HESLING, R.G. (1975) Wedding the new to the traditional in bus transit: door-to-door and fixed-route systems combined in California. *Traffic Engineering and Control*, **16** (4), pp. 182–4.

Details are given of the integrated transit system adopted by Santa Clara county, USA, which had to provide a service to 1.07 million people spread over 1300 square miles by means of 200 buses. It was decided to use 110 of the buses for a fixed route service operating on major arterial roads only, and linking all important centres of activity, and to use the other 90 buses to provide a door-to-door service which would supplement the fixed route service; a control system was then selected which would integrate the entire bus fleet. Details are given of the computer assisted scheduling system adopted for the control of the door-to-door service. It is estimated that the combined system reaches 97 per cent of the population and public response has been very favourable.

6C18 PRESCOTT, J.R. and LORBER, W.G. (1977) Transportation planning in rural regions of Iowa. *Transportation Research Record*, 638, pp. 51-4.

Changes in population, population density, and travel patterns, as well as economic changes, in the state-designated transport planning regions of Iowa from 1950 to 1970 were analysed in order to determine the validity of the present planning region boundaries. It was found that, as a result of the substitution of manufacturing for farm employment the rural regions have become less self-contained with inter-regional commuting, and shopping trips more the norm than intra-regional travel for such purposes. It is suggested that rural transport planning regional boundaries may have to be redrawn in order to avoid the interjurisdictional problems that would arise with the present boundaries.

6C19 PUBLIC TECHNOLOGY INCORPORATED (1979) Elderly and handicapped transportation: eight case studies. US Department of Transportation, Final Report, DOT-I-79-32, September.

The report, while not covering the complete range of approaches to the problem of providing more adequate transport for and increasing the mobility of elderly and handicapped persons, is illustrative of a variety of approaches that have been taken in communities of all sizes throughout the United States. Case studies of: Austin, Texas; Pomono Valley, California; Akron, Ohio; Chattanooga, Tennessee; Bridgeport, Connecticut; Spokane, Washington; Brockton, Massachusetts, and San Mateo County, California, are presented.

6C20 RUPPENTHAL, K.M. (1980) Benefits and beneficiaries—A Canadian highway case study. Paper presented at the IRF Inter American Regional Meeting, Buenos Aires, May.

In order to develop areas in the northwestern part of Canada, the national Canadian government and the Province of British Columbia entered into an agreement which provided that certain new highways would be constructed, and other existing highways would be improved to a given set of standards. Having made that agreement, the two governments entered into a contract with the Center for Transportation Studies of the University of British Columbia to determine how the costs of these highway improvements should be shared. The author describes the types of procedures anticipated by the Center, the problems actually encountered in the course of the study, the study methodology and results, and the lessons. The study was specific to Canada, British Columbia, the Yukon Territory and the State of Alaska, but the problems encountered can be expected anywhere.

21 SHORT, J. (1978) Iowa's approach to transit marketing. *Transportation Research Record*, 696, pp. 55–7.

This short paper describes one particular state's response to transport inaccessibility, especially in rural areas. Here, special programmes like congregate meals, medical services and sheltered workshops have been linked through specific transport provision and marketing of the services.

22 SIRIA, B.S., SMITH, D.E. and SMITH, W.A. (1978) Morehead, Kentucky, school bus demonstration project. *Transportation Research Record*, 696, pp. 73–6.

Recent public policy has demonstrated increased concern for the effectiveness of existing transport systems as a cost-efficient alternative to major capital expenditures. One such programme in Kentucky uses a single school bus to provide transit service in the community of Morehead. A 36-passenger school bus operates hourly along a 12.1 km (7.5 mile) route from 8.30 a.m. to 4.30 p.m. on weekdays and from 9.30 a.m. to 2.30 p.m. on Saturdays. Service is provided to Morehead State University, several public housing projects, the central business district, a principal manufacturing house, and the hospital. The one-way fare is $0.25. The Kentucky Department of Transportation, the Rowan County Board of Education, and the City of Morehead all share in the management of the project.

Net operating costs during the 12-month demonstration period are shared between the Department of Transport and the City of Morehead (75–25 per cent, respectively). To date, farebox revenues have equalled 8.78 per cent of the total operating costs. Initial patronage during the first 5 months of the demonstration programme was low, increased drastically during severe winter weather, and moderated somewhat when warmer weather arrived. Weekday patronage averages 33.6 persons/d and Saturday patronage averages 16.8 persons/d.

6C23 STRINGFELLOW, W.G. (1977) County-wide transit dependent study—Lincoln/Lancaster County, Nebraska. Final Report to the Urban Mass Transportation Administration, UMTA-NE09-0009-78-1.

This report describes the analyses and findings resulting from a technical study to investigate the special transport requirements of the handicapped, elderly, and economically disadvantaged persons in Lancaster County, Nebraska. It inventories the existing transport available to transit dependents, defines target groups and latent trip demand, establishes ridership objectives, and evaluates the costs and benefits of various alternative improvement concepts. The key to the overall focus and purpose of this study is to ensure that the mobility needs of urban and rural transit dependent groups in Lancaster County are being adequately met, and that their role in the planning and development of improved transit services is secured. In order to achieve these goals, a programme has been initiated which consists of the following elements: maintain the existing Handi-Bus system (a demand responsive service to elderly and handicapped persons); institute procedures to increase system productivity; increase weekend and evening hours of operation; implement shared-ride taxi service as a supplement; institute a reduced fare programme on fixed-route service for qualified low-income persons; expand Handi-Bus service to rural areas; give additional study to a medical service shuttle on the regular LTS system; expand the Handi-Bus system if shared-ride taxi service cannot be implemented; and ensure that the transit dependent groups are included in the continuing planning process for special transport needs. The study points out that the programme must include continuous review and monitoring and should be updated annually.

24 Sullivan, B.E. and Suen, S.L. (1981) Surface rural public transportation in Canada. *Transportation Research Record*, 831, pp. 63-9.

Events and activities in rural public transport in Canada during the past 10 years are described based on material drawn from government reports, transport guides, and field observation. All surface modes that provide common-carrier 'public' access service are included as well as certain paratransit services that do not completely fit this definition but are nonetheless judged to be relevant. In Canada, most rural public transport services are medium-distance operations (80-400 km (50-250 miles)) and perform an intercity function as well. Short-distance rural transport can be found in a variety of forms across the country but is less widespread. Existing service arrangements and government programmes are outlined, and a number of case summaries that illustrate new activity in recent years are discussed.

25 US Department of Transportation (1974) Rural transportation in the South East. Department of Transportation, Washington.

This document is designed to be of practical value to those charged with the responsibility of establishing and improving rural transport systems to fill the recognized needs for short-haul passenger transport service between central business districts and adjacent rural communities. Existing rural transport operations in Sumter, South Carolina and in Boone, North Carolina are discussed. Observations and recommendations applicable to any rural transport system include a step-by-step outline designed for the layman who wishes to establish a rural system from scratch, followed up by advice gleaned through experiences at the local, state and federal levels. There is a helpful discussion of federal funding programmes available and the limitations of each. The appendices contain a variety of information ranging from vehicle rules and regulations to state enabling legislation for regional transport authorities.

26 Van Sickel, K. and Heathington, K.W. (1979) Transportation needs for the elderly, handicapped and low income of Mississippi. Report prepared for the Mississippi State Highway Department and Mississippi Council on Ageing.

The purpose of this report is to examine the elderly and disadvantaged population of Mississippi and define how transport fits into their needs for daily living. Essential segments of this study are the identification of existing transport resources within the state, categorization of deficiencies in existing facilities, and appraisal of future efforts needed to provide the transport services for the elderly and disadvantaged. In view of the problems of the transport disadvantaged defined by this study, i.e. need for critical trips due to rural isolation, coordination of existing programmes, facilities, and support systems within local government bodies as well as private sources emerges as the most promising approach to providing better services to meet the needs in Mississippi. Five alternatives are noted for coordinating the existing resources of the state: coordination of social service providers who need transport for their clients; coordination of transport systems and social service agencies who are or could be potential transport providers; equipment purchasing coordination for all agencies; coordination of site location; coordination and integration of funding sources and user restrictions.

6C27 WEAVER, V.C. and LUNDBERG, B.D. (1977) Rural public transportation: North Dakota transportation case study. *Transportation Research Record*, 638, pp. 44–6.

A rural public transport programme has been developed for westcentral North Dakota which consists of two levels of service. One level is the formation of local transport associates which would coordinate the travel demands of those in need of transport and the automobile drivers in the community who are willing to provide transport and which would actively pursue the expansion of a pool of volunteer drivers who would be willing to provide rides for those in need. The other level is specialized transport vehicles (designed for the handicapped) being leased by the community to institutions such as nursing and retirement homes in order to serve groups such as the elderly and handicapped whose needs cannot be met by the private automobile service.

6C28 WHITE, H.P. (1983) The provision and funding of rural roads—the New Zealand example. Paper submitted to the UTSG Annual Conference, January, London.

Comparatively little is known of the cost and cost effectiveness of the provision and maintenance of the road system serving a rural community of low population density and with high economic and social expectations. Rural areas of New Zealand are characterized by low population densities, highly evolved farming systems and high social expectations. The cost of providing adequate services, especially roads in relation to population density, rateable income, and traffic volume is high under these circumstances. Fortunately, statistical data available and the method of funding roads in New Zealand provides sufficient information to make such a study possible.

The paper sets the background of the problem and then continues with an analysis of the method of funding roads, which shows a much closer relationship between fiscal income from vehicle and fuel taxation and expenditure on roads than in UK. The vehicle taxation system based on 'user pays' and which attempts to relate payment to wear and tear on surfaces is also examined. The data available are next considered and an attempt made to show how these can be used to arrive at road provision and maintenance costs. Some sample Counties will be looked at in detail to illustrate the points. Some of the problems facing Local Authorities in the provision of roads will also be examined. In conclusion it is pointed out that the problem is becoming of increasing importance in the UK as Local Authorities are faced with retrenchment policies and some useful lessons can be learnt from the New Zealand example.

6D Developing countries

D1 ABAYNAYAKA, S.W., HIDE, H., MOROSIUK, G. and ROBINSON, R. (1976) Tables for estimating vehicle operating costs on rural roads in developing countries. *Transport and Road Research Laboratory*, LR 723.

Tables are provided for estimating vehicle operating costs by component on free-flowing low volume rural roads in developing countries. They provide a convenient and easy reference manual for road appraisal and investment studies. The components evaluated are fuel and oil consumption, maintenance parts and labour charges, tyre wear, depreciation, crew costs and standing charges. They are estimated on a quantity or non-dimensional basis so that costs can be determined for any monetary system or environment by applying the appropriate set of unit rates. Operating costs may be estimated for different road geometries, surface condition and altitude and for vehicles of different types with different prices, ages, loads and engine power. The tables are based on research carried out in Kenya by the Overseas Unit of TRRL in collaboration with the International Bank for Reconstruction and Development. Examples are given for paved, gravel and earth road surfaces.

6D2 BARWELL, I.J. (1977) Notes on simple transport in some developing countries. ITDG Transport Panel, Information Paper No. 2, Oxford.

6D3 BARWELL, I.J. (1979) Development of indigenous equipment for rural transport. *Transport and Communications Bulletin for Asia and the Pacific*, 53, pp. 20–5.

6D4 BARWELL, I.J. and HOWE, J.D.G.F. (1978) Appropriate transport facilities for the rural sector in developing countries. International forum on appropriate industrial technology held at New Delhi, International Labour Organisation, Washington DC.

6D5 BARWELL, I.J. and HOWE, J.D.G.F. (1979) Appropriate non-automotive technology urged for rural needs in developing countries. *Transportation Research News*, 85, pp. 7–8.

This paper reviews the recent policy approach to the 'rural transport problem' in developing countries and it contains opinions of how that policy should be changed. The basic approach to the problem has been providing or improving the quality of access which has meant almost exclusively road access. Past road investments have favoured construction or improvement of major rural highways rather than urban or minor rural roads. The generally accepted design standards for highways in developing countries recommend essentially US Standards, which results in a lavish system to accommodate sophisticated vehicles that the average rural dweller does not have and cannot afford. A study of 93 developing countries showed that, in 1968, the average vehicle ownership was only 9.2 per 1000, and it is expected to rise to only 11.8 by 1980. The result of this policy is skeletal road networks that plainly do not serve effectively the majority of the population, and vehicles so expensive that they are beyond the means of all but the most affluent. In this paper, it is recommended that simpler and cheaper vehicles might be appropriate for rural societies. Slower and lighter vehicles would allow the alignment, strength and width of roads to be reduced, which would result in a considerable saving in costs. Six categories of basic vehicles for rural areas of developing countries were defined: aids to carrying loads on the head, shoulders, and back; handcarts and wheelbarrows; pedal-driven vehicles; animal transport; motorcycles; and basic motorized vehicles.

)6 BARWELL, I.J. and HOWE, J.D. (1979) Appropriate technology and low cost transport. *Transportation Research Record,* 702, pp. 22-30.

This paper is concerned with the provision of appropriate transport facilities in the rural areas of developing countries. It is argued that the technologies applied in the past have been inappropriate to, and ineffective in meeting the transport needs of their poorest people. Further, that there are alternative and more appropriate transport technologies which can better meet many of these needs. Past transport strategy has been dominated by an institutional preoccupation with the provision of roads suitable for conventional motor vehicles. The supply of those vehicles has been left largely to the private sector and their technological appropriateness unquestioned to the extent that the type of vehicle is not a variable in road design. The result has been high road construction costs, slow network development, and the neglect of the movement needs of small scale farmers and of traditional forms of transport. A range of basic vehicles is described whose technology is shown to be more appropriate to the needs of many rural developing communities. It is suggested that attention should be focused on improving the technology of basic vehicles with a corresponding re-appraisal of track requirements. The application of a more appropriate technology requires that rural transport planning should explicitly include an appraisal of the small farmer's movement needs and the constraints within which these must be met.

D7 BLAIKIE, P., CAMERON, J. and SEDDON, D. (1979) The relation of transport planning to rural development: the implication of road construction in Nepal. University of East Anglia, Development Studies Discussion Paper 50.

The main thesis is that the construction of three main roads in Nepal has had very little effect on the crucial prerequisites for any significant development of the region. Moreover new roads do not begin to resolve any of the main problems of the predominantly agricultural economy.

6D8 BLAIKIE, P., CAMERON, J. and SEDDON, D. (1979) Road provision and the changing role of towns in west-central Nepal. University of East Anglia, Development Studies Discussion Paper, 49.

Road provision is shown to have accelerated the process whereby towns are ceasing to be craft centres and trading points for export products, and are becoming merely distribution centres for foreign goods.

6D9 BOVILL, D.I.N., HEGGIE, I.G. and HINE, J.L. (1978) A guide to transport planning in the roads sector for developing countries. Ministry of Overseas Development, London: HMSO.

6D10 BRADEMEYER, B., MOAVENZADEH, F., MARKOW, M.J., EL-HAWARY, M. and OWAIS, M. (1979) Road network analysis for transportation investment in Egypt. *Transportation Research Record*, 702, pp. 229-37.

The Road Investment Analysis Model (RIAM) has been applied to the analysis and planning of highway investment decisions in Egypt. Ten alternative maintenance policies were analysed over the network study zone, reflecting three types of investment concerns important to the Egyptian Transport Planning Authority. Among the questions addressed were: the relative frequency of the maintenance activities; the relative magnitude of the investments as reflected in the overlay thickness; and the relative levels of investment among the three road classes—primary, secondary and tertiary—to achieve the most effective overall investment strategy in the network. Additionally, the heavier the level of investment, the greater was the economic return from that investment, given that the investment was distributed fairly evenly among the various road classes. The optimum alternative identified was found to consist of frequent, light overlays on the primary system (where additional strength is not required) and initial heavy overlays followed by frequent, light overlays on the secondary and tertiary systems (where additional structural strength is needed to meet future traffic demands). These results held true whether the performance was judged on economic efficiency or user satisfaction (consumer surplus).

)11 CONRAD, P.E. and SCHOON, J.G. (1979) An integrated nationwide rural road system for the Gambia. *Transportation Research Record*, 702, pp. 222–8.

The rural road system in The Gambia, West Africa, comprises over 2300 kilometers of paved, gravel and earth roads. These connect rural communities with each other, to riverside staging points, to the larger towns and cities, and to produce storage and trans-shipment depots. The role of the road system is considered in regard to these functions and as related to needs for future rural development consistent with national goals and objectives. Data based upon recent studies in The Gambia are presented, particularly those which address future agricultural development potentials and road integration with river linkages. The categories of primary, secondary and principal feeder roads are examined from the viewpoint of current function, traffic, and existing deficiencies. Future highway needs based upon optimum use of the River Gambia and the road network for transporting a variety of import and export commodities are described and a tentative road investment programme is proposed. Guidelines are then outlined to assist in the geometric and structural design of future highways in The Gambia and a review is made of material types and availability for future use.

)12 DE VEEN, J.J. (1980) The Rural Access Roads Programme. Appropriate Technology in Kenya. International Labour Organisation, Geneva.

The text provides information on an alternative way of road construction to planners and chief executives in developing countries who are interested in applying employment-generating indigenous technologies, provided these can be implemented efficiently and effectively without adverse effect on the cost and quality of the product. The Rural Access Road Programme (RARP) was initiated in Kenya to provide all-year farm-to-market access throughout the country. The text consists of 11 parts; including a description of the inception and implementation of the programme and the scope of the technical and financial assistance given to RARP, a description of the organizational structure and the work of the technology unit, and a description of the selection and technical aspects of the construction of the access roads. The planning, organization and management of a large-scale labour-intensive project, both at headquarters and at site level are described and evaluated. Recruitment procedures and motivation of the workers including the payment systems are discussed, and there follows a description of site arrangements and construction activities, the training of personnel, the recruitment of supervisory personnel, and the curriculum contents. The organization of road maintenance, the relevance of the RARP to other developing countries are outlined in the final section. Appendices provide further information on the structure of the RARP, design standards, average task rates, expenditure control procedures, procurement, planning, programming and reporting at site and unit level, gravelling, and time and location chart.

6D13 EDMONDS, G.A. (1979) Appropriate technology for low volume roads. *Transportation Research Record*, 702, pp. 11-21.

This paper describes construction work that has been carried out on rural low volume roads in Iran, Thailand, the Philippines, Nepal, Kenya, Guatemala and India. It shows how the initial concern with increased productivity and economic evaluation gave way to an emphasis on institutional, administrative and managerial problems. The paper highlights the major problems of the implementation of an effective labour-based programme. It is argued that the use of labour-based methods requires a reappraisal on the part of engineers of their traditional attitudes not only to the details of design, management and organization of low volume road programmes but also to the integration of these programmes into the general development of rural areas in the developing countries. Finally, it is suggested that to provide an environment in which labour-based techniques are considered as an alternative technology will require changes in fiscal and institutional measures to ensure that there is no inherent bias against these methods.

6D14 EDMONDS, G.A. (1980) Road construction and resource use, in Edmonds, G.A. and Howe, J.D.G.F. (eds) *Roads and Resources. Appropriate Technology in Road Construction in Developing Countries*, London: Intermediate Technology Publications Ltd, pp. 22-5.

)15 EDMONDS, G.A. and HOWE, J.D.G.F. (1980) (eds.) *Roads and Resources. Appropriate Technology in Road Construction in Developing Countries.* London: Intermediate Technology Publications Ltd.

)16 FOURACRE, P.R. (1977) Intermediate public transport in developing countries. *Transport and Road Research Laboratory*, LR 772.

A review of intermediate forms of urban public transport used in the developing world. The controversy surrounding these modes is discussed and issues and problems identified with illustrations taken from the practice of organizations and operations. It is concluded that these forms of transport can and do offer a significant contribution to urban and rural transport.

)17 HARRISON, R. and SWAIT, J.D. (1980) Relating vehicle use to highway characteristics: evidence from Brazil. *Transportation Research Record*, 747, pp. 97-105.

Data derived from a large-scale user-cost survey currently being conducted in Brazil are presented and analysed. Equations for six vehicle classes that are used to predict rates of vehicle use (defined as kilometres travelled per month) as a function of highway characteristics are presented. The highway characteristics studies are surface roughness and three measures of vertical geometry. These data were collected by two specially instrumented vehicles that measured a network of 597 routes totalling 38,000 km. Vehicle-use data representing 1220 vehicles were used as the main analysis set; the set comprised 265 cars, 37 utility vehicles, 655 buses, and 243 trucks. A further 261 heavy vehicles were used to derive predictions for this class after the main analysis had been conducted. Equations derived from the analyses were tested against a further set of 145 vehicles. Reference to previous studies is made, and an example that shows the derivation of differential depreciation costs per kilometre is included. Preliminary results on the effect of vehicle age are given, and details of further work are specified.

)18 HENNES, R.G. and SACHDEV, L.S. (1969) Planning rural highways in India. *Traffic Quarterly*, **23** (3), pp. 573-86.

The manifest problems of transport in the rural areas of India are highlighted and this study focuses on the twenty year Road Development Plan. Progress is criticized as it has concentrated on providing access to market centres and their development rather than providing access to rural villages. The evaluation criteria need to be carefully established if the best use of scarce resources is going to be made in the rural road sector.

6D19 HERATY, M.J. (1980) Public transport in Kingston, Jamaica and its relation to low income households. *Transport and Road Research Laboratory*, SR 546.

This report is based on a study of public transport in Kingston, Jamaica, carried out with the cooperation of the Jamaican government. It is one of a series of similar studies in developing countries carried out by the Transport and Road Research Laboratory. The results of local investigations into the organization and operation of the conventional bus undertaking and of the privately-operated minibuses are described and Jamaican government survey data are used as a basis for analysing the characteristics of the users of the two different services. An analysis of the attitudes of passengers, as elicited from this survey and from in-depth research with low income households, helps in formulating the ways in which both bus and minibus services may be improved. The role which public transport plays in the lifestyle of low income households is discussed with particular reference to expenditure on transport compared to other budget items. The Jamaican findings are compared with previous studies of the role of paratransit in two cities in South-East Asia.

6D20 HINE, J.L. RIVERSON, J.D.N. and KWAKYE, E.A. (1983) Accessibility and agricultural development in the Ashanti region of Ghana, *Transport and Road Research Laboratory*, SR 791.

Using a cross sectional framework of analysis, data was collected from 33 villages (all but two with vehicle access) in the Ashanti Region of Ghana located between 8 and 102 km from the Regional Capital, Kumasi. By comparing a number of development parameters and the transport costs of moving farm produce between each village and Kumasi (and also between each village and its respective district centre) the link between accessibility and agricultural development was investigated. Within the range of accessibility considered little evidence was found to indicate that market agriculture was promoted directly by accessibility. However, loan finance was easier to obtain the nearer the farmer lived to Kumasi.

Overall there is evidence to suggest that the most accessible villages tended to concentrate more on non-agricultural activities (such as rural industry and the provision of services, including marketing) while the less accessible villages concentrated rather more on agriculture. The study supports the view that where road investment can induce only a small change in transport costs then little impact on agricultural development may be expected.

D21 HOWE, J.D. (1973) Estimating the composition of rural traffic in developing countries. *Traffic Engineering and Control,* **15** (8), pp. 393-8.

Modern methods of highway design require more than simple estimates of current and future traffic volumes, and this is particularly prevelant in developing countries where data are often inaccurate or non-existent. This paper discusses the general problem of estimating the composition of rural road traffic, considers the accuracy problems and highlights some of the common mistakes made.

D22 HOWE, J.D. (1976) Valueing time savings in developing countries. *Journal of Transport Economics and Policy,* **10** (2), pp. 113-26.

After reviewing methods used to value savings in money costs resulting from time savings to persons, goods and vehicles by transport improvements, the author concludes that there is too little evidence that the claimed benefits are real. Willingness to pay must be a more reliable criterion. There is a comment and rejoinder on the issues raised in *JTEP* **11** (2), pp. 195-200.

D23 HOWE, J.D.G.F. (1979) Some thoughts on intermediate technology and rural transport. *Development Digest,* **16** (4), pp. 73-9.

Simple vehicles lower in cost than modern trucks, less demanding for repair or local manufacture, and requiring less costly roads, can have wide application in rural development. Rural transport planning requires careful study of local conditions and resources.

D24 JACOBS, G.D. and FOURACRE, P.R. (1976) Intermediate forms of urban public transport in developing countries. *Traffic Engineering and Control,* **17** (3), pp. 98-100.

Although the examples given relate to urban areas in developing countries, it is concluded that intermediate public transport provides a useful service, although not in a coordinated way. Research is required on the economics of their services as well as their political and social implications.

6D25 KADIYALI, L.R. (1979) Road user cost study in India—Objectives and methodology. *Indian Highways,* **7** (1), pp. 45–52.

This paper reports on a road user cost study being carried out in India at an estimated cost of rs60 lakhs out of which the World Bank will be contributing about rs20 lakhs. The major components of the study, which is scheduled for completion by May 1981, are described as road user cost survey, which seeks to develop the relationships between the cost component of vehicle operation in relation to road characteristics, based upon data obtained from a large number of vehicles; traffic experiments which include determination of free-speed as governed by roadway characteristics; determination of speed-flow relationships for different road types; and determination of accurate fuel consumption data on different vehicles under different road conditions; and special studies including the determination of the accident rate and accident cost under different roadway characteristics, the determination of the rate of depreciation of vehicles and the value of time saved by road users and vehicles. Reference is made to earlier studies in India and abroad, the objectives of the study are described, and details provided on the research methodology associated with each section of the study.

6D26 THE NATIONAL COUNCIL OF APPLIED ECONOMIC RESEARCH (1981) Transport Technology for the Rural Areas: India. World Employment Programme Research Working Paper 83, International Labour Organisation, Geneva, July.

6D27 ORGANISATION FOR ECONOMIC CO-OPERATION AND DEVELOPMENT (1977) *Paratransit in the Developing World—Neglected Options for Mobility and Employment.* Proceedings of the First International Paratransit Workshop, Asnières-sur-Oise, France, July.
Vol I Workshop Proceedings and Programme Recommendations.
Vol II Paratransit in the Developing World: Background Documents.

28 REDDY, K.C., SINGH, R.C. and GUPTA, D.P. (1979) Rural roads in India—achievements and task ahead. *Journal of Indian Road Congress*, **40** (2), pp. 349–89.

29 SADDLER, J. (1981) A review of the road requirements of Zimbabwe. Paper presented at the 9th International Road Federation World Meeting, Stockholm, June.

The Government of Zimbabwe has an avowed commitment to improve the quality of life for the African inhabitants. The proposed programme of rehabilitation and reconstruction includes the improvement of road services, particularly into remote rural areas. This paper endeavours to review the situation in respect of road communications, and makes recommendations to give wide-spread relief using a phased programme of construction.

30 SIMMERSBACH, P. (1980) Rural roads in third world countries: design, construction and maintenance. Paper presented at the 4th IRF African Highway Conference, Nairobi, January.

The author discusses the shortcomings of the traditional economic analyses which are unsuitable for rural roads and the producer surplus-oriented type of analysis which is more appropriate for rural areas of low economic activity. The theory is illustrated with case histories in Honduras, the Dominican Republic, the Sudan, and Zambia, and there follows a description of the engineering and contractual aspects of rural road projects, covering design to appropriate standards, construction and rehabilitation work, and maintenance operations. Project implementation for a rural road construction programme requires a different set of monitoring, procurement, management, and control tools than those suitable for other highway projects. A case study on a rural road in Bolivia, is presented and this demonstrates how the development of a remote area has been stimulated by the construction (through different stages) of a typical feeder road.

31 SMITH, J.D. (1981) Transport Technology and Employment in Rural Malaysia. World Employment Programme Research Working Paper 88, International Labour Organisation, Geneva, December.

32 SMITH, J.D. (1982) The use of simplified techniques in project ap-

praisal—application to a rural roads programme in peninsula Malaysia. Paper presented at the PTRC Annual Summer Conference, Warwick, July.

The provision of new rural roads can improve or extend existing transport networks and contribute to a wider socio-economic development process. Benefits from such projects result directly from the construction and use of the new facility and indirectly from the wider socio-economic impact.

Appraisal techniques have therefore become more complex in an attempt to model rural transport improvements in the context of rural development. The use of producer-surplus techniques has often been carried out with the assistance of international aid agencies. When such assistance has been made available and the institutional background favourable for efficient programme coordination and phasing, project objectives can be achieved.

However external assistance cannot be provided in the case of many rural road projects and complementary programmes phased in accurately. In addition the use of producer-surplus methods is not appropriate in every situation, for example when social objectives are to be achieved. When in these circumstances resources are limited and institutional improvements present problems, at least in the short-term, alternative techniques are required to make the best use of rural road investments.

This paper is based on a situation where rural road projects are implemented independently of other sectoral investments. It suggests that simplified techniques will be more appropriate when expertise and data are limited. The aim of the work is to prepare techniques suitable for use by local government officers that can assist in the decision-making process. Reference is made to the appraisal and implementation of a rural road programme in Peninsular Malaysia where current techniques were found to be impracticable.

Following a brief review of this programme, the paper outlines the need for a planning framework in which the various types of rural road project can be fitted. The framework relates both to the wider rural development structure and to the specific transport requirements in the project area. From programme objectives and the planning framework a simplified model has been developed for use in project appraisal based on the level of data and expertise available. The model is then applied to a selection of rural road projects and results compared with those obtained from more elaborate methods.

Benefits from the use of a simplified approach include the potential for standardizing data collection and forecasting procedures between different government departments and reductions in project preparation time. Improved understanding between transport planners and politicians in the appraisal and decision-making processes will also be aided.

)33 SQUIRE, L. and VAN DER TAK, H.G. (1975) *Economic Analysis of Projects*, Baltimore: Johns Hopkins Press for the World Bank.

)34 SRINIVASAN, N.S. (1980) Planning and research activities in the field of traffic transportation. *Indian Highway*, **8** (2), pp. 96-102.

)35 TINGLE, E.D. (1977) Rural road planning in developing countries, in Visser, E.J. (ed.) *Transport Decisions in an Age of Uncertainty*, The Hague: Martinus Nijhoff, pp. 531-5.

Outlines the relevance of transport planning techniques to the decisions on rural roads in developing countries and suggests that research should concentrate on two main areas. These are the evaluation methods that should be appropriate to the situation and cost-effective systems for rural areas.

)36 WEIGHTMAN, D. (1979) Designing intermediate vehicles for rural development needs. *Development Digest*, **16** (4), pp. 84-9.

The demand for transport in rural areas should be met by choices from among a variety of vehicles intermediate between heavy trucks and primitive carts. The range is already wide but designs should be specific to the conditions prevelant in developing countries.

7 Bibliographies

There have been no previous systematic and comprehensive bibliographies on rural transport and planning. A number of specialist bibliographies, most unannotated, have been produced on parts of the field and these have mainly related to individual research projects. Principal among these are the Moseley *et al.* bibliography on rural transport and accessibility, and the Alpert and Lesley bibliography on the role of public transport in new towns. At the end of this section on bibliographies is a selection of the principal abstracting services and information services that can be used for further investigations.

ALPERT, M. and LESLEY, L. (1981) *The Role of Public Transport in New Towns, A Bibliography*, Liverpool: Department of Town and Country Planning, Liverpool Polytechnic.

An attempt has been made to categorize the references by subject within one of eight main sections. Although the principal concern is with new towns, there are sections on transport and mobility, methods, policy and a range of transport modes. Some of the references relate to rural areas.

BLACKSELL, M. and GILG, A. (1981) *The Countryside: Planning and Change*, London: George Allen and Unwin.

This volume has a bibliography with some 300 references on rural issues and would provide a useful starting point. Transport is not an integral part of the study.

GB DEPARTMENT OF THE ENVIRONMENT (1976) Economic and Social Problems of Rural Communities: Review of Research. DoE, PSC 5.

GB Department of the Environment and Department of Transport (1976) Roads and transport in rural areas. Bibliography No. 17B, DoE, London.

Covers all aspects of the rural transport problem with the material arranged chronologically. It includes books and pamphlets as well as articles published since about 1970. There is a short section on rural research in progress.

GB Departments of the Environment and Transport (1983) Rural Transport 1977-1983, Bibliography 17B: Supplement No. 1, DoE/DTp, London.

This bibliography updates the previous DoE/DTp library listing over the six years from 1976. The information is based on the acquisitions to the library and is arranged chronologically by year.

Haight, F.A. and Tung, J.S.N. (1976) Traffic and Transportation: a Permuted Title Index and Research Guide. Boalsburg, PA: Pennsylvania Technical Publications.

Contains titles and authors of all papers in six transport journals for the period 1966-1975. The journals are Traffic Engineering and Control, Journal of Transport Economics and Policy, Transportation, Traffic Quarterly, Transportation Research and Transportation Science.

Hoggart, K. (1981) Rural Development: A Bibliography, Parts One and Two, Public Administration Series, P-789, Illinois, August.

Concentrates on rural development in Western nations and includes about 150 references on transport out of a total of some 3000 citations.

Kihlman, B. (1980) Inventering av existerande forskning rörande kollektiv persontransport. Kulturgeografiska Institute, Göteborgs University, Göteborg, March.

This Swedish volume covers the literature of all passenger transport both in Swedish and overseas (1970-1980). There is a section on rural areas (Glesbygdsomraden).

MOSELEY, M.J., HARMAN, R.G., COLES, O.B. and SPENCER, M.B. (1977) *Rural Transport and Accessibility*, Volume 2, Appendices and Bibliography. Final Report to the Department of the Environment, Norwich: Centre for East Anglian Studies.

This bibliography which is a direct output of a large research project contains over 400 references. Most relate to the British and American experiences and the vast majority to work that was published in the 1970s. This emphasis related to the accelerating interest in the subject area. Accessibility is interpreted in a wide context and includes studies on rural society, settlements, socially disadvantaged groups as well as transport. The transport references are categorized under general reviews and area studies, management issues and specific modes. This bibliography has until now been the most comprehensive guide to the literature.

NEATE, S. (1981) *Rural Deprivation*. An annotated bibliography of economic and social problems in rural Britain. Norwich: Geo Abstracts, Bibliography No. 8.

Other information sources

Chartered Institute of Transport. Library Transport Bibliographies, 80 Portland Place, London W1N 4DP.

Duplicated, annotated lists compiled from the Library's resources are available to members and non-members. The lists are primarily prepared for the requirements of students who are taking the Institute's examinations.

Council of Planning Librarians. Exchange Bibliography Series. Available from the Council at Post Office Box 229, Monticello, Illinois 61856, USA.

This is a nationally organized group of librarians, planners and organizations interested in the provision of information about city and regional planning. A complete list of bibliographies is available on request.

DAVIES, E.M. (1980) (ed) *Inlogov Register of Local Authorities' research projects*. University of Birmingham: INLOGOV.

Has a section (E) on transport including a range of rural based research projects.

GB Department of the Environment Library Bulletin, DoE Library, 2 Marsham Street, London SW1P 3EB.

This publication is a fortnightly digest of annotated references covering most aspects of planning, and refers to journal articles, books, official publications, plans and a wide range of published and unpublished material from many countries. Each issue contains between 300 and 500 entries arranged according to subject material. Annual author and subject indexes are compiled.

Geographical (Geo) Abstracts, University of East Anglia, Norwich NR4 7TJ.

A bi-monthly service in six separate series. Section F is devoted to regional and community planning. Each issue contains between 300–500 abstracts from journal articles and other sources collected from all over the world.

Greater London Council, Department of Planning and Transportation, County Hall, London SE1 7PB.

Urban Abstracts is published in two series, each with eight issues per year. Transport, mainly with an urban focus, is part of series one.

Highway Research Information Service, 2101 Constitution Avenue N.W., Washington DC 20418.

HRIS abstracts is a quarterly publication compiled from computer tape records and contains selected abstracts of research reports, technical papers in conference proceedings and journal articles. In each issue there are four sections. The abstracts themselves form the main part with a source index, an author index and a retrieval term index providing the other three sections.

Transport and Road Research Laboratory, Old Wokingham Road, Crowthorne, Berkshire, RG11 6AU.

The library operates a computer based data and information retrieval system. Through this, literature searches can be carried out on request, but enquiries must be specific and precisely formulated.

US Department of Transportation, Technology Sharing Program, US Department of Transportation, 400 Seventh Street SW, Washington DC 20590.

The Technology Sharing Program makes the results of recent research on transport topics available to state and local governments. Documents are available on request to them.

WHITE, B. (1974) *The Literature and Study of Urban and Regional Planning*, Routledge and Kegan Paul: London.

This book discusses the processes of spatial planning and the range of subject knowledge which is required to contribute to it. It describes the physical forms in which the literature relating to planning is usually presented and the ways in which this information is made available. The author gives details of the most useful libraries whose facilities are available, and of the research which is being undertaken. The second part of the book consists of a subject bibliography, including one on transport, and each contains annotated references to books, official publications, development plans, legislation and other material. The subject bibliography is followed by lists of journals, bibliographies and abstracting services.

Selected periodicals

1 *Transport*

Highways and Transportation (from January 1984, formerly *Journal of the Institution of Highway Engineers*, and *Highway Engineer*).
Institution of Highway Engineers, 3 Lygon Place, Ebury Street, London SW1W 0JS.
Monthly, 1954–

International Journal of Transport Economics
8 Via GA Guattani, Rome 00161, Italy.
Three issues per year, 1974–

Journal of Transport Economics and Policy
London School of Economics and Political Science, Houghton
Street, Aldwych, London WC2A 2AE.
Three issues per year, 1967–

Planning Transport Research and Computation
PTRC Education and Research Services Ltd, 110 Strand, London
WC2
Irregular.

Proceedings of the American Society of Civil Engineers, Journal of the Engineering Division
American Society of Civil Engineers, 345 East 47th Street, New
York, NY 10017.
Quarterly, 1956–

Traffic Engineering and Control
Printerhall Limited, 29 Newman Street, London W1P 3PE.
Monthly, 1959–

Transport (formerly *Journal of the Chartered Institute of Transport*)
Chartered Institute of Transport, 80 Portland Place, London W1N
4DP.
Bi-monthly, 1920–1979. New Series 1980–

Transport Reviews
Taylor and Francis, 104, John Street, London WC1N 2ET.
Quarterly, 1981–

Transportation
Elsevier Scientific Publishing Company, PO Box 211, Amsterdam,
The Netherlands.
Quarterly, 1972–

Transportation Planning and Technology (formerly *Transportation Technology*)
Gordon Breach Science Publishers Ltd, 42 William IV Street, London WC2.
Quarterly, 1972–

Transport Policy and Decision Making
Martinus Nijhoff Publishers, PO Box 566, The Hague, The Netherlands.
Quarterly, 1980–

Transportation Quarterly (formerly *Traffic Quarterly*)
Eno Foundation for Transportation, Box 55, Saugatuck Station, Westport, Connecticut 06880.
Quarterly, 1947–

Transportation Research
Pergamon Press, Headington Hill Hall, Oxford OX3 0BW.
Bi-monthly, 1967–

Transportation Research Record (formerly *Highway Research Record*)
Transportation Research Board, 2101, Constitution Avenue NW, Washington DC 20418.
Irregular

Transportation Science
Operations Research Society of America, 428 East Preston Street, Baltimore, Maryland 21202.
Quarterly, 1967–

2 Planning

Built Environment
Alexandrine Press, PO Box 15, 51 Cornmarket Street, Oxford OX1 3EB.
Quarterly, 1975–

Environment and Planning
Pion Limited, 207 Brondesbury Park, London NW2 5JN.
Monthly, 1969–

Journal of the American Planning Association
American Planning Association, 1776 Massachusetts Avenue NW, Washington DC 20036.
Quarterly, 1917–

Planner: the Journal of the Royal Town Planning Institute.
26 Portland Place, London W1N 4BE.
Seven issues per year, 1914–

Policy and Politics
School for Advanced Urban Studies, Rodney Lodge, Grange Road,
Bristol BS8 4EA.
Quarterly, 1972–

Practicing Planner
American Institute of Planners, 1776 Massachusetts Avenue NW,
Washington DC 20036.
Quarterly, 1971–

Progress in Planning
Pergamon Press Ltd, Headington Hill Hall, Oxford OX3 0BW.
Quarterly, 1973–

Regional Studies
Journal of the Regional Studies Association, Cambridge University
Press, Trumpington Street, Cambridge CB2 1RP.
Quarterly, 1967–

Socio-Economic Planning Sciences
Pergamon Press, Headington Hill Hall, Oxford OX3 0BW.
Bi-monthly, 1967–

Surveyor—Public Works Weekly (formerly *Surveyor* and *Municipal Engineer and Surveyor—Local Government Technology*)
IPC Buildings and Contract Journals Ltd, Surrey House, 1 Throwley Way, Sutton, Surrey, SM1 4QQ.
Weekly, 1892–

Town and Country Planning
TCPA, 17 Carlton House Terrace, London SW1Y 5AS.
Monthly, 1932–

Town Planning Review
Liverpool University Press, 123 Grove Street, Liverpool L7 7AF.
Quarterley, 1910–

Transactions of the Institute of British Geographers
Institute of British Geographers, 1 Kensington Gore, London SW7 2AR.
Quarterly, New Series 1976–

8 Additional entries

8.1 ANON (1980) Socio-economic and environmental impacts of low-volume rural roads—a review of the literature, Devres Inc, Washington DC, Program Evaluation Discussion Paper 7, pp. 184.

8.2 BELL, W.G. (1983) Mobilizing volunteers in community transport for elderly and handicapped in Great Britain. *Specialized Transportation Planning and Practice,* **1** (3) pp. 237–62.

Findings from an exploratory study in 1982 of volunteers in community transport programmes in England indicate that the volunteer concept is working reasonably well in local programmes, particularly in rural areas. While data on several issues such as cost savings achieved with the use of volunteers are sketchy, the survey found the net impact of volunteers in community transport resources was positive. Three recommendations are suggested which are designed to increase the flow and scope of volunteers.

8.3 BUCHANAN, J.M. (1982) Survey of the Mobility of Disabled People in a Rural Environment, Royal Association for Disability and Rehabilitation (RADAR) Monograph.

The main object of this study is to provide factual information on the problems disabled people have in coping with everyday things in a rural environment. A rural area (Wiltshire) was chosen to see whether problems of mobility encountered by disabled people were similar to those already documented in an urban area using the same methodology and whether the recent decline in rural transport was affecting disabled people more adversely than able-bodied persons. This report sets out the findings of the survey carried out in 1978/9. Details are given of the sampling method, demographic characteristics, medical diagnosis, degree of handicap, household

composition, work status, income, housing, mobility on foot, vehicular transport, employment, shopping, use of local facilities, treatment from doctors, social interaction, attitude to disability, and the
results of the survey are discussed.

8.4 BUTTON, K.J. (1983) Regulation and coordination of international
road goods movements within the European Common Market: an
assessment. *Transportation Journal*, **22**(4), pp. 4–16.

This paper looks at the experiences of the EEC in developing a
Common Transport Policy. The focus here is on international road
goods movement, with intermodal coordination, and the coordination of domestic road haulage policies within the EEC is reviewed
where relevant. The role of road haulage in Europe is described
with historic background and retrospective comment. The impact of
the Common Transport Policy on international road haulage is considered and ways of circumventing some of the current problems in
policy are suggested.

8.5 CHARNOCK, D.B., ROBBINS, J. and BROWN, C. (1983) Public transport coordination in Shire Counties—the East Sussex approach.
Traffic Engineering and Control, **24**(10), pp 471–6.

East Sussex County Council needs to coordinate both urban and
rural transport. This article describes two projects: SHUTTLE in
the urban area of Brighton and Hove demonstrates the development
of the 'tram track' or trunk network; and ESCORT in rural Lewes
and Wealden districts shows the cost effectiveness of properly coordinated complementary services. The services coordinated in the
rural areas use vehicles from several local authority departments as
well as contract hire services, community services, voluntary services
and the private sector, and a broker matches up the requirements
for transport against the wide range of suppliers. In this way a better
service is provided at a lower cost.

8.6 COE, G.A. and JACKSON, R.L. (1983) Developments in Stage Carriage Bus Fares before and after the Transport Act 1980. *Transport
and Road Research Laboratory*, LR 1098.

Prior to the Transport Act 1980 stage carriage bus fares were controlled by conditions attached to road service licences by the Traffic
Commissioners. In October 1980 the Act removed such control in

all but exceptional circumstances. The study discussed in this report was designed to track the development of stage carriage bus fares in a sample of areas from January 1978 to January 1983 to discover whether or not any significant differences between the pre- and post-Act periods could be discerned. The results indicated that there had been no increase in the rate or magnitude of fare rises, that there was some evidence of moves away from overall fare scales by large public bus companies, that promotional fares were being used on a wider scale, that most fare agreements set up in sites of competition prior to the Act were holding, that there were relatively few examples of new competition and that the use of Traffic Commissioner reserve powers to prevent either undercutting or over-pricing was almost non-existent. Because of the limited emergence of new competition, it appeared that factors other than the Act had had a greater influence on the general course of events: these were the economic recession, the falling rate of inflation, the outcome of local government elections in May 1981 and the differing subsidy policies of county councils.

8.7 FIELDING, G.J. (1982) Transportation and the handicapped: the politics of full accessibility. *Transportation Quarterly*, **36** (2), pp. 269–82.

In order to comply with federal legislation, US transit systems began to provide full and equal accessibility for handicapped and disabled people. The costs of the programme were enormous compared to the use made of the facilities. On May 26 1981, the US Appeals Court ruled against the imposition of the programme. The article describes the legislative background concerning so-called 'mainstreaming' and accessibility rights for the handicapped, and the political climate which precipitated it. Describes the attitudes of the transit industry, which was unhappy about appearing restrictive towards handicapped people's rights. The transit system of Milwaukee is used as a short case study.

8.8 GAND, H. (1984) 'Bottom Line' business standards versus public service obligations: The case of the German Federal Railway. *Transportation Research*, **18A** (2), pp. 151–61.

The publicly-owned German Federal Railway Corporation (DB) is technically very proficient but economically very inefficient. The financial burden that its revenue shortfall has imposed on the State has become nearly intolerable. There are external and internal reasons for the DB's financial problems. External factors include: competition from other modes, changes in demand for bulk goods, and a shift in national traffic flows from east-west to north-south. Internal causes are: low productivity growth, confused regulations about reimbursing costs for public service burdens and lack of freedom for management to pursue cost-lowering measures. The article describes four different periods of policy aimed at consolidating and modernizing the German Rail System. The latest set of proposals for a financial cure involve a transfer of the track and infrastructure to direct government responsibility and putting transport operations into a for-profit corporation. The debate still continues over precise details of a proposed remedy but the political interests involved will likely prevent a novel or clear-cut solution.

8.9 GB Department of Transport (1984) Buses, London: HMSO, Cmnd 9300.

This White Paper outlining Government policy proposes major changes to promote competition in local bus services which will, it claims, be to the benefit of travellers. The measures include the abolition of road service licensing and its replacement with a scheme that allows competition for each route, a new transitional grant for operators of rural services (£20 million in the first year), the provision that all operators will be able to participate in concessionary fares schemes for the elderly and the disabled, the increase in quality control standards, the wider use of services run by education, health and social services authorities, the Post Office and others, and restructuring of the bus industry to allow it to change to meet market needs. The proposals to change the structure of the bus industry include the reorganization of the National Bus Company into smaller free-standing parts which will then be transferred to the private sector. The funds for rural services include an innovation grant of up to £1 million a year to be administered by the Development Commission. Transitional grants amounting to £20 million in the first full year will be paid directly to operators to help maintain rural services. The grant will be phased out in even steps over four years. Fuel duty rebate will continue.

10 LESTER, N. (1983) *Subsidising Rural Public Transport*, London: Transport 2000.

A local public transport service is needed, but in rural areas it is effectively impossible to provide one adequately on a commercial basis. Revenue support is important in making a contribution to easing this problem. Considerations that this leads to waste are exaggerated and much depends on the way in which the subsidy is administered. Given the predetermination of needs, followed by a 'buying in' of necessary services, and fares levels whether for conventional or experimental services, an efficient use of public money can be made to benefit the whole community.

11 McSHANE, M.P., KOSHI, M. and LUNDIN, O. (1984) Public policy towards the automobile: A comparative look at Japan and Sweden. *Transportation Research*, **18A** (2), pp. 97–109.

This article compares two different national approaches to regulation and promotion of the automobile. It examines how the problem was perceived, what styles of intervention developed, and how the implementation of seemingly standardized solutions differed. Japan tended to view the private automobile as a socially expensive luxury until quite recently. Some features of its policy response, for example low spending on roads, high motor vehicle taxes, flow from this outlook. Other aspects, such as the effective mass public safety campaigns, and the coordination between industrial and regulatory policies flow from Japan's social and cultural patterns. Sweden's policies are aimed at 'civilizing' the car, not restricting it. They tended to develop in a relatively straightforward manner on the basis of an underlying social consensus, as contrasted with the adversarial approach common in the US.

12 NASH, C.A. (1984) Rail policy in Britain—What next? *Transportation*, **12**(4), pp. 243–59.

The 1974 Railways Act set British Rail (BR) the rather vague objective of providing a passenger service broadly comparable with that then existing within a given level of support. For the first few years under the Act, BR succeeded in operating within the financial constraints imposed, but only by considerable increases in charges and by negotiating wage settlements which implied declining real wages. From 1978 on, rising labour costs and reductions in traffic led to a rapidly developing crisis in BR's financial position.

The position of each section of BR's business is discussed briefly. It is shown that the designation of some sectors as being purely commercial is inappropriate, since it means that benefits to users and to the community at large are ignored in decision-making. Similarly, the decision to maintain 'social' passenger services at a given level means that finance and investment are concentrated unduly on preservation of the existing pattern of service, rather than on providing value for money. In both sectors, the likelihood is that in general fares are too high and services too frequent.

At the operational level, the criterion of maximizing the (weighted) volume of traffic carried is advocated as a practical way of choosing between alternative fare and service level packages. More broadly based strategic studies would be needed to decide on the weights to be adopted, the level of finance to be made available, and the overall strategy.

8.13 NUTLEY, S.D. (1983) *Transport Policy Appraisal and Personal Access-ibility in Rural Wales*, Norwich: Geo Books.

8.14 NUTLEY, S.D. (1984) Planning for rural accessibility provision: wel-fare, economy, and equity. *Environment and Planning A*, **16** (3), pp. 357–76.

Although there have been a great many studies of rural accessibility, the vast majority have been concerned only with basic survey and evaluation, with very little systematic attempt at developing meth-odology for improving rural access standards. This paper is based upon previous work using the time-space approach to evaluation and policy appraisal, and considers its extension into planning. This can only be done under the guidance of crucial policy-decisions on the accessibility targets desired, cost limits, and criteria for the dis-tribution of (access) benefits such as the degree of social/spatial equity. Policy options and their implications are discussed, and a planning framework outlined.

8.15 RALLIS, T., MEULENGRACHT, K. and VILHOF, P. (1984) The organ-isation of public transport in Denmark. *Transportation Research*, **18A** (2), pp. 163–75.

The sharp contrast between the public transport needs of Greater Copenhagen and provincial Denmark has led to significant differences in policy and organizational structure for public transport in the two regions. Outside Copenhagen the period 1965-75 saw a rapid decline in rural public transport supply and a rise in special services (school buses, etc). A 1978 law requiring county councils to prepare comprehensive regional transport plans reversed this trend. Most counties now have economically responsible transport corporations which contract with public and private operators for service. School routes have been opened, train and bus schedules have been coordinated and zonal fare systems have been introduced. In Greater Copenhagen urban sprawl has promoted a gradual public take-over of most transport services in the region, culminating in an almost all-pervasive 'public works' type of transport corporation under regional authority in the late 1970s.

16 SALOMON, I. (1984) Telecommuting—promises and reality. *Transport Reviews*, **4** (1), pp. 103-14.

The use of modern telecommunication facilities enables, technically, the substitution of physical commuting by telecommuting. The assessment of the potential substitution between transport and telecommunication requires not only that telecommunications be recognized as an element in the transport system, but furthermore, that the broad implications of physical and electronic movement be considered.

Various studies of this issue have suggested that telecommuting will have positive effects on urban areas as more jobs cease to require physical travel. By contrast, this paper takes a critical approach to the actual potential of telecommuting. Although the social benefits may be larger, the non-monetary costs borne by the individual telecommuter are likely to discourage wide scale transitions to this type of work. This assessment is based both on theoretical reasoning derived from research in sociology of work, as well as some preliminary empirical analysis.

17 STANLEY, J. and STARKIE, D.N.M. (1983) Grant aiding rural local roads—an alternative approach. *Transportation Planning and Technology*, **8** (3), pp. 209-15.

The paper points first to the significance of rural road expenditure in Australia and to the limited success of attempts to place grants for these roads within a framework of economic efficiency. Attention is then drawn to the merit good issue and to the findings of recent research which suggest that spatial equity and changing levels of aspiration are important determinants of road user attitudes. From this we conclude that disequilibrium between expected and actual road performance levels will be a salient characteristic and that road grants should be directed to reducing this discordance. A methodology for distributing grants is suggested and illustrated by reference to South Australian data.

8.18 TANNER, J.C. (1983) International Comparisons of Cars and Car Usage. *Transport and Road Research Laboratory*, LR 1070.

Statistics relating to cars and their usage have been assembled for 19 countries for the years 1958 to 1980. These are then analysed in relation to population, national income, petrol prices and other relevant factors. Aspects considered are car ownership rates per person, numbers of new cars, the average life of cars, their average engine capacity, the average kilometres driven per year and the tonnes of petrol consumed per year. Despite problems with the availability, compatibility and reliability of the data, a number of consistent patterns emerge. Among the clearest and strongest influences are those of income levels on the number of cars, and of petrol prices on the sizes of cars and hence how much petrol they use. Changes in kilometres per car appear to be related in the short-term to changes in petrol prices and in the longer term to the rate of growth of car ownership.

8.19 WISTRICH, E. (1983) *The Politics of Transport*, London: Longman.

This book begins with an overview of trends and developments in transport policy and in the main operating systems since 1945. The guiding ideology of the professionals, the policymakers, the politicians and the pressure groups is then discussed, and key policy issues are analysed from two viewpoints—the pressure groups and political party stance. These issues include: the battle for the environment in the 1970s when local resistance groups were formed as a result of proposals for new motorways and a Third London airport; the conflict over increased lorry weights; and the dramatic confrontation over subsidies to public transport in 1981–2, when the House of

Lords ruled that subsidies by the Greater London Council to London Transport were illegal. There is a short section specifically on rural issues that concentrates on the accessibility problem, but much of the material on transport policy changes is also relevant.

20 YAGAR, S. (1984) Predicting speeds for rural 2-lane highways. *Transportation Research*, **18A** (1), pp. 61–70.

A procedure is developed for estimating highway speeds as a combined function of both traffic volumes and the geometric and environmental conditions surrounding the highway. The proposed method applies a general set of passenger car equivalent units (pcu's) for trucks, recreational vehicles, and opposing flows, in order to reduce traffic volumes to a single variable, which can then be introduced at either an average level or at contrasting high and low levels, along with geometric/environmental conditions into a multiple linear regression equation which treats all of the factors simultaneously. The procedure is applied to estimate various operating speeds on rural 2-lane highways in Ontario, using a data bank compiled in 1980. Equations are developed for the 10th, 50th and 90th percentile operating speeds. Speeds in Ontario are found to be affected by: traffic volumes, by direction and type of vehicle; access to adjacent land use; access from other highways; speed limit; existence of an extra lane; and grade. These Ontario findings are tempered by a lack of severe grades on high-volume roads, and by standard road widths. Thus it is recommended that the described procedure be re-applied in another jurisdiction using data which incorporate a wider range of grades, and road widths.

Subject index

Note: page numbers are in italic, all other numbers refer to entries.

accessibility *8*, 1A2, 1A34, 2A18, 2A38, 2A39, 2A62, 2C9, *89–150*, 3A2, 3A4, 3A5, 3A13, 3A17, 3A21, 3A23, 3A27, 3A28, 3C21, 3C26, 3D5, 3D16, 3D29, 3D39, 3D40, 4C64, *251*, 5A19, 6A14, 6A24, 6A30, 6B9, 6C4, 6D12, 6D20, 8.7, 8.13, 8.14

accessibility measurement 3A3, 3A6, 3A8, 3A10, 3A11, 3A12, 3A13, 3A18, 3A19, 3A24, 3A25, 3A27, 3A30, 3A31, 5B19, 5B48, 6A12, 6A36, 6A40, 6A42, 6B7

accidents 5C26, 5E1, 5E6, 5E9, 5E15, 5F9

activities *93*, 3A18, 3A29, 3B12, 3C32, 4D14, 5B7, 5B48

activity based methods 5B7 5B17

administration 2A59, 2B2 (*see* organization)

agriculture *6, 7*, 1A4, 1A10, 1A24, 5C1, 5C3, 5C6, 5C12, 5C14, 5C32, 5C59, 5F19, 6B3, 6D7, 6D20

Alaska 2B36

ambulance services 4C6 (*see* hospitals and hospital car service)

appropriate technology 6D2, 6D3, 6D4, 6D5, 6D6, 6D13, 6D23, 6D24, 6D36

Argentina 5C4

attitudes 1A2, 3A1, 3B24, 3C29, 4A79, 4B12, 4B28, 5B1, 5B21, 6A4, 6A30, 6C19

Australia 1A8, 4A25, 5C51, 5F24, *343–4*, 8.17

Austria 5A4

Avon 5F34

Ayrshire *34* (*see* Scotland)

Bangladesh 3B35, 5A20

Bedfordshire 4A31, 6A6

Belgium 6B7, 6B12

Berkshire 3C30, 6A5, 6A48

Bolivia 5C14, 6D30

Brazil 5B18, 5D25, 5F32, 6D17

British Railways 4B4, 4B8, 4B10, 8.12

brokerage 4C1

Buckinghamshire 3B30

bus, general 9, 1B2, 2A18, 2A28, 2A32, 2A50, 2A58, 2A62, 2B42, 2B45, 2B46, 2B47, 3C23, 151-2, 4A44, 4A45, 4A48, 4A52, 4A75, 4C59, 4C85, 8.9

bus licensing 33-34, 2A19, 2A23, 2A26, 2A27, 2A33, 2A43 (see deregulation and trial areas)

Busmodel 3B11

bus operations 1B8, 2A12, 2A33, 2B1, 2B10, 2C10, 4A32, 4A63, 4A65, 8.6

bus ownership 2B10

bus patronage 1B6, 2A53, 2C9, 2C10, 151, 4A4, 4A30, 4A51, 4A56

bus service withdrawal 2C2, 152, 4A58, 5B7, 6B6

Buurtbus 156, 4C13, 4C53

California 2B33, 3B23, 3C33, 4C83, 5B8, 5D22, 6C2, 6C17

Cambridgeshire 6A6, 6A43

Canada 1A8, 3C19, 4B25, 4C3, 4C20, 4C71, 5A22, 343-4, 6C13, 6C15, 6C20, 6C24

car 156-7, 4D13, 4D14, 4D18, 5B32, 5D2, 6C28, 8.11, 8.18

car availability 3A1, 3B9, 4D5, 4D8, 4D12, 4D14

carless 91, 3A18, 3B13, 3B16, 3B33, 3C13, 4A41, 4D17

car ownership 5, 8, 9, 1B6, 1B9, 2A18, 2A33, 92, 3A18, 3A19, 4A29, 4D6, 5D13

car passenger 4D15

car sharing and pooling 2A27, 2A33, 2C9, 3A1, 3C12, 3D42, 154, 156, 4C1, 4C25, 4C27, 4C29, 4C51, 4C62, 4C68, 4C70, 4C89, 4C97, 4D11

Carolina 2B44, 3D17, 5F20, 6C25

Cheshire 2A45, 2A46

Chile 5C26

Clwyd 4D18, 6A17, 6A46

Common Transport Policy 38, 2C7, 2C12, 2C17, 8.4

community initiatives 7, 2A18, 93 (see self help)

community rural 1A7, 1A21

community transport 2A22, 2C3, 3D42, 154, 156, 4C7, 4C12, 4C13, 4C17, 4C26, 4C41, 4C91, 6A1, 6A17, 6A19, 6A43, 6A54, 8.2 (see unconventional public transport)

company cars 5D3, 5D18
competition *151–4, 157*
computer manuals *252*, 5B24, 5B25, 5B29, 5D25, 6C17
concessionary fares 2A1, 2A21, 2A24, *92*, 3A7, 3C1, 3C14, 3C15,
   3C16
Connecticut 4C25
conservation *7*, 5C68, 5D3, 5D9, 5D10, 5D11, 5D23
consumer preferences 3A1, 3B4
contingency planning 5D3, 5D5, 5D10
coordination 2A1, 2A11, 2A12, 2A14, 2A47, 2A56, 2B10, 2B11,
   2B19, 2B35, 2B47, 2C3, 3C3, 3C22, *152*, 4A21, 4A46, 4A54, 6C26
cost benefit analysis 4B8, 4B9, 4C58, 5C17, 5C25, 5C29, 5C41,
   5C44, 5C50, 5C52
costs *see* transport costs
cross subsidization *34, 151*, 4A67
Cumbria 3D2, 5B15, 5E8
cyclists 2A25, 3C30, 3C31, *157*, 4B11, 4D1, 4D3, 4D4, 4D9, 4D10

Dakota 2B33, 6C27
decision makers 3A22, 3A28, 3B6, 5C19, 6A29
demand 3C24, 3C29, 3D9, *151*, 4A9, 4A78, 4A81, 4B17
demand based measures of need *89–94*, 3B5, 3B18, 3B20, 3B27
demand modelling 4B17, 4B32, 4C92, 4E15, *252*, 5B5, 5B6, 5B10,
   5B15, 5B16, 5B21, 5B22, 5B27, 5B28, 5B30, 5B34, 5B35, 5B36,
   5B38, 5B40, 5B41, 5B42, 5B43, 5B45, 5B47, 5C63, 6A1
demand responsive services 4A1, 4A22, 4C1, 4C3, 4C4, 4C11, 4C18,
   4C34, 4C45, 4C86, 5B10, 5B46 (*see* dial-a-bus)
demonstration projects 2B1, 2B28, 2B31, 2B33, 2B46, 2B47, 3B24,
   3C33, *155*, 4A43, 4C1, 4C73, 6C3 (*see* RUTEX, unconventional
   public transport, policy US)
Denmark *39*, 2C10, 4A60, 4C52, 5B34, 5B35, 5B39, 8.15
depopulation *6*, 1A24, 1A32, 1A44
deprivation *8*, 1A1, 1A2, 1A34, 1A37, 1A47, 1A48, *91–92*, 3A1,
   3B14, 3B15
Derbyshire 4D1, 4D2, 4D3, 6A13, 6A14, 6A20
deregulation *34*, 2A27, 2A34, 2B17, 2B40, *152*
derived demand *90*
developing countries *156*, 4C81, *254–5*, 5C6, 5C10, 5C12, 5C16,
   5C18, 5C36, 5C37, 5C40, 5C47, 5C49, 5C69, *344–5*, 6D1–6D36
   (*see* appropriate technology, individual countries)

development 1A23, 1A50, 2A12, 2B12, 2B18, 2C5, 2C17, 4B25, *251*, 5A2, 5A16, 5C5, 5C18, 6D13

Devon 1A1, 1A5, *34*, 2A14, 3B21, 4C12, 4C26, 4C27, 4C28, 4C29, 6A4

dial-a-bus 4C31, 4C36, 4C40, 4C45, 4C54, 4C59, 4C72, 4C85, 4C87, 5B14, 6A41, 6C2, 6C8 (*see* demand responsive services, disadvantaged, handicapped)

disadvantaged 2A42, 2B22, 2B24, 3A20, 3A23, 3A31, 3B22, 3C4, 3C5, 3C8, 3C13, 3C17, 3C37, 4D7, 5C30, 6C12, 6C23 (*see* poverty, housewives, elderly, young people, handicapped)

distribution *253*, 5B11, 5C28, 5D3

disused railways 4B1, 4B11, 4D9

diverting bus *154*, 4A22, 4C67, 4C79, 4C92

Dorset 4A22

Durham 2A31

dual purpose vehicles *154*, 4C56

Dyfed *34*, 2A44, 3B29, 3B32, 3B39, 4C30, 6A32, 6A37

economic appraisal 1A26, 1A49, 4A40, 4A70, 6D33 (*see* evaluation)

economics and economic growth 1B5, 4A30, 4B5, 4B23, 5A17

Egypt 6D10

elasticity of demand 1B6, *152*, *153*, 4A4, 4B15, 4B22, 4B32, 5B31

elderly *6*, *36*, 2B34, *92*, 3A7, 3A29, 3C1, 3C12, 3C14, 3C16, 3C21, 3C22, 3C23, 3C24, 3C27, 3C28, 3C29, 3C32, 3C33, 3C34, 3C35, 3C36, 4A79, 4C14, 6A27, 6A52, 6B12, 6C9, 6C11, 6C19, 6C26, 8.2

employment *6*, *7*, 1A3, 1A28, 1A32

energy 2A11, 2C11, 3D1, 3D19, *255-6*, 5B10, 5B32, 5D1-5D25

energy and planning 5D2, 5D3, 5D10, 5D16, 5D17

energy and settlement patterns *256*, 5D15, 5D17

engineering *256-7*, 5F1-5F34

England 3B5, 3B37, 3C15, 3D13, 3D40 (*see* UK)

environment *7*, 1A22, 2A25, 2C11, 4E6, 4E7, 4E12, *256*, 5E3, 5E4, 5E12, 5E13

environmental appraisal 5C7, 5C38

environmental groups 1A33

Ethiopia 5A16, 5C10

Europe 1A18, *39-40*, 2A1, 4B21, 4C18, 4C35, 4E1, 4E4, 4E9, 4E10, 4E14, *342-3*, 6B1-6B24

Europe East 6B19, 6B21 (*see* USSR)

evaluation 1A15, 2A36, 2B1, 2B10, 2B31, 2C13, 3A9, 3B37, *153*, *155*, 4A8, 4A13, 4A14, 4A66, 4A83, 4B27, 4C58, 4C86, *253-5*, 5A8, 5B33, 5C2, 5C5, 5C12, 5C13, 5C14, 5C21, 5C25, 5C26, 5C27, 5C29, 5C30, 5C33, 5C34, 5C35, 5C39, 5C40, 5C41, 5C45, 5C47, 5C48, 5C49, 5C52, 5C56, 5C62, 5C63, 5C64, 5C69, 5C71, 5E2, 6A5, 6D30, 6D32

fares and revenue *153*, 4A4, 4B9
finance 2A30, 2A40, 2A49, 2A59, 2A60, 2B8, 2B12, 2B13, 2B19, 2B21, 2B22, 2B23, 2B27, 2B32, 2B48, 2C16, *151-5*, 4A55, 5B39, 5C15, 5F33, 6C28 (*see* transport policy and programme, transport supplementary grant)
Finland 5A10
forecasting 5A11, 5B9, 5B17, 5B23, 5B31, 5B39, 5C19, 5F17
France 1A8, 1A23, *38*, 3D28, 5A8, 5C21, 6B3
freight 2A25, 2B3, 2B17, 3D14, *157*, 4B21, 4E1, 4E3, 4E8, 4E10, 4E12, 4E15, 5C47, 5D23, 5F7, 8.4

Gambia 5C14, 6D11
Georgia 2B25, 6C12
Germany *39*, 2C8, 2C9, 4A21, 4A26, 4A61, 4B3, 5C21, 6B13, 8.8
Ghana 6D20
Gloucestershire 5F34, 6A52
goals achievement matrix 5C34, 5C35, 5C57
gravity models 5B2
Great Britain *see* UK, England
Guyana 5C7
Gwent 3B10, 5B16, 6A33, 6A36
Gwynedd 2A53, 4A17

Hampshire 3B10, 4A39, 6A26, 6A28
handicapped 2B34, 3B18, 3C10, 3C12, 3C19, 3C33, 3D39, 4A79, 4C3, 4C14, 4C20, 4C46, 6A27, 8.2, 8.3, 8.7 (*see* disadvantaged, elderly)
health care *93*, *94*, 3C1, 3C2, 3D11, 3D30, 3D31
Hertfordshire 1A43, 4E13, 6A2, 6A22, 6A31
hospitals and hospital transport *93*, 3B3, 3C9, 3D16, 3D29, 3D39, 3D40, 4C9, 4C68, 4C80, 6A30, 6A36, 6A40
housewives *93*
housing *7*, 1A25

Illinois 2B2, 2B4, 4A83

income 4A29, 5D3

India 5C27, 6D18, 6D25, 6D26, 6D28, 6D34

Indiana 4D7, 6C6

information 2B45, 3D2, 3D6, 3D7, 3D8, 3D10, *152*, 4A62

inquiry 5C20, 5C24, 5C42

institutions 1A8, *156*, 4C75, 5C54, 6C10

interchange 4A27, 5F12, 6A23

investment appraisal *253-5*, 5C1, 5C5, 5C9, 5C10, 5C16, 5C21, 5C36, 5C37, 5C53, 5C61 (*see* evaluation)

Iowa 2B12, 2B13, 3B18, 3B20, 3C22, 5A2, 6C7, 6C18, 6C21

Ireland *39*, 2C1, 2C13, 3D26, 5B45, 5D7, 6A3

isolation *8*, 2A18, 3B26, 3B36

Italy *38*, 6B1

Jack Committee *33*, 2A28

Jamaica 6D19

Japan 8.11

jitney *154*, 4D16, 5B10

Kansas 3B20, 5E11

Kent 4D5

Kentucky 6C22

Kenya 5C10, 5C55, 5E9, 5F29, 6D1, 6D12

Lancashire 6A35

latent demand 3A1, 3B24

Leitch comprehensive appraisal framework 5C2, 5C7, 5C21, 5C23, 5C42, 5C53, 5C58, 5C73

life styles 5B7

Lincolnshire 3B15, 3D6, 4A24

local plans 2A52

locational accessibility *90*

long distance travel 3D13, 5B15

lorry routes and planning *157*, 4E3, 4E5, 4E6, 4E7, 4E12, 4E13, 4E15

Malaysia 5C61, 6D31, 6D32

management 1A8, 1A18, 2B41, 2C13, 4B14, 5C2 (*see* organization)

managerialism 3A22

market analysis project *34*, 2A25, 2A26, *152*, 4A3, 4A6, 4A11, 4A39, 4C37, *254*, 6A6

marketing 2A34, 3C22, 4B2, 6C21

Maryland 5C67

Massachusetts 2B37, 4A13, 5A46, 5C13, 5C46, 6C3, 6C9

Michigan 5B22

minibus 3C27, *154*, 4C26, 4C39, 4C42, 4C59, 4C77, 4C85, 6A1, 6A39, 6A43

minimum levels of service *91*, 3B2, 3B5, 3B8, 3B28, 6B9, 6B10

Minnesota *6*, 5B40

Mississippi 6C26

Missouri 3B20, 3C35, 4A12, 5D5

mobile services 1A34, 2B4, *93*, 3D2, 3D22, 3D33, 3D35

mobility *8*, 1A2, 1A6, 2A37, 2A38, 2A42, *89-150*, 3A1, 3A14, 3A17, 3A26, 3A29, 3A31, 3B4, 3B13, 3C10, 3C21, 3C36, 3C37, 6A29, 6B12, 6B21, 8.3

mobility allowance 3A7

mobility club 4C32, 4C98

modal split 4D5, 4D12, 4D15

monitoring 3C22

Montgomeryshire 4A24

multicriteria analysis 5C53

multiflow assignment 5B4

National Bus Company *34*, 2A19, 2A26, 4A64, 4C37, 4C59, 8.9

national travel survey 1B6, 3D21, 4A51, 4A56, 4C21, 5D12

Nebraska 3B20, 6C4, 6C23

needs 1A1, 1A2, 2A39, 2A56, 2A61, 2B25, *91-92*, 3A29, 3B5, 3B6, 3B11, 3B16, 3B24, 3B31, 3B32, 3B33, 3B37, 3B38, *254*

needs measurement 3B1, 3B3, 3B6, 3B7, 3B8, 3B10, 3B12, 3B17, 3B18, 3B19, 3B20, 3B21, 3B22, 3B23, 3B24, 3B28, 3B29, 3B30, 3B34, 3B35, 3B38, 5B6, 5B11, 5B12

Nepal 6D7, 6D8

Netherlands *38*, *39*, 2A12, 2C2, 2C3, 2C4, 2C5, 2C10, 2C16, *156*, 4B3, 4C13, 4C31, 4C53, 4C91, 5B44, 5E10, 6B4, 6B5, 6B6, 6B9, 6B10, 6B14, 6B15

New Jersey 5B23

New York 2B33, 4A76, 4C99, 5B31, 5D9, 5D10

New Zealand 5B20, *343-4*, 6C28

Nicaragua 5C14

noise 5E7

non motorized transport 2A36, 2A37, 2B26 (*see* cyclists)

Norfolk 1A24, 1A34, 2A17, 2A29, 3A23, 3C21, 3D16, 3D23, 4A30, 4A52, 4C17, 5F33, 6A11, 6A19, 6A29, 6A30, 6A42, 6A43, 6A44, 6A51, 6A54, 6A55

Northamptonshire 3B9, 3D37, 4A24, 6A6

Northumberland 4B15, 6A32

Norway 4C36, 6B16, 6B17, 6B18, 6B22

Nottinghamshire 2A10, 5F3, 5F4

Oklahoma 2B33, 3B20

Oregon 2B27, 2B33

organization 2A47, 2A59, 2B14, 2B37, 2C4, 2C6, 2C9, 2C10, 3A23, 5B26, 6B4

Oxfordshire 1A2, 2A4, 2A37, 3A1, 3B4, 3C18, 5B17, 6A41, 6A45

paratransit *see* unconventional public transport

participation 2B12, 2B14, 5C8, 5C57, 5C72, 6B5 (*see* inquiry)

pedestrians *see* walk

Pennsylvania 2B33, 3D38, 4A9, 4A43, 4B19, 4D7, 5B5, 5E1

personal accessibility *90* (*see* accessibility measurement)

planning approaches *5, 6*

planning balance sheet appraisal 5C43, 5C44, 5C45

planning documentation 1A17

planning general 1A22, 1A27, 1A36, 1A45

planning problems 1A11, 2A51, 4A8

planning process *6*, 1A30

policy UK 1A2, 1A5, 1A15, 1A26, 1A34, *33–39*, 2A6, 2A13, 2A19, 2A27, 2A30, 2A35, 2A37, 2A43, 2A63, 2C7, 3A1, 3A2, 3C26, 8.13, 8.19

policy US 2B1, 2B5, 2B6, 2B7, 2B9, 2B15, 2B20, 2B29, 2B30, 2B31, 2B44, 2B45, 2B47, 2B49, 4C82

policy other countries 2C4, 2C5, 2C9, 2C15, 6B23 (*see* common transport policy)

politics and planning *8*, 1A33, 3A28

postbus 3D42, *154*, 4C2, 4C30, 4C35, 4C77, 4C88, 4C93, 4C94, 6A9, 6A10, 6A17, 6B11

poverty and the poor *8*, 1A10, 1A17, *36*, 2B43, *92*, 3B35, 3D17, 6D19

prediction 4A56

private hire car 6A26

privatization and private operators 2A3, *152*, 4A25, 4A37, 4A38, 4A71, 4A72, 6C7

public passenger transport plan *34*, 2A5, 2A39, 2A44, 2A54, 2A61, 3C16, 4C64, 6A55

public transport *9*, 1B5, 2B5, 2B7, 4A2, 4A5, 4A7, 4A10, 4A17, 4A18, 4A19, 4A20, 4A23, 4A28, 4A33, 4A36, 4A42, 4A43, 4A47, 4A49, 4A50, 4A54, 4A57, 4A68, 4A69, 4A77, 4A80, 5B12, 5B34, 5B35, 5C33, 5C39, 5C63, 6B2, 6B9, 6B24, 8.5, 8.10, 8.14

queueing models 5F10, 5F18, 5F31

railbus *153*, 4B4

rail closure 4B16, 4B18, 4B20, 4B24, 4B30

rail conversion *153*, 4B6, 4B13, 4B26

rail performance measures 4B21

rail reorganization 4B19

railways *9–10*, 1B1, 1B3, 1B4, 2A18, 2A19, 2A20, 2A25, 2A31, 2A53, 2C6, 2C13, *153*, 4B1–4B32, 5A5, 8.8, 8.12

rate support grant 2A48, 5B11

recreation *6*, 3D13, 3D21, 4A15, 4B1, 4B7, 4B12, 4D1, 4D2, 4D4, 4E2, 4E8, *253*, 5B2, 5B9, 5B14, 5B16, 5B21, 5B28, 5B42, 5D4, 5D20, 5D21, 5D22, 6A13, 6A14, 6A15, 6A16, 6A18, 6A21, 6A22, 6A33, 6A51

regional policy and planning 5A4, 5A9

regression analysis 4A38, 5A3, 5B8, 5B19, 5E12, 5F15, 5F26

resources 1A1, 1A18, 1A49, 1A51

road design 5F12, 5F16, 5F19, 5F21, 5F22, 5F29, 5F30

road investment analysis model 6D10

road maintenance 5F24, 5F27, 5F28, 5F29

road transport investment model 5C10, 5C55

roads 2B4, 2B24, 2B32, 2B43, 5A3, 5A5, 5A6, 5A8, 5A10, 5A13, 5A19, 5B24, 5B25, 5B29, 5B31, 5B38, 5C1, 5C2, 5C3, 5C4, 5C6, 5C7, 5C11, 5C12, 5C14, 5C15, 5C16, 5C17, 5C18, 5C19, 5C20, 5C21, 5C22, 5C24, 5C25, 5C27, 5C29, 5C31, 5C36, 5C40, 5C48, 5C51, 5C54, 5C58, 5C59, 5C61, 5C62, 5C68, 5C69, 5F8, 6B1, 6B3, 6D9, 6D10, 6D11, 6D14, 6D15, 6D18, 6D28, 6D29, 6D35, 8.1, 8.17, 8.20

rural change 1A15

rural community *6*, 2B16

rural community council 3D42, 4A53
rural definition 5
rural general 1A39, 1A42, 1A46, 1B7
rural sociology 1A10, 1A40, 1A41, 1A43
rural typology 1A53
rurality 1A13
RUTEX 1A1, *34*, 2A12, 3C26, *155*, 4C8, 4C9, 4C10, 4C21, 4C26,
    4C27, 4C28, 4C29, 4C30, 4C37, 4C56, 4C60, 4C67, 4C68, 4C69,
    4C70, 4C77, 4C78, 4C79, 4C80, 4C81, 4D20

safety *256*, 5E1, 5E5, 5E10, 5E11, 5E14, 5E19, 5E23
school transport 2A1, 2A27, 2C9, *92*, 3C6, 3C11, 3C12, 3C18, 3C30,
    3C31, 3C42, *154*, 4A21, 4A34, 4C6, 4C30, 5B17, 6A48, 6C22
Scotland 3B25, 3B26, 3B27, 3B34, 4C56, 4C77, 4C78, 4C79, 4C80,
    4C88, 5B9, 5C29, 5C31, 6A9, 6A10, 6A24, 6A25, 6A27, 6A39,
    6A50, 6A53
self help 2A3, 3D24
service levels and provision 6, 3D12, 3D24, 3D34, 3D37, 3D42,
    4A16, 4A76
settlement policy 6, 1A5
settlements 1A9, 1A12, 1A15, 1A17, 1A19, 1A20, 1A31, 1A52
severance 5C3, 5C11
shared car hire *154*, 4C28, 4C69, 4C78, 4D20 (*see* car sharing and
    pooling)
shop 7, 2A16, 2A17, *93*, 3A10, 3C1, 3D23, 3D32, 3D33, 3D35, 6A36
Shropshire 3C9
simulation methods 5A11, 5B5, 5B6, 5B14, 5B18, 5B28, 5B37, 5B39,
    5C60, 5E14, 5F20
social impact analysis 5C66, 5C67
social services transport 2B22, *92*, 3B3, 3C3, 3C24, 3D32, 4C6
Somerset 4A39
speed limits 5D11 (*see* traffic flows and speeds)
Strathclyde 3B10, 3B27, 4C79, 6A49
structure plan 1A38, 1A45, 2A12, 2A52
subscription bus *154*, 4C15, 4C49, 4C55, 4C92, 5B10
subsidization 1A1, *38*, 2A6, 2A34, 2A45, 2B18, 2C10, 2C15, 3B37,
    152, *153*, *155*, 4A70, 4A73, 4A74, 4A83, 4B3, 8.10
Suffolk 2A16
Surrey 3C15, 3C16, 6A48
survey 4C21, 4C26, 4C62, 4C92, 4C97, 5B3, 5B13, 5B15, 5B16,

5B17, 5B20, 5B33, 5B46, 5B48, 5D10, 6A12, 6A26, 6A27, 6A33, 6A44, 6A48, 6C10 (*see* attitudes, national travel survey)

Sussex 2A56, 6A7, 8.5

Sweden *39*, 2C15, 4A41, 4A54, 4A82, 4B3, 4B29, 4B42, 4D16, 6B2, 6B20, 6B23, 6B24, 8.11

Switzerland 4A63, 6B10

taxi 3C33, *154*, *156-7*, 4C46, 4C83, 4C99, 4D7, 4D16, 4D21, 5B14, 6A26

telecommunications *93-94*, 3D1, 3D3, 3D4, 3D5, 3D8, 3D9, 3D11, 3D14, 3D15, 3D18, 3D19, 3D20, 3D25, 3D26, 3D27, 3D28, 3D32, 3D36, 3D38, 3D41, 5A11, 8.16

telemedicine 3D11

telephones *94*, 3D4, 3D20, 3D25, 3D28

Tennessee 2B33

Texas 3C6, 4D7, 5A14

time geography *90*, 3A15, 3A16, 3A25, 3A27, 3C26, 6B20

trade off analysis 3A1, 5B1

traffic commissioners 2A57, 4A24

traffic flows and speeds 5F1, 5F2, 5F3, 5F13, 5F14, 5F15, 5F25, 5F26, 5F31, 6D21

training 3B22, 3B23

transit *see* bus

transmigration 5C14

transport and land use 2A37, 2A39, 2B26, *252*, 5A12, 5B19, 5B20

transport costs 2B5, 2B9, 2B19, 2B35, 4A9, 4A13, 4A31, 4A84, 5C46

transport general 1B10, 2A15, 2A42, 2B38, 2B39, 2B40, 2C14, 4A53, 4A85

transport investment and development *251*, 5A1, 5A2, 5A3, 5A4, 5A5, 5A6, 5A10, 5A13, 5A14, 5A15, 5A18, 5A20, 5A21, 5A22

transport planning 2A38, 2A59, 2A60, 2B38, 2B39, 5B35, 5D2, 5D3, 6A35

transport policy and programmes *33*, 2A2, 2A7, 2A9, 2A12, 2A18, 2A25, 2A41, 2A46, 2A55, 5C56

transport supplementary grant *34*, 2A7, 2A9, 2A25, 2A41, 2A48, 5B11

travel *9*, 2A38, *89*, 3D9, 4C97, 4D14, 5D2, 6A41

Treaty of Rome *38*

trial areas 2A27, 2A29 (*see* deregulation)

trips *9*, *89*, 3A18

unconventional public transport 2A19, 2A23, 2A26, 2A32, 2C9, 2C13, 3A2, 3A14, 3C8, 3C17, 3C19, 3D14, *153-5*, 4A30, 4C17, 4C19, 4C22, 4C23, 4C24, 4C33, 4C37, 4C38, 4C43, 4C47, 4C48, 4C50, 4C57, 4C58, 4C61, 4C63, 4C64, 4C65, 4C71, 4C74, 4C75, 4C76, 4C81, 4C84, 4C90, 4C95, 4C96, 4C99, 5C13, 6B22, 6D16, 6D24, 6D27 (*see* appropriate technology)

United Kingdom 1A8, 1A18, 1A23, *33-36*, 2A1-2A63, 2C10, 2C12, 3D22, 4C13, 4C40, 4C72, 4C93, 4C94, 4D8, 4D17, 4E1, 4E12, 4E15, 5A1, 5A13, 5A15, 5A18, 5B11, 5C21, 5C22, 5C23, 5C41, 5C42, 5C48, 5D2, 5D3, 5D8, 5D12, 5D13, 5E15, 5F7, *341-2*, 6A1-6A55, 6C28

United States 1A8, 1A18, *36-38*, 2B1-2B49, 4A20, 4A59, 4B31, 4C3, 4C5, 4C23, 4C39, 4C71, 4C89, 4D17, 4E1, 5A3, 5A11, 5B32, 5C21, 5C41, 5C70, 5D14, 5D19, *343-4*, 6C1, 6C5, 6C8, 6C9, 6C16, 6C19 (*see* individual states)

USSR 4B25, 6B7

utility assessment 5C40

value of time 6D22 (*see* evaluation)

vehicle design 3A7, 3C1, 3C20, 4A12, 5F11, 6C9, 6D36

vehicle operating costs 6D1, 6D25 (*see* evaluation)

video conferencing 3D3

village car *156*

Virginia 3B12, 3B24, 3C24, 6C5, 6C10, 6C14

visual amenity 5E2, 5E8

voluntary sector *156*, 4A81, 4C13, 4C82, 5C65, 6A19

voluntary transport 3B3, 3C3, 3C17, 3C34, 3C35, *155*, 4C6, 4C29, 4C30, 4C44, 4C66, 4C80, 6A17, 6A27 (*see* community transport)

Wales 3A24, 3A25, 3B37, 3C15, 3C25, 3C26, 3D39, 4A39, 4A84, 4B5, 4B9, 4B23, 4B28, 6A40, 6A47, 8.13

walk *89*, 3A18, 4D17, 4D19, *256*, 5E6, 6B18

Warwickshire 6A8

waterways *157*, 4E1, 4E2, 4E4, 4E8, 4E9, 4E10, 4E11, 4E14, 5C9

Westmorland 4A24

Wiltshire 5E13

Wisconsin 4C82, 5C65, 6C11

Worcestershire 4A39

works bus services 4A36, 4A38, 4A39, 4C49

Yorkshire *34*, 2A63, 3A10, 3A32, 4A65, 4B7, 4B12, 4B15, 4C9, 4C67, 4C68, 4C69, 4C70, 6A1, 6A12, 6A23, 6A38
young people *92*

Zimbabwe 6D29

Author index

Abaynayaka, S.W. 6D1
Abbiss, J.C. 5F1
Abkowitz, M.D. 4C1
Ackroyd, L.W. 5F1, 5F2, 5F3, 5F4, 5F5, 5F6
Adams, D.E. 4C2
Adams, L. 6A1
Adler, T.J. 5B39
Aex, R.P. 4C3, 4C4
Age Concern 3C1
Allard, M.D. 3C2
Allen, B.J. 2B3
Allen, W.B. 5D1
Allsop, R.E 5F7, 5F8
Alschuler, D. 4C75
Altshuler, A. 4C5
Anderson, J.R. 3C28
Anon 3B1, 3D1, 8.1
Apicella, V. 6B1
Appleton, J.H. 4B1
Ario, O. 4A1
Asp, K. 4A2, 6B2
Association of County Councils 1A1
Association of Transport Coordinating Officers 3B2
Awdas, D. 2A1
Axelsson, B. 6B24
Ayton, J.B. 1A19

Baanders, A. 3B33
Baden, A. 5A19
Bailey, J.M. 3B3, 3C3, 3C4, 4C6, 4C7
Baker, R. 6A2
Balcombe, R.J., 4C8, 4C9, 4C10, 4C11, 4C12
Baldwin, M. 4E1

Ball, R.R. 2A2
Banister, C.E. 5D2
Banister, D.J. 1A2, 2A3, 3A1, 3A2, 3B4, 3B5, 3B6, 4C13, 5B1, 5D2, 5D3
Barb, C.E.J. 4C23
Barbour, K.M. 6A3
Barker, W.G. 4C14
Barre, A. 6B3
Barrett, B. 4A3, 4B2
Barrow, J.F. 2A4
Barwell, I. 6D2, 6D3, 6D4, 6D5, 6D6
Baumel, C.P. 4B20
Bautz, J.W. 4C15
Baxter, M. 5B2
Baxter, R.S. 3A3
Bayliss, B. 4B3
Bayliss, J. 2A5
Beale, C.L. 1A3
Bebbington, A.C. 3B7
Beenhakker, H.L. 5C1
Beesley, M.E. 2A6, 5C2
Beetham, A. 2A7, 3B8
Bell, C. 1A41
Bell, M. 5C3
Bell, W.G. 8.2
Benacquista, R.J. 2B1, 2B31
Bendixson, T. 5D4
Benedick, R. 5C4
Bennett, G.T. 5F9
Bentham, C.G. 3D16, 6A30
Bents, F.D. 5E1
Benwell, M. 3A4, 3B9
Berg, W.D. 2B2, 3A14
Berger, L. 5C5
Berthoud, R. 5B3

Best, R.H. 1A4
Bettison, M. 5F2, 5F3, 5F4
Bhatt, K.U. 4C49, 4C50
Biderman, J. 5C12
Bird, C.M. 3B10
Blackesley, E.J. 1A6
Blacksell, M. 1A5
Blaikie, P. 6D7, 6D8
Blanchard, R.D. 3C36
Blomberg, R.D. 5E6
Blonk, W.A.B. 6B4
Blowers, A. 2A8
Blunt, J. 4C16
Bly, P.H. 4A4, 4A56, 4A78
Bohn, D. 6C3
Bonney, R.S.P. 4A5
Botham, R.W. 5A1
Bovet, D. 5C12
Bovill, D.I.N. 5C6, 6D9
Bovy, P.H. 4C17
Bowen, S.P. 4C62
Boynton, C.H. 4C4
Bracey, H.G. 1A6
Brademeyer, B. 6D10
Bradshaw, K. 1A7
Brancher, D.M. 6A4
Brander, J.R. 5A22
Breen, D.A. 2B3
Breen, W.G. 3D26
Breur, M.W.K.A. 4C18
Brewell, K.A. 5A2
Brewer, K.A. 5D19
Bridle, R.J. 5C7
Briggs, R. 3C5, 3C6, 5A3
Bright, M.J. 6A5
Brilon, W. 5F10
British Railways Board, 1B1
British Road Federation 6A6
British Waterways Board 4E2
Britton, F. 4C19
Brogan, J.D. 5C33, 5F11
Brookes, T. 4A6
Brooks, J.A. 5B4
Brown, C. 8.5
Brown, N.A. 6C1
Brown, W.M.M. 5B33
Brownlee, A.T 3B27
Bruggeman, J.M. 6B5

Bruton, M.J. 5C8
Bryant, C.R. 1A8
Bryant, P.W. 6A7
Buchanan, J.M. 8.3
Buchanan, M. 3B11
Budhu, G. 5C9
Bulman, J.N. 5C10
Bunce, M. 1A9
Bunker, A.R. 2B4
Burkhardt, J.E. 2B5, 2B6, 2B7, 2B8, 2B9, 3B19, 3C7, 4A7, 4A8, 4A9, 4A10, 5B5, 5B6, 5C11, 6C11
Burns, I. 4C35
Bursey, M. 4A11
Bus and Coach Council 1B2
Butcher, H. 3D2
Butler, D.A. 5F22
Butler, D.L. 5D19
Buttel, F.H. 1A10
Button, K.J. 5A13, 8.4
Buxton, M.J. 1B9, 4D18
Byrne, B.F. 5B3

Calson, R.C. 6C2
Cameron, G.R. 6A8
Cameron, J. 6D7, 6D8
Canadian Department of Transport 4C20
Canner, L. 4A13
Cantilli, E.J. 3C13
Carapetis, S. 5C54
Carnemark, C. 5C12
Carpenter, T.C. 6A9, 6A10
Casey, R. 4A12
Ceglowski, K.P. 2B8, 2B9
Centeno, K. 5B25
Central Transport Consultative Committee 4B4
Chammari, A. 5B1
Charnock, D.B. 8.5
Chartered Institute of Public Finance and Accountancy 2A9
Chatterjee, A. 4A66
Chavis, L.K. 3B12
Chernyuk, G. 6B8
Cherry, G. 1A11
Chew, K.S. 5C40
Chisholm, M. 1A12

Christie, A.W. 4E3, 4E13
Christie, B. 3D3
Chudleigh, P.D. 5B20
Clamp, P.E. 5E2
Clark, D. 3D4, 3D5, 3D6, 3D7, 3D8, 3D9
Clarke, M. 5B7
Clayton, G. 4B5
Cloke, P.J. 1A13, 1A14, 1A15, 1A16, 1A17, 1A18, 1A19, 1A31
Clout, H. 1A20, 4A52, 6A11
Coates, V. 3B13
Coe, G.A. 4C21, 8.6
Cole, I. 3D2
Coles, O.B. 3A5, 3A23, 3B14
Collins, B. 2A10
Collura, J. 2B10, 4A13, 4A14, 5B46, 5C13, 5C46, 6C3
Comsis Corporation 6C4
Connell, K.M. 4C73
Connor, J. 3B15
Conrad, P.E. 5C14, 6D11
Constantine, T. 5F12
Cook, A.P. 4C22, 4C23
Cook, C. 5C54
Coombe, R.D. 5F26
Cooper, J.C. 4B5
Cooper, J.S.C. 6A12
Cooper, T.W. 5C15
Cope, D. 4A13, 4A14
Coras Iompair Eireann 2C1
Corcoran, P.J. 4E3
Cornwall, P.R. 5C16
Cottrell, B.H. 6C10
Council for the Protection of Rural England 2A11
Countryside Commission 4A15, 4B7, 4D1, 4D2, 4D3, 4D4, 6A13, 6A14, 6A15
Countryside Review Committee 1A21
Cowan, P.D. 3D10
Crain, J.L. 3C8
Cresswell, R. 2A12
Cross, K.W. 3C9
Cutler, D.A. 2B11
Cutler, M. 4C24
Cutrell, J. 5B25

Dallmeyer, K.E. 3C10
Daly, A.J. 3A6
Daly, P.N. 6A12, 6A38
Dare, C.E. 5D5
Dartington Amenity Research Trust 6A16
Davidson, J. 1A22
Davies, B.P. 3B7
Davies, C.H. 5E12
Davies, E.R. 6A17
Davies, P.W. 5C17
Davis, C.E. 4C25
Davison, P. 2B31, 6A18
Dawson, T.C. 4A59
Deak, E. 5A11
Dean, C.L. 5B8
Dean, N. 2A13
Deavin, P. 6A19
De Boer, E. 2C2, 2C3, 6B6
De Hamel, B. 5E3
Dehampers, J.M. 4A16
De Kogel, C.G. 2C4
De Lannoy, W. 6B7
Demetsky, M.J. 3C11, 6C5, 6C10
Denisyuk, L.M. 6B8
Dennis, S.J. 3D13
Deomas, T.H. 5E4
De Queiroz, C.A.V. 5F32
Derbyshire County Council 6A20
Deshpande, G. 5B36
De Veen, J.J. 6D12
Devon Rutex Working Group 4C26, 4C27, 4C28, 4C29
Dhillon, H.S. 3D11
Dickey, J.W. 3B24, 6C14
Dijkhius, H. 6B9
Dinefwr Rutex Working Group 4C30
Dirkse, G.J. 4C31
Dobbs, B. 4A17
Dodd, A. 3B39
Dodge, R. 5B38
Dodgson, J.S. 4B8
Doermann, A.C. 3D11
Doherty, M.J. 4C32
Donald, R.G. 4D5
Dredge, A.S. 4C12
Drewett, R. 1A30

Drinka, T.P. 4B20
Drudy, P.J. 1A23, 1A24
Druitt, S. 5C29
Dueker, K.J. 3C22
Duffell, J.R. 6A21, 6A22
Duffield, B.S. 5B9
Dumble, P.L. 3A19
Dunn, M. 1A25

Eagle, D.M. 5B40
Eastman, R. 5B33
Ebner, J. 5A4
Eckmann, A. 2C5, 3C12
Edmonds, G.A. 5C18, 6D13, 6D14,
    6D15
Edwards, D.A. 4D6
Edwards, M. 3D12
Edwards, S.L. 3D13
El-Hawary, M. 6D10
Ellson, P.B. 6A23
Elton, M. 3D3
Emerson, D. 3D34
England, H. 2A14
Englisher, L.S. 5B10
Ennor, P.D. 4A18
Ernest-Jones, S.R. 5F6
Ernst, U. 2B29
Esch, R.E. 5B32
Etschberger, K. 4A1
European Conference of Ministers of
    Transport 2C6, 3D14, 4C33, 4E4,
    5D6
Evans, A.W. 5B11
Evans, R.D. 4B9
Ewing, G. 5B2
Ewing, R.H. 4C34
Executive Office of the President
    4A20

Fain, R.P. 3C35
Fairhead, R.D. 4C21
Falcocchio, J.C. 3C13
Farrington, J.H. 3B34, 6A24
Farthing, D.W. 5F13
Faulks, R.W. 2A15
Fausch, P.A. 4A21
Feeney, B.P. 5D7

Fichter, D. 4C98
Fielding, G.J. 4C83, 8.7
Fischer, J.F. 5B18
Fleishman, D. 4C35
Fletcher, J. H. 5F14
Flynn, E.J. 6C6
Fogel, R.W. 5A5
Forde, M.C. 6A25
Forkenbrock, D.J. 2B12, 2B13
Fouracre, P.R. 6D16, 6D24
Fritz, T.L. 6C7
Frøysadal, E. 4C36

Galin, D. 5F15
Gallacher, R.W. 4D7
Gallacher, W.E. 5C19
Gallop, K.R. 4A22
Gamble, P. 5B12
Gand, H. 8.8
Ganser, K. 4A23
Gant, R. 6A52
Garden, J. 3A7, 3B33, 4C7, 6B10
Garland, A.D. 2B14, 4A10
Garratt, M.G. 6A5
Garrison, W.G. 5A6
Garrity, R. 2B14, 4A10
Garton, P.M. 2A49
Gauthier, H.L. 5A7
Genton, D.L. 6B11
Gerrard, M.J. 5B14
Gilder, I. 1A19, 1A26
Gilg, A.W. 1A5, 1A27, 1A28
Gilmour, P. 4A25
Gipps, P.G. 5F18
Girnan, G. 4A26
Gladin, S.T. 3D31
Glassborow, D.W. 4C38
Glen, A. 3D2
Glennon, J.C. 5E5, 5F19
Glover, J.G. 3C15, 3C16
Goldberg, A. 6C10
Gonzalez, S.M. 5C26
Goodhue, R.E. 4C83
Gordon, S. 4A13
Goyder, J. 1A33
Gracey, H. 1A30
Grandjean, A. 5A8
G.B. Department of the Environ-

ment 2A16, 2A17, 2A18, 2A19, 3D15, 4D8, 4E5

G.B. Department of Transport 1B3, 2A20, 2A21, 2A22, 2A23, 2A24, 2A25, 2A26, 2A27, 3C14, 4B10, 4B11, 4D9, 4E6, 4E7, 5C20, 5C21, 5C22, 5C23, 5C24, 5D8, 8.9

G.B. Department of Transport Assessments Policy and Methods Division 5C28

G.B. House of Commons 4C37

G.B. Ministry of Transport 2A28, 4A24, 5B13, 5F16, 5F17

Green, R.J. 1A29

Greenbie, B.B. 4A27

Greening, P.A.K. 4C39, 5B15, 6A26

Gregory, P. 6A27

Gregory, W.R. 6A28

Griffin, L.J. 5E12

Grigg, A.O. 4B12

Grimmer, M. 4C40

Groff, W.H. 4C25

Gubbins, E. 4C41

Guenter, K.W. 6C8

Guha, S. 5C27

Guild, A. 2A29

Guiliano, G. 4C83

Gunnerson, S.O. 4C42

Gupta, D.P. 6D28

Gur, Y. 5B23

Gurin, D.B. 4C43

Gwilliam, K.M. 2A6, 2A30, 2C7

Hale, A. 5E6

Hale, C.W. 5C28

Hale, D.M.J. 4C86

Hall, C. 4A28

Hall, P.G. 1A30, 4B13, 5A9

Halla, N. 5A10

Hamilton, T.D. 2A31

Hanna, K. 3D17

Hanrahan, P.J. 1A31

Hansen, W.G. 3A8

Harboort, J. 6B12

Hargroves, B.T. 3C11, 6C10

Harland, D.G. 5E7

Harman, J. 6C9

Harman, R.G. 3A23, 4A29, 4A30, 5C68, 6A29

Harris, M.R. 5B4

Harrison, A. 5C29

Harrison, A.J.M. 4E8

Harrison, R. 6D17

Hartgen, D.T. 5D9, 5D10

Hartley, J.M. 4B14

Hauser, E.W. 3C17, 5C30

Hawker, M.E. 4C44

Hawkins, M.R. 2A32

Hawthorne, J.H. 4C93, 4C94

Hayes, J. 2B15

Haynes, R.M. 3D16, 6A30

Hayton, F. 5C31

Headicar, P.G. 6A12

Hearne, A.S. 5C3, 5C32

Heathington, K.W. 5C33, 6C26

Heels, P. 4B15

Heggie, I.G. 6D9

Heimbach, C.L. 5E20

Heinz, E.E. 5A11

Heinze, G.W. 2C8, 2C9, 6B13

Heldund, J.H. 5E1

Henderson, I. 2A37, 2A38

Hennes, R.G. 6D18

Henry, C. 5A8

Heraty, M.J. 6D19

Herbst, D. 2C9, 6B13

Hesling, R.G. 6C17

Hewitt, J. 4E15

Hewitt, J.R.A. 4A31

Hibbs, J. 2A33, 2A34

Hide, H. 6D1

Higginson, M. 4A32

Hilewick, C.L. 5A11

Hill, M. 5C34, 5C35

Hillman, M. 2A35, 2A36, 2A37, 2A38, 4B16

Hine, J.L. 5C36, 5C37, 6D9, 6D20

Hislop, M. 6A31

Hoare, AG. 4A33

Hobeika, A.G. 5C9

Hodge, I. 1A32

Hodge, P. 1B4

Hoekert, M. 6B10

Hoel, L.A. 2B41, 6C5, 6C10

Hoey, W.F. 4C45

Hofstra, M. 6B14
Holder, A. 2A39
Holding, D.M. 6A32
Hollings, D. 4B28
Hollis, G.E. 6A11
Holt, S.R. 4B17
Hood, T.C. 4D11
Hounsome, K.R. 2A40, 2A41
Howe, J.D.G.F. 6D4, 6D5, 6D6, 6D15, 6D21, 6D22, 6D23
Howie, M.R. 3D17
Huddart, L. 4B12, 5B16, 5E8, 6A33
Huddleston, J. 2B16, 5B38
Hudson, H.E. 3D18
Hudson, W.R. 3A9
Hunjan, J.S. 5C17
Hutchinson, T.Q. 2B4
Hutton, J. 4A34
Hyde, P.J. 6A48
Hynes, C. 2B17

Independent Commission on Transport 2A42
Irwin, L.H. 5A12

Jackson, A.F. 4A35
Jackson, R.L. 4A36, 4A37, 4A38, 4A71, 4C39, 6A26, 8.6
Jackson, R.T. 6A34
Jacobs, G.D. 5E9, 6D24
James, N. 2A43
Janssen, S.T.M.C. 5E10
Jefferson, J.R. 5C38
Jelley, C.A.B. 4A39
Jensen, O.H. 5C39
Jewell, M.C. 6A35
Jofre, F.A. 5C26
Johnson, R.J. 3A10
Johnson, W.D. 2A31
Johnston, I. 2A36
Johnston, S.A. 3C17
Johnstone, M. 5C31
Joint Working Group of TRRL and Gwent County Council 6A36
Jones, A.D. 3A11
Jones, P.M. 3A12, 5B17
Jones, S.R. 3A13

Jones, T.S.M. 2A44, 3C18
Judge, E.J. 5A13

Kadiyali, L.R. 6D25
Kaesehagen, R.L. 5B18
Kane, A. 5C15
Karash, K.H. 4C46
Katteler, H.A. 4D10
Kau, J.B. 5B19
Kaye, I. 2B18, 4A10
Kearney, E.F. 5E6
Keen, P.A. 4B18
Keith, R.A. 4C47
Kellett, J.T. 2A45
Kemp, J.B. 2B19
Kemp, M.A. 4C50
Ketola, H.N. 2B20
Kettle, P.B. 5C2, 5C45
Khasnabis, S. 5F20
Kidder, A.E. 2B21, 2B22, 2B23, 4A40
Kihlman, B. 4A41
Kilsby, D. 4A6
Kilvington, R.P. 2C10, 3B16, 4A42, 6A42
Kinder, J.D. 6A5
King, E. 5B36
King, R.L. 5B20
Kinstlinger, J. 4B19
Kirby, R.F. 4C48, 4C49, 4C50
Klein, D.H. 5B21
Klinkenberg, J. 2C3, 6B15
Knapp, S.F. 6C11
Knight, V.A. 2A46
Knighton, R.C. 4A76
Knowles, R.D. 6B16, 6B17
Koch, J.A. 5C40
Kocur, G. 4C51
Korompai, G. 4E9
Koshi, M. 8.11
Koushki, P.A. 3A14
Koutsopoulos, K.C. 3B17, 3B18
Kraemer, K.L. 3D19
Krayenbuhl, V. 4C17
Krogh, F. 4C52
Krogsaeter, K. 6B18
Kropman, J.A. 4C53, 4D10
Kuhn, H.A.J. 5B22

Kurth, D.L. 5B23
Kurth, S.B. 4D11
Kutter, E. 4C54
Kwakye, E.A. 6D20

Lago, A.M. 2B8, 2B9, 3B19, 5B5, 5B6
Larsen, M.B. 5F21
Larson, R.A. 2B24
Larson, T.D. 2B32, 4A43
Latham, G.R. 3C19
Laudenbach, A. 2C11
Lawler, K.A. 5D12
Lazarus, P.E. 2C12
Leach, S. 2A47
Leake, G.R. 5D11
Lee, J. 3B20
Leistritz, F.L. 5D14
Lemer, A.C. 5C41
Lenntorp, B. 3A15
Lenzi, G. 3A3
Lester, N. 8.10
Levin, P.H. 5C42
Lewis, A.D. 4A44
Lewis, G.J. 6A37
Lewis, K. 3B11
Lichfield, N. 5C43, 5C44, 5C45
Lienesch, W.C. 3C28
Lima, P.M. 4A43
Lineham, R. 5A14
Lippoy, R. 4A45
Litz, L.E. 5B24, 5B25
Llewelyn, F.J. 5F22
Local Government Operational Research Unit 4A46, 4C55
Lombaers, J. 3C20
Lorber, W.G. 6C18
Loutzenheiser, R.C. 5E11
Lowe, P.D. 1A33
Lowe, S. 5E15
Lucarotti, P.S.K. 4D12
Lucchini, S.F. 5B26
Lugton, J. 4C36
Lundberg, B.D. 6C27
Lundin, I. 6B24
Lundin, O. 4A2, 6B2, 8.11
Lyles, R.W. 5F23

MacAnge, T.R. 4C62
MacBriar, I. 4A11, 4B2
McCallum, B. 4A11
McCoomb, L.A. 4D15
McGillivray, L. 3C17
McGillivray, R.G. 2B29, 4C50
McKelvey, D. 2B45, 3C5, 3C22, 4A35, 4C63
McKelvey, F.X. 5F11
Mackie, A.M. 5E12, 5E13
Mackie, P.J. 2A48, 2A49
McKinsey International 2C13
McLaughlin, B.P. 1A36, 1A37
McLellan, A.G. 1A8
McMillan, A.W. 2A52
McShane, M.P. 8.11
Madden, A.J. 5F5, 5F6
Maddocks, T. 3B21
Maggied, H.S. 2B25, 6C12
Male, J.W. 5C46
Maltby, D. 5D12
Marche, R. 5B27
Marin, R.L. 4C57
Maring, G. 2B31
Markow, M.J. 6D10
Marks, J.V. 4C83
Markve, K. 2B26
Marotel, G. 4D13
Martensson, S. 3A16
Martin, B.V. 4A47, 6A38
Martin, P.H. 4A37, 4A38, 4A48, 4C58, 4C59
Mauro, G.T. 4A49
Mayer, W.N. 5C47
Mayne, J.W. 6C13
Mentz, H.J. 4C54
Metcalfe, A. 2A50
Meulengracht, K. 8.15
Mieczkowski, B. 6B19
Milefanti, D.C. 4C50
Miles, J.C. 5B15, 5B28
Millar, A. 6A39
Millar, W.W. 4A9
Miller, A.J. 5F31
Miller, C.E. 3D20
Miller, J.J. 4B20
Millikin, N.G. 3B22, 3B23
Mills, D. 2A51

Mills, G. 5C48
Mills, K. 4A11
Ministere des Transports 4A50
Ministry of Overseas Development
    5C49
Mishan, E.J. 5C50
Misner, J. 4C51
Mitchell, C.G.B.   3A17,   3A18,
    3D21, 4A51, 4C87, 4D14
Mix, C.V.S. 3B24, 6C14
Moavenzadeh, F. 5C40, 6D10
Mobolurin, A. 4A14
Mogridge, M.J.H. 5D13
Monteath, I.G. 5D12
Montoulieu, C.F. 2B8
Moore, D.H. 2B27
Moore, N. 2A47
Morgan, R.D. 2B28
Morosiuk, G. 6D1
Morrall, J.F. 6C13
Morris, D. 6C10
Morris, J.M. 3A19
Morris, P.O. 5F24
Moseley, M.J. 1A34, 1A35, 2A60,
    3A20, 3A21, 3A22, 3A23, 3C21,
    3D22, 3D23
Moser, B. 5B18, 5D25, 5F32
Moser, L. 5F32
Moyes, A. 6A40
Mulinazzi, T. 3B20
Muller, K.W. 4A26
Munton, R.J.C. 4A52, 6A11
Murdock, S.H. 5D14
Murphy, H.W. 5C51

Nash, C.A. 1B5, 4B14, 4B21, 5C52,
    8.12
National Consumer Council 4C64
National Council of Applied Eco-
    nomic Research 6D26
National Council of Social Service
    1A38, 4A53, 4C65
National Council for Voluntary Or-
    ganisations 3D24, 3D25
National Executive Committee of
    the Labour Party 1A39
National Swedish Road and Traffic
    Research Institute 4A51, 4D16

National Technical Information
    Service 5B29
National Waterways Transport
    Association 4E1
Navin, F.P.D. 6C15
Neely, G. 4A55
Neumann, E.S. 5B30
Neumann, L. 4C51
Neveu, A.J. 4A79, 5B31
Newby, H. 1A10, 1A40, 1A41
Newell, J. 5B32
Nicholl, J.P. 5F8, 5F25
Nkonge, J.H. 4A14
Noortman, H.J. 4E11
Norman, A.J. 4C66
North Yorkshire Rutex Working
    Group 4C67, 4C68, 4C69, 4C70
Notess, C.B. 3C23, 3C24, 3C29
Nutley, S.D. 3A24, 3A25, 3B25,
    3B26, 3C25, 3C26, 8.13, 8.14

Ochojna, A.D. 3B27, 6A41
O'Cinneide, D. 3D26
O'Flaherty, C.A. 5F26
Ogden, K.W. 4E12, 5F31
Olander, L.-O. 6B20
Oldfield, R. 1B6, 4A56, 4B22
O'Leary, D.P. 6C3
Olney, G.P. 6A42
Olsson, L. 4C42
Olsson, M.L. 2B29
Oppermann, M.C. 4C57
Oregon Department of Transporta-
    tion 3D27
Organisation for Economic Co-
    operation and Development 1B7,
    2C14, 5F27, 6D27
Orriss, H.D. 6A43
Orski, C.K. 4C71
Ostenfeld, T. 4A57
Ott, M.T. 4C1
Owais, M. 6D10
Owens, S.E. 5D15, 5D16, 5D17,
    6A44
Oxfordshire County Council 6A45
Oxley, P.R. 3A26, 4A58, 4C72

Paaswell, R.E. 4D17

Pacione, M. 1A42
Packman, J. 3D22
Pahl, R. 1A43
Panebianco, T.S. 2B30
Paramo, J.A. 5C4
Park, C. 1A18
Parker, E.B. 3D18
Parkinson, M. 5A15, 5B33
Patten, C.U. 3C27
Patton, C.V. 3C28
Paulhus, N.G. 4A59
Pavlik, Z. 6B21
Pearce, D.W. 5C52
Pearman, A.D. 5C53
Peat, Marwick and Mitchell 3B28, 3B29
Pedersen, P.O. 4A60, 4C52, 5B34, 5B35
Perloff, H.S. 4C73
Persson, T. 6B20
Peters, C.M. 6A21, 6A22
Peters H.A.J. 4C53
Peters, R.J. 5F28
Pfefer, R.C. 6C16
Pflug, W. 4A61
Phillips, M.H. 6A46
Picha, K.C. 5D22
Pirie, G.H. 3A27, 3A28
Plassard, F. 3D28
Plummer, R.W. 5B35
Poka, E. 2B31
Popper, R.J. 3C29
Pott, J.T. 6C17
Potter, S. 5D18
Prato, R. 5C4
Prescott, J.R. 6C18
Pritchard, B. 3B30
Prudhoe, J. 4E13
Public Technology Incorporated 6C19

Radwan, A.E. 5E14
Rallis, T. 8.15
Randolph, W. 1A44
Rankonen, O.J. 5C54
Rao, K. 2B32
Rathey, G. 6B11
Rawson, J. 3B31

Rawson, M. 1A25
Rayner, W. 5A16
Reddy, K.C. 6D28
Rees, G.L. 2A53, 6A47
Rees, J.H. 4B5
Reichart, B.K. 2B33
Renold, J. 6A1
Reske, D. 4E14
Revis, J.S. 2B34, 2B35
Rhys, D.G. 1B8, 1B9, 4D18
Richards, K. 4B33
Richards, P.J. 3B35
Richards, R.O. 5A2
Rickaby, P.E. 5D17
Riekic, G. 5D18
Rigby, J.P. 2A54, 3C30, 3C31, 3D29, 6A48
Riipinen, M. 4D19
Rimmer, P.J. 4C74
Ring, S.L. 5D19
Riverson, J.D.N. 6D20
Robbins, J. 8.5
Robert, S. 1A44
Robertson, D.M. 3B8, 3B32, 3B39
Robertson, I.M.L. 6A49
Robins, D.L.J. 1A45
Robinson, G.K. 5B37
Robinson, L. 2B36
Robinson, R. 5C10, 5C55, 6D1
Roblin, R.A. 2B37
Robson, P. 3C32
Roe, M. 5C56
Rogers, A.W. 1A25
Rogers, G. 5A22
Rooks, E.H. 3C17
Roos, D. 4C75
Rose, D. 1A41
Rostow, W.W. 5A17
Rühl, A. 3B33
Ruppenthal, K.M. 6C20
Rural Voice 1A46
Russwurm, L.H. 1A8

Sachdev, L.S. 6D18
Saddler, J. 6D29
Sager, T. 5C57
Sahaj, L. 3C33
Salomon, I. 8.16

Saltzman, A. 2B38, 4A10, 4C76
Sammon, J.P. 4B24
Samuels, A. 5C58
Saunders, P. 1A41
Sayer, I.A. 5E9
Schmidt, R.H. 5C59
Schneider, J.B. 3D30
Schneider, M. 5B23
Schoon, J.G. 6D11
Schühle, U. 2C9, 6B13
Schuldiner, P.W. 5C46
Scottish Association for Public
    Transport 6A50
Scottish Development Department
    2A55
Scottish Rutex Working Group
    4C77, 4C78, 4C79, 4C80
Searle, G. 2A56
Seaton, R.A.F. 3A26
Seddon, D. 6D7, 6D8
Self, G.E. 4E15
Shannon, G.W. 3D31
Sharp, C. 5A18
Shaw, J.M. 1A47, 6A51
Shepherd, N. 5E15
Short, J. 6C21
Short, J. 3D32
Shucksmith, D.M. 5D20
Sigalov, M.R. 4B25
Silcock, D.J. 4C81
Simmersbach, P. 6D30
Simmons, J.M. 5A19
Simpson, J.A. 5F29
Singh, R.C. 6D28
Sinha, K.C. 5E14
Siria, B.S. 6C22
Skelton, N.G. 3A29, 3C24
Skiner, J.L. 3D31
Skinner, D.N. 5F30
Skorpa, L. 5B38
Slee, B.J. 5C60
Smerk, G.M. 2B40
Smith, D.E. 6C22
Smith, D.R. 2A57
Smith, E. 4B13, 4B26
Smith, J. 6A52
Smith, J.D. 5C61, 5C62, 6D31,
    6D32

Smith, N. 5B28
Smith, R.L. 4C82, 5C63, 5C64,
    5C65
Smith, W.A. 6C22
Sobel, K.L. 5B10
Soot, S. 4A62
Sparrow, F.T. 4C32
Spaven, D.L. 4B6
Spencer, M.B. 3A23, 3D23, 6A30
Spratley, J.M. 6A30
Spreiter, H. 4A63
Sprouncer, S.M. 3D33
Spurlock, C.W. 3D31
Squire, L. 6D33
Srinivasan, N.S. 6D34
Stabler, M.J. 4E8
Stanley, J. 5C52, 8.17
Stanley, P.A. 3B34, 6A24
Stapleton, B. 3B35
Stark, D.C. 4C93, 4C94
Starkie, D.N.M. 4B27, 8.17
Steahr, T.E. 4C25
Steer, J.K. 4B28
Stein, M. 5C66, 5C67
Stenson, H.H. 4A62
Stephanedes, Y.J. 5B39, 5B40
Steuart, G.N. 4D15
Stoakes, R. 5D21
Stone, J.E 2B41
Stone, J.R. 6C5, 6C10
Stone, K.H. 3B36
Stopher, P.R. 6C16
Strand, S. 6B22
Stringfellow, W.G. 6C23
Suen, S.L 6C24
Sullivan, B.E. 2B42, 5B41, 6C24
Sullivan, E.C. 5D22
Sunden, E. 4B29
Surti, V.H. 3C10
Swait, J.D. 5D25, 6D17
Swedish Institute 2C15
Sweetnam, J.L.G. 6A25
Symons, J.G. 3D30
Sze Ming Chan, M. 3C11

Taggart, R.E. 5C67
Taitz, L. 5C68
Tamakloe, E.K.A. 3B20

Tanner, J.C. 8.18
Tarrant, J. 5A20
Tarrius, A. 4D13
Taylor, C. 3D34
Taylor, D.H. 3D35
Taylor, J. 4A64
Taylor, M.A.P. 5F31
Teal, R.F. 4C83
Tebb, R.G.P. 4A65, 6A23
Tendler, J. 2B43
Thelen, K.M. 4A66
Thomas, D.St.J. 1B10
Thomas, R. 1A30
Thompson, J.M. 5C14, 5C16
Tice, R.K. 3C35
Tingle, E.D. 6D35
Tipping, D.G. 5C69
Tokerud, R. 5C70
Tolle, J.E. 3D38
Tolson, F. 2B29
Topham, N. 4A67
Tourism and Recreational Research Unit 5B46
Town, S. 3A18, 3D21
Transport and Road Research Laboratory 4C84
Transportation Systems Center 4A68, 4A69
Trench, S. 4A70
Trower-Foyan, M. 2A58, 3B37
Tudor, D.N. 2B44
Tunbridge, R.J. 4A71, 4C85, 4C86, 4C87
Turner, R.D. 3C9
Turnock, D. 4B30, 4C88, 6A53
Turns, K.L. 4A72
Tyler, E. 4B22
Tyler, M. 3D36
Tyson, W.J. 4A73, 4A74, 4A75

Ugolik, W.R. 4A76, 5B43
Ulstrup Johansen, C. 4C52
Underwood, W.C. 2B45, 5C71
Unwin, K.I. 3D6, 3D7, 3D8, 3D9
US Department of Transportation 2B46, 2B47, 2B48, 4A77, 4C89, 4C90, 6C25

Van Ampers, J.M. 4A16
Van der Ree, L. 6B9
Van der Tak, H.G. 6D33
Vank, C.M. 5C3
Van Knippenberg, C. 5B7
Vanoon, C.C. 4C91
Van Oudhensden, D. 6B7
Vanrne, A.S.E. 5C32
Van Sickel, K. 6C26
Van Tol, H. 5B44
Vaudois, J. 6B3
Venhuizen, D. 3C6
Verdonck, W. 4C18
Verhoeff, J.M. 2C16
Vick, C.M. 5C3
Vickerman, R.W. 3A30
Vilhof, P. 8.15
Visser, A.T. 5F32
Vlcek, I. 6B21

Wachs, M. 3C36
Waksman, R. 4C61
Walcoff, P. 3D11
Walker, A. 1A48
Walker, N.S. 5C67
Walsh, J.A. 5B45
Walters, J. 5C28
Walton, C.M. 2B16, 3A9, 3C37, 5A14, 5B38
Warburton, S. 2A58, 3B37
Ward, D.E. 4C92
Warman, P. 4A47
Warren, R.P. 5B46, 5C13, 6C3
Warren, W.D. 4B31
Waters, M.H.L. 5D23
Waters, W.G. 5A21
Watt, R.S. 4C63
Watts, P.F. 4C93, 4C94, 4D20
Wayne, F. 5D24
Weaver, V.C. 6C27
Webster, F.V. 4A56, 4A77
Weekley, I.G. 3D37
Weeks, N.E. 5C62
Wegmann, F.J. 4A66
Weightman, D. 6D36
Weiner, E. 4D21
Weiss, D.L 4A79
Weiss, E. 3B13

Wellman, B. 5C72
Wells, G. 2A59
Wells, M. 3D38
Welsh Consumer Council 6A54
Welsh Council 3D39
Werczberger, E. 5C35
Wesseling, F.W. 3C19
Whalley, A. 2A37, 2A38, 4B16
Wheeler, M. 3D40
Whitbread, M. 5C45
Whitby, M.C. 1A32, 1A49
White, H.P. 6C28
White I. 3B9
White, P.R. 2A44, 4A80, 4A81, 4B15, 4B17, 4B32, 4C95, 4C96, 5B47, 6B23
Whitelegg, J. 2C17
Wibberley, G.P. 1A22, 1A50, 1A51, 3A31
Wiberg, U. 4A82
Wickstrom, G.C. 3B38
Wiese, A.E. 2B49
Wigan, M.R. 3A19
Wiklund, L. 6B24
Wilkes, P.F. 6A54
Wilks, D.F. 3D41
Williams, E.L. 5F33
Williams, M. 4A83

Williams, S.R. 4B32
Willis, E. 4A84
Willis, K.G. 1A49, 4A85
Wilmers, P.H.M. 2A60, 6A55
Wilson, F.R. 5A22
Winfield, R. 2A61, 2A62, 3B32, 3B39
Wistrich, E. 8.19
Wohl, M. 4C50
Wood, K. 4C97
Woodruffe, R.J. 1A52
Woollett, S. 3D42
Wootton, J.H. 5F34
Worthington, H. 6C11
Wragg, R.F.W. 2A53, 6A47
Wytconsult 1A53, 2A64, 3A32, 5B48

Yagar, S. 8.20
Yass, I. 5C73
Young, S.L. 5B20
Yukubousky, R. 4C98

Zaelka, D. 4C51
Zaniewski, J.P. 5D25
Zapata, R.N 3C29
Ziegler, E.W. 4C4, 4C99

Abbreviations

BRB	British Railways Board
CBD	Central Business District
CIE	Coras Iompar Eireann
CPRE	Council for the Protection of Rural England
CRC	Countryside Review Committee
CTP	Common Transport Policy
DGH	District General Hospital
DOE	Department of the Environment
ECMT	European Conference of Ministers of Transport
EEC	European Economic Community
FHWA	Federal Highway Administration
GAO	General Accounting Office
HMSO	Her Majesty's Stationery Office
LGORU	Local Government Operational Research Unit
MAP	Market Analysis Project
NBC	National Bus Company
NCSS	National Council for Social Services
NCVO	National Council for Voluntary Organisations
OECD	Organisation for Economic Cooperation and Development
OUP	Oxford University Press
PEP	Political and Economic Planning
PMM	Peat, Marwick and Mitchell
PTC	Public Transport Plan
PTRC	Planning and Transportation Research and Computation
RSG	Rate Support Grant
RUTEX	Rural Transport Experiments
SAE	Society of Automotive Engineers
SDD	Scottish Development Department
STA	Surface Transportation Assistance Act

TPP	Transport Policy and Programme
TRRL	Transport and Road Research Laboratory
TSG	Transport Supplementary Grant
UMTA	Urban Mass Transportation Administration